My Chinese Experience
A Personal Story

BILLY COSTINE

Orla Kelly Publishing
27 Kilbrody, Mount Oval,
Rochestown, Cork,
Ireland.

Dedicated to all those people that never
got a second chance.

Contents

Prologue

Have a look at the name of my book. A lot of people might say, what's all this about then? When you mention the word 'Chinese', what do people think about first? Most likely it's their local Chinese restaurant or takeaway. Only when you go in to order a Chinese takeaway or you sit down in one of their restaurants to order your food, is the picture of a Chinese person or the country of China uppermost in most people's minds. One of the reasons is because China is so far away and as the saying goes, 'Out of sight, out of mind'. Then another thought might occur to you, 'I wonder what that country is really like?'. When the takeaway is ready or you are after eating your meal in the restaurant, the thought of China disappears again, until the next time you enter the premises when hunger strikes. All natural thoughts, I would think. Also, you'd probably be thinking 'Ah well, what does it matter anyway? I'll never get the chance to visit that country in my lifetime…'

One thing I would like to mention, and I think most people would agree with me, is that to the best of my knowledge Chinese people have been accepted into every country all over the world. One of the reasons I think they have been accepted is because of their work ethic. They have a willingness to work hard and they get an honest return for their labour. That is testimony to their success and their nature from past generations.

After a change of circumstances in my personal life which I never thought would happen to me, I was fortunate enough and privileged to have visited the People's Republic of China on ten separate occasions. These visits were between November 2005 and April 2019.

I'm sure my story, in fact I'm certain, will absorb and captivate you from start to finish in a lot of aspects, especially about this fascinating country. The places I saw, the cities I visited, the people I met and the things I have done – all of these things intrigued me about China. I think my story will certainly intrigue you too.

You're looking at its culture, its history, its traditions, and its beautiful natural landscape, but most importantly, the Chinese people themselves are a resilient, friendly and strong race of people. I have been very privileged to have had all these experiences. I never imagined in a million years my life would end up in the precarious position that it did. I never thought I was as close to the edge, as I was. But, as in my first book *The Flight of a Magpie,* I believe that fate has played such a big part in my life to date. Can I explain it? No not really, but it has occurred. All I can say is that it happened to me and in the cold light of day, I have to live with the thought (be it good or bad) and believe that it was all meant to happen.

So my friends, don't ever take things for granted in life. Do make the most of what you have and treasure it. Never put something off until tomorrow if you can do it today. Where is the guarantee in life that you will be around tomorrow? If you want to do something whilst here on this planet, just go ahead and do it. Never have any regrets about what you should have done! Some things happen in life for a reason, which we cannot explain or find an answer to. In my case, I now know the reason why a lot of things happened to me.

Your choices are limited. I believe it's all about what you choose. Making choices can determine so much about events the next day, the next week, the next month or year. But more importantly, it's about survival and I made it to the finishing line. I was lucky!

The present date is Thursday February 13th (the day before St. Valentine's Day) in the year 2014. I'm now ready to write my story, to bring you into my world and to tell you all about the experiences I've had in China. I firmly believe the reason I first went to this fascinating country was all to do with fate.

Where it all started

For me, this intriguing and fascinating story all started on September 5th, in the year of 2003 and of all places, at a bus stop in the picturesque town of Killarney in the beautiful county of Kerry, in the far south west of Ireland.

'A far place from China', you might say.

Well, this was the way it happened for me.

A month earlier, my twenty-six-and-a-half-year marriage had come to an abrupt end. Indeed, sad times for all concerned in what easily brought about the biggest changes ever in my personal life. But as the lines in the famous Frank Sinatra's song *My Way goes, Regrets, I've had a few and then again too few to mention. To think I did all that and saw it through without exemption. Oh yes, much more than this, I did it my way.* How ironic that these words should reflect so much of my life story. My job then was as a bus driver for Bus Eireann (the national bus company) in Ireland.

I was in the town of Killarney to pick up passengers for their return trip on the Euro Lines bus service to London. This route also served Cardiff, Bristol and Reading. This service which I had done for several years, involved rotating driving shifts with another driver every second week. It always started out early in the morning in Waterford city. I would clock in at around 07:30, as the Euro Lines bus service from London would normally arrive into the city around 08:20, having left London the previous night. When the coach arrived, I would change with the incoming driver, relieving him of his duty. Usually, a ten-minute break would be sufficient for the passengers to go to the toilet, the shop or have a quick smoke. We would then continue the service leaving Waterford city at approximately 08:40, with our final destination being the town of Killarney.

We would have several designated stops en route, where certain passengers would exit the coach. Most of these passengers would have been locals returning home on holidays at various times within the year and for other reasons, like funerals, marriages, birthdays, or other family gatherings and social occasions within their own communities. Then there were people like the long-lost Irish emigrant, (of which I had many as passengers over the years) who had left these shores, through forced emigration in sad and bad economic times, from the 40's through to the late 80's and even some into the early 90's. Some of these people would all be part of this daily service which ran throughout the year, except for Christmas day. On occasion, you could also have had passengers from any part of the world. Some were holidaymakers, while most others would have been seeking their Irish roots.

To keep it simple, any distances I'll be talking about, will be in miles. This bus journey covered a road distance of around one hundred and seventy miles, with a driving time of just over four hours. We would usually arrive in Killarney at around 12:50. Firstly, I would go and get the bus fuelled and cleaned. Then I would go for something to eat myself. Feeding my empty stomach was a must! After all, the body needed re-fuelling too (mine was no different) for my return journey, which would be departing again at 14:30 the same day.

On this particular day, as I was about to depart on my return journey, there was only one passenger at the bus terminal. She was a Chinese lady.

Looking back now, I often ask myself, was all this meant to be?

She had long black hair and was of slim build. As she ascended the steps of the bus, I greeted her with a warm smile, as I did all passengers intending to travel on this long bus trip. By checking her ticket, I could see she was London bound. She told me her name was Fengqin. It soon became clear to me that her English was good and better than I expected. I quickly sensed that this lady was well-educated. I also wondered where she had come from and what she was doing in the town of Killarney in

County Kerry. These were my initial thoughts in those first few moments of our meeting.

Fengqin sat in the front seat opposite me, separated by a space of about two feet. I just felt early on that the chemistry for conversation was there. I suppose, you just might call it to a degree, curiosity. As it happened on that day, there were no other passengers on board the bus for that particular part of the journey.

It was a wonderful summer's day. The sun was out in all its beauty and splendour as we departed from the bus stop. Being blessed with a good memory and being a perfectionist by nature, it was exactly 14:30. I remember this chance encounter quite vividly. Little did I know then, of the significance of this meeting, the impact it would eventually have on my life and how it would determine my future. Not in a million years would I have imagined or guessed what was going to unfold further down the road of life for me. I always believed in fate and its consequences, let it be good, bad or indifferent. In my book, as the title in the name of that other famous Frank Sinatra song goes, *That's life*. Well, so be it.

This journey started, as did our conversation, when the road ahead was clear and at intervening periods. Safety was still paramount in my mind, while doing a professional job. I still had that gut feeling, that I had one very interesting lady on board.

Throughout the first leg of the bus journey, our intermittent conversation was on more general topics. Where had she come from? Was she working in Ireland? What was she doing in Killarney? How long had she been here in Ireland? What did she think of Ireland? What did she think of the Irish people? Why was she returning to England on this particular day? All of these initial questions were answered by the time our bus journey stopped in Cork city bus station. This was where the main body of passengers boarded the Euro Lines coach daily. After being stopped there for a few minutes, all of the intending travelling passengers booked on board my bus were waiting. The usual scenes would greet my eyes: tears were visibly evident with friends, relatives and families all saying goodbye to their loved ones, until the next time they saw them.

As we departed the bus station on time at 16:45, our conversation was put on hold. Fengqin and I spoke very little on the journey from Cork city to Waterford city.

On our arrival at the bus station in Waterford city that evening (usually around 18:30) there would normally be a fifteen-minute official break. This was where my driving duty ended for the day. It was also where the relief bus driver who was preparing for the outbound journey to London took control of the bus.

Fengqin got off the bus for a bit of fresh air and to stretch her legs. She was also looking to buy a bottle of water. Showing her the way to the shop in the bus station, our conversation continued. We spoke for a further few minutes. She thanked me for buying her the bottle of water. She did briefly mention to me, that she would be returning to Ireland in a few weeks' time.

I said, "Perhaps our paths will cross again."

"Maybe," she replied. With seconds to spare, she disappeared back out and onto the bus as it was about to depart.

Does the word fate ring a bell? Well, fate did play its part some weeks later, when the Euro Lines coach from London arrived back into Waterford city on its scheduled daily morning stop. As luck or fate would have it, I was relieving the inbound driver on that particular day. This was the normal procedure, mainly in the interest of safety, as drivers are only allowed to drive for a certain number of hours in a twenty-four-hour day. While I was checking the bus passengers' names and the drop-off locations on my list prior to departing, low and behold, there was Fengqin's name. I made my way down the aisle of the bus. Finding her, I said hello with a welcoming smile.

"Hello, nice to see you again," I said.

"Nice to see you too," was her reply. She smiled and said no more, neither did I.

I returned to my driving seat shaking my head and resumed my official duty, before we were to depart. Although, when I think about it now, I did ask myself the question, why had she returned to Ireland?

We departed the bus station at the usual time of 08:40 to begin our journey. As usual, I dropped passengers en route at various destinations. Some two and a half hours later, Fengqin got off the bus when we arrived at the bus station in Cork city. She didn't have much luggage with her, which also made me curious. Having a few minutes to spare, I took the liberty to ask Fengqin if she would like a quick cup of tea or a bottle of water.

"Alright then," she said, "but I mustn't miss my bus to Bandon."

Again, I wondered why she was going to Bandon and not Killarney. Our brief conversation struck up again and I was to find out a little more about this woman. Even now, (some seventeen years on) I often think back at the circumstances of our chance meeting. If I had known then, what I know now, as the line in that other famous song by Louis Armstrong goes, *What a wonderful world it would be.*

When the time arrived, we said goodbye and parted, going to our separate buses. Fengqin gave me her mobile number, which moments earlier I had taken the liberty of asking her for. In return, I gave her mine, genuinely thinking that was the last I would see of this woman. I thought no more of it.

A few weeks went by and I continued with my work on the Euro Lines bus service as usual. Living by myself gave me plenty of time to reflect on my present life and my circumstances. It was not easy for me and, to be honest, the thought of ending it (my life) did cross my mind on occasion. Turning to excessive drinking was certainly not the answer. Neither was taking drugs – not that I ever gave them a thought! There was a river across the road from where I lived at that time and I could easily have been its next victim. But I choose to say no thanks to all of those thoughts. Though I still made time to have a few drinks on the weekend with some of my close friends. Mainly, just to relax and unwind. Football still played a big part in my life – it always has and always will, regardless of what life may throw at me. After all, it is still the beautiful game. But I have learned through experience that life goes on. Life is about choices. You make the calls and you live with them. It's like being on a long train journey, you can stay on or get off, the choice is yours, but the train keeps going.

A few years earlier, through football circumstances, I had met a famous footballer called Dave Wigginton at his place of work. It was in a pub/ restaurant, called The Galley which was in Schull, in West Cork. He lived in the small seaside town and coincidently it was in the same direction as Bandon. When I met him, I spoke about his very early football career with Derby County Football Club in England and in his latter days, with the famous Cork Hibernians Football Club. I had in my possession that day a few clippings of old newspapers in which Waterford FC and Cork Hibernians had done battle in previous years in the League of Ireland. Dave was included in a few photographs, and he was a little surprised to see them. It brought back memories to him and the light sound of laughter echoed around the room. I found the time spent with him to be quite interesting. Throughout our hour-long conversation and listening to some other stories from his playing days, I found him to be a very nice and friendly man.

One day, I was more than surprised to get a phone call telling me that Dave Wigginton had died unexpectedly of a heart attack in his new place of work, which was in a factory. I got in contact with his wife and sympathised with her while also apologising for not being able to attend Dave's funeral owing to work commitments. But I did promise her that when the opportunity arose, I would pay my respects and visit his grave.

Coincidently, a few weeks after meeting Fengqin on the bus, there was a bank holiday coming up. I decided to travel to Schull and to do as I said I would and pay my respects to this late footballer's family and visit his grave. I still had Fengqin's number, so I decided on impulse to ring her and put a question to her. It was on a Tuesday morning and I didn't even know at this stage if she was still in the country.

Gathering my courage and making the call, I made contact.

"Hello Fengqin," I said, "this is Billy Costine the Euro Lines bus driver."

"Oh yes, I remember you," she said. "Hello Billy, how are you?"

"I'm okay thanks," I said. "I'm heading to Schull in West Cork to do a message next Friday morning and was wondering would you like to come for a short trip and see this beautiful little town. I can meet you in Bandon and pick you up on the way, if you like?"

"Oh, alright then," she said.

Our conversation only lasted for a few short minutes. Fengqin made arrangements with me to meet her outside the church on the hill that overlooks the small town of Bandon.

The following few days passed and soon Friday came, as I knew it would, like every other Friday. I left the warmth of my bed after hearing the alarm and saw that the clock was just after striking 04:00. Having showered and shaved, breakfast was put on hold for a few hours. Although, I do remember taking some fruit, some apples, bananas and grapes. Leaving Waterford city an hour later and under the cover of darkness, I started my journey to Bandon in West Cork. Anticipation of what this day might bring was at the back of my mind. How would I deal with meeting Dave Wigginton's family and their sad loss? The other one was would the Chinese woman named Fengqin turn up and what conversations would we have.

A few hours later at 08:30, I was crossing over the bridge into the small, but beautiful town of Bandon. The sun in the sky was already waiting to lay siege on this beautiful part of Ireland. The council workers were busy cleaning the streets, weeding the flower beds and emptying the litter bins. Approaching two of them I asked, "Well lads, I can see you're busy at work and doing a good job too, I might add."

"What can we do for you?" one of them said.

"I was wondering where the church is?" I asked.

"Ah, you're only a stone's throw away from it," he replied. "Just go around the corner and it will be looking at you."

"Thanks lads! Have a good day," were my parting words.

I drove around the corner and there was the church on the hill. I parked my car close to the main gates and turned off the engine. I got out and waited anxiously, anticipation grew by the minute – I suppose from not knowing what to expect next.

As I counted down the minutes, my watch soon showed 08:55. There was no turning back now. Would Fengqin turn up? Would she be late? Would she forget completely? Yes, all of these thoughts crossed my mind in those closing minutes, as finally another look at my watch showed 09:00. Then I saw this dark-haired lady appear into my line of vision. She was coming around the bend on the main street, riding a bicycle. Her long black hair flowed in the gentle breeze as she cycled closer and closer. I quickly recognized her. Yes, it was Fengqin.

When she arrived, I nervously shook her hand and said hello. "Right then, you're all set to come on this journey with me?" I said.

She answered, "Yes Billy, I have never been there before, but I will go with you."

"We will be gone for a few hours, is that okay?" was my reply. "We can get something to eat and drink, whenever you like."

"That's okay, Billy. I don't eat much anyway. I'm not a big eater." Going from what I could see of how thin a figure she had, that was certainly true. Fengqin then chained her bicycle to one of the railings surrounding the church. She sat into the front passenger seat of my car and we both put on our seat belts. We departed from outside the church and drove for one of the exit roads out of the town of Bandon.

I do remember, the rest of my fruit was eaten on the way. A few thoughts were to cross my mind on this journey. I just had a feeling this was going to be a very interesting day, in more ways than one. We spoke about the weather, the passing scenery, the people and the country of Ireland. Fengqin made our conversation easy, which was welcomed by me. Interesting, intelligent and sometimes surprising were the answers I got, from my casual questions. I knew as before and without being told, this was no ordinary Chinese woman.

Prior to me meeting Fengqin a few weeks earlier, on that initial bus trip, I had never before even spoken for any length of time to a Chinese woman, except in a restaurant or a take-away outlet, when giving my order. All of the questions that I had asked myself about her were being answered, although slowly and cautiously. After about an hour's relaxed drive, the small little seaside town of Schull appeared on the horizon.

Finding the address of the late Dave Wigginton, I stopped the car outside this small terraced house and approached the front door. Fengqin stayed in the car, patiently awaiting my return. On knocking on the door, it was answered by a small boy.

"Is this the Wigginton house?" I asked.

"Yes," said the small boy, as he looked at me curiously.

"Would your mum be at home?" I enquired.

"One moment and I will get her for you," was his reply.

A few moments later, Mrs Wigginton approached the front door. Having only previously spoken to her on the phone at the time of her late husband's untimely demise, I introduced myself to her. "Hello Eileen, so nice to meet you," I said, as I shook her hand.

"Ah yes, I remember you now. You're Billy Costine from Waterford city," she said.

"That's correct. Well, I'm here to offer my condolences to you and the family and to visit Dave's grave, if I may?" I said.

"That's very kind of you, to have travelled such a long distance to get here," Eileen said.

"Well, I would love to see his grave," I asked.

"Sure Billy, it's not too far from here," she replied. Eileen then gave me the directions to the local graveyard. After a further few minutes talking and the offer of a cup of tea and a sandwich, I declined gracefully, as I told her this was a long trip and I had to return to Waterford city that evening. I gave her a departing hug and offered my sympathies once again. Leaving behind their family home and doing a U-turn back up the road, I followed the instructions Eileen had given me. It was a glorious morning, absolutely beautiful. The sun was now starting to make its mark, in the really clear blue sky. I thought to myself, days with weather like this should be savoured, particularly when I thought of where I was about to enter. Good weather and sunshine in Ireland, usually transforms the whole country into a blanket of green.

After a few short minutes driving, it was quite easy to find the graveyard. Fengqin and I stopped at the entrance and got out of my car. We entered through the small gates of the cemetery. This neat and tidy graveyard overlooks the lovely sailing harbour in Schull. What a picturesque setting it is, except on this occasion, I was there on a very poignant errand. Within a few minutes of searching around the graveyard, I found the late great Dave Wigginton's grave. All the memories I had of this famous footballer whom I had met personally and seen play in Kilcohan Park in Waterford city on many occasions came flooding back to me. Here I was, standing over his final resting place. How sad it was for me, thinking about a player who had graced the green sod with such distinction during his playing career. He was a hero to so many football fans in Cork city and the surrounding areas.

Dave Wigginton was a key player in that great Cork Hibernian team of the late 60's and early 70's. He was affectionately known as Wiggy.

They had many a memorable battle royal with Waterford FC, in those entertaining and never to be forgotten years in League of Ireland football. Sadness descended on me as I stood there with my inner thoughts.

Meanwhile, Fengqin had wandered off to sit on a little piece of high ground overlooking this beautiful bay. After spending several private minutes with my thoughts at Dave's graveside, I joined her on the grassy knoll. It was there that she opened up and told me a little bit more about her life, her past and present.

She was born in a city called Anshan, which is north east of Beijing. It's a city that is most famous for its steel. The best steel in China comes from Anshan city. Fengqin had married into a well-off family and had one son. Her life then was one of ease, but something was missing. Through a spiritual experience she had, she decided to leave her life of comfort and came to England, having divorced her husband back in China. She had entered a world of prayer and meditation. Later Fengqin married an Englishman and they had two children, a boy and a girl. Through all of this time, she devoted herself to the power of meditation. While her children were at a young age, she decided to leave everything and travel on her mission in life. She spent a period of time sleeping rough and helping the homeless in Soho in London. After some time there, she came to Ireland and lived in Dublin city. Again, Fengqin mixed with the poor and helped the needy, while all the time staying focused through meditation. From Dublin city Fengqin then went to Cork city and stayed there for a period, again helping the homeless and needy. She then moved to Bandon town and this was where she was presently? A kind of strange story, you'll admit.

Our conversation lasted about two hours, in these beautiful surroundings and this peaceful place. The time flew by and then it was time to go, as the calling for food was beckoning. Reaching the cemetery gates on the way out, I gave one more glance back and thought of the late great Dave Wigginton.

We left the solemnity of the graveyard behind us and went to a pub/restaurant in the town called The Galley. If you remember, this was actually the place, where I had first met Dave Wigginton! We had a nice meal there! I had fresh fish-n-chips with a salad, and a cool pint of Guinness. Fengqin just had a small portion of salad with a handful of chips and a glass of water. I find most Chinese people are very disciplined in their eating habits…. unreal! An hour later, when we emerged from the pub after our delightful meal, the sun was still out in force and shining gloriously on all its victims below.

Returning to my car and during our relaxing return journey back to Bandon, our conversation continued. A picture of Fengqin's personality and make up was now beginning to become a little clearer in my mind. She did curiously ask me what Waterford city was like. I gave her my honest opinion, for what it was worth. Sometime later we arrived on the outskirts of the town of Bandon and a few minutes later, the church was back in view.

Fengqin exited my car when it stopped and as she was preparing to unlock her untouched bicycle from the church railings, she thanked me for a most enjoyable and delightful day. We then shook hands and I gave her a small hug.

"No problem Fengqin, you look after yourself," I said. "If you ever want to come to Waterford city, do let me know."

On my long journey back home, I had mixed feelings on the day's events. Sadness, joy and intrigue to name but three. Darkness had again descended on Waterford city as I arrived home. I didn't have any problems sleeping that night! Tiredness ruled.

I continued working away, while I also continued with my usual weekend routine in football of scouting all over Ireland for the English Premier League side, Newcastle United Football Club. They were then and still are the sleeping giants of the North East.

A few weeks after that particular and interesting weekend, I got a phone call one evening on my return home from work. It was Fengqin's voice on the end of the line.

"Hello Billy," she said.

"Hello Fengqin, this is a nice surprise," was my reply.

"Billy, my work in Bandon and Cork city is finished. I want to stay in Ireland and was wondering could I move to Waterford city. Could you have a look for some small place for me to stay around the city centre perhaps? Nothing elaborate," she finished with. As regards accommodation, I knew by now that she was a woman of little needs and comforts.

"Okay, give me a few days and I will see what I can come up with. When I have some news, I will get back to you," I replied.

"Okay Billy. God bless you," was Fengqin's reply. I made several inquiries around the city over the following few days, for suitable and safe accommodation for her. After all, this was a middle-aged Chinese woman, shortly to be living alone, in a big city. Eventually, I got Fengqin suitable accommodation in a flat on a quiet and safe street, close to the city centre. I knew it would suit her needs and give her, her own space. When the time was right, I duly notified her. At that time, she had been renting a room in a house in Bandon, where her landlord was a man called John. A few days after getting her a place to stay and when her mind was made up, I travelled very early one Saturday morning to Bandon. This was to help Fengqin move her belongings to Waterford city. On my way to Bandon, I took in a schoolboy soccer match in Cork city to look at a certain player. This was in my official scouting capacity for Newcastle United Football Club. Immediately after the game and having taken down my notes of importance on the player and anyone else that caught my eye on that day, I headed for Bandon.

When I got there and found the house, Fengqin was pleased to see me. She had just a few basic things in plastic bags, like clothes, toiletries, books and food. The bare essentials, that's all. She was a woman of little needs, which didn't surprise me. I was now beginning to get a truer picture of this woman. While we were there, I met her landlord John. John was a separated father of four and a very quiet person by nature. I could see he was sad to see her go, as she had been living there for a while. She said her goodbyes to John, as did I and we left. Fengqin had no interest in relationships, as all her time was spent on meditation, prayer and helping the needy.

On our arrival back in Waterford city some hours later and meeting her new landlord, Fengqin settled into her new surroundings and acclimatised quickly, as I knew she would. She never ever questioned where she was staying, or even who her neighbours were. These things were of trivial concern to her. This woman had seen and done a lot!

Shortly after that, the end of 2003 arrived. I wondered what the year of 2004 would hold for me. Obviously, getting my book *The Flight of a Magpie* finished and published was my main priority then. As regards Fengqin, that was anybody's guess. This woman could leave at the drop of a hat, or just up roots and go in the blink of an eye.

Over the next few weeks, I called on her occasionally to see how she was getting on and also to make sure she was safe from any undesirable people, some of whom lived in the same building. But surprisingly, in all the time that she lived there, no unsavoury incidents ever occurred. Fengqin kept to herself and continued her vocation of prayer and meditation quietly, undisturbed. That was the way she wanted it to be. It was totally her choosing, with no hassle! Fengqin did her own thing, but we kept in touch from a distance.

One Friday evening she received word that her old landlord (John) was seriously ill in Cork's Regional Hospital and he wanted to see her. She rang me and asked could I bring her to the hospital in Cork city, as she wanted to visit John. Without a moment's hesitation, I said I would.

This we did the following morning (Saturday), having left Waterford city some two hours earlier. When we got there, the news was bad! We saw John straight away in a bed in a private room. He told us up front that he was close to death. He was just over major surgery and his stomach had been removed, due to a huge cancerous growth. Fengqin comforted him for the following five hours that we were there. She prayed with John and told him that it was God's will what was in store. She re-assured him not to be afraid of death, as he was going to a better place. Also, saying that God would be waiting for him. It was heart-breaking and even worse to see, but John's time on this earth was up. When you think about it and if you believe, God is in fact waiting for us all!

I was now seeing the spiritual side of Fengqin in practice and how she was able to portray it. This was a very moving and new experience for me. Surprisingly, while I was in the room, John called me over to his bed. He reached out his hand, which I held firmly. I have never forgotten the words he said to me.

"Billy, thank you for bringing Fengqin to see me before I die," he said in a low voice.

"John, that's not a problem whatsoever. I just don't know what to say to you at this sad time," I said.

"Billy, don't you worry. I have to make way for someone else to be born," he said.

What humble words from a person in John's position. I took this sad and final moment on board, and it remained in my thoughts for a long time. I was still holding John's hand as he spoke these solemn words to me. I couldn't but help filling up and crying. He was as thin as a skeleton under the bed clothes. It broke my heart to see him just lying there like this and being so close to death with no escape. The reality of everything and how precious life really is was brought home to me that day.

Eventually, it was time for both of us to say our farewells to a very gentle man who had accepted his fate with great dignity and raw courage. Fengqin approached John first and gave him a final hug and kiss. I was lost for words and broke down, as I too said my final goodbye. As I was the last of us to leave the room, I looked back to see John give me a wave, a smile and a thank you sign. The atmosphere in the car on the return journey home was a lot quieter.

Two days after that sad experience, on the Monday morning, Fengqin rang me to tell me that John had died. His brother had broken the sad news to her with a phone call, earlier that morning. His ex-wife and four daughters were at his bedside in his final hours, before he departed this life. Over the years, John has come into my thoughts on occasion.

The year of 2004 came and went quickly. When time was available, I was writing as much of my book as possible. It was still paramount for me to get it finished. It was written as an achievement, and certainly not for any monetary gain.

The year of 2005 started the same as all the others, but there was to be a twist in my life, before that year was out. Little did I know then, of what lay ahead! Again, I was kept busy with work, football and writing my book. My life was lonely as regards having someone to share it, to give me stability and a further purpose to it all. These thoughts I kept to myself but continued with my usual routine. I also kept in touch with Fengqin from a distance. She did her own thing, as I did mine, that was the way it was.

Early in March of 2005, Fengqin returned to England to visit her children. She had kept in touch with her ex-husband. They had remained on good terms and amazingly, they still are to this day. As it should be, why bring bitterness into the situation. Life is too short, for a lifetime of conflict. She remained in England for a few weeks and then returned to Ireland in April. When she got home, I kept in touch with her through the occasional visit.

A few months later Fengqin informed me that she was going back to China to visit her family, whom she had not seen for a number of years. A few days before Fengqin left for the People's Republic of China, I visited her twice in her flat. On the last occasion, it was to see if she wanted or needed anything. The answer was as I had expected. "No Billy, I have everything, thank you," was her reply. While there, I also made arrangements to bring her to Dublin Airport for her scheduled flight. The time rolled by and the day of her departure arrived. I duly collected her from her flat, at the break of dawn. I remember it well. It was August 15th in the year of 2005.

This was the way it happened for me. In the course of our conversation en route to Dublin Airport, I turned to her and thoughtfully said, "Fengqin, when you are in China for the next few weeks, will you have a look for a Chinese woman for me?"

"Are you serious, Billy?" she said.

"Yes, I'm serious," I said.

"What age group are you talking about?" she asked.

"I don't care about her age, as long as she is genuine," I finished.

"Okay. I'll do that and have a look for you," said Fengqin.

And that was the way it happened for me.

On our arrival at the airport and once Fengqin had checked in her luggage, we had some time to spare. Our conversation over early breakfast continued for an hour or so. Then it was time for her to go through security and to her departure gate. I gave her a hug and a kiss on the cheek, as we said goodbye. I waved to her as she disappeared out of sight in the midst of the other travelling passengers. Then she was gone. Just like that! This woman wasn't into saying any long goodbyes. It was a long and boring return journey back home to Waterford city for me, on that particular afternoon. But life for me went on as per usual.

A few weeks passed until Fengqin returned. I collected her at Dublin Airport and naturally, I was delighted to see her. On the homeward journey, our conversation was about everything except the main question I had requested on her departure. Believe it or not, we never even touched on the subject. It wasn't at the forefront of my thoughts and Fengqin never mentioned anything regarding it to me either.

One day, about a week after she had arrived home, I went to visit her in her flat. While there and in the course of casual conversation I said to her, "Fengqin, did you manage to have a look for someone for me while you were in China?" Not being over-confident, or over-excited about what the answer might be.

I was taken aback when she replied, "As a matter of fact, Billy, I did have a look for someone for you while I was there," she said.

"Oh, this could be interesting," was my reply.

"Billy, I want you to have a look at this photograph and see what you think," she said reaching for a folder in one of her still half-opened and unpacked suitcases. I stood there in the middle of the small room in the flat and wondered what was coming next. "Here," she said, "have a look at this and see what you think."

Opening the folder cautiously, being a little nervous of its contents, I duly obliged her request. There were two photographs in an inner envelope when I opened it, which caught me by surprise.

"Well Billy, what do you think of that girl?"

"Oh, she looks rather nice," was my reply.

Fengqin told me her name was Hong Wei, also of her background and circumstances (she was divorced and had one grown up son) which was a little surprising to me. "Do you think you might go to China to see her sometime?"

I said without reluctance or hesitation, "Sure, I'll go and meet her. Why not? What have I got to lose? As a matter of fact, I'm going to make arrangements without delay," I said.

"That's good news, Billy. You won't be disappointed. I promise you," she said. We finished our conversation and I said no more about the proposition that was put to me that day. Never thinking I'd ever see China in my lifetime.

The following few days for me, were spent with my inquisitive thoughts of visiting this country which we in the west know so little about. I wondered what this far off country was like. What was it going to hold for me, as regards my future? I must say, I was intrigued at the thought of going to China to meet Hong Wei and see some of this country. I was going to take up the challenge and see what this part of my life had in store for me. There was to be no going back for me now. Nope, I was going and that was that! As I said earlier in this book, if only I knew then of what lay ahead for me. Within a week or two, I had put in a request for some time off work, for the second week in November. In the meantime, Fengqin had given me Hong Wei's address. I sent her a letter and two photographs of me, saying that I was looking forward to our meeting and also telling her the date of when I would be travelling to Beijing. Obviously, she would have gotten an interpreter to read my letter and would have to bring him with her. I also told her other things about me that she needed to know. This was all duly done, but the choice was still hers of course!

Shortly afterwards, Hong Wei gave me the go ahead to make my arrangements. You would be surprised just how many Chinese people have good English, as I was to find out for myself, when I finally got there. I had to make arrangements to get a Chinese visa. I visited Dublin city shortly afterwards accompanied by Fengqin. There I handed my filled-out visa application form into the Chinese Embassy.

Into the unknown

❦

y visa was granted on returning there a few hours later, that same day. As long as all the paperwork was correct, then there weren't any problems. Back in that year of 2005 when I applied for my first visa, you just filled out the form. You then brought it to the Chinese Embassy and handed it in with the appropriate fee and waited a few hours before calling back to collect it. You could and still can apply for a visa for up to three months, six months, or even a year in some cases. This of course depends on your needs and circumstances. On this, my first trip, mine was to be for just over a week, within a three-month period. That was the application practice then, but it changed a few years ago. Now you would hand in your application form with the appropriate fee and wait a few days. Then you would go back and collect it, or if you preferred, it would be sent out to you in the post. If you wanted a visa quickly, you would have to pay extra money. The location and address of the Chinese Embassy was on Merrion Road in Dublin city then. It is still on Merrion Road but the address has changed. As far as I'm aware, Chinese people don't need visas if they have Chinese passports when they are returning to their native land, on holidays or permanently.

In between, Fengqin had made arrangements with Hong Wei for me to meet her in Beijing International Airport. She would have to leave her own city of Anshan by car in the early hours of the morning, drive ninety kilometres to the nearest airport which was in a city called Shenyang and then take a flight to Beijing. I had pencilled in Saturday November 12th as my departure date from Ireland. One week after my birthday, on November 5th.

Eight days were to be the duration of my stay. What was I going to expect? What was I going to see? Where was I going to go? What was I going to do? Where was I going to stay? Apart from Hong Wei, who else was I going to meet? All of these initial thoughts ran through my mind, over and over again as my departure date drew closer by the day.

There are several ways you can go to Beijing from Ireland. Regardless, you will have to break your journey with two flights. First a short one, followed by a long one. The travelling time going to Beijing for me was around eighteen hours. That was from leaving my own doorstep, getting to Dublin Airport, taking two flights, plus the waiting time spent in the airports. Don't forget, China is seven hours ahead on the clock in summertime and eight hours in the wintertime.

You can go from Dublin via Frankfurt in Germany (Airbus) to Beijing. You can go from Dublin via Amsterdam (KLM) to Beijing. You can also go from Dublin via London Heathrow (British Airways) to Beijing. Or you can go from Dublin via Charles de Gaulle airport (Air France) to Beijing. Alternatively, you can go from Cork via Charles de Gaulle airport (Air France) to Beijing. Lastly, you can also go Cork via London Heathrow (British Airways) to Beijing. Since 2019, there is now a new direct service from Dublin to Beijing, but a little more expensive. So you see, you have several ways to get to Beijing. I decided to go Dublin (Aer Lingus) via Amsterdam (KLM) to Beijing. Over the course of the intervening years, I have tried all of these routes and in my opinion, the Dutch Air company KLM are by far the best.

The day before I left, I went to see Fengqin in her flat. It was around midday, I remember it quite clearly, like it was only yesterday. She made a bit of lunch for me while I was there, which was most welcome. We naturally talked about my trip and what to expect.

"Billy, Hong Wei will be waiting for you at the arrivals area at Beijing International Airport. When you go through customs, continue walking and just follow the signs which will also be in English for the arrivals area. She will be there, Billy. Don't worry," said Fengqin. She reassured me all would be well.

With that, I thanked her for all her help, which had now brought me to this point in my life. "We will see where this takes me," I said.

It was around 15:00 when I said goodbye to her and left her dwelling. Sleep and rest were now the most important factor on my itinerary for the remainder of that day. This was to prepare me for my long journey the following day. I can safely say I found it hard to sleep that night. Wouldn't you? China beckoned me now! I never thought in a million years, this would happen to me.

It was in the early hours of Saturday November 12th in 2005, when I left my house by car, going across Rice Bridge which spans over the famous river Suir, and drove to Dublin Airport. Waterford is the oldest city in Ireland and the capital of the south east of the country.

Apprehension was certainly evident in my demeanour, on my way to Dublin Airport one hundred and ten miles away. After this two-and-a-half-hour journey, I finally arrived at my destination. I parked my car in the long-term car park and gathered my two suitcases. The shuttle bus which I had been waiting for arrived a few minutes later and took me to the terminal. Checking in on time is always so important to me, when you're going on any long-distance flight. I always took the view that it's better to be at the airport early and kill a bit of time, than to be leaving things late, as you might have a hold up on the way. Think of all the things that could go wrong, all for the sake of being there a little earlier. A puncture, a crash, some fault with your car. Even by bus, things can go wrong. Why take the risk by being late? For sure, the plane will still go without you.

Checking in at the appropriate time and with my suitcases now gone through, I went through security. At this time, I was just carrying one shoulder bag with all of my travel documents inside. When I was finished with security, I went for a meal. After that I headed for the departures area. Going through the departure area, all of my documents were in order. From Dublin to Amsterdam was the first and easy part of my journey.

The second part was going to be a long and tedious flight, but I was ready for what lay ahead. I had been to America a few times before, but this was to be a lot longer travelling time and going to another country with a different culture. I suppose you could say excitement was building too. The thought of what to expect in this far off country was also in the back of my mind. My plane departed Dublin Airport on time and arrived in Amsterdam on time.

After a period waiting in the terminal, the time for my next plane arrived. Everything was in order at the departure gate, so I was free to make my way to the waiting plane. I took my seat on this giant plane and waited for take-off. How these planes stay up in the air is still a mystery to me. The size of them alone would frighten you. It's quite amazing really when you think about it! You get on a plane in London, Amsterdam, Frankfurt or Paris and when you get off, you're in Beijing, the capital of China. Think about it, I find the thought of it, just amazing.

Eventually, this monster of a plane took off at the appropriate time. I had a book with me to relieve the boredom that accompanies you on long journeys. It's about eleven hours flying time. Also to keep you occupied, you can watch films or play music on your own personal control unit and screen. This is on an electrical system throughout the plane and is built into the back of the head rest of the passenger in front of you. The stewardesses will bring you food and drinks on a regular basis, but it is still a long and boring trip in general. That's my thoughts on this journey. Other people might not think the same. For me it doesn't get any easier and I would find it very hard to ever get used to it. How the stewardesses do it on a continuous work cycle is beyond me. I wouldn't do it for any money!

Eventually, the time came when the plane was a few miles out from the city of Beijing. The thought of it alone was mind boggling to me, to say the least. Here I was, about to touch down in a country that I never thought I would see in my lifetime. The moment of truth had arrived for me.

My plane touched down in Beijing International Airport on time, to the minute in fact. This I found quite amazing, considering the distance we had travelled. After alighting from this huge plane and breathing in my first breath of Chinese air, I couldn't quite believe I was actually in China, until I looked around and saw loads of Chinese airport staff. Some of them were moving around on small loading vehicles, while others were re-fuelling different planes for their return journeys to all parts of the world.

I entered the nearby designated terminal. Then I found myself going through the security section first. All of my papers were in order, which was a huge relief. Believe you me, excuses here would have fallen on deaf ears. You would naturally be a little nervous, especially in a strange country, plus the thoughts of the language barrier. In today's world and with the threats that are out there from certain individuals and terrorist groups, I can fully understand countries' security. I never have, nor will have any problem with this code of practice.

I continued through to the baggage reclaim area, where after a number of minutes, I collected my two suitcases. Next, it was on to the customs area. I think if we are honest, this is always a nerve-wracking experience for most visitors to foreign countries. Even though you would be carrying nothing illegal, it's just the thought, I guess. I was waved on by the custom officer, which then brought me into the main arrivals area.

Make no mistake about it, everything was for real now! I must admit, while I was a little nervous, the bigger part of me was still positive and confident of what was going to confront me. Fengqin had reassured me and that was good enough for me. I then proceeded to push my luggage trolley into the main arrivals area. Away in the distance, I could see crowds of people behind barriers, all waiting for their families, friends or foreign tourists. Or whatever the case may be! This was a wide-open area, where everyone came into view at the same time. Obviously being by myself, it was tough, as one would find it hard to pick someone out immediately from the huge and excited crowd. As I got closer, I tried to focus on seeing Hong Wei.

Then suddenly, from somewhere in the midst of this crowd, I heard a most welcoming shout. "Billy! Billy! Billy, over here!" I looked to my left and focused all along the continuous lines of excited people. Then, I spotted an equally excited Hong Wei. 'Ah, there she is,' I said to myself. I could see she was in the middle of a few people and waving her hands frantically trying to get my attention. Making my way over to her, we met, and a bunch of flowers appeared from nowhere.

In her very, very broken English she said, "These are for you Billy," followed by a hug and a peck on the cheek.

"Oh, how kind of you, Hong Wei!" I said. "Thank you so much for such a kind thought and especially for being here."

At least the ice was now broken, and contact was made. Hong Wei looked a little different from what I had seen in the two photographs that Fengqin had shown me back in Ireland a few weeks earlier. She was even nicer looking in reality! Then again, from a personal point of view, this was all about getting to know her. Hong Wei then introduced me to a friend of hers, a Mr. Wang who was going to be our interpreter. She had obviously brought him along, as it was a case of having to! She herself had practically no English, just a few words! Then again, who was I to talk – I had no Chinese either! A nice mix you might say, so make of it what you will! But I could see we were on a level footing, in this context anyway.

Just an observation, for what it's worth: I would stick with the opinion that it's easier for a Chinese person to learn English, than it is for an English-speaking person to learn Chinese. I have said that to a lot of people over the years and I have no reason to change that view.

Hong Wei and Mr. Wang summoned a waiting taxi for us outside the terminal building. Going out into the sunshine at around midday, in another land was all new to me. So, this was my first introduction to China. This was Beijing International Airport in the capital of China. Mr. Wang sat in the front of the taxi and gave strict instructions to the driver of where our destination was. Hong Wei and I occupied the back seat, where she was excitingly pointing out all of what was occupying my wide-open eyes. The traffic outside the airport was chaotic. Everything on four wheels was moving at a fast pace, like buses, trucks, vans, cars and taxies. I noticed a lot of the cars were new, big and fashionable, which rather surprised me. A lot more than I would have thought!

The taxis – they were there in their hundreds! So many that when hailing one, you would literally be waiting less than a minute. This trend continued when using taxies during my stay, never waiting more than a minute! I will stand over that statement, as this was the case everywhere else I went on my other nine visits to China. When it came to two wheels, well there were hundreds of motor bikes, mopeds and push bikes. When you mention push bikes, listen to this, while I was in Beijing for the eight days and as the line in the song goes… *there are nine million bicycles in Beijing*… Well, I must have seen all of them during my stay there! All of these vehicles were going about their daily routine with their own destinations in mind. I thought the Tour the France was big when it came to bikes. What a sight this was to see, especially where I had come from. It was the same story here in this place, every day. I found it absolutely amazing.

In the year 2014, there were roughly 1.35 billion people living in China. In the year 2019, there were roughly 1.40 billion people living in China. The most populated country in the world. The population of Beijing alone was around twenty-one million people then. This will tell you about the sheer volume of people I was expecting to see on landing in the capital of this country.

The sights that greeted me on the way into the city were real eye-openers in their own right. Thousands of old-style high-rise apartment blocks greeted my eyes. Obviously, these buildings were from the earlier days. These were now being overtaken by tall modern apartment skyscrapers that dotted the landscape. Huge cranes hung over the sides of these buildings that were still under construction. I could see hundreds of workers on different levels of these buildings, all working away, all doing what they had to do. On some buildings, the men were just like ants, such was the sheer amount of them. I would visually say, looking from a distance, the foremen had a very responsible job in directing all of these workers to their daily targets and what's more, to see that they were met.

The infrastructure was also fabulous, as the highways had four lanes, in both directions. The last time I saw something like this, was when I was in Los Angeles in America. I could see the highways intertwine with the flyovers on this taxi journey towards the centre of Beijing city. In China, they too, drive on the opposite side of the road to us! When you are in four lanes of traffic and see it going in both directions, you are talking about a lot of vehicles on the road.

It was like snakes and ladders, with continuous movement up, down and across. I know you get traffic jams in most countries in the world and particularly at certain times of the day, but there were none to be seen here. It was just after midday and all the traffic was moving so freely that it caught my unsuspecting eye. As we continued our journey to the city centre, all the aforementioned sights were still very much in evidence.

Gradually though, the landscape changed to one of high-rise neon signed factories, shops and large apartment blocks. Hong Wei was continually pointing out things of interest to me and I was taking note! The centre of Beijing was eventually coming into view. The adrenalin was now starting to flow even more within me. Now you're talking about serious crowds of people, thousands of them. As I said, I had been to America a few times, but this was just mind boggling. The streets were just one continuous flow of traffic, not to mention the bicycles. The footpaths were overladen with Chinese people of every description. They were tall, small, thin and very few fat. I suppose I would have to say most of them were really thin. You had the business fraternity, the well off, the ordinary, the poor, the old and the young. Our destination was soon on the horizon.

"Not too far to go now, Billy," was the call from Mr. Wang in broken English.

"Oh that's okay, Mr. Wang," I said. "I'm fascinated by what I'm seeing, it's unbelievable to see all of this."

Five minutes later, we arrived at our residence. It was the well-known and much used hostel called Jade International Youth Hostel. This was just a stone's throw from Tiananmen Square, right smack in the middle of Beijing city centre. As we were checking in, Mr. Wang and Hong Wei did all of the talking for me. I just stood there with my mouth open, my eyes open and my ears pricked, as the two of them produced their ID. My passport, travel arrangements and documents were shown to prove same, as the receptionist had requested.

While all of this was going on, I could see a lot of foreign people around the place. Some of these were at the long reception desk, checking in or checking out, or gathering information on their itinerary for the day. All these hostels and hotels, especially the big and well-known ones, would have a few staff at the reception that would be able to speak English as well as a few other languages. Other tourists were in the lobby with their suitcases while some more had different size back packs. I could see there were different nationalities from all over the world there. Obviously, this was a well-known landmark building and was being used regularly by students and tourists alike. It was like a little safe haven, where the atmosphere was relaxed and friendly.

I suppose it was particularly pleasing for those people who were probably visiting Beijing for the first time and perhaps did not have an interpreter to call on. This was where I was so lucky with Mr. Wang! I would have to say, even at this early stage that the staff were helpful and friendly, which put my mind at ease. I was now heading into the unknown for the next eight days.

I could see Hong Wei was anxious to show me around as much as she possibly could in close proximity to the hostel. I too, was excited about going out to see what I could in this monstrous city. I didn't want to disappoint her, but this was a day where my body had taken a lot of punishment, with all that travelling. Remember, I had gotten up early on the morning of my departure from Waterford city and drove to Dublin Airport. Then I waited for my flight to Amsterdam from where I then had to wait again before boarding my flight to Beijing.

When all of the preliminaries were done and we were checked in, we were then shown to our rooms. Mr. Wang had a single room and Hong Wei and I had a double room. The rooms were neat, tidy and spotless. The same layout as is in most other countries I would imagine. Hong Wei had arranged for us to have some food next. What was in store for me here, I said to myself, as the three of us made our way down to the restaurant, in this fine International Hostel. It really was first class. These were my introductory thoughts at first. This was now to be my first taste of real Chinese food. I could see Hong Wei was excited about showing me the menu and all its contents. Going back then and even now, as on our other visits to China, she can eat anything. I mean anything that is put in front of her. She just amazes me how she never lost her original taste of Chinese food. Over the last few years, most of the big and well-known hotels, especially in Beijing also serve English and European food. You also have the choice of using chopsticks or a knife and fork.

We sat down in this beautiful and relaxing restaurant. We studied the menu for several minutes, before Hong Wei and Mr. Wang first ordered. For them, it was a clear watery soup first; this was followed by dumplings with beef meat in them and a selection of vegetables. Their main meal was then washed down by one glass of hot milk and one glass of hot water. What we would describe as dessert, like ice cream or confectionary, here it was different. To my surprise their choice was fruit! A selection of apples, oranges, bananas and grapes appeared.

Whatever Hong Wei and Mr. Wang ordered in the following days of my stay, it didn't last too long on their plates. There was no wastage of food from these two Chinese people. The mindset is indoctrinated into their upbringing, waste not, want not. By the time my eight-day stay was over and seeing what I was to see in the following few days, I was of the same mindset also, when I left. Food for me of course was a different matter! Even though it was early afternoon, my choice of food was to be of a safe nature and I ordered soup. Expecting it to be the regular bowl of creamy mushroom or thick vegetable soup, as I was so accustomed to back in Ireland, boy, was I in for a big surprise. This was to be my very first taste of Chinese food on Chinese soil!

When my soup arrived in a lovely silver bowl, I thanked the waitress. It had a lid on it, and I could feel it was piping hot. remember saying to myself, I'm going to enjoy this. To my ultimate surprise, on lifting the lid and looking inside, yes it was soup okay, but there looking up at me were two fish heads, with eyes intact. What a shock I got! The fright nearly killed me! Needless to say, I declined immediately, even though Hong Wei tried to persuade me it was just for flavour. It was also customary and totally safe to eat. Customary or not, I wasn't for letting any of this go past my lips.

There were to be other shocks in store for me when it came to food in the following days. My main meal (with knife and fork or chopsticks) arrived a few minutes later. It was a piece of pork, two boiled eggs, two rashers and some bread. The bread was a little sweeter than I thought. The boiled eggs were okay too. The rashers were a bit like back home, but different in size. They were really only narrow strips of bacon, but very tasty and nice. This all had to be washed down. As I had never drank tea or coffee in my entire lifetime, I certainly wasn't about to start now, not even in China! So, it had to be beer for me. I had not seen any Guinness (Ireland's favourite alcoholic drink) in the large upright fridge that was close by in the corner of the restaurant, so it had to be a bottle of lager. With all the different names on the bottles of lager, one caught my eye, it was called Tiger beer. I said to Hong Wei, I think I'll try that one. In fact, I ordered two of these bottled beers. These were gladly sunk in quick succession, while at the same time, it enabled me to wash down this meal.

For me the rest of the menu was at a standstill. Some of the things I saw on it, I just couldn't have imagined eating them.

When our meal was finished, Hong Wei suggested to Mr. Wang (it was great to hear them speaking in Chinese) that we should all go for a walk. It was now close to 17:00 and it was starting to get dusk. We wouldn't have to go too far, as there would obviously be something to see, in close proximity to the hostel.

What I was shortly about to see was going to be interesting! This was certainly a sight that caught my eyes! The famous Tiananmen Square was just around the corner, as was The Forbidden City. These two famous landmark sights were booked in for me for the following day. Armed with my camera, Hong Wei, Mr. Wang and I left the confines of the hostel.

It was now approaching teatime, as we crossed the main road, where the traffic was now moving thick and fast. Cars, taxis, buses, trucks, motor bikes and ordinary bicycles in their hundreds greeted my eyes. For those who started early, work was finishing for the day. School was over too and it seemed that everybody on view was trying to get home. The exception of course being, the people that were only starting to go to work. At my request, we stopped a few times and I just stood there and watched this evening sight, as it happened. Obviously, Hong Wei and Mr. Wang had seen it all before. But, in fairness, they gave me loads of time to sample it for myself. You'd want to see the amount of people on the move. I definitely wanted to take all of this in. After all, I had only been in China a few hours!

I remembered and being realistic with my thoughts, I said to myself, would I ever be back here again? Who knew at this stage? It was anybody's guess! I said to myself, God knows what I'm going to see next!

I think seeing the masses of people in all of the big cities and at other social events, on my trips to China, is something that sticks in the visitor's mind, big time and forever!

We proceeded further down the street. Then we turned into another main street. What greeted my eyes here was the sight of food being cooked openly on the public road. This was the famous Wang Fujing Street. This is one of the most unique and fascinating streets in the whole of China. In fact, I would go as far and say, anywhere in the world! This street in Beijing is known all over the world to both locals and tourists alike. This main street has loads of cooking stalls, on both sides of the road, with everything you could imagine, being cooked. Most of this food would be described by the Chinese as a delicacy. I'm sure to most of us westerners, seeing some of this food at first sight, would think otherwise.

We started on stall number one and worked our way forward amongst the crowds. Our plan was to go up one side of the street, and down the other side. At the same time, take in all of the unique sights that would greet us, on this world-famous street. I would say at a guess, there were around sixty to eighty of these family run cooking stalls. Remember, the stall holders only have about five hours to sell what they have on offer. They desperately try to get your attention in the hope you will buy some of their perishable goods from their stall, before the clock runs out on them. I found it fascinating to watch this whole operation in action. This unique cycle continues every day at the same time and at the same spot. Some of these stall holders were so good at selling their wares; they could sell sand to an Arab.

The locals and other Chinese people that were there knew exactly what they wanted and which stall to go to. It was a routine shopping trip for them. Everything was being cooked, from starfish, to octopus, eels, beef, chicken, pork, steak and a whole host of other things that I couldn't even describe or even tell you what they were. But this was one big cooking sight in front of us. The tourist that were there, were like me, fascinated by what they were seeing. Some of them were sampling the different types of cooked food that was before them. Others took a more cautious approach and treaded carefully amongst the hundreds of people that frequent this famous street every evening, between the hours of 17:00 and 22:00. Most of them were taking photographs and tasting some of the very strange dishes that were on offer. Hong Wei, Mr. Wang and I also took photographs in similar poses with starfish, octopus, eels, but they were not for eating by me. Hong Wei and Mr. Wang had no problem consuming small portions of them, after pleading with me to try them also.

'Wait I'll try something in a minute', was my continuous reply! Eventually, I plucked up the courage and decided to go for the beef on the skewer stick. I remember saying to myself, I should be safe enough eating these. Hong Wei ordered six beef skewers for me. These are small pieces of beef that have been pierced with a very fine stick and cooked on an open charcoal grill or fire. Once you know what you are getting, these can be quite tasteful and satisfying to eat. They wouldn't fill you mind; they're really like appetisers I suppose. Don't forget also, we weren't long over our meal in the hostel.

Yes, these tasted really nice; in fact, I said to Hong Wei through Mr. Wang, "Can I have another six of those please?"

So she made her way to a stall to order six more of these for me. While she was gone, my eyes were scanning and looking around the place with curiosity and unabated interest in all that I was seeing. There were hundreds of people all over the place. But, out of the corner of my eye, I did see a sad sight. There were a lot of litter bins scattered around at various points, where as you can imagine, all of the different types of leftover or unfinished food are dumped when finished by everyone that frequents this crowded and very busy street. I saw the sad figure of a poor old man, with his head gone into a refuge bin, nearly followed by his body, in search of food. I watched him frantically going through some of the freshly thrown away leftovers. This sight greeted my eyes with sadness and surprise! Nobody even gave him a second glance, as he horridly moved his hands through a lot of the garbage that was also amongst the pieces of discarded food. I saw him retrieving mere scraps of food, to satisfy his hunger.

Just then, Hong Wei appeared out of the crowd and arrived back with the skewers of beef. I said to Mr. Wang, "Can Hong Wei get me six more of these please? Give me those and wait here," I said. They both looked at me in amazement, as I made my way through the crowds and in the direction of the old man. I tapped him on the shoulder, as his frantic search for food continued, before being interrupted by me. "Would you like to eat these?" I said. The language barrier was not a problem, he knew what I meant! He looked at me in astonishment, followed by a wide smile and a thank you gesture. I gave him the six skewers of beef, which disappeared inside his aching stomach, as if piranha fish had got a hold of them. Such was the hunger of this old man. It was something I had to do, even though I know it would be the same story for this poor individual and others the following day. It's the same the world over I guess, but it shouldn't be like this. There has to be an answer out there somewhere!

Hong Wei and Mr. Wang were still looking at me in surprise, as I returned to their company. Then Hong Wei gave me the extra six skewers of beef, which went down a treat. We then continued on our journey around this fabulous street. The sight of all the different foods being openly cooked was everywhere. To my disappointment, having gone up one side of the street and down the other side, our journey finally finished. I was enjoying watching all of the activity that was taking place. It truly was and still is an amazing street to see.

There was to be a lot more fascinating sights to catch my eyes before this first trip to China was over! I would say this opening sightseeing trip took us about two hours. There was no need to rush, as we had all night. We eventually made our way back to the hostel, through the maddening crowds and chaotic traffic that was still to be seen. For me, this was still a magical sight to see. After entering and exiting the lift on our designated floor, Mr. Wang said goodbye to us and said he would see us early for breakfast in the morning, around 09:00. Then Hong Wei and I made our way to our own bedroom. It was a normal bedroom with all the familiar surroundings. Everything was neat and tidy, and I could see from looking around, that it was cleaned thoroughly on a daily basis. This was a well-run international hostel, with a reputation to uphold. Hong Wei just had a little English, but I could see she was relaxed in my company and we communicated okay.

I slept soundly, as fatigue from all of the travelling had played a big part in me getting the sleep that I got. My body had been put through the mill. We slept until the following morning, when the early sun shone through our window, and awoke us. It was Monday November 14th!

We got up at around 08:00, showered and met Mr. Wang at the arranged time in the restaurant. As regards my breakfast, I chose from the menu, two eggs, two rashers and some bread. The only difference was, it was a buffet service in the morning time. You just went up to the counter and got what you wanted. Luckily, I was able to get what I wanted. Plus the two Tiger beers from the fridge were a welcome sight too. I had to play it safe, as it was early days on this maiden trip. Hong Wei and Mr. Wang got a bowl of boiled rice each, eggs, a thing called Tofu and various colourises to mix with other delicacies that were on their plates. They both drank several glasses of hot water each. No, this change over of food was not for me yet, if ever! The three of us finished breakfast at around 09:30. What was in store for me was anybody's guess, but I was here for a serious reason and that was to see what bearing this trip would have on my life, if any!

So, what was next for me, on this journey into the unknown? Hong Wei, spoke through Mr. Wang and directed him to tell me what our itinerary was for the day. He told me we were going around the corner to see The Forbidden City and then Tiananmen Square. Thanking Mr. Wang, the three of us set off, on what was going to be a mystery tour for me. After a ten-minute walk, we entered from a side road, out onto the main street. As I looked across the ten-lane road (yes ten lanes), five each way, I could see Tiananmen Square in the distance.

There were a few monuments there which I presumed were replicating Chinese history. There were other buildings there also, but I did not know then what they represented from the distance I was at. I knew time would tell me in due course! One building I did know (from reading about it) was at the far end of the square. It was a mausoleum, where their great leader Mao Zedong (to us in the west, he would be known as Chairman Mao) lies in state. Tiananmen Square is directly across the main road from

The Forbidden City. The entrance to the first phase of The Forbidden City was parallel to the footpath on which we were walking. As we got to the entrance, I looked up to see a giant photograph of the late Chinese leader, Mao Zedong.

Bright lights, big city

❦

He was born on December 26ᵗʰ in 1893 and died on September 9ᵗʰ in 1976 at the age of 83. Yes, this was definitely a new experience for me!

Here I was standing at the entrance to one of China's greatest landmarks. Firstly, one has to walk through The Meridian Gate and then over The Golden Water Bridges. This is a set of five bridges (Take your pick!), to enter the first phase of The Forbidden City. This place was originally known as, The Purple Palace or The Grand Palace. It is now known as The Palace Museum. It is one of the five most important palaces in the world and one of the most visited World Heritage destinations. In one day alone, on October 2ⁿᵈ in 2013, one hundred and seventy-five thousand people visited this historic place. Now isn't that an unbelievable amount of people? You'll agree, quite staggering to say the least!

There are around ninety palaces and court yards. There are nine hundred and eighty buildings and some eight thousand, seven hundred rooms. The Forbidden City is divided into two parts, called the outer courts and the inner courts. The three main buildings in each are central to the history. The inner courts housed the Emperors' families, which were off limits to the ordinary man. In history, trespassing here was punishable by death or a long prison sentence. The outer courts, as you can imagine, were outside of these areas. At the four corners of this gigantic complex, there are four main watch towers, called the Corner Towers. These were obviously built for security, as you can imagine. There is also a moat running around the entire perimeter of this amazing place. This was home to twenty-four Chinese emperors, from the Qing Dynasty to the Ming Dynasty, over a period of years, from 1420–1911.

Thousands of tourists from around the world and Chinese people from all over China visit this group of buildings every day. Never would you see such a selection of cameras on view. Practically every second person had a camera to capture and take in this unique and historical place. The layout of these buildings is like a funnel. You go through one to get to the other and so on. We would only be going through the main spine of The Forbidden City.

After entering The Meridian Gates and crossing The Water Bridges, the first building comes into view. This building is called the Gate of Supreme Harmony. This is followed by the Hall of Supreme Harmony. Then you continue on through the Hall of Central Harmony followed by the Hall of Preserving Harmony. To me, these buildings all looked like those in the outer court! You continue on further, which to me brings you into the inner court. These were, the Gate of Heavenly Purity, followed by the Hall of Heavenly Purity. Then you had the Hall of Union, followed by the Palace of Earthly Tranquillity and then the Gate of Earthly Tranquillity. The Imperial Garden followed and then towards the rear was the Hall of Imperial Peace and the Gate of Loyal Obedience. Lastly through the rear exit was the Gate of Divine Prowess.

As I said earlier, that was just the main spine of The Forbidden City. I presumed Hong Wei and Mr. Wang had been to Beijing at some point in their lives. Obviously they had seen it all before!

At the entrance to the first building and the ancillary buildings (there were loads of these) that followed, there were huge signs depicting the history that is attached to the relevant buildings. It's obviously written in Chinese first and then English. But in some cases, they are written in more than two languages (I think I saw German and Italian) used in some, although I stand to be corrected!

We took in all the sights as I simultaneously read all of the history relating to the buildings and the rest in rotation. This all takes time and you would need plenty of it. It starts with the Ming dynasty and goes right back through history. Right from the beginning with all of the different emperors! The first buildings and the rest all had different artefacts, such as paintings, antiques, cloths, jewellery, furniture and war memorabilia such as swords, knives and a lot of other instruments which were used in battles. There were other eye-catching sights also, such as museums, libraries, rare books and historical documents, bronze ware, jade, timepieces and sculptures. After nearly three hours of walking in and out of buildings, we had seen a lot. I thought that was that, but on our way back out of the outer court yards a sign caught my eye; it simply said Ceramics.

"Hong Wei," I said. "Look at that sign over there."

Hong Wei in her wisdom beckoned to Mr. Wang. He asked me did I want to see over there.

Obviously, we had missed this attraction on the way in, as it was off the main walkway. "I sure do," I said. "No way am I going to miss anything inside these four walls."

You see I'm like that. I wanted to know what was hidden behind these doors. On entering this three-building section, boy, was I in for a surprise. There was one to the right, one to the left and one in front. We headed for the building in the front first. The sight that greeted my eyes was unbelievable! There were ceramic vases of all sizes, pots, statues, bowls, plates and figures, all dating back in history.

Some, even as far back, as the 16th and 17th century. What I was seeing was unreal, compared to the rest of the contents in other buildings in the Forbidden City. As far as I was concerned, this was the jewel in the crown for me! The other two buildings contained similar artefacts. In each of the buildings there were security attendants. In rotation, Hong Wei asked them in Chinese of course, could I take a photograph. To my surprise, 'Yes', was the reply that greeted my ears with great joy and satisfaction. These three buildings were like Aladdin's caves, such was the treasures that they contained. After spending some satisfied time there, it was finally time to go! So as you can see, you could easily spend the day there, just trying to take all of this in. This was all fascinating for me to see. I tried to grasp the enormity of what I was looking at. But for me, or I guess any westerner to take it all in one go, was a tall order! Hong Wei took a lot of photographs throughout the entire tour. Also through our interpreter,

Mr. Wang, she told me lots of things about the different aspects of what I was looking at.

As you can imagine with all of these priceless and irreplaceable artefacts from history on view, I could well understand and see why security was extremely tight. Believe you me, when I say tight, I mean tight! The visible presence of security personnel was everywhere and who could blame them? After all, you are dealing with one's own country's heritage! We must have spent the best part of four hours in there, with that extra sight included in The Forbidden City. Having spent that amount of time walking around the place, it felt like my legs weren't there anymore, such was the tiredness. I would still recommend to anyone given the chance, to go and see The Forbidden City. If you are in Beijing, you really can't miss it! It's a must, you won't be disappointed! There should be no excuses, go and see it.

We emerged back into the busy everyday life that is Beijing, while still shaking my head with all that I had just seen. The main road outside The Forbidden City and next to Tiananmen Square is called Chang'An Avenue and caters for ten lanes of traffic, five both ways. I stood there with Hong Wei and Mr. Wang for a few minutes and just watched. What a sight to behold!

Both of them, then directed me to the underground that goes beneath this massive road. Walking across it was definitely a non-runner! When we emerged from underneath it on the other side, Tiananmen Square was looking straight at us. Do you know it's the fourth biggest square in the world, on a par with St. Peter's Square in Rome in Italy or The Kremlin in Moscow in Russia, to name but two. Being one of the largest public squares in the world, it can hold up to one million people. You'll agree that's worth thinking about!

As it was now nearing 14:00, it was time for a quick rest off our feet and a snack in any one of the hundreds of restaurants that surround these two most important places. Again, caution was uppermost in my mind as regards food! Hong Wei's intentions were good, and my welfare was to the forefront of her mind. We settled into a small restaurant and she asked me through Mr. Wang what I would like to eat. Of course, me looking at the menu here was like looking up a bull's rear end. Whatever Hong Wei and Mr. Wang had, I didn't have! Even though it looked nice, I was not for sharing this food. There are colourizers on offer at every mealtime. These are mainly for adding flavour to your meal, whatever it might be. They look nice and colourful but try tasting them. For my taste, I found it was a different story. I explained to Mr. Wang, I did not mean to offend anyone as regards not appreciating the hospitality that was being afforded to me, on this my second day in China. There would be lots more days and nights, in my other visits to China, where I ate food in many more restaurants and hotels.

As regards the food, I finally settled for beef slices with chicken flavoured noodles and roast chicken. These were all served on separate plates; with potatoes and vegetables in soup (without the fish heads) I might add. I used chopsticks and a spoon for the potatoes, vegetables and soup. I was learning fast in this amazing place! This, of course, all had to be washed down with two bottles of Tiger beer. With me it was a case of the devil you know is better than the devil you don't.

I had Chinese currency (which is called yuan) with me, which I had given to Hong Wei that morning, for safe keeping. The value of Chinese money then in 2005 was roughly, ten yuan to one euro in Ireland. For example, to simplify it, ten euro was worth one hundred yuan. Over the course of the few days that I was there, we had to visit the bank a few times to change money. Here my passport was produced by Hong Wei on my behalf. It was scrutinised and double checked by the teller, before any transaction was done, or any money changed hands. If the notes are torn or damaged, the teller won't accept them. Outside some of the banks, you will have certain Chinese people who will approach you and ask do you want to change your money. These people can be very persuasive and seem at times like they will not take no for an answer! You have to be strong here and do as I did, give them a bit of the old foul language (you know, it starts with an F and ends with off) and this usually works. They will offer to change your money but will want commission for doing so.

Hong Wei advised me not to entertain them under any circumstances. I would pass the same advice on to any westerner visiting Beijing; stay well clear of these people. Just be alert and careful and keep all of your money and documents out of view, until your well inside the safe confines of the bank.

When our meal was finished and my body rested, particular my legs, it was time to see Tiananmen Square. Well yes, Tiananmen Square, what can I say! The one thing I did know about it, was that Mao Zedong's body lay in state there, in a Mausoleum. Seeing is believing and believe you me, it is worth seeing! It is a big wide-open space, with hundreds of people on it at any given time.

The Chinese flag flies proudly at one end of the square, directly across the road from The Forbidden City. We made our way over to the flagpole which is set on a raised platform and surrounded by decorative Chinese stone. I stood there and looked at the flag and thought of what it meant and represented to the Chinese people. Like any national flag of any country, it symbolises your heritage, the country's history from its origins to the present day and the future. It's the one thing that unites any country and its people? It's what you believe in and in some countries' history, people have died for it. My own country of Ireland is just one example. If you lose that identity, you lose everything as a nation. Standing and pausing there for a few more minutes, I reminisced with my thoughts.

Every day in the presence of hundreds of Chinese people and visitors alike, the flag is hoisted with great pride, in a ceremony every morning at sunrise and lowered every evening at sunset, in similar fashion. As it was the early afternoon, I remember speaking to Hong Wei, through our interpreter Mr. Wang.

"We must find out what time the flag will be lowered at this evening," I said. "I definitely want to see this ceremony and what it entails."

"Sure Billy, we will come back later, when we find out the time and see it," said Mr. Wang.

"Can you find out the time now and at least we'll know for sure?" I said. Mr. Wang and Hong Wei then asked a few Chinese people that were close by. They were duly informed that the flag would be lowered at around 17:30 that evening. That was good enough for me and I thanked them.

Something which I was to learn a few years later on one of my other visits to Beijing, I found quite astonishing. Do you know you can actually check months in advance through the internet and get the exact time, practically to the minute, of what time the Chinese flag will be raised at sunrise and lowered at sunset on any given day? I found that information to be quite useful and unreal.

As I curiously looked around where we stood, I could see there were a lot of unarmed soldiers in different locations around the square, all standing to attention in their green uniforms and white belts. They all looked very young and smart but were very alert in doing their national security duty. It is not advisable to continuously ask them to stand in for photographs. They are under strict orders not to participate and don't take kindly to being asked. Remember, there are hundreds of foreign tourists walking around the square all day long. Imagine if they were all to start posing for photographs for every second visitor. You can imagine the interruptions and lapse of concentration these soldiers would have in doing their daily duty. So, I'm sure you've heard the old saying, 'When in Rome, do as the Romans do'.

We obeyed the rules and I resisted from asking for a photograph with one of them, even though I would have loved one. We then headed towards the opposite end of Tiananmen Square. This was towards the Mausoleum building where Mao Zedong lies in state. I knew the chance of seeing him now at this time of the day was slim, particularly when I saw the crowds that were still there from a distance. This has and still remains the daily routine (since his death in 1976) where Chinese people and visitors alike from all over the world come to see him. This event for me would now have to wait until the following day. But there were still a lot more for me to see! I then made the point to Hong Wei and Mr. Wang,

"Tomorrow morning I want to visit the Mausoleum. I don't care how long it takes. I'm prepared to wait like everybody else in the queue of hundreds to see Mao Zedong."

"Okay," said Mr. Wang, "that will be done for you Billy."

You know, I think most of us Irishmen have loads of patience and endurance; it's one of our strong points. Little did I know then, but the following day, I was going to need it, in fact all of it!

The other building on the square to our right was The Great Hall of the People. Straight in front of us was The War Heroes Monument. This was a huge structure of solid stone, standing upright and towering over Tiananmen Square. We made our way to this, as it was directly in front of us. On our way I could see from her body language that Hong Wei was excited at the interest I was showing in wanting to learn all about the Chinese history attached to these amazing sights. I said to her, through Mr. Wang, "I love history and learning about other countries cultures and seeing as much as possible of their historical sights."

After several minutes we arrived at The War Heroes Monument. This has a decorative solid base of stone in a block appearance and rising to a second level on which this gigantic piece of carefully cut stone is sitting. It is huge and can be very deceptive when you are alongside it, compared to seeing it from a distance. But what a piece of stonework it is, in its entirety. It was incredible to think someone could actually create this from stone.

Lots of Chinese people and visitors alike were getting photographs taking in groups or individually around this huge structure. I suppose in some cases it was to prove to their friends and family that they were actually there. Other reasons were probably historical, due to the fact that there is a lot of Chinese engraved writing all around the stone, dictating past events and what 'The War Heroes Monument' is really all about. Of course, looking at all the Chinese writing was non-sensical to me, as I couldn't speak or read Chinese. It did fascinate me though how the writing was carved into the stone and how beautifully painted in red (The Chinese National colour) it was.

Mr. Wang and Hong Wei through talking and sign language tried their best to tell me what the writings meant. But I did know it all related to past war events and historical dates, such as Liberation day in 1949 and Martyr's Day on September 30th to October 1st.

As I admired all that was before me, I was very respectful of all of this, where I was and what this monument represented and meant to every Chinese person, dead or alive! Naturally I got a few photographs taken in close proximity to this monument. It was then time to move on! There was a lot more to see and a lot more to do!

To the far right, was The Great Hall of the People. This is one of the places where the Chinese National People's Congress (government) meets a few times a year. It's a magnificent building with the Chinese National flag proudly displayed on the front of it, high above the entrance. Then across the top of the roof and at several intervals there are more Chinese flags fluttering in the wind.

A beautiful sight to see and I acknowledged how the Chinese honour their National flag. There are steps leading up to the main entrance. The day we were there, it was closed to the public. Even now, I'm still not quite sure if it is in fact open to the general public at all. But it's a beautiful building to see and how it stands out on the skyline. Mr. Wang and Hong Wei were again busy trying to explain to me what the building was all about. I acknowledged their contribution and was grateful for their input.

Just a passing point, the meeting hall can hold up to ten thousand people at a sitting. Furthermore, there is also a banqueting hall there with seating for five thousand people. I thought to myself and in a joking way, how many chefs and servants, would you need at one of those functions?

Turning on our heels, it was now time to move on. We were on Tiananmen Square and from where the Chinese flag flies, we were moving from left to right. As the clock moved on, so too did the tourists and Chinese people to see the other historical sites that are there. Our next objective was just to have a customary glance at the Mausoleum where Mao Zedong lays in state. As we walked towards it, Hong Wei (while keeping a tight grip on me) and Mr. Wang were in conversation. I was still able to communicate at times through body language. Then, from a distance I could see two separate long stoned sculptures of Chinese soldiers in battle. These stood in front of the Mausoleum and on huge platforms of stone. A few minutes later, we arrived at these magnificent stone sights. I was amazed at the length, height and detail of these sculptures.

I was to learn later through Mr. Wang that they depicted the history of the Chinese people's revolution in 1949. As I thought initially, that's what these were all about. This information intrigued me, when listening about past Chinese events. There were people there admiring these stone carvings and taking photographs, as I was. The amount of detail in the stone figures was unreal. Their faces, their clothes and the weaponry they each carried, were nearly lifelike. They all had one thing in common though! They were all looking the one way and totally focused on their enemy in pursuit of victory. This was my impression of these sculptured stone carvings. These two sights impressed me. I must have walked around each of them at least five times and studied every detail. Again, we took a few photographs, between the three of us. Rotating positions and in different poses around these stone sculptures. With that intense observation finished, it was time to move on again! It was also time to have a visual look at the Mausoleum. It was a short distance from where we stood! What a sight this was to see! It was still another huge and magnificent building from the outside. The visiting times during the year of 2005 were from 08:30 to 11:30 and from 14:00 to 16:00. It was now close to 16:00, as the last of the visitors were just entering the building.

We approached the security barriers that surrounded the visitors entry and just stood there, observing the last of the day's proceedings. I knew I would have to wait until the following day to see the inside of this building and more importantly, the body of Mao Zedong lying in state. After spending some time there, and studying the structure of this building, the mere sight of it in its entirety and what I had seen on Tiananmen Square over the previous hours had left me in awe! The clock was moving on and so were we.

We headed back to the opposite end of Tiananmen Square to wait our turn, amongst the hundreds of Chinese and tourists from all over the world that gather twice daily for the raising and lowering of the Chinese national flag. As I said earlier, the flag is raised at sunrise and lowered at sunset. In our case it would be sunset, so patience would be needed. It's not every day one is going to see this ceremony. In my case, I was only too well aware, I might never see it happening again.

It took the three of us a while to reach our destination. We then took our places, having got a good vantage spot (because we were early) amongst the waiting crowds. It was just a matter of waiting and being patient for the moment, which was scheduled for 17:30, something to this Irishman, was not a problem; I couldn't speak for Hong Wei and Mr. Wang. Who would have guessed (least of all me) where I would be on this particular day in the year of 2005. I never thought I would be standing on Tiananmen Square, in Beijing city, in China, but I truly was!

As in life, one never knows what lies around the corner. There are a million things that can happen to any individual person in one's lifetime. Some good, some bad and as regards your health – well that is a complete lucky dip. So, the real question is, how does one cope? Well, that my friends, can only be answered by oneself. The way I see it, everyone has to make the most of the cards they are dealt with in this life. Understandably I'm afraid, some people are weaker than others. That's the human nature of us, something that we will never quite fully understand. My motto in life is and always has been, while we are here on this planet, let's make the most of it. I say, don't have any regrets about making certain decisions or not making other decisions in your life. Although, I do fully accept, it's easier to be wiser after the event.

The moment for the flag lowering ceremony did finally arrive and on time. What a moment to saviour, I thought to myself. The ten-lane traffic (five each way) on Chang' An Avenue between The Forbidden City and Tiananmen Square is given a direct command to stop by the traffic police. Immediately, all the traffic stops in an instant! Then, from one of the private entrances to The Forbidden City emerges a platoon of armed soldiers, led by a higher-ranking officer.

The precision and pace with which they march straight out onto the road is eye-catching. Cameras are continuously flashing from every vantage point, as mine was. Also bear in mind of course, how many tourists and Chinese are witnessing this. For some, it would have been a once in a lifetime experience, knowing they would probably never be back. Could this have been the case for me also, I wondered.

Back in the year of 2005 it was the practice, or so I believe, as I had heard when I was there that there was a private military tunnel under the main road. The soldier that was to lower the flag would surface a few minutes earlier through a trap door, having used the tunnel, and wait for the armed party to arrive. From where we were, it was hard to distinguish whether this was true or false.

When the platoon arrived, orders were given and several drill movements were carried out, then the soldiers all stood to attention. The timing in their movements were immaculate and to the second. What a sight to see, I'm sure it was the same for everyone present. Then the flag was slowly lowered, while the platoon of soldiers saluted its movement and was eventually folded in the same exercise, by the appointed soldier. You could hear a pin drop, as this most sacred of ceremonies was taking place. If memory serves me right, the soldier with the carefully folded flag disappeared back down the trap door and returned to The Forbidden City through the tunnel. At the conclusion of this exercise, more drill orders were given to the platoon as they made their way from the now vacant flagpole and marched across the still and motionless main road before entering the same entrance they had emerged from a few minutes earlier.

When this exercise finished and not until it finished, the traffic must wait until a signal is given and then it continues to flow. This was the centre of Beijing at teatime, with hundreds of cars in the ten lanes. I would have guessed the whole ceremony from start to finish would have lasted about ten minutes. I would advise anyone to go and see this ceremony if at all possible, at sunrise or sunset. It really is a must and it has to be seen in reality to really take it all in. The military precision at which it is carried out is breath-taking! With that eye-opening ceremony over, it was time to head back to our much-publicised hostel. When we got back to our temporary dwelling, it was after 18:00. Hong Wei and I made our way to our room, while Mr. Wang said goodbye. As he retreated his instructions were that he would see us at 20:00 in the main lobby, as we would be going out for dinner somewhere.

Hong Wei's English was very poor, but we were able to communicate through body language. She was relaxed in my company, as I was in hers. We rested our tired bodies with a relaxing sleep for about an hour. On awakening we had a quick shower and changed into some clean clothes. We arrived in the lobby at one minute to 20:00, where Mr. Wang greeted us with a broad smile.

"Billy," he said, "we are going someplace nice for dinner. This restaurant was recommended to me by a friend. Is that okay with you?" he said.

"Yep, that sounds okay by me," I said. Who was I to argue with a Chinese man in the middle of Beijing?

We hailed a taxi from outside the hostel on the main road. As I have said earlier, it only takes about a minute of waiting time. We departed through the busy streets as the neon lights, shop fronts and busy food stalls all lit up the many streets we passed through. Ah yes, this was a different Beijing at night, than what we had seen a few hours earlier. As regards people, well they were everywhere! Each going their separate way, as if they were on a mission.

My stomach and curiosity were now calling the shots, as I wondered where this taxi was taking us. After a few minutes, we arrived at this rather impressive looking restaurant. As we walked up the steps, with Hong Wei holding my hand tightly, I could see there were a lot of people entering and exiting this restaurant, which indicated to me that this was a busy and well-known eating establishment. When you enter the main lobby or reception area, usually there are one or two waitresses there in Chinese costumes.

They warmly greet you with a Chinese welcome, especially westerners. Usually, you are escorted to your table, but if you prefer, you can still pick one of your choice anywhere within the restaurant. The waitresses won't argue with you, as they know there are lots more competition out there on the streets from other eating establishments. On this occasion, we were guided to a table facing onto the busy road that could be seen through the large window that separated us.

I had noticed on our way in, a large fish tank in the lobby, with lots of fish swimming around in it. I asked Mr. Wang what the purpose of all this was. Were the fish all for show, like back home in the fish tanks you see in most Chinese restaurants? He bluntly told me if you want a fish on the menu, it has to be cooked. You just pick whichever fish you want, and they cook it for you. It would be taken out, killed and cooked in a few minutes.

I said to him, "Just like that?"

He said, "Yes Billy, just like that."

Needless to say, I declined his offer.

Service always comes immediately, which is great to see. Hong Wei and Mr. Wang ordered hot water to drink, which really amazed me. For the duration of my stay, both of them always drank hot water. For me it was different, I ordered two bottles of Tiger beer, as had been the case until now. So far, so good – why change? Though I did have intentions of sampling other beers before my eight-day stay was over. But for now, Tiger beer was my preferred choice. When it came to ordering food, I felt it was time to be a little braver.

Hong Wei was excited showing me (through pointing out) all of the different choices on the menu that were before me. There were various things like chicken wings, chicken legs, slices of beef and pork, cow's tongues, other choices and fish, of course. They were lots more for me to see there. Some I could describe, but you mightn't like me to describe others! Then you had loads of various delicacies, plus all different soups. You also had things like chow mein, barbecued spare-ribs, chicken balls in batter, spring rolls, noodles, meat dumplings and obviously boiled or fried rice. All dishes that we Europeans would be accustomed to seeing in our local Chinese restaurants and takeaway back home.

Again, I had to play it safe. Going just a little further, I thought about tempting fate. Was now the time I thought? For the starters, Hong Wei ordered some chicken wings for me. They had some strange fruit that I had never even seen before, nor did I even ask what it was. The chicken wings arrived and were eaten by me, much to my satisfaction. Then through Mr. Wang, I ordered the chicken balls in batter, the slices of beef and pork and some boiled rice. I also ordered a few spring rolls. I felt I was safe for the moment going that route. I'm afraid soup and fish were off the menu for me and even at that early stage they would remain off my menu for the duration of my stay. Even now looking back on my other subsequent visits that were to follow, fish by itself has never been consumed by me, nor will it ever be!

Hong Wei and Mr. Wang ordered too. What they ordered I didn't know, as they understandably spoke in Chinese and therefore left me in the dark until it arrived, and l got a look at it. For me, I reckoned seeing would be believing. Hong Wei, in her good nature, kept asking Mr. Wang had I ordered enough. Even today, she is always concerned about my welfare, day or night and wherever we go. This I took great notice of and it had me thinking inside a bit more.

Remember I mentioned colourisers earlier? And how they always accompany the food. They were presented to us in all colours again. They came in small beautiful decorated Chinese bowls and are there to add a little flavour to your particular dish. Chopsticks or a knife and fork arrive before any food. It was all about learning for me, so I stuck with the chopsticks.

Naturally, the hot water and Tiger beer arrived first. A few minutes later the food followed, all on different plates and piping hot. It all looked rather beautiful. I was looking at all the different foods displaying their own identity with colour and flavour. We tucked into our food, and with every mouthful I took, the hunger pains were slowly easing for me. I couldn't really imagine washing this food down with hot water. As you know, most Chinese food is served hot and I think to us westerners, the thought of drinking beer or a mineral to wash it down instead of water makes more sense.

After all that, it was now time for dessert. Looking at the menu and trying to figure out what was what, the only choice I saw that I recognized were banana fritters in batter and syrup. Oh yes, I said to myself, I'll have them! Hong Wei and Mr. Wang skipped desert and just sipped away on their hot water, while waiting for me to finish my third course. The banana fritters were delicious, the syrup was just a little too sweet, but edible. Throughout my meal and when finishing it, I had noticed a lot of other Chinese customers continually looking in our direction. Sometimes you could be the only westerner in a restaurant, so I think it's natural for them to be curious and understandable from their point of view. I took no offence to it, as I knew where they were coming from. I must also add, they were very friendly, constantly smiling and also inquisitive to hear me talking English to Mr. Wang. This has always been the case and still is on my visits; I return the acknowledgement in body language with a smile.

With starter, dinner and desert finished, plus an extra Tiger beer consumed, you could say I was now full. I felt the choices I had made with my food were right and most pleasing to eat. Restaurants in Beijing and all over China are completely different to the European way in terms of service and price. They are mainly visually graded in tiers and laid out in different ways. For example, restaurants on the main streets of the big cities, or well-known restaurants with a good name are obviously dearer than others. That is understandable and I suppose, the same in every country. But the cost factor in China is a lot cheaper, due to their economy. Like the meal we had just consumed and what we had paid for it. It would have been a lot more expensive back home in Ireland.

Back in that year of 2005, one Euro was worth ten Yuan. Our bill was about four hundred Yuan, which was the equivalent of forty Euros in Ireland. The other restaurants, while working their way down the pecking order, can be seen in lesser streets and poorer parts of Beijing. They are obviously cheaper, and the choices of food are limited. It boils down to just basic food, which is well cooked and will have its own flavour. I'm afraid that's life, the world over! The imbalance is there in every country on the planet. The rich, the well off, the working class, the poor and the desperate who just keep searching for survival, by whatever means they can.

After paying our bill and saying goodbye to the excellent and friendly staff, it was time for some fresh air and a walk. The time was around 22:00, as we walked outside the restaurant and into the night air. It was a little chilly, but not too cold. I noticed the nightlife in Beijing was in full flow. Taxies, cars, buses, trucks and of course motor bikes and bicycles in their hundreds were all going with the flow. When it came to people, well what can I say? There were people everywhere; they were all going somewhere, in their own planned schedule. As I said earlier, there were around twenty-one million people living in Beijing in 2005. It was not an unusual sight to behold, even at that time of night.

Mr. Wang said to me, "Billy, we will go for a little walk and then get straight back to our hostel, as tomorrow is going to be a long day for you. Okay?"

"Sure, that's okay by me," I replied.

With Hong Wei holding me closely to her and Mr. Wang in company with us, we strolled through a few streets, with me observing all the surrounding sights. Shops, restaurants, clubs and food stalls were scattered all around everywhere. The neon lights on some of these buildings were flashing brightly. This was such a rare sight for me to see.

After about fifteen minutes of walking, Mr. Wang hailed a taxi. Within a minute or even less, we were on board a taxi bound for our hostel. Mr. Wang took the front seat and Hong Wei and I sat in the back. Within ten minutes, our public service vehicle was screeching to a halt at the hostel. These taxis don't hang around waiting, as time is money. They literally go from one job to another, or they are constantly flagged down on the streets every few minutes. They move quickly through the heavy traffic. I mean fast, but within the speed limit! Then again in Beijing, the capital, the pace of life and the traffic are what you would expect. I suppose you could say, they're both in the fast lane. The majority of the taxies in Beijing are green and yellow in colour. I was to learn over the years that in the cities that I visited, most if not all of them had their own different independent coloured taxies.

Hong Wei and I said goodbye to Mr. Wang and we went our separate ways, with instructions to meet for breakfast the following morning at 09:00 in the restaurant. Tiredness had again hit my body, as this had been another long day. Hong Wei and I communicated through body language, as she still had very little English. My feelings for Hong Wei were cautiously getting stronger and I detected hers were too. We both fell into a deep sleep.

I awoke first the following morning and got up. It was around 08:15. I observed that Hong Wei was still asleep. I showered and freshened up, as I knew we were in for a long day. Where would my thoughts lie at the end of this third day in China, I wondered. On my return from the en-suite to our bedroom, Hong Wei had awoken and hurriedly followed the same routine.

For those fifteen or so minutes, while I was waiting for Hong Wei to re-emerge, I was left alone with my thoughts. This was where my life had brought me to now, I thought. Who would have believed it? But I was positive in my thinking that this was where I wanted to be. After all, I knew what waited back in Ireland, as regards my lifestyle. Was fate beginning to surface again in my life?

When Hong Wei re-appeared, within minutes we were on our way to the restaurant for our 09:00 deadline. Mr. Wang was waiting and greeted us on our arrival. His English was good, and I was beginning to understand him better with each passing hour. The buffet service was up and running – you just took what you wanted. It was pre-cooked and in hot platters laid out on tables. The presentation was top class and spotless. I got the same breakfast as the previous morning and was content with that, for the moment. Hong Wei and Mr. Wang also practically got the same breakfast as the previous morning. We tucked in and when we were finished, we returned all our empty plates, cups and glasses to the service area. It was a bit early for me to be drinking beer, but never having drunk tea or coffee in my lifetime, what other choices did I have? The time was 09:45 as we got up from the table.

Our first port of call was to go and see Mao Zedong lying in state in the mausoleum on Tiananmen Square. It was within walking distance, so we set off. Nice and fresh and eager to see this most privileged of viewings and not knowing what to expect, added to the excitement within my thoughts. Hong Wei was sticking to me like a plaster and kept a firm grip on my arm. Mr. Wang was level with us on the pavement, as we mingled with the continuous flow of people that passed us both ways, en route to our destination. I could see that the Chinese flag had been raised earlier that morning. I knew the protocol had been carried out, as was the norm. We got onto the main footpath adjacent to Tiananmen Square and followed it to a certain point near the end. This was where the queue started. When we reached it, there were already lots of people there.

People were in the queue from earlier that morning, as was the practice every day. We took our place at the back (there were no skipping queues here) and had to be prepared to be patient. This long and winding queue took its time while moving along slowly. I could see that there were a few westerners ahead of us scattered in the long queue. We were all here for the same reason, to see the embalmed body of the man who had changed the culture and future of China all of those years ago. Whilst moving along slowly, I could see that more crowds were joining the tail end of the queue, as we had done some time earlier.

As we drew closer to the mausoleum that houses the body of Mao Zedong, I could see that security was getting tighter and tighter. As we slowly made progress in this long and winding queue, you reached a point where you eventually hit a security checkpoint. After passing through this area, it brings you into another security zone, where you would now be on Tiananmen Square. Mr. Wang informed me that the building is called Chairman Mao Memorial Hall and that he lies in the North Hall. From here the volume of people grows and slows down as the main entrance to the Memorial Hall draws closer. Excitement was now building within me with every step I was taking. Hong Wei was holding me even tighter, as curious eyes were looking at us from all around. Mr. Wang was coolness personified.

There are flower sellers in small cabins close by and a lot of Chinese people in the queue were continually rushing over to buy flowers from them. Worshipers obviously buy these flowers to honour Mao Zedong. If memory serves me, I think the flowers were either roses or tulips. I watched all of this with great interest, as Hong Wei and Mr. Wang kept me up to date with what to expect. For me, a westerner in a foreign land, it was far from the famous quays of Waterford city in Ireland, where I was standing now. I kept asking myself, what was I going to see inside the walls of this magnificent building in one of China's most sacred places, while honouring their most famous of all leaders?

Eventually it was our turn with others in the orderly queue to climb the entrance steps. I never did count them, but there were certainly more than thirty-nine steps. When we got to the top and entered the huge doors that make the entrance, a large and magnificent hall awaited us. Inside the main doors and across the huge hall was a real life giant white marble statue of Mao Zedong. He was in a sitting and relaxed position.

Visitors formed two queues that eventually separated and went in the direction of the statue; each entering a huge door on either the left or right side of this impressive sight. The former charismatic Chinese leader looks out on all those that enter his mausoleum. Mounds of flowers given by the visitors that went before us lay at the foot of this statue in respect to their former great leader.

The people that I had seen buying the flowers on the outside, prior to entering the great hall, made their way to the same area to do likewise. This was a continuous exercise from Chinese people within the two queues. We stayed in the left one and moved slowly towards our intended door. I looked at the statue of Mao Zedong from a distance and knew I was now about to see a privileged sight.

Security was present and strict in the great hall, but not uncomfortable. I was well aware of the vast number of visitors that visit this place every day. As we entered the door, another large room appeared. This room is called The Hall of Last Respects. Across from where we had entered was the embalmed body of Mao Zedong. He was about one hundred feet away and lay in a clear glass coffin, mounted on a solid base and draped to his upper chest in the Chinese flag. He was flanked by four armed soldiers, at the railed off area and standing to strict attention. There were no photographs allowed and the queue had to keep moving.

I think the main reason for this was to stop a build-up of people, which would then become congested and uncomfortable. You would have enough viewing time, but the enormity of what you were looking at, what this great leader meant to the Chinese people and the history that was attached to him was still a sight to behold. It was hard to take it all in at that moment. You would feel privileged, as I did, to be in the same room with Chinese people and visitors from all over the world. There and then, I still couldn't believe where I was! This was as real as it gets.

As we continued moving, Hong Wei was holding my hand tightly. After a few minutes walking we were finally close to the exit door. We then emerged out into the beautiful bright sunlight. I looked to my left and there was the back of the queue forming again and so it went on. This continuous cycle is to be seen every day and certainly a sight to behold. I would also say this is a must for everyone to experience if they visit Beijing.

When we were a good distance away, I looked back and thought of where I had been a few minutes earlier and the enormity of what I had seen. It was now gone 12:30 and that word hungry was raising its regular head again. Mr. Wang asked me was I hungry. I said I was. He pointed across the road and said we will try that little restaurant over there.

It took us a few minutes to cross the busy road, which was at the side of Tiananmen Square. This restaurant looked nice from the outside and was clean on appearance inside.

"This looks a nice place to eat," I said.

"What will you have to eat, Billy?" said Mr. Wang.

Hong Wei was all excited again in showing me the well laid out menu.

"I will try a few of those dumplings with the beef in them, some chicken wings and two or three of those spring rolls," I said. "Oh, and can I have two bottles of that Tiger beer, please?"

Mr. Wang and Hong Wei then ordered from the menu. It was fish, dumplings, boiled rice and of course, the customary glasses of hot water, which was served from a teapot. We were waiting only a few minutes before our food arrived. Before that Mr. Wang had asked me where I wanted to go next or what did I want to see.

"Well Mr. Wang, I have always wanted to see the pandas, which are synonymous with China and especially Beijing," I said. He said we would go to the zoo after our meal. He then told Hong Wei of our next port of call, where I could see from the expression on her face that she was excited at the prospect of going to see the pandas too.

We finished our meal without too much delay, although I threaded carefully with mine. When our lunch was finished, the clock was striking 13:30, as we emerged in the sunlight on the main street outside.

Beijing Zoo is situated in downtown Xicheng district of the city. Obviously with transport, there are several ways to get around this monstrous city, namely the subway, the metro, taxis and of course the old reliable bus service. Mr. Wang said we'll take a taxi to get there quicker.

On hailing a taxi, one arrived at our feet in one-minute flat. How's that for service, I thought. It is incredible! Within a few minutes we were at our destination. There were lots of tourists and Chinese people around the entrance, as you would expect. Some were going in separately, others with groups, but mostly with families. We saw the same sights coming out as we were going in, as you can imagine, to this popular venue. Mr. Wang paid the taxi man and within seconds his vehicle had disappeared into the afternoon traffic.

Hong Wei was holding my hand and I could see she was excited. I suppose you could say, I too was excited at the thought of seeing the pandas. I'm sure it's the same the world over, everybody loves the zoo, man, woman or child. The entrance to the zoo is through three big arches, which look quite impressive. This was also the largest and oldest zoo in China. Around six million visitors pass through these arches each year. This zoo was built in 1906 and was known as The Wansheng Gardens. But then in 1955 the Chinese Government kept it simple and changed the name to just Beijing Zoo. There are between five thousand and seven thousand animals and between four hundred and six hundred different species to be seen there. The first successful birth of a giant panda in captivity took place in the zoo in 1963.

We entered through one of the arches. Mr. Wang went and got us our tickets. There was a huge tourist map of the zoo to be seen on a wall close to where we were. It is a great idea, as one could pick which animals they wanted to see first and just go there. I knew first off, one could easily spend the day in here, but the pandas for me were a priority, anything else was a bonus. Where and when would I see these beautiful and rare animals again? If I'm being honest, I think they would be everybody's first choice too. We made our way to one of the two entrances. The Beijing Panda House is composed of two parts, namely The Asian Games Panda House and The Olympic Games Panda House. The Asian Games Panda House was built in 1990 and the giant panda named Pan Pan was chosen as the official mascot for the 11th Asian games in Beijing.

The giant panda Jing Jing was chosen as one of the mascots for the 29th Olympic Games in Beijing in 2008. Beijing Zoo actually built The Olympic Games house. We arrived at one of the two areas and I was taken aback by the amount of people that were there. There were huge glass panels that separate the tourists from the pandas themselves. Their natural habitat and environment was as it should be, with trees, plants and huge boulder like stones, which also formed a resemblance to small caves. There was an outer space for them to wander around in and an inner area also. When we made our way to the front, one of several pandas was out curiously observing the tourists from within their protected glass wall. There was loads of their favourite food of bamboo shoots lying around. This panda and the others were clutching these and stripping them first with their teeth and then munching away to their hearts content. It was just incredible to see them stripping the shoots. We were allowed to take photos, which we gladly did.

The children around us with their parents were all excited and of course they were trying to draw the attention of the pandas by banging on the glass surrounds with their hands. I'm sure all of these glass panels would definitely have been reinforced, just in case the inevitable was to happen.

I observed the closest panda to us. I must say they are beautiful, with their big black eyes and their black and white colouring. When we were there, around five could be seen. They do look lazy and lie around on raised wooden structured platforms, sleeping when they are not eating. But that's their nature and in their breeding. They look terribly affectionate and cuddly with their thick fur. I imagine they are quite heavy too. Hong Wei was excited too, at both seeing them and being with me. I could see Mr. Wang also shared his delight in being there. Even at this early stage and it only being my third day in China, I felt the chemistry between Hong Wei and I was now slowly starting to mix.

After spending about an hour there and being privileged to have seen them, it was time to have a look around at a few other animals. The obvious ones come to mind, lions, tigers, elephants, hippopotamuses', zebras, snakes, and other reptiles. Then there was the huge variety of the feathered kind. There were birds of all sizes and colours. This all took time, to go to the different areas of this massive zoo, but I was happy to be there. I would say we spent between three and four hours in there. Of course, everywhere we went, there were lots of tourists and Chinese people to be seen. Tiredness of the feet was again beginning to take a serious toll. We decided to call an end to the day's proceedings. Also, the zoo's closing time was approaching fast. It was nearing 17:00 as we left the entrance to this magical, historical, exciting and interesting international zoo.

Mr. Wang turned to me and said, "Billy, we will get back to our hostel quickly, even though we are heading into the teatime traffic. We will have a quick freshen up before dinner. Then we will go out and get a nice dinner in a restaurant. I'm sure you must be a little tired, as it's been a long day already."

A little tired, now that was an understatement, I thought.

"Tomorrow will be a big day for you, as we will be going to see The Great Wall," he said.

"Right, Mr. Wang, that's okay by me and I'm sure Hong Wei will go along with that too," I said.

It took the usual waiting time of one minute as the taxi pulled up at our feet. Within twenty minutes our destination was in view. It was also pleasing to be back at our welcomed accommodation. We went to our separate rooms, with Mr. Wang saying, "I will see you in the lobby, Billy, around 19:30." He said the same thing I presumed to Hong Wei in Chinese, as she smiled and answered back. Hong Wei and I both got washed, showered and then relaxed with a short nap. Shortly after, I awoke first and called Hong Wei. It was time to go and meet Mr. Wang as 19:30 was approaching fast. After meeting Mr. Wang in the lobby and exiting the front door, we hailed a taxi.

"We are going to a different restaurant tonight, Billy. Is that okay?" he said.

Shortly afterwards, we arrived in downtown Beijing. On entering another impressive eating establishment, with all the customary welcomes for westerners, a table was pointed out. Mr. Wang and Hong Wei studied the menu and ordered but not without asking me first.

"Oh, I'll have chicken wings, slices of beef, spring rolls and some fried rice, please," I said, also requesting, two bottles of Tiger beer.

Within minutes the food arrived, all piping hot and with a smile. Hong Wei and Mr. Wang had ordered all kinds of everything, some of which I just couldn't imagine eating. Not in a million years, it was like jelly and I still didn't know what it was! The customary teapot with the hot water and two glasses also arrived. The thoughts of being on The Great Wall the following day intrigued me, as I slowly ate my food and quickly drank my drink.

"Mr. Wang, could I have another two bottles of beer, please?" I asked.

"Sure," he said, "you're our guest. Whatever you want, just ask."

When we were finished, just over an hour later, my stomach was full and my thirst was quenched, Mr. Wang said, "Billy, tomorrow will be a long and tiring day, with an early start."

"Don't worry Mr. Wang, Hong Wei and I will be prepared and ready to go the distance. I'm really looking forward to this part of my visit," I said. I could also see Hong Wei was excited too, by the expression on her face. Although there were other personal thoughts too, running through my head. Why was I really here in this strange land? When we left the restaurant, it was around 20:30. We hailed a taxi and were at our hostel in a matter of minutes. It would be an early start in the morning. 08:00 was the designated time given by Mr. Wang when we said goodnight. Hong Wei and I retired to our bedroom and eventually fell into a deep sleep.

My fourth day in China was on the horizon and probably the most interesting to come. At 08:00, as requested, we were at the busy restaurant, where it was all hands on deck. The three of us had the same breakfast as the previous morning. My motto was, why change at this early stage. Although, drinking a beer or two normally would not be my habit at that hour of the morning, but who cared – not me. After all, my choices were limited! Mr. Wang and Hong Wei spoke in Chinese about the itinerary for this long day that lay ahead. The weather was a little cooler when we left the hostel at around 08:50 and hailed down the first passing taxi. Mr. Wang gave the driver strict instructions to take us to a certain place. After about fifteen minutes driving through the busy traffic – remember it was also part of the morning rush hours, with schools, shops and factories being the designated destinations for a lot of people and children.

We arrived at our destination, called Deshengmen bus terminal in downtown Beijing. This was the main departure area, where buses or coaches were in readiness every day for all who wanted to visit The Great Wall of China. The Great Wall is about thirty to forty miles outside of Beijing. There are different sections of The Great Wall that one can visit.

Everyone doesn't go to the same part, at the same time, as there wouldn't be room for everyone to stand on that historical piece of history – not with the number of tourists that go there every day of the year. It's commonly known that upwards of ten million people visit The Great Wall every year. There were lots of buses there and we went to our designated bus after Mr. Wang had bought our travel tickets at the small office.

As luck would have it, we managed to get the first two seats. Being a professional bus driver myself back in Ireland with the national bus company (Bus Eireann), I wanted to observe the driving on the right-hand side of the road and see what way the driver would handle it. When we were about to depart, the driver donned a white pair of gloves and took off his outer jacket, to reveal a smart blue shirt with a company logo on it. I didn't bother to look any closer, as it was of no great concern to me. I just wanted to see what his driving was like. I couldn't tell you either what kind of a bus it was, as I'm not into buses. The only things I can tell you are that it had manual gears, it was not new, it had a rather big steering wheel and the seats were comfortable but looked a little old.

Hong Wei was sitting with me and trying to explain in what little English she had all about The Great Wall. I could see she was happy to be in my company. Mr. Wang sat opposite us and remained cool. Everyone getting on the bus was excited. I could see it in their body language. Some people could have visited the wall before and could have been going back to see another section of it. The distance from Beijing to different sections of the wall varies. You could be talking about forty, fifty or even sixty miles away.

Just to give you some further facts about this seventh wonder of the world. The Great Wall lies on the outskirts of Beijing. It is more than 13,000 thousand miles long and covers some ten to fifteen provinces across China. It was built more than 2,300 years ago and in different sections, by different dynasties. The Qin Dynasty started it first around the 5th century and its construction ended during the Ming Dynasty's reign around the 16th century. The Great Wall stretches in the far west of the country, at a place called Jiayu Pass in Gansu Province. This is in a vast desert area of China. From there it continues its journey all the way through to the Shanhai Pass in Hebei Province and down to the eastern seashore at a place called The Old Dragon's Head and into the Bohai Sea. The Great Wall is roughly around twenty-five feet high, but in certain places it can be around fifty feet in height, depending on the terrain and it is just less than seven metres in width. That would be wide enough for ten people walking abreast.

Its width was also calculated to be wide enough for two carriages to be drawn in opposite directions while going to and back from the towers with supplies of food, water and weapons. The beacon towers were mainly used as lookouts across the wide areas of rough land. The signalling process was a series of different fires creating smoke signals by numbers, from beacon to beacon. There are around ten thousand watchtowers and beacon towers scattered all along The Great Wall.

In the Badaling section alone, there are forty-three watchtowers. Some of these watchtowers, when we encountered them were quite vertical and a little awkward to climb. The bottom of The Great Wall is wider than the top. This was for strength and also to preserve it. When you study it and think about it, they really did think about everything. There were over a million people used in the construction and around four thousand died, mostly from hunger or sickness while it was being built, as work went on day and night. When any worker died, they were just entombed in the foundation and the work carried on. Cruel as it seems, that was the way it was. There were to be no slackness or slowing down in the construction of The Great Wall. This was all about keeping out the invaders; whoever they might have been in those times.

It's reported that a few years ago, on one day alone some seventy thousand people visited a certain section of the wall. In recent years, it is widely accepted that the best time to visit The Great Wall is in springtime. This is when the apricot trees and apricot flowers are in full bloom. I was told, they are a sight to behold in this wonderful and rare place. So my friends, you can see why people would be getting excited at the prospect of seeing this phenomenal sight for the first time. In our case it was just under two hours' drive to the Badaling section. This is one of the most visited parts of The Great Wall, as it is one of the best preserved.

As you exit the city, the infrastructure was intriguing and catered for thousands of vehicles of all descriptions. These vehicles had two, four, six, eight or even ten wheels and had a destination in mind. We had our destination too, which was uppermost in my mind. There were numerous tourist coaches that passed us coming from The Great Wall. I knew this by the signs that were on the front of them, indicating The Great Wall in English. This is the continuous cycle all day, every day, with buses coming and going to The Great Wall.

I did notice the volume of traffic was heavy in the early part of our journey, but not to the same degree as we neared our destination. At this point, I could see The Great Wall a few miles away in the distance. From where we were, it was small, but I could see it was in a mountainous region.

This was really rough terrain, with hills and heavy forestry all around. The roads were now of a slightly minor nature, though still wide enough to take the heavy traffic that was on it. Excitement was building from within me again, as Hong Wei was pointing out sights to me. Mr. Wang remained cool throughout, but what would I have done without him!? He was a godsend to me, in more ways than one. I could see too that the other tourists on our full bus were getting excited too.

A distance away from our destination, I noticed that our bus was now on an upward journey and climbing up a long and winding road. This was a change of view from minutes earlier, but I took it all in. Hong Wei was excited and spoke a little in her broken English. We ran into a series of hairpin bends where I noticed the driver's experience in dealing with them. His driving skills were top class and I knew he had been up and down this road on numerous trips; too many to count I would imagine.

Finally, we arrived at our starting point, where our bus parked in the designated parking area. Having come from the centre of Beijing, we now found ourselves way, way out on the outskirts of the city. The three of us disembarked and made our way to the start of this part of The Great Wall. There were lots of shops and stalls selling their wares. There were also restaurants and toilet facilities there to cater for the many tourists. Others wanted you to have your photograph taking on The Great Wall for a homebound souvenir. Hong Wei and I decided just to get this done for the moment and collect it on the way back. Mr. Wang advised me to ignore all of the other outlets for the moment, and we could reconsider on the return leg. Basically, you just get on the wall and start walking. It's as simple as that. The day was humid, bright and there was a sort of crispness in the air, even though it was November. We wore light clothing and light shoes. This was not an expedition to the North Pole, but it had been just as exciting for me on my return to the starting point, some four hours later.

There were crowds of people going in the same direction as us and in their own time. Other people were on their return walk. I must say I noticed tiredness written all over their faces and exhaustion oozed from their posture. You would be surprised how your stamina would be tested during this unique experience.

I suppose the first thing I noticed as we started our walk was the steepness of this part of The Great Wall. Yes, you would be fresh and all enthusiastic about how far you could go at the start. I noticed that both sides of The Great Wall were different as regards their shape. On my left there were huge blocks of stone, of all shapes and sizes. There were cut-outs in The Great Wall every ten yards or so looking out onto the rough terrain. I tried to picture the scene of battle, as it was way back then. Obviously, these wall openings were giving you good vantage points, when looking down on your enemy, used for defending by whatever means possible against the invaders. The other side of The Great Wall was a little lower and was all of the same height. This was the inner wall to the cities that lay on the right side of the wall.

After walking for a few minutes, I noticed that a lot of The Great Wall in front of us was uphill and then downhill again at all different stretches. You had the watchtowers scattered along the way, as well as the beacon towers in between. You could see way ahead of where you were going to walk eventually, if you ever got there. With the humidity and the amount of people on The Great Wall at the same time as us. Yes, you could say it became a little crowded. After walking for around half an hour with Hong Wei holding me close, I noticed my energy levels beginning to be affected. It was enjoyable, but you were still climbing upwards for periods and then going down again. I would say every second person on The Great Wall had a camera, which was in constant use. We took lots of photos too. The magnificent surrounding scenery all around us was just breath-taking.

What I found fascinating when looking out over The Great Wall at different times was the rough ground that it is actually built on. There were huge boulders that were left in their original positions and they were still used in the construction. They just built them into The Great Wall as they went along. It was a work of genius really, when you think about it. I noticed when looking down at the flagstones under our feet, that every so often there was a channel running across our path. This was created to take the excess water that would gather at the end of the gully. This channel continued out through a small opening on the inner side of The Great Wall. It is still as visible today as it was way back then. This meant you never had any excess water building up on The Great Wall. The Chinese really did think of everything, didn't they?

We continued on our walk for another hour or so, not forgetting that whatever distance we walked, we still had to come back. There were no back doors on The Great Wall. All the time I was continually looking around at the people, the land and the way ahead. At a designated area we saw some stallholders and there was also a facility there where you could get a souvenir of The Great Wall on a brass plate and the date included. Hong Wei indicated to Mr. Wang that she wanted to get this done for me as a memento of the occasion. The Chinese person set about doing this for me. You also get it in a red presentation box that accompanies it. This only took a few minutes and I was delighted to get it. What a nice thought and gesture it was from Hong Wei. It was one that I took on board, as I gave her a hug and a kiss in appreciation. It is something I value greatly and feel privileged to have gotten. The thought of where I was born and grew up, to where I was now, entered my head at that moment for some strange reason. You could have knocked me with a feather as who would have believed it? Not me!

We continued on, passing through about four more watchtowers and two or three beacon towers, which was still quite a distance to have travelled. But then it was decision time as regards what to do. Do we keep going or turn back? Had we seen enough or was it to be more of the same. I also knew that whatever distance we walked forward, we had to walk back. I knew Hong Wei was getting tired and Mr. Wang was undecided, but easy. I had the casting vote and I opted to turn around and head back.

Looking back down on The Great Wall behind us, I could see where we had started out from. It was like a giant snake heading back across the rough terrain. When you looked at it from our high vantage point, it was a magnificent sight to see. I knew then The Great Wall was truly a sight to behold and knew why it is one of the Seven Wonders of the World. Surprisingly we made our return walk on The Great Wall slower than when we were on the ascent. When we did eventually reach our starting point again, tiredness and hunger had taken over our bodies. The stallholders were still out in force and the souvenir shops were all enticing us in. We collected our photograph which was glazed onto a mug. How they did it, I don't know, and I didn't even ask. But I had my other special souvenir and now, some four hours after we started, my stomach ruled.

We sought out one of the restaurants there and entered the dark interior from the outside bright sunlight. What was I going to get in here, I wondered, but on this occasion there was no time for me to be choosey or particular. Mr. Wang and Hong Wei went to the counter and ordered dumplings, boiled rice and some fish dish, plus their usual hot water. I ordered through Mr. Wang a mixed dish of noodles and beef, chicken wings and two bottles of Tiger beer. The restaurant had wooden benches with long tables there, and we just picked one and sat down. The relief on our tired limbs was palpable. Shortly, the relief on our stomachs was going to ease too. Hong Wei asked Mr. Wang was I after enjoying myself. I assured him to tell her I was more than happy and privileged to have seen what I saw.

After spending a welcome hour resting there, our plates were now empty. I ordered another beer before we left. I found the food okay, better than I thought it would be. But when hunger takes over, everything can taste nice. However, it was now time to go. We made our way to the coach departure area to get our bus back to Beijing. We took our place in the long queue and waited our turn. The way it works is when the bus is full, it goes. There is no need to panic because there are a continuous supply of buses returning all day. It was now late in the afternoon and returning to Beijing city took a little longer than on our outward journey, but I was patient. I would say it took us close on three hours. This was mainly due to the build-up of teatime traffic. Although we were not at a standstill, the closer we got to the city, the slower the traffic went.

Eventually we did get to the hostel. It was a little just after 18:00. A quick shower and a change of clothes, then the three of us were ready to go out for dinner. I was tired, but my stomach ruled for now. It was around 19:00 when we left the hostel, with Mr. Wang saying to me, "Billy, we won't go too far as we are all tired and tomorrow is going to be another busy day for you."

"That's okay with me," was my reply.

The taxi arrived as usual and we departed, as our destination was just a few streets away. It was a different restaurant on a different street, that's all I knew. I was just going with the flow. Hong Wei was keeping me close by her side. I knew what way I was thinking as regards our relationship. It was beginning to take root. I wondered what way Hong Wei was thinking? Was it the same as me?

When we got to the restaurant and sat down at our table, I realised this table was different. I noticed there was a hole in the middle, which contained a stainless-steel basin. I asked Mr. Wang what was all this about. He told me this was another way of cooking food. We ordered our food and it arrived a few minutes later. It was strips of beef, strips of lamb, chicken and small portions of various meats. They were all raw and on separate plates. Of course, I didn't forget to order my Tiger beer. Mr. Wang and Hong Wei ordered their usual glasses of hot water. How disciplined they were in their daily routine. What happens next, I asked Mr. Wang? That question was answered a few minutes later when a man entered the room with a steel bucket of red-hot charcoals and a metal rod. We moved back and the man then used the metal rod to lift out the charcoals from the bucket. These were then lowered quickly into the waiting steel container in the middle of the table. Then a steel grill was put over the charcoals and the various foods were separately put on it.

This method is a little slow at first but believe you me, the food cooks in minutes given the heat from the red-hot charcoals. The strips of beef, lamb, chicken and the rest are all continually turned in the cooking process. All this food tasted like something I had never tasted before. Given the choice, this was to be my favourite way of eating Chinese food in the following few days. This was a whole new experience for me! This request was conveyed to Hong Wei by Mr. Wang when our meal was finished. It was now close to 20:45 when we said our goodbyes to the pleasant and mannerly restaurant staff. Up to this point in time, Hong Wei had looked after all our food bills. We arrived back at our hostel as the clock struck 21:00. It was the end of another unique and exciting day for me.

I had spoken to Mr. Wang briefly during the week and had repeated a suggestion to him earlier that day on our return bus journey to the city, from The Great Wall. He said, "Billy, I have a surprise for you. Tomorrow we will be going to see one of the top professional football club academies doing some training. They are called, Beijing Guoan FC. I have got a special invite for you to attend a training session," he said. "We must be there at a specific time and cannot afford to be late."

"Oh, that's great! I'm really going to look forward to that," I said. "Don't worry, I'm never late for appointments, especially one as important as this one, I can assure you! Mr. Wang, thank you for doing that for me," I finished.

Beijing Guoan Football Club plays in the Chinese Super League. They were semi-professional from 1951–1992 and went full-time professional from 1992 to the present. Their colours at home are all green and away all white. They are nicknamed, The Imperial Guards.

At this point of time in my life, I had been an officially registered football scout in Ireland since 2000 for Newcastle United, the Premier League football club in England. I had asked Mr. Wang previously would it be possible while I was in Beijing to see some football in any Chinese club academies. He had been in touch with a few people and one had offered me an invitation to go and see their academy in action. I was thrilled to take up the invitation. With only having three days left in Beijing and it was important to see what I could from a tourist and a football point of view, but equally it was important to judge was there a relationship between Hong Wei and I developing. Time would tell me over the next few days, when it would be decision time.

Thursday morning arrived, with the same breakfast eaten by me. It was around 09:30, when we left the hostel and got a taxi to this well-known football club. The specific time to be there for was 10:00.

Firstly, we went to see the general manager in his office in this rather large complex that joins the many playing fields that were on view. Mr. Wang introduced me to him, where I then showed him my credentials and identification as regards my scouting role with Newcastle United Football Club in England. Obviously, I forget his name at this stage, as you would. It was in November in the year of 2005. He firstly offered us some food and a drink and then we chatted for a few minutes through Mr. Wang. He was very interested to know what an Irishman was doing in Beijing, what my interest in football was and he was surprised that I was working in a professional manner for such a famous football club. Hong Wei listened intensively to what was being said at all times. After a while in conversation with him, he then invited us to follow him out onto the playing fields.

This giant playing area met my eyes with surprise and excitement. We picked a spot on the side of these playing fields and I watched with a high level of intensity and concentration. There were about twelve football fields (if I can remember correctly) with boys of all ages, from about seven or eight upwards to full adults. There were one or two coaches with each group of boys on every pitch all conducting their own sessions.

We were asked not to take any photographs and I assured Mr. Wang this was not a problem for me, as I was more than happy to see what I was seeing, having gotten this unique opportunity. After a while and accompanied by the general manager, we moved around to other pitches. I studied the different age groups and waited to see which of the boys on view showed what I would have considered potential to have a football career. This was a challenge in itself and I was enjoying every minute of it. While this was going on Mr. Wang and Hong Wei spoke to the manager and informed him that I took the game of football very seriously, when playing, when managing myself and now in a scouting capacity.

On each of the pitches that we viewed, I picked out one or two boys that caught my eye. I looked for control, vision, positional sense, work rate, concentration level and creative ability. I told Mr. Wang of my observations and he duly passed them on to the general manager. I could see by his body language and expressions that he took my opinions for what they were worth on board. I could also see that all the coaches were excellent at their jobs. The players listened closely to what they were being told, at different stages of their sessions. I could read the body language and didn't have to have it translated to me. All of these sessions and matches were going on at the same time. I was spoilt for choice.

We were there for about one and a half hours and when the time came to go, I told Mr. Wang to thank the manager of the academy football club most sincerely and that I appreciated the hospitality that was shown to me by him and his staff. I thought he was a very pleasant and friendly man, with a lot of responsibility in his job. It was a great experience for me to see football on the other side of the world. I also knew this was not an opportunity that was offered to every westerner. I felt very grateful and privileged to have seen what I had seen. However, it was now time to say goodbye and thanks.

It was also time to move on, this we did by way of a taxi. We went to get some lunch from a waitress served restaurant and I stuck to the same menu as did Mr. Wang and Hong Wei. While we were having lunch Mr. Wang asked me where I wanted to go next. I asked could we go and see The Temple of Heaven Tiantan Park. They agreed to do that as soon as we finished there. After one hour our lunch was finished as we exited the restaurant. The first part of the day had been both pleasing and rewarding from my point of view. Now I wondered what the second half of the day would offer me. I noticed Hong Wei looked happy, and I was happy too!

It was now around 14:00 as we got into the taxi, which a few minutes later, dropped us off at the appropriate point for tourists. The Temple of Heaven Tiantan Park is in the southern Chongwen district of Beijing. It was first built in 1420, a long time ago. Within the park, there are three main sights to see: The Circular Mound Altar, The Hall of Prayer for good harvest or The Temple of Heaven and The Imperial Vault of Heaven. The whole area is encircled by a wall and is actually bigger than the surrounding wall of The Forbidden City. Now that I found hard to believe, but it was actually true!

We entered from the southern side through the Zhaoheng Gate. It's really three square archways of stone with beautiful carvings on them. When you go through them, you walk a short distance on a white marble road until you encounter The Circular Mound Altar. There are four series of steps (north, south, east and west) leading to the top. It is an area with a raised circular stone platform. On top of it are carved stoned rails all around it. Here a spacious area awaits the visitor. In the middle you can see a round heaped stone protruding from the surface. This stone is known as The Heaven Heart Stone, or The Sun Stone. This was the area where the Winter Solace ceremony of thanksgiving and calls for a good future to the God's took place every year. Close by there is a pole called The Lantern Viewing Pole.

There were three, but two were destroyed over time. This pole (ninety-five feet in height) was used for indicating the location and for the start and finishing times of the ceremony. I stood there with Hong Wei and Mr. Wang close by and wondered what it really must have been like in those days in the early 14th century. Having entered from the most popular south steps we exited back down the north steps and onto the marble road again which brought us to the Imperial Vault of Heaven. This building looked like a wooden tent in appearance and was on the one level.

This holiest of places was used for storing the God's tablets, which were to be used in worshiping heaven. Hong Wei was sticking close by me, as Mr. Wang explained a few historical things to me. The inside is like the underside of a dome. The ceiling is beautifully painted, decorated with different types of coloured stone and other affects. There is a stone chair on view with various patterns on and around it. In times past, The Heavenly great tablets were placed on this chair. The three of us spent a few minutes there as I was anxious to see and take all this history in. Hong Wei and Mr. Wang didn't mind. When we left, we continued on the north side and went over the small Danbi Bridge. This short walk again took us to a place of greater interest. It was The Hall of Prayer for a Good Harvest. This really was another jewel in the crown!

When we arrived there, it was fairly populated with a lot of tourists of all nationalities and Chinese people. This was where the emperors prayed for a good harvest and for good times in the future. It's built on three levels of marble stone which forms the base. There are a small number of steps leading to the entrance. This building again looked like a three-tier tent from a distance. You would imagine that there are three levels on it, but there is only one. It stands thirty-eight metres in height and thirty-six metres in diameter. The Ming and Qing dynasties believed that this exact spot was where the Heaven and Earth met. They believed that the heaven was round, and the earth was square.

One amazing thing Mr. Wang told me as we stood in the building and while I was admiring the structure from the inside, he said, "Billy, do you know this building was built without nails? There are basically just beams holding up the side walls." "Now I find that quite amazing, Mr. Wang," was my reply. I wondered how they ever managed to do that. The roof is something similar (with its paintings on the underside of the dome) to The Imperial Vault of Heaven building. This holy building intrigued me greatly. We spent some extra time there and then moved on to the other interesting sights that are in this giant complex. Hong Wei didn't leave my side and I knew she was enjoying being in my company, as I was in hers.

We looked at The Terrace of Worshiping Heaven, The Firewood Stove, The Divine Kitchen Courtyard, The Palace of Abstinence, The Imperial Hall of Heaven and The Lingxing Gates. As the saying goes 'Time flies by when you're having fun!'. On checking my watch, I could see that the time really was flying by! We had spent a few hours in this very interesting and holy place. It was now close to 17:00, which meant it was either time to go for food and a rest or to go back to the hostel for a rest and then go for dinner. Having been asked my preference by Mr. Wang, and with Hong Wei's approval, I informed him that I would prefer the latter.

After arriving back at our base and having a rest, it was time for dinner. I was hungry now and my stomach was rumbling with the echoes of 'Get me food now!'. We departed around 19:00 and took a taxi to another designated restaurant of Mr. Wang's choosing. Everything had been good up to now. All these restaurants that I visited were top class, for service and food, even though I still thread carefully. Again, we were warmly greeted at the main door by the customary Chinese welcome and took our seats. It was going to be the charcoal hole in the table job for me again on this occasion. Most of the food is brought in raw and cooked over the fires. Some other dishes were served cooked. Hong Wei always sat with me and Mr. Wang opposite us. They ordered what I didn't order. They could eat anything, and I mean anything. As with me, I was still choosey. I ordered chicken wings, strips of beef, strips of lamb and fried rice. A few bottles of Tiger beer for me were a welcome sight to wash the food down.

Hong Wei spoke to Mr. Wang, continually asking him was my food okay. I assured him and her that it was. From start to finish, we spent probably around two hours there. The names on these restaurants I'm afraid have eluded me. The one thing I can say was the food was very good. As we made our way back to the hostel through the Beijing nightlife and with Hong Wei holding me tightly and speaking what she could of the English language, I felt the chemistry was beginning to mix a little more. It had been a good day and I was happy! After arriving back at the hostel, Hong Wei and I got a good night's sleep.

Friday was Friday, as it always is, in any country. Another long day awaited us as we finished our breakfast and departed from the hostel at 10:00 sharp. Mr. Wang informed me that the traffic was very busy.

"Billy, today we are going to The World Park. Did you ever hear of it?"

"No, I can't say I have," I replied.

"Well, you will be impressed when you see this place," he said.

"I'm sure I will, as I have been impressed with everything I have seen to date," I told him.

So naturally, optimism reared its head as we neared our destination after a twenty-minute spin to the southwestern Fengtai district of Beijing. On our arrival, Hong Wei paid the taxi fare. This place looked impressive. What awaited me here, I thought. I wasn't waiting too long, to find out. There was an entrance like a castle, with huge gold lettering overhead which said, Beijing World Park. Also on view and blowing in the slight breeze were a lot of national flags from around the world. Hong Wei was again holding me ever so tightly as the three of us went through the entrance. There were huge wide-open spaces, with lots of flowers and trees all around us, but I wasn't prepared for what I saw next.

Away in the distance I thought I could see the famous French Eiffel Tower. I said to Mr. Wang, "What's going on here?"

"Keep looking and you will see a lot more," he said.

As we drew closer, I could see this was a perfect replica of the famous French landmark. It was obviously not as high, but it was perfect in detail, I couldn't believe it. I studied it, felt it and photographed it. We took lots of photographs of these sights while we were there. Hong Wei was constantly asking Mr. Wang was everything okay for me. This really should have been a case of bringing your walking shoes, because several hours later having walked around this fascinating giant park, my feet weren't there. I wished somebody had told me what to expect, before I had taken on this adventure.

Looking around from where we were, I could see in the distance some other world-famous buildings and landmarks. This place was unreal with its contents. You could go in any direction and one of these magical sights would greet your eyes. I found out later that there are one hundred of these world-famous replica miniature buildings and landmark sights from fourteen countries and regions. The park is divided into five main areas, Africa, Asia, Europe, America and Latin America.

We continued on walking and took in whatever sights came our way. Next up was the Leaning Tower of Pisa and was exactly as it looks in reality. We continued on to see the statues of Easter Island from South America, the Vatican in Rome, the Rialto Bridge and the Coliseum from Rome in Italy too. From London you had the Tower Bridge, St. Paul's Cathedral, Buckingham Palace, the Houses of Parliament and Big Ben. The Karnak Temple from Greece, the Cathedral of Notre Dame and the Arc de Triomphe in France, the Pyramids from Egypt and also, the Aztecs Pyramids, Red Square in Moscow in Russia, the Taj Mahal in India. From America you had the Twin Towers and surrounding buildings in lower Manhattan. There was also the Statue of Liberty, the Capital Building, the White House and the Washington Monument. There was also a replica of the Golden Gate Bridge in San Francisco, plus the Netherlands Windmills as seen in Holland and the Opera House in Sydney in Australia.

These were all exact replicas and complete in every detail. We saw lots of other buildings and sights that were not familiar to me, but this place was really quite amazing. After about four hours of walking and taking photographs of these wonderful sights, we took a well-deserved break at a small restaurant inside the confines of this fascinating place. Hong Wei was tired, but Mr. Wang was relentless in his task to keep me happy and interested while in Beijing. I thought as he was probably thinking that we would never meet again. The one thing we all had in common, irrespective of what nationality we were from, was that we were all hungry at the same time.

We had a meal, but I cannot even remember what I ate, although I do know I drank two bottles of Coca-Cola. We took a long break to gather our strength and to continue on. As I said at the outset of my book, the Chinese people are a resilient race within a resilient nation.

Mr. Wang turned to me and said, "Billy, we are ready to continue, are you okay?" Mr. Wang and Hong Wei quite clearly showed me this by their actions, in wanting to continue. "Yeah, I'm ready to continue too," I said. I was letting them know, that this Irishman was also resilient. We continued on our journey further into the unknown. We came upon other sights and rather interestingly, we came upon a fountain operated by laser beams. It was quite incredible to see all of this. There was also a plant maze and a fairyland amusement park for adults and children.

All of this took time and its toll on our bodies from the waist down. Eventually it was time to go. We made our way back to the main entrance. I would say we were in this very popular park for about five hours in all. In reality we could have even spent another five hours in there. A taxi took us back to the hostel ahead of the teatime traffic, where we had time to spare. A long rest followed for all three of us, with a 19:30 meeting time in the lobby before a restaurant of Mr. Wang's choosing was the order of the night. After a rest, Hong Wei and I freshened up and arrived in the lobby to be met on time by Mr. Wang. A taxi brought us to another restaurant; again, the open charcoal fire in the middle of the table was on offer. We basically ordered similar food to the previous few days. The same Tiger beer was also ordered by me.

Separately the chicken wings came cooked and I made my presence felt, with another plate of them ordered. We took our time and Hong Wei was asking Mr. Wang was everything okay for me. The two hours drifted by as we conversed as best we could. Mr. Wang had told me privately during the week that Hong Wei really liked me. I took this message on board but kept it to myself. With our meal finished and a few bottles of Tiger beer drank, the magic time of 21:00 arrived and it was time to go. I must say that although this was only my first visit to China, I found the people were very friendly.

A few minutes later, we were back in the lobby of the hostel. Before Mr. Wang went to his room, he said to me, "Billy, tomorrow is Saturday. It's your second last day in Beijing. There is still a lot you could see tomorrow. But we'll decide where to go in the morning after breakfast."

"Yes, that's okay, Mr. Wang, whatever you decide," I said.

"I will see you at 09:00 in the morning," he said.

Hong Wei and I both nodded our heads in agreement. It had been another long day on our feet and just to be off them for the next few hours was pleasing. Within minutes of us hitting the sack (bed), we were fast asleep. Tiredness had ruled and there was no one awake to argue. But we did wake the following morning around 08:00, which was Saturday.

Hong Wei and I chatted as best she could in her broken English. I was able to understand her through body language as well. We showered, dressed and were in the restaurant for 08:55, to be met by Mr. Wang. We all got the same breakfast as previous mornings, with one exception – I drank cold water. When asked, I refused Hong Wei's request to drink it hot. This was my second last day in Beijing. Understandably I was curious and also anxious to know what effect this encounter with Hong Wei would have on my personal life and where it might be heading. Would I be back here again in this intriguing and historical city of twenty-one million people?

My flight was on Monday morning from Beijing International Airport. What would happen between now and then was anybody's guess, but an answer would be coming soon. I knew what way my feelings were for Hong Wei, even at this early stage. I wondered what her thoughts were, having spent the last few days with this Irishman. But what I did know was that Hong Wei was a beautiful woman, she was cool out, with a great sense of humour.

Over our hurried breakfast, Mr. Wang said, "Billy, we can visit two more places today if we move early. We will go to The Fayuan Buddhist Temple and finish with a visit to The Summer Palace."

"That's okay by me and thank you for being so helpful over these last few days," I said. By 09:30 we were on our way in the hastily hailed taxi.

The Fayuan Temple is on a street called Fayuansi in the southwest part of central Beijing, in the Xuanwu district. When we arrived there, tourists and Chinese people were starting to go through the main entrance. I quickly read the history of this temple and found out it was one of the oldest in China. It was mainly made up of six courtyards and several halls.

Hong Wei was holding me tightly, which I was becoming accustomed to by now. We made our way through the main entrance, which is called The Mountain Gate. From there I could see another entrance further on where two huge black lions flanked the doorway. This temple was first built in 645 during the Tang dynasty and rebuilt again in 1436. My God I said to myself, what history we have here. Over the course of the next few hours, we went through the courtyards and visited all the halls. Namely the Hall to Mourn the Loyal, the Hall of Heavenly King, the Hall of Great Buddha, the Mercy Hall and the Pilu Hall. There was also the Pavilion of Buddhists Sutras, a Buddhists library, the Buddhist Academy of China and a museum of culture where the Buddhists study.

While we were there, we saw several Buddhist monks working in some courtyards and others in prayer at different shrines. There were to be a lot more Buddhist temples in the country. I would recommend seeing this temple if you ever visit Beijing.

We came outside and went to the nearest restaurant. It was beef dumplings, chicken wings and fried rice for me with Tiger beer. Hong Wei and Mr. Wang had soup, boiled rice, veggie dumplings and some other food, which didn't appeal to me by its looks. Oh and a few glasses of hot water. I did ask myself, why they both look so healthy! It was around 13:30 when we left the confines of the restaurant. With much haste and without delay, it was on to The Summer Palace by taxi.

When we arrived at the drop off point, I could see that this place was unique in its own right. This picturesque and tranquil place is situated about ten miles outside of Beijing. It was known as The Museum of Royal Gardens and was first constructed in 1750 as a royal garden, at the end of the Qing dynasty. It was only opened up to the public in 1924.

We wandered leisurely along the pleasant walkways, amidst numerous visitors. We encountered a lot of different gardens which were in winter bloom and had lots of all-year plants, shrubs and flowers on display. These paths were decorated with overhead structures like tunnels and painted in the finest of detail, dictating all of Chinese history through figures, emblems, animals and past Chinese emperors. This huge complex runs along the edge of the Kunming Lake on one side and at the back it is slightly divided by another interior lake called The Black Lake.

Why I don't know, but this place was definitely worth seeing. There was also a prominent building there called The Hall of Joyful Longevity. The weather was cold, but nice and fresh. We stopped for a short break several times where it was appropriate and a little sheltered to take in the fabulous views that were offered to us.

Mr. Wang had said to me earlier on one of these occasions, "Well Billy, what do you think of this place?"

"It's just fabulous, what scenery and the gardens are just beautiful, even for this time of the year."

"What must they be like in summertime?" I wondered.

"Beautiful beyond belief", was his reply. "You have seen a lot in your first visit to Beijing."

"Yes, and I'm very grateful to you for showing me all of the places I have been so privileged to have seen," I said. The thought kept reoccurring to me, would I be back here again? Hong Wei was the only person that could answer that question for me, when the time came. In the following hours, my mind kept saying to me, when was that time going to be, when would she give me her answer. My mind was made up. I wanted to see her again. But this was her choice and hers alone.

Visiting the Summer Palace was an added bonus, but this all took time and naturally the clock was moving on. A saying my father used always say, 'Time and tide waits for no man'. It was time to get back to our base before the teatime traffic gathered momentum. We made it back to our accommodation with plenty of time to spare. The taxis don't hang around in Beijing.

After our relaxing rest, our departure time was scheduled for 19:00. I just went with the flow, as Mr. Wang instructed the taxi driver where to take us. He knew by now, my first choice of taste for restaurant food was when it was being cooked over the charcoal fire. A few minutes after leaving the hostel, we arrived at this restaurant. It was of a higher standard, but the usual greeting was in store for us. When seated, we ordered. Why change now, was my thinking when dealing with food on this maiden voyage. I ordered chicken wings, strips of beef, pork and lamb for the charcoal fire. The bottles of chilled Tiger beer followed as usual. Hong Wei and Mr. Wang ordered all kinds of everything and insisted on me trying some, but a stern no way was my answer. I knew they meant well, but I was not for changing now.

Mr. Wang asked me about what I thought of Beijing over these past few days and what did I think of Hong Wei. I told him what he wanted to hear, and he smiled.

I said, "I will come back to see Hong Wei again, if she approves."

Mr. Wang answered with, "Hong Wei would love to see you again, Billy."

After two hours our meal was finished and then it was a short spin in the taxi back to the hostel. Mr. Wang said goodnight and gave us a time of 09:00 for breakfast. This man had been such a big help to me, which I appreciated so much. Without him I would have been truly lost! I called him aside and gave him a monetary gift for all of his help. He did not want to take it, but I insisted he did. We retired to our appropriate rooms, as darkness fell, but Beijing's nightlife kept shining brightly in the darkness. After a few minutes, Hong Wei and I fell into a deep sleep. Sunday morning came, like all the rest of them came, whether you're in Beijing or Ireland or any other part of the world.

All three of us were to take it easy after breakfast, as I thought. But on impulse, Hong Wei decided to go shopping. With the places I had been and the sights I had seen, shopping was the furthest thing on my mind. It certainly wasn't a priority for me and nowhere near the top of my list, but I said why not to Mr. Wang. We took a taxi straight to the main shopping area in the centre of downtown Beijing. At our leisure, we decided to have a look around the shops. What an understatement that was and little did I know what I was letting myself in for. Is there any woman who doesn't like shopping? Not that I know of and Hong Wei was no different.

At our ease, we ventured into a few shops that were in close proximity. There were sports and clothes shops everywhere. All around us there were souvenir shops and food outlets in their hundreds. A few small souvenirs caught my eye in one of them and I managed to pick up a few bits and pieces for friends back home. In one of the many impressive jewellery shops we visited, just for a look, I might add, the prices on the jewellery items were very reasonable to me. In one of the jewellery shops and to my surprise, Hong Wei wanted to buy me a present. What could I say – she wouldn't take no for an answer? Mr. Wang looked on impartially and smiled, then shrugged his shoulders. She purchased an item for me, and I thanked her repeatedly. A kiss and a hug followed. It was mutual. Hong Wei continually asked Mr. Wang was everything okay and had my stay been okay for me. Through Mr. Wang, I assured Hong Wei that I was very pleased with the sights that I had seen and all that we had done and how I was looked after. I further told him that Hong Wei had been fantastic company and I was delighted to have met her. He then conveyed my message to her.

Saying goodbye wasn't easy

igh noon arrived and an early lunch was called for. We walked to a nice nearby restaurant and ordered lunch, which consisted of spring rolls, chicken wings and strips of beef. The Tiger beer was always needed to wash it down. It was another restaurant with the open charcoal fire which pleased me. This was my favourite way of cooking the food then and believe it or not, it still is today. After lunch we returned to the International Hostel, as it was now time to wind down. My flight was early the following day, so it was all about rest and taking it easy. This we did, with Hong Wei and I conversing as best we could. Soon the hours passed until darkness fell over Beijing city and soon it was time for my last supper. We got a taxi to another restaurant around 19:00 and dug into the food that was served. My last Tiger beers were sunk with great satisfaction. We took our time, as there was no rush over the following two hours. On arriving back at the hostel for the last time, we said goodbye to Mr. Wang and retired for the night.

It was Monday morning when the alarm struck at 06:00, to get us up and out of the bed. When I was showered and shaved, and Hong Wei had freshened up too, we packed our cases and made our way to the restaurant, where the reliable Mr. Wang was waiting for us. All three of us had our breakfast at 07:00, as arranged. At 08:00 we were checking out with Hong Wei insisting on paying the bill at the reception. I told her to thank them for their hospitality over the course of my stay there. The two receptionists smiled back and said goodbye in Chinese. The early trip in the taxi to the airport was of mixed emotions for me. Having been privileged to have seen what I saw, there was also the emotional side of saying goodbye to Mr. Wang and of course, Hong Wei. After all, she was the reason I had come in the first place. As we neared Beijing International Airport, Hong Wei said to me in her broken English, "Billy, I will learn English when you are gone and look forward to seeing you come back again."

"Okay Hong Wei, I have your telephone number and your e-mail address."

Mr. Wang said, "Billy, we will go to the check in desk with you and spend a little time in the waiting area, until it is time for you to go to your departure gate."

My departure time was 12:00 (high noon, like in the western films), but luckily, I was not about to be hanged! On all the international flights that I have taken, I always make a point of being at the airport well in advance of my departure time. Some two hours after checking in and with much talking done, the three of us had a light meal in one of the many restaurants there.

As the clock struck the appropriate time, it was now about heading to my departure gate. I kissed and hugged Hong Wei tightly. I felt it and I knew she felt it too. Words became lost and sadness struck inwards. I thanked Mr. Wang and shook his hand with sincerity and appreciation. The big terminal clock was showing the time as we parted company. As I headed to my departure gate, the distance between us grew. When I was at the point of no return, I waved back for a final time at Hong Wei and Mr. Wang. They continuingly kept waving at me, until I was out of sight. It was an emotional few minutes for me, having to say goodbye and I genuinely felt it.

The Big Bird (plane) took off on time. I looked out my window on the magical city of Beijing way down below me, disappearing fast. I wondered where Mr. Wang and Hong Wei were now. My mind was filled with memories of the past week, of where I had been, of what I had seen, of what I had done – all to do with meeting Hong Wei.

These thoughts accompanied me on the long and tedious ten-hour flight back to Amsterdam. This giant plane touched down in Amsterdam on time, where I then had to wait a while before boarding my second plane on this return journey to Dublin Airport in Ireland. My plane touched down on time here too. Within an hour I was in my car and on the road back to my home city of Waterford.

After the one-hundred-and-ten-mile drive home, I was coming over Rice Bridge and down the quays to my then address in William Street. After ten minutes of entering my abode, tiredness hit me like a sledgehammer. But before I went asleep, there were two thoughts that entered my head. The magical city of Beijing was a long way away now and what was Hong Wei doing right now?

Even after that first trip into the unknown, I think the bug had slowly bitten. Tomorrow I would go and see Fengqin in her flat and tell her all she needed to know. My eyes then closed firmly, and I went into the darkness!

It was bright the following morning when I woke. A full Irish breakfast from a nearby local restaurant was a welcome sight on my plate. It didn't last long and was washed down with a mug of hot chocolate. Right then, let's go and see Fengqin at her place, I said to myself. Fengqin was in when I called. I could see she was surprised and happy to see me.

"Come in, Billy, and tell me all about your trip," she said.

"You were right about Hong Wei being a nice girl," I said. "I'm going to stay in touch with her through email and I might be even able to get to see her on Skype. Boy, would you be tired after making that trip! I'm going to have to get some more sleep today, as I'm back in work tomorrow."

"You do that, Billy, and keep in touch," Fengqin replied.

I sent Hong Wei a few introductory short emails over the course of the next few days and I received replies back from her. In them we exchanged thoughts and feelings for each other. She also told me she was learning English and looking forward to seeing me sometime in the New Year. The month of December arrived in Ireland and obviously Christmas day is the main feast in that month. Christmas in itself meant nothing to me at this particular time, except my son Keith and daughter Lisa kept in touch with me. My work on the Euro Lines bus service continued and I just got on with the job. I still had my close friends who I shared a well-earned drink with on the weekends. My love of football at local level in Ireland continued, as did my scouting job and following the fortunes of

Newcastle United, as I had done since the season of 1961/62. I stayed in touch with Fengqin and kept her up to speed on developments as the end of the year turned and 2006 entered the equation.

Deep down I knew I wanted to go back to China sometime in 2006 to see Hong Wei. This was where I was, and this was where I wanted to be at this point in time in my life. When you are in the situation that I found myself in from the middle of 2003 onwards, I came to the realisation then and still agree now that when it comes down to it, nobody really cares. Unfortunately, that's the way the world is gone! No one really gives a damn. People might say they care, but do they? I'm afraid that in the world we live in today, this is the way it is. It's sad to have to say that, but it's the law of the jungle out there and it's all about survival. If you can't survive, you go under, simple as that! That was my overall reading of the situation then and still is today. I make no apologies to anyone, why should I? But I had made my mind up – I wasn't going under for anybody.

As the weeks passed, I continued to send emails to Hong Wei, and she continued to reply to them. She asked me in one of her emails when I was coming back to China again. She said she would love me to meet her family in her home city of Anshan. I said I would go in January for around seven days, as my job could not give me any extra time off. I went ahead and made the same arrangements as before, regarding booking my flight and getting my visa.

My departure was to be on January 13th and a Friday would you believe it. Superstitions and all that stuff were the furthest thoughts from my mind as regards that date! I was going to alter my flight pattern slightly, by going from Cork to London, then on to Beijing with Air China and finally fly to Shenyang. This was the nearest airport to where Hong Wei lived. Then it would be another ninety miles by road. This was going to be even longer than my maiden journey to China, as I would be taking an extra flight. But I was prepared to go the distance (literally) to see Hong Wei.

With regard to getting my visa, the same procedure applied. Fengqin came to Dublin with me to apply for it and we collected it the same day.

Everything was in order, there wasn't a problem. The following few weeks passed, and anticipation grew again. The day of my departure from Cork Airport finally arrived. I drove there from Waterford city and parked my car in the car park. As regards time, I always gave myself plenty. I didn't care what other people thought of my plans or actions, who gave a damn about me, nobody really.

My flight took off on time and landed on time in Heathrow Airport in London. After waiting in the airport terminal for a while, I was eventually seated on my second flight to Beijing. It took the same time to get there as before. When we landed in Beijing, I had to wait a short time to get my next flight to Shenyang. The flight time is just over an hour, but although I was getting tired, I was motivated and kept myself alert with the thought of meeting Hong Wei again. My plane took off at the correct time and gently touched down on the runway at Shenyang Airport on time. I still don't know just how they manage to fly those planes!

It was now Sunday and into the early hours of that morning. Was I tired? You bet I was! When I had retrieved my two average size suitcases, I went through security, then through the customs and finally found myself in the arrivals area. It was still hard to imagine finding myself back in China again, only a few weeks after I had been here in 2005.

It was a case of 'Hello' again

With my suitcases in tow and my eyes peeled, I had only one target in my sights and that was Hong Wei.

I heard the call in the distance, just like I had heard it before in Beijing in November. "Billy, over here!" was the shout from the small crowd that were there at that particular time. It was Hong Wei and there she was again waving her hands frantically trying to get my attention. She needn't have worried, I saw her.

When we met, I hugged her warmly. She then introduced me to a Mr. Liu who was her brother-in-law and then to a Mr. Lee who was another interpreter. There was no need for flowers on this occasion, as her presence was all I wanted. Mr. Wang, our previous interpreter, was not available at that time. Hong Wei held on to me tightly as we made our way to the car belonging to Mr. Liu. We got in the back and snuggled up to each other. It was a big black car, but don't ask me what make it was. I knew Hong Wei was delighted to see me, as I was to see her. Mr. Lee was friendly, and I found after a few minutes in his company that his English was a little better than Mr. Wang's had been. That's just the way it was.

When we exited the airport car park it was dark. A light fall of snow was falling all around us and it looked picturesque. Christmas was gone a few weeks, but I still felt it in the air. We were now about to go cross-country and through open countryside which I was told was a shorter route to get to Anshan city. I really didn't know what to expect, but even though I was tired, I wouldn't have missed this spin for the world. The weather was a lot colder in that January than what it had been on my first visit in November the previous year. The light snow was like a blanket on the ground, but not hazardous for driving. What an experience I was about to have.

It was fascinating riding along in the dark, not at any great speed I might add. The sights that greeted my eyes in the still of night were obviously all new to me. We passed a lot of old farmhouses, some looked like deserted outbuildings. The snowflakes continued lightly on their downward journey, as we continued on ours. The headlights on our car told my tired eyes that we were passing red bricked buildings of all descriptions.

There was also lots of farm machinery of every description by the roadside. Most of them had plastic coverings of some sort, but you could still roughly identify them by their shape. We met very little traffic on the road, but then again, it was in the dead of the night. Although, in between the start and the finish of this car ride, we had passed a small number of people walking or cycling in the dark, possibly going to someone's house or getting ready for the long working day that lay ahead in the countryside. I felt then, as I still do now fourteen years on, that there was something magical and unique about that trip in the car that night. Let's just say, it stayed with me. Dawn was breaking and it was starting to get bright as all four of us continued our journey towards Anshan city in Mr. Liu's car.

Whilst in transit and with Hong Wei cuddled closely to me, we conversed as best we could in her broken English. Her English had improved slightly in the few weeks since I had last seen her. I also knew she wanted and was determined to learn the English language quickly. It was approaching 05:00 as we drew closer to our destination.

While we were on the outskirts, away in the distance, I could see the skyline of Anshan city. This was my first visit to this industrial city, which was known the world over, because it was most famous for its steel. We were going to Hong Wei's sister Pan Pan's house first, where her mum was scheduled to meet us. The streets leading to the address where we were going to were starting to get busy with citizens on the move for an early start at work. At that hour of the morning, it was mostly bikes, trucks and to a lesser extent, cars. Anshan is still a big city in itself, with a population of around three million in 2006. In 2010, the census showed there were 3.6 million people living there. It was a city, like all the rest, whose population was continuingly growing.

As I said earlier, the city would be most famous and noted for its manufacturing of steel. The production started in a factory in 1948. It is said that the best quality steel in China comes from Anshan city. It was the second largest steel manufacturer in China and at one time was called The Capital of Steel. Coincidently, the previous year in 2005, there were plans for the company to merge with a competitor called Benxi Iron and Steel Group. To the best of my knowledge, they formed a new company called Anben Steel Group. Have a look at the name, the first two letters for Anshan and the first three for Benxi. There are also three large iron ore mining pits surrounding Anshan city.

Surprisingly, the city is twined with the city of Sheffield in England, which I didn't know. Plus, it holds one third of the world's talcum supply. The famous philanthropist Guo Mingyi was born in Anshan city and still lives there. There are also five museums in Anshan, four of which are smaller than the main one. These are just a few little points of note, which I thought you, the reader, might find interesting.

Naturally, I was a little nervous of where we were going, but Hong Wei reassured me that all would be well meeting her mum and some other members of her family. When I asked her about her dad, she informed me that he had died a few years' earlier. As I said before, did I ever think I would find myself here? Not in a million years, would I have guessed it. But as in my life and dealing with fate, I stayed positive!

We eventually arrived at her sister's house. This sister was called Pan Pan. As I glanced at it before leaving the car, I could see it was a small one level terraced house, with a small garden in the front and a long concrete path leading to the front door. We reached the front door with Hong Wei holding my arm, Mr. Liu just ahead of us and Mr. Lee bringing up the rear. Again, this was further into the unknown for me. Pan Pan opened the door and hugged me warmly. I responded with a peck on the cheek and a smile.

We made our way into a small room which was now crowded with a group of people, where I knew a lot of excitement and curiosity about my presence would be. Her mum, Wei Qui Wen, was next to be introduced to me. I immediately hugged her and warmly kissed her on the cheek. She was an old lady who'd had nothing easy in her life while rearing her six children. I could see this in her body language, which was also written across her face. But I knew she had a strong nature and her family were all that mattered to her. Among the group were Hong Wei's other sisters and a few children. I was introduced to all of them in turn, which took quite a few minutes. There are five sisters. In order, they are Hong Yan 1, Hong Wei 1, Hong Wei 2, Hong Yan 2 and Pan Pan. Hong Wei 2 is my wife.

Going by custom, they began talking amongst themselves about what I was going to eat. Believe you me, food was the last thing on my mind. There is a word called sleep and I had to go in search of it quickly. My eyes were now beginning to close without effort. Hong Wei made arrangements for me to get some sleep in a nearby bedroom. She spoke in Chinese to those present, with Mr. Lee interpreting for me. She told them I needed to sleep after my journey, and I would speak with them later. Hong Wei whispered into my ear, that she would make something for me to eat when I wake up and would that be ok. With barely having the energy to answer her, I said to Hong Wei that was okay with me, but sleep was essential at that point.

With the passing of time, I eventually opened my tired eyes and looked at my watch, it was around 13:00. The sleep had done me a world of good and had brought me back to the land of the living. I returned to the sitting room, where I had first been, and everyone was still there. Excitement was still in the air as all present threw their eyes on my second coming. Then all of the questions began flying: What's Billy going to have to eat? What does he want to drink? Would he like this? Would he like that?

Hong Wei was being bombarded with hurried questions. Mr. Lee told me all of this in English, but I knew what was going on by the body language alone. Hong Wei herself then made me an omelette. It had eggs, tomatoes, mushrooms, cheese and onions. When it was cooked, I drank a glass of cold milk to accompany it. Ask me was it nice – it was just beautiful and delicious. The Chinese people in general I find they will bend over backwards when they welcome you into their homes. I found this has always been the case with me on my visits to other people's homes too. Well this has been my experience. Being a westerner, I know was one reason, the other was probably because Hong Wei's family took to me. It was so nice to see love and feel wanted. Hong Wei's cooking was top class and still is to this day. She is a wonderful cook and can cook wonderful Chinese dishes.

After another hour or so there, we said goodbye, as it was time to go to our accommodation which was in the city centre. It was a beautiful five-star hotel called Huan Qiu. Hong Wei had booked us in there earlier, and now we just needed to check-in. After doing that, we then had to go and see her brother and son. Mr. Liu drove his car and Mr. Lee accompanied us across the city. All of Hong Wei's family had no English, but I knew by their body language how much they had welcomed me. I must say, all of them then and even now, have shown the same level of courtesy and friendliness to me, as on all of my other visits.

We met her brother Hong Yao Bin and spent a few minutes with him. He came across as a rather quiet, but a very friendly man. Then we went to another part of Anshan and met her son, Jin Yang. Immediately I detected he was a very pleasant and good-mannered young man. His warm handshake and embrace were all the proof I needed. I could see by his actions how anxious he was to help me in any way possible to make my stay as enjoyable as he could. Reading his body language while he was talking to his mum in Chinese, even then, I could see he was very close to her and loved her dearly. He had no English, but Mr. Lee was able to communicate with him for me.

We had made arrangements earlier to have dinner with the rest of Hong Wei's family that evening. We just relaxed for the few hours in the hotel and then freshened up before being collected by Mr. Liu in his car with Mr. Lee. Mr. Lee was still a very important person to have by my side, in those early days. The thought did obviously cross my mind, that this could be my one and only visit to Anshan city. But who knew that? I certainly didn't. We went to a hotel called Sheng Li and then to a private room, where the rest of Hong Wei's extended family were gathered.

She introduced them to me, and I must state again, they were all friendly. I'd say there could have been up to twenty people there. We all sat down at two very long tables, where it was service with a smile by the waitresses. I went for chicken wings, cooked beef and lamb and I tried a new beer called Qing Dao. It was a little different in taste to Tiger beer. I stuck with that for the remaining few days of my visit. When the waitresses were finished taking our orders, they returned shortly afterwards with plate after plate of different dishes. The two tables were laden down with all kinds of food. I tried and sampled a few of their contents, but only in a small way. Hong Wei could eat anything. What a woman!

A few of Hong Wei's family made short speeches and welcomed me to Anshan. I returned the invitation and spoke for a few minutes and stressed to her family that Hong Wei was the reason I had come back. I knew they were all so proud of their home city, as they should be, like us all. Again only a few of them had some broken English. Mr. Lee sat next to me and interpreted what they were all saying and at times asking questions. He returned the same favour to them, what I was saying and asking too. I must say that the food I ate that first day in Anshan city was tasty and on a par with the food I had eaten in Beijing. After about two hours our meal was finished, and pleasantries had been exchanged between me and them. It was around 20:00 when we left the confines of this nice restaurant. Hong Wei and I returned to our hotel where we had a relaxing night together. The next few days for me were all about seeing Anshan city and the surrounding areas and meeting more of Hong Wei's friends.

When I awoke it was Monday morning and with just under a week of my stay to go, I wanted to see as much of this city as I could. Not forgetting the most important question of why I had really returned to China. We arrived in the restaurant at around 09:00. The breakfast in this five-star hotel was a self-service buffet. You just took what you wanted and grabbed yourself a table. I tried two small glasses of hot milk for a change, which took a bit of getting used to, but I adjusted to it. Though I am not saying I would have it every day! I had some meat dumplings, bread rolls and two eggs. This was to be my main breakfast intake for the week. At around 10:00, Hong Wei told me we must meet Mr. Lee and go see a few places of interest.

"I want to know as much about Anshan city as I can while I'm here," I said.

"Okay, we will do that," was Hong Wei's reply.

On leaving the warm confines of the hotel lobby and making our way to the main entrance of the hotel, weather-wise it was different than before. A fresh fall of snow had descended, which was now covering the ground. The temperature had dropped down to around minus ten degrees on that particular morning. Even though we were both wrapped up, my two ears were exposed to the elements. They felt like they were cut off from my face. This was cold, I mean, real cold - colder than anything I had ever experienced before.

When we got to the entrance of the hotel, Hong Wei got talking to a Chinese lady. While she did, I just happened to look out on the pavement and saw a sad sight. There was a man with one leg and one arm just sitting there. He only had a large sheet of cardboard beneath him. You can imagine how cold it was and what the conditions must have been like for him. He had his one arm outstretched with a box, holding it out to passers-by. I couldn't help but notice, he wore little clothes and they were lightweight in appearance. There was a walking crutch lying nearby and that was it. Some people were just passing him by like he wasn't even there. As I have already spoken about what I had seen in Beijing a few weeks earlier, I wondered where does the fault lie. It's the same the world over, but I find it sad. He looked like he was in desperate need of help. All I could do was go over and give him a few yuan. He just looked up at me and nodded in appreciation. I felt it was the least I could do, under the circumstances. After that act of whatever you want to call it, we were then waiting to wave down a taxi.

Most of the taxis in Anshan city were Volkswagen Jetta's. They were red and grey in colour. They carry four people and at times can be a little cramped with a full load, but then again you are never in a taxi for more than a few minutes. They do move quickly around this city, from dawn until dusk. There are hundreds of them to be seen, going nonstop. The speed of the service here is the same as in Beijing. A smaller city but yet there was plenty of taxies to be found. We were only waiting two minutes for a taxi to arrive.

Don't forget the road conditions were a little hazardous due to the snow, thus explaining the extra minute or two waiting time. We picked up Mr. Lee shortly afterwards at a rendezvous point. He sat in the front and gave strict instructions of our destination to the driver. The fares around the city started at a fixed rate of seven yuan and obviously work upward for the distance of your journey. Most trips are only for a few minutes, as you are going from one area to another, which would involve just a few streets. But most of the streets are very long, you wouldn't walk more than one or two anyway. So, ten or fifteen yuan on average would get you from A to B. That's roughly about €1.50 in euros at an exchange rate of ten to one at that time.

Our first destination was the old Anshan Cheng Gate on the far outskirts of the city. This was the former entrance to this ancient city when it was called Anshan Cheng. It goes way back in time to the Ming Dynasty. After a few minutes and a briefing from Mr. Lee on the way there, we arrived at this structure. It was a huge big stone entrance and looked like the Arc de Triomphe in Paris, France from a distance. It was still standing after all these years and wearing well. We spent a few minutes there and I observed it from both sides. Obviously, a photograph with Mr. Lee and Hong Wei as befitted the occasion. From there we hailed another taxi and headed to the famous Jade Buddha Palace Museum.

Within a few minutes we arrived at this impressive sight. The museum is actually in a complex that is adjoining the well-known 219

Park. The 219 national park is so called, because Anshan city was under Japanese rule in 1931, until they were defeated in 1945. Then you had the civil war for three years between the National Government and the Peoples Liberation Army. The city itself was liberated by the PLA on the 19th of February (2nd month and 19th day) in 1948. Thus, the name of the park and also of course Anshan city was once again under Chinese rule.

The museum itself I found very interesting, with all types of jade and other precious stones on view. They had a tourist shop there and we purchased three small items as souvenirs and a reminder of our visit there. But the real prize was to see the world's largest jade Buddha statue housed here. It was a magnificent sight to see, as it stood eight metres high and weighs two-hundred and sixty tons. It is made entirely of jade and looks green in appearance, but yes, it is a magnificent sight to see.

After spending an hour or so in there, we went out to 219 Park and relaxed with a leisurely walk. There were kids playing on the many children's playgrounds that are there. It is not like in Ireland where when playgrounds are vandalised. We have a tendency to shrug our shoulders and accept it as the norm – Ah, someone will fix it on Monday morning! I have often said publicly and continue to say that there is no deterrent. That's the real reason for vandalism. Why should one person or persons by their actions cause damage to a public amenity and deprive other members of the community the enjoyment these facilities provide. I say this type of behaviour should not be tolerated anywhere. It certainly would not be tolerated in China. Vandalism of other public places like bus shelters, toilets or interfering with planted trees, which are sacred to the Chinese people, would not be acceptable either. All of the above-mentioned things are left alone in China for the enjoyment of everyone. Why, because the deterrent is there, and I agree with it completely. If you cause wanton vandalism or destruction to public property, you should pay heavily for your actions. I couldn't agree more with this policy. It should be the same the world over.

Hong Wei was holding me closely and not letting me out of her sight. I knew she was happy to be in my company. As it was coming to lunch time, we got ourselves a snack from one of the nearby restaurants that are there. I had two little burger buns with meat and a salad dressing on them. This was washed down with a coke, as it kept the wolves (hunger) from the door for another few hours. Hong Wei told me that we would be going out for dinner later with a few of Mr. Liu's friends.

The next few hours were spent strolling around and looking at all that was to be seen in this well-kept park. Mr. Lee was a patient man and I valued his company immensely. Even though Hong Wei's English was improving, where would I have been without this interpreter? When the time was right, Hong Wei, Mr. Lee and I decided to get a bus back to our hotel.

The bus route was passing Mr. Lee's home on the way, and he disembarked at a certain point. Mr. Lee had left word with Hong Wei that he would pick us up at 19:00. Both of us got a nice relaxing rest for a few hours. After waking at 18:30, we had a quick shower to freshen up and a change of clothes. Mr. Liu duly arrived on time with Mr. Lee and we departed. Where to, I didn't know, nor did I care; all I knew was that I was in Hong Wei's company and that was good enough for me.

We soon arrived at a hotel called Wu Huan, which was in the centre of Anshan city. On arrival we received the same Chinese welcome from the door staff as in Beijing. The four of us made our way upstairs to a large private room. This could be interesting, I said to myself as we were about to enter the room. Several males and females were present. Mr. Liu introduced me to all of them individually. They were all personal friends of Mr. Liu and I ended up calling them 'The gang of eleven'. They were all friendly and the females present all in turn got a peck on the cheek from me, while the men got a good Irish handshake. I don't think Hong Wei minded too much. I was just making it customary from a western point of view. The large round empty revolving table was completely new to me. I instinctively had to give it a small spin or two. Hong Wei placed my order with the rest of the orders from the people present.

I could see they were all inquisitive about my background and how I had come to Anshan city. Hong Wei told all of them collectively in

Chinese and answered all their questions in turn. They were all friendly and they kept asking Hong Wei did I want this or did I want that. One thing I did want though was a drink. I found shyness disappeared very quickly in this company. With a click of his fingers from a certain Mr. E and a few words in his native Chinese language to the waitresses, a few boxes of beer arrived within minutes. I loved listening to Chinese people talking together in their own language then and still do to this day. I find it fascinating to listen to them. I soon realized that all of Mr. Liu's friends had very little English between them. But Mr. Lee was invaluable here and kept the lines of communication open.

When the food and the drink did arrive, it was in abundance. What a sight to see on the table – with every kind of Chinese food you could imagine on display within minutes. It was all laid out on plates, bowls and trays of every description. With Hong Wei by my side, it was time to set off on this food adventure. What an adventure it turned out to be in the following two hours. I tried practically all the different foods that were on offer. Some I liked and others I just refused to eat, irrespective of what Hong Wei, Mr. Liu or Mr. Lee thought. Nope, if I don't like it, I just won't eat it. That was the case then and is still the case now. I know I might sound awkward, but believe you me, I am anything but. Just take the message on board that if you don't like it, don't eat it.

A lot of people and especially people I know back in Waterford city have this misconception about Chinese food. I keep on telling them, the Chinese food in China is completely different to that of the Chinese cuisine we eat all over Europe. There is a world of a difference, slightly visual, but obviously more so in taste. The European Chinese food is of a certain flavour. You could eat any dish you like and it would go down okay. In my opinion and having been to China on ten occasions now, I think some of the food you just would or could not eat. Don't get me wrong, it's all cooked well and looks nice, but it's when you taste it, it's different. Some of it is overpowering, as the flavour is too strong, too hot or in other cases, it just doesn't go with your constitution. I think that's just the way it is, others might think differently. It's all about opinions and one's taste, I guess. But as I have told countless people over the years, when they ask me about China – don't let the food put you off. This is just my taste and opinion!

As regards food, I always tell people there are plenty of choices, but stick to what you like and don't change your mind. There is always a wide selection of cold meats to sample too. Fish is a product I eat a lot of back home in Ireland, but in China, I just refuse to eat it. Most of the fish dishes are steam cooked and when presented on the table look beautiful, which it is to those who like to eat it, but not me. It's cooked whole with the head and tail attached and they can be served in flavoured gravy. The Chinese eat fish with chopsticks, and it is a terrific sight to see them in action. When they are finished, all you see is the spine, the head and the tail. It is like something you would see in a cartoon, such is the sight. But I must stress, this is a perfectly healthy dish, only it is not for me. Funnily enough, the one food that I ate the most of was chicken wings. I must have eaten thousands of them over the years. The reason was because I liked them. Simple as that! Most of them are oven-cooked and appear crispy on the plate. They are piping hot and very tasty to eat.

Back to the meal. I would say when we were finished, I was full. I found, you are hungry when you start, but you would be surprised how quickly you get full. With every mouthful or two, the custom is to wash it down with a small glass of beer. They really go hand-in-hand, because most of the food is hot. But if that's the way it is, I wasn't complaining. The bottles of Qing Dao beer went down a treat. I think my consumption on the night was just short of double figures.

During the course of this delicious meal I was offered some Chinese wine, but I declined. All Irishmen know not to mix your drinks, irrespective of what you started on. Experience came into play here, although I had to refuse it nicely without causing any offence to my hosts. Amazingly, throughout this meal and as was the case with others up to now, Hong Wei just drank hot water. She just refused to break her lifetime's habit. No wonder she was the picture of good health and still is today.

We said our goodbyes and they collectively said, "We will see you again before you go back to Ireland, Billy."

"Yes, I'm sure you will. Thank you for accepting me into your company," I said.

Mr. Liu and Mr. Lee drove Hong Wei and I back to our hotel. When dropping us off, Mr. Lee said they will see us in the morning after breakfast at around 10:00. I thanked him for his help over the previous days and expressed how much I appreciated it.

We had an early and relaxing night and got a good night's sleep before daylight again entered through our bedroom window around 08:00. It was morning, it was Tuesday. After our breakfast was finished around 09:50, Mr. Liu and Mr. Lee arrived to be our guides for the day. Mr. Lee told me they had a place called Garden of Birds and asked me whether I would like to see it. I said I would. So, within twenty minutes, we had arrived at this rather unusual place.

As we approached from the car park, it became apparent to me that this was something that I would not have seen before by what greeted me. It was like a forest, with loads of trees and a rocky surface all around, with wooded paths going in all directions. It really was like a forest, with all of the greenery around us. But the amazing thing that one could not miss was the giant strengthened green net that covered the whole of this forest area. It was like a canopy spread out on support poles at different intervals. Like the poles you would see holding up the tent in a circus. This was to get the correct height.

We also noticed that there were a few men, like gamekeepers on the outside of this huge netted area and walking around checking the netting. We then heard noises coming from all of the different species of birds around us. Now, I couldn't tell you one bird from another, but I was able to recognize a few parrots perched on some trees and a few peacocks walking around the surrounding areas. They would come quite close to you, but still keep their distance.

Mr. Lee told me there are a lot of rare and tropical birds there. The main reason the netting is there is to make sure none of these precious birds escape out into the modern life that exists outside of this netted area. Outside of this environment, these birds would not survive. There were all different kinds of birds around us. Some were lively and singing, while others were stationary and quiet. Others were cautious and eyed us from their safe vantage points. They were used to the many visitors that pay a visit to this most unusual of places every day. Mr. Liu and Mr. Lee looked on with casual glances at all the different birds. I think Hong Wei showed a little interest too. We relaxed there and had a long walk around the whole area. You would be naturally drawn to looking upwards at the different type of birds that live their lives under this covered area. Hong Wei was on my arm for the two hours that we were there. I found it was well worth the visit, especially because of its rarity.

As it was close to lunch time, we decided to get a snack. There was a small restaurant close to this place and we went out there. I tried a large pancake with beef in it and a Coke-Cola to wash it down. Mr. Liu, Mr. Lee and Hong Wei had some kind of soup and beef dumplings. Three glasses of hot water accompanied their meal.

An hour later, Mr. Lee informed me that our next port of call was to see Qian Shan Mountain Buddha. It's next to another national park on the outskirts of Anshan city. It translates to a Thousand Mountains and there probably are. Just like Anshan city translates to Saddle Mountain.

It wasn't snowing at the time, but it had left its calling card in a thin layer on the ground. It was only a car ride away, and Mr. Liu again took control of the steering wheel of his car to ferry us there. It didn't take us too long before we got there. The National Park is full of forest trails and scenic routes through it. It borders a range of mountains, one of which is shaped like a massive stone Buddha – it is the natural shape of the mountain. We took the cable car service, which brings you up so far. Then you have to get off at a certain point on the last landing stage and make your way further up on foot. On the way up in the cable car, the views were stunning. Especially as you look down on the National Park below.

Hong Wei and I were in one cable car (as they only hold two at a time) and Mr. Lee and Mr. Liu were in the other. I found out then that Hong Wei was not scared of heights, but then again, neither was I. After disembarking, we went through one of the forest trails. There were several areas where we had to step up on a level and this was aided by steps cut into the stone. It really was some piece of craftsmanship to see from all those years ago.

Most of the steps were now smooth, which indicated to me that a lot of people had travelled on this well-worn path. We eventually came out into a clearing and there was the giant stone Buddha across from us. They say this Buddha resembles Maitreya, an ancient Buddha. I could see that he had trappings of red on him; a big red clothed necklace and also a red cloak hanging from him. We took a few photographs and I studied the view from where we stood. This truly was magnificent scenery that was bestowed upon me. At that moment in time, I thought to myself if only the people in Waterford city could see me now! I laughed to myself. I never thought I'd be here in this unique place.

When we were finished there and after admiring the views, we made our way back down the mountain. We soon arrived at the entrance to a Buddha's monastery. There was a monk there, mainly I think to give tourists and people who visit an insight into their lifestyle and the history surrounding the monastery. The four of us had a few words with him. My questions were translated by Mr. Lee. They were on the lines of: How long have you been here? Where in China were you born? Do you miss the modern world? Did it take you long to adapt to this way of life? Could you see yourself here forever?

I must say, that all the rest of the monks and Buddha's priests that I was to meet over the years in other temples and monasteries, came across as being very content people. They were after adapting to a quiet, stress-free, peaceful life. They all seemed positive and content with the lifestyle they were leading. They occasionally do smile and also come across as gentle human beings. Just inside most of the temples and other monasteries that I had visited on this maiden occasion and in the following years, there was an altar. It was like a big bath with ashes from past users, with huge and small coloured candles that also look like giant crackers. These burn slowly and give off a rather strong smell of incense. Visitors buy these coloured sticks and light them, then kneel and say a prayer to Buddha. And the cycle continues, in the sense that there are always some of these sticks burning there. Hong Wei, Mr. Liu and Mr. Lee firstly lit their own incense sticks and put them in the sandy base that holds them upright for the duration of their life. They then individually made their way to the altar. They each in turn knelt on cushions and bowed to Buddha. What they said and murmured, I don't know. It was between them and their God. Who was I to question their actions?

After spending a few minutes there, it was time to go. The thought did occur to me as we waved goodbye to the monk that in a few days' time I would be back in Ireland and this monk and the rest of the order, would still be here in this solemn place. It was a contrasting thought which flashed in front of me. They live in their own content world and we live in ours. I have often wondered who are the happiest, them or us. Whatever your belief is, I think it's a thought that is worth thinking about sometimes or even often. For some strange and unknown reason, my own thoughts momentarily turned back to Fengqin in Ireland. What was her path in life? What was she doing with herself now? How was she filling in her twenty-four-hour day? It's all about choices I guess, but who are we to judge anyone! With dusk approaching and tiredness slowly creeping up on my body, we re-entered Mr. Liu's car and headed back to Anshan city. We arrived back at the hotel at teatime. Hong Wei had made arrangements for that evening to go out for a meal.

Mr. Liu and Mr. Lee would call back at 19:30 and take us to our pre-planned destination. A two-hour sleep for myself and Hong Wei was followed by a quick shower and my body was as good as new, and ready to go. As punctual as ever, Mr. Liu and Mr. Lee arrived on time. We were soon on our way to a restaurant called Hai Feng. A few of Hong Wei's school friends wanted to see her and meet me. I was happy to oblige. When we got there, they were all waiting to greet us. They were all naturally a little bit excited at seeing Hong Wei and being introduced to me. It was understandable, I suppose, and I understood where they were coming from. There was a peck on the cheek and a smile from me for all of them. It wasn't every day that they had a westerner in their midst and to be about to have a meal in their company.

It was close to 22:00 when we were finished our meal and said our goodbyes. Mr. Liu accompanied by Mr. Lee, dropped us back at our hotel with the parting words from Mr. Lee, "See you around 10:00 tomorrow, Billy. We will have somewhere else lined up for you."

"Okay Mr. Lee, see you then and thank you for all your help up to now," I said.

Hong Wei and I had a relaxing night. Her English was slowly improving, which meant our communication was also getting better. My thoughts were still within myself, but the direction my life was taking me in, all sounded right to me. I was going with the flow in a positive manner.

The following morning (Wednesday) came, as it comes every week, in whatever part of the world you might happen to be. With breakfast finished, excitement was high as to where we would be going. Hong Wei was as cool as ever and I could see she was in a happy mood in my company, as always. Mr. Liu and Mr. Lee arrived, as punctual as ever, on the stroke of 10:00. Mr. Lee said, "Billy, today we are going the short distance to the main Anshan city museum. We think you will find it very interesting there."

"Good," I said, "I love museums and anything to do with history." Also adding, "Ye have a lot of it here in this country, going on what I have seen already."

After about twenty minutes of Mr. Liu's careful driving through the mid-morning traffic, we arrived at our destination. The main Anshan city museum is a large long building with modern brick work and panelled glass on the outside, which leads you to the main entrance. This leads you into a foyer area, from there you can go in any direction you like. Most of the museums I was to visit over the years in different cities have a layout that you basically start at one end and work your way around in a clockwise direction, or you can also go anti clockwise.

We started on our left and proceeded to take in the displays. There were areas there dictating where the history of jade and porcelain was found within Anshan city. This dated back from very early on as I could see from the many recovered pieces displayed in closed glass cases. The history of Anshan city obviously took precedence with its cultural background being explained through the many large photographs that were also on display. We saw models of people in the early century and what Anshan city looked like way back then. I was enjoying this no end, and with Hong Wei on my arm, I couldn't have been in a better place.

Meanwhile Mr. Liu and Mr. Lee had wandered off at their leisure. No one was in any rush, as we had all day. This was a most relaxing experience for me. We took in the ground floor with other interesting sights. Eventually moving upstairs where there was more of the same on display. There were arts and crafts areas which I also found very interesting. All of these were accompanied by big signs which were in two languages, Chinese and English. We came to the part about the steelworks. We saw it from the beginning with a huge model of the early plant laid out, to the spectacle that it is today. I was impressed.

We saw Mr. Liu and Mr. Lee at different intervals, and they asked me was I enjoying what I was seeing, to which I said I was indeed. The museum is very interesting. I enjoyed it immensely. The whole history of Anshan city was laid out before me in different areas. I remember quite vividly that I was the only westerner in the museum at that particular time, on that particular day. They were other tourists there, but they were all Chinese people.

Security personnel were very much on view too, but they were relaxed and kept their distance, even though their trained eyes were keeping a watch on all visitors. There was one particular sight that I thought was very interesting, especially to the western tourist. It was a large group of wax figures from all the different tribes and cultures from all over China. They were from the north to the south, the east and the west. They had their own costumes portraying their identities and traditions within the borders of China; such as the Mongolians, the Eskimos and so on. We spent about two and a half hours there and I enjoyed every minute of it. We took photographs in different areas of the museum.

Mr. Liu and Mr. Lee met us as we were leaving the building and Hong Wei told them in Chinese that I had enjoyed it very much. Now it was time to get a snack somewhere. There was a small eating place within walking distance. We just had a few dumplings with vegetables. Mr. Liu and I had two Tiger beers each. Mr, Lee and Hong Wei just stuck with the hot water. What was next on this cool dry sunny day, I wondered. Hong Wei was as happy in my company as I was in hers.

Next up was a trip to see an uncle and aunt of hers who lived in a retirement apartment complex in another part of the city. Mr. Liu and Mr. Lee dropped us off there and said goodbye. We would meet them later for dinner that night with members of Hong Wei's family again. These modern apartment complexes all have lifts because the occupants are all in their late years. They all have security systems inside their dwellings too, which is reassuring for them. Although I stand to be corrected, but I think vandalism and robberies are not as common here as in European countries or certain cities across the world. The deterrent is there, and you pay the price for your actions.

After a little bit of searching at the front entrance for their apartment number and finding it without any great difficulty, we entered the lift and choose the right floor. Exiting the lift, we found the right door and we rang the bell. It was a real surprise to this elderly couple when they opened the door, as they weren't expecting us. Hong Wei was all excited introducing me to them in Chinese. A kiss and a hug were given to her aunt and a strong handshake was offered and accepted by her uncle. I thought at a guess, they were in their late 70's. In actual fact they were in their early 80's; Hong Wei told me that afterwards, when I enquired. They looked in such good health and had all of their faculties. They were very happy and content where they were living and amid the security that surrounded them. They had no English, but I could see from their body language that they were pleased to see us, especially their niece Hong Wei.

Straight away their hospitality came into focus with their offering of fruit or some other nice items of food. This was also accompanied by a question in Chinese of what I would like to drink. I told Hong Wei just a drink of orange juice and some grapes would be appreciated. I think every household in China has fruit of some description. It's as common to them, as potatoes and bread is to us. They understandably asked Hong Wei a lot of questions about my background and where I lived. Whilst their conversation was in Chinese, my thoughts turned to the life and times of this devoted couple. I could see by their body language that they were a strong couple, that was for sure.

Hong Wei told me their backgrounds in her broken English, and I was able to understand her. I tried to get a picture in my mind of the China they grew up in. When they were younger and Mao Zedong was in power, they had hard times bringing up a family (the one child policy was not in force in those days) and thinking about their future. But through their love and sacrifices, their family all got good educations and jobs and are now parents themselves. It was also good to hear that their families come and visit them regularly. It's so respectful and thoughtful to your parents, to practice that. Remember when they are gone, they are gone! As the line in the other Frank Sinatra song goes, *That's life, funny as it seems.*

We spent about two relaxed hours there in their company and took a few photographs with them. They offered us more food and drink before we left, but once was enough. We didn't have any room left in the body's eating department.

One of the main things I have learned over the years is the Chinese secret of eating food little and often. This practice has been evident on all my trips to China. How true and relevant it is to one's health. I think us Irish have a tendency to go for long periods without food and then sit down and eat your hand (just a saying) if needs be. I liken it to a camel going for long periods without food. But it is bad practice, when you think about it, even though we grew up with it. How many Chinese people do you see in China who are overweight? Very few. We said our goodbyes and left them in their happy environment. As we left the building, I turned to Hong Wei and spoke slowly in English so she would understand, "They look like such a devoted and happy couple and they have been together for so long." This lovely sight was so nice for me to see in a foreign country.

We hailed a taxi and arrived back at the hotel a few minutes later. Sleep was my request to Hong Wei for the two hours that followed. After waking and having a quick shower, we were ready for our next engagement. Mr. Lee and Mr. Liu arrived around 18:30 and we departed into the cold night air. We arrived at another hotel, which believe it or not, I actually forgot to get the name of, but the Chinese welcome was the same as in all the other hotels.

Entering another private room, members of her family greeted me with the same friendly welcome. The rotating table was there again. I picked and choose carefully from the wonderful display of food that was on offer. I fancied Tiger beer, and I had a few to wash the meal down. There were loads of conversations going on around me, all in Chinese and wonderful to hear. Admittedly some members present tried a few words of English but left it at that. I must say, the atmosphere was welcoming, and they were friendly to me.

Finishing early, we arrived back at our hotel around 21:30 to where Mr. Lee said, "We will see you two in the morning about 10:00."

"That's okay by me, Mr. Lee and thank you," I said.

Hong Wei and I got an early night, some very welcome sleep. I found that walking around every day, however short it is, saps your energy and naturally does make you tired.

My thoughts and feelings for Hong Wei were getting stronger. Although I did have a strong inclination that her feelings were similar to mine, I couldn't help but wonder would I be back in China sometime soon? I was left alone with these thoughts in the still of the night, while Hong Wei slept soundly. I also slept soundly shortly after these thoughts as well. So, that was where I was at that point in time in my life.

Thursday morning arrived. The weather was around minus five degrees and the snow was still lightly spread over Anshan city. But it was nice and fresh and not too bad to travel around in. After finishing breakfast around 09:45, Mr. Liu and Mr. Lee promptly arrived on schedule and we departed on what was going to be another mystery tour for me. As ever, Hong Wei was by my side and constantly trying to converse with me in her broken English. With me helping her with her English words, we communicated okay. Mr. Lee turned to me and said, "Billy, today we are going to take in the shopping areas and get you a few souvenirs to bring back to Ireland."

"Okay Mr. Lee, whatever you think, I will go along with." I agreed.

As Hong Wei's English was improving slowly, I still needed Mr. Lee to interpret at times and Mr. Liu obliged with transport. We eventually parked the car in close proximity to one of the main shopping malls. There were hundreds of people all going on their own separate journeys with their own agenda. As we approached this spectacle of shops, the neon lights were out in force, indicating to the shopper the store's own identity, their brands of clothing or footwear or electrical or furniture that were available to purchase. Other buildings had big giant posters of well-known Chinese television and the bigger film screens stars and more of music artist, advertising for all different brands of cosmetics, perfumes, electrical goods and sporting clothing.

All four of us entered one of the main shopping complexes named Jing Zhi Jie. Well now, this was everything you could think of wrapped up in one. The sights that greeted my eyes more than surprised me. Back in Dublin, Ireland's capital city, they have a few major department stores which cater for everything and these are quite impressive sights. They are constantly thronged with thousands of shoppers. I have been to stores in London, Newcastle-upon-Tyne (my second home) in England, also in New York, Boston and Los Angeles in America, and they have all impressed me no end. What was before me now was just as impressive as any of those.

There was a basement floor, a ground floor and then five floors shooting upwards towards this huge glass roof that let in the natural daylight. Access to these was done on corresponding lifts and moving escalators, all going up and coming down, non-stop. These were all leading to different floors with shops of every description on view. A magnificent sight to see and they were all thronged with people. Hong Wei said to me, "Billy, you stay close to me, because you are not Chinese." Thinking I was suddenly going to wander off, but with the grip she had on my hand, there was going to be no fear of that. This was another side of her personality that was being shown to me. There was a caring side to her too, which I took into my private thoughts. Mr. Lee and Mr. Liu were in attendance and had seen all of these shops before.

We got off on the first floor and wandered around to the many sights that greeted me. Some of the shops I recognized, especially the sporting brands, like Nike, Puma and Adidas. They were all selling footwear, coats, jackets, tracksuits and jerseys with the crests from most clubs in the Premiership in England, like Manchester United, Liverpool, Arsenal, Spurs, Chelsea and Manchester City. These were the main ones, but I did see the Newcastle United one there too. Then there were smaller shops in their hundreds, in little small outlets that were crammed with all sorts of everything. You name it, they had it – just about anything you would want.

Going through the other floors slowly I saw department stores selling clothes for men, women and children. Also on sale were footwear, perfumes, toiletries, furniture, gifts and lots of Chinese artefacts. These were mainly for the tourists, although I did not see too many. It must have been the time of the year, I guess. Most of the goods that were on one floor could be purchased on the other floors too. But I just wanted to go through all the floors, in our own time and finish at the top. Hong Wei was happy being with me. In all the shops, both then and even now, the shop assistants know you're a westerner (obviously) by your looks and try to get your attention at every opportunity. But I just said 'Ni Hao' (Hello in Chinese) and carried on. I left all of the picking and choosing to Hong Wei.

We eventually got to the top floor and finished the shopping expedition some three hours later. A sudden bout of tiredness hit me like a brick wall, without any warning. There was a natural balcony with a railing around this whole complex and from the top floor you could look down on all that moved, both human and mechanical. What a fascinating sight it was to see. Hong Wei held me just a little bit tighter during my aerial view of this giant shopping mall. I thought respectfully, you would make a fair splash on the tiled floor down below, if you were unfortunate enough to fall over the railings. I have been back there several times since and the shopping centres in small doses never lose their appeal for me. Hong Wei picked up a few things on the way, like gifts, footwear and a beautiful Adidas tracksuit for me. With the time moving on, as it does every day, it was time to descend the escalators.

My body was now shattered. I certainly would not have been capable of walking down the five flights of stairs. My two faithful friends, Mr. Liu and Mr. Lee stayed with us for the whole of the exercise and I thanked them for their patience. "Hong Wei," I said, "let's get some food into all of us." With the huge number of small restaurants in close proximity to the vast array of shops, it was easy to find one. When we entered one of these and I sat on the chair, the relief to my tired limbs was never so welcome. The tiredness was on a par with The Great Wall expedition some three months earlier. I wasn't choosey about what Hong Wei ordered for me, as long as it was something I had eaten before. She ordered for herself and the two lads also. Mr. Liu and Mr. Lee drank tea for a change. I drank a beer of some description. I can't even remember which brand it was, but I drank it. I got two. They were small and I was thirsty. We spent over an hour in there, until recovery was signalled by me.

Mr. Lee said, "It is now midday and we are going to bring you to the other side of Qian Shan Mountain. You will see Anshan City from another side. There is also a Buddhists retreat which I want you to see."

"That's okay by me," I said.

Although it was cold and the snow was falling ever so lightly, there wasn't going to be a problem. After a few miles we were outside the city suburbs and heading into what looked like a country setting, as we went uphill for a further few miles. It was getting more isolated by the mile with less and less people to be seen. But the driving conditions were okay, as they were used to this type of weather at that time of year. We eventually stopped in this secluded area, where through the light snow I could see a clearing and still see a rather well-worn walking path. Mr. Lee told us all to wrap up as it was cold outside.

He turned to me and said, "Billy, we are going walking up this mountain. It's easy, just a little awkward in places."

When we got to the starting point, Mr. Lee turned and said to me, "As you can see, Billy, the path is well-worn. This took time over the years, so there won't be any major problem, irrespective of the weather. These male and female monks here are totally cut off from the outside world. They spend a period of time here in isolation; mostly I think to reflect on their lives. They're a little shy and don't usually communicate with visitors."

"Okay," I said, "I will take that on board and see how we go."

After going further up this path, we came into this clearing which was on a high level. We stopped and looked back over a white picturesque Anshan city from another angle. It was so perfect to see another view in the tranquil of these different surroundings. I thought I was standing on the spot in the famous film that was made about Shangra-la. It was about the mountain climbers that found the hidden city in the snow in the mountains, where all was never-ending and perfect.

But when we looked directly down below, we could see the red buildings where the monks lived. We spent a short time there from our vantage point observing this view of Anshan city from this angle. The tranquillity of this magic spot had to be seen to be believed. When we were ready, we then started our return journey back down the mountain where my intentions were to call into this peaceful place. I just love meeting people and conversing with them. But I knew it was going to be a little different to meet any of the inhabitants. We eventually did find the entrance of this very secluded and quiet place. There was nobody visible in the area. We were definitely the only outsiders there, on this particular afternoon. I remember it well and how quiet it was. The three or four buildings there were all painted red and there was a light layer of snow all around the courtyard.

Hong Wei said to me, "Billy, we will go now."

I said, "No, not until I see a monk of some description."

Then in the corner of my eye, a thin Chinese female monk emerged from a closed doorway. She was heavily wrapped in a long shawl layered over other clothing and she was wearing a thick furry hat (like the Russian ones) on her head, with only her face visible. She was extremely shy, and her body language suggested to me that she did not want to engage with us. Particularly as I was the only westerner there in the midst of these four Chinese natives.

Mr. Lee said to me, "Billy, I will see what happens."

He approached her cautiously and asked her in Chinese could I have a word with her as I had come a long way and was from the other side of the world, from a country called Ireland. She nodded an agreement in body language that said okay. I remember the snowflakes were falling very lightly on her black clothing. I then approached her with Hong Wei by my side and Mr. Liu who was in close attendance. When I was one foot from her, I reached out my hand, but she refused hers. I was not offended and went with her wishes. Her face was young, and she was absolutely beautiful but unbelievably shy. We communicated through Mr. Lee interpreting my questions and her answers.

I asked her, "Have you ever heard of Ireland?"

She replied in Chinese, of course. "No, I have not."

To which I further answered, "It's a beautiful country, particularly in the summertime." I then asked her, "How long does everybody spend up here?"

"Two years, but it's optional. You could stay longer if you preferred," she said.

I asked, "What do you do about food and how do you survive up here?"

She said, "We grow some food and the rest is brought up from Anshan city at different intervals."

I asked, "Do you miss the hustle and bustle of city life and is this place not just too quiet? Surely you must find it lonely at times up here in the wildernesses?"

Surprisingly, she answered with a smile. "No, not at all. I have God for company amid this peace and tranquillity. That's all I need. No, as a matter of fact, I don't miss the city life at all."

"What about the weather?"

She replied through Mr. Lee, "We get used to it and it's only for a short time in the year."

I found it unbelievable to hear her views on life and felt humbled to be in the company of such a contented individual. I could see and feel a presence glowing from within her, as if there was a halo on her head. With these few questions answered, I could see she was reluctant to continue our conversation any further. I thanked her through Mr. Lee, and she nodded her head in agreement. I got a photograph taken with her even though I felt a little uncomfortable doing it. She nodded her head again as she turned and retreated to the doorway from where she had emerged. I stood there in silence, while looking at Hong Wei, Mr. Lee and Mr. Liu. I shook my head in sheer amazement. I wondered what someone like her was doing in this isolated place. But, as I said previously, life is about choices, and that was hers. I thought there has to be a presence here and I certainly felt it in that woman's company that day. It was an uncanny feeling and one which I have never encountered before or since.

As a matter of fact, I thought about my short meeting with this woman in the following few days. Later on I pondered the following questions: Where was she now? Was she still there? What was she doing with herself, if she was not there? Did she ever return to civilian life? I wondered, but also knew I was never going to get an answer to these questions. I considered it to be a most unique and special spiritual place. I would say between going up and coming down the mountain, timewise was in the region of about two hours. With all the walking I had done over the few days, I suppose you could say it was one way of keeping me fit. We made our way slowly back down to where the car was parked and returned to Anshan city through the light snow that was falling on the city-bound roads. As my days were slowly disappearing in the month of January, my remaining time was precious. Dinner was planned for that night with Hong Wei's family.

After Mr. Liu and Mr. Lee dropped us back to our hotel, we had a good three-hour break, where a sleep was welcomed by me. I think Hong Wei agreed too, as she accompanied me. After our sleep and a relaxing shower, it was time to go and meet Hong Wei's extended family again. At 19:00 we took a taxi outside the hotel and were at our designated destination within a few minutes. As usual, the nightlife continues every night in Anshan city. It was at another hotel called Sheng Li. Our greeting on arrival was courteous and friendly. The round table was again in operation here. Her family were all glad to see us and inquired where I had been, what I had seen and who we had visited. Hong Wei was on my left-hand side and Mr. Liu was on my right. I basically stuck to the chicken wings, slices of duck and beef and, surprisingly, scrambled egg. I accompanied these with a few beers at regular intervals. The usual photographs and conversation were carried throughout our meal. Mr. Lee was talking to me in English, while Hong Wei was talking to everyone else present in Chinese. A great night came to an end and we returned to our hotel by 22:30.

Friday morning came and after breakfast was finished at 08:30, Hong Wei said to me in her broken English, "Billy today we will be on our own. We are going to see some more of my cousins and some other friends around Anshan city. Together, we spent the day in several houses (about an hour in each), where everyone was intrigued to meet me in the company of Hong Wei. Food was offered to us in all of these households. At certain times we accepted (mid-morning, dinnertime and late afternoon) and at other times in between, we declined.

I noticed then and have noticed since, that Chinese people in general all keep their houses, however big or small, neat and tidy. Taxis were hailed after each of these visits, to ferry us to the next house Hong Wei had on the roster. It was only minutes from one dwelling to the other, but still too far to walk. I took visual sights on our travels of all the buildings and shops that we passed in different parts of Anshan city. The number of customary pecks on the cheeks or hugs for the women that were given out by me during the course of that day was well into treble figures. The men were different, as they all had to make do with an Irish handshake. I said to myself in a joking fashion, now I know how a politician feels when he is out canvassing, particularly back home in Ireland.

The evening time came and after relaxing for a time, Hong Wei and I went to a small restaurant called Wu Huan. It had the charcoal fire for cooking, which pleased me no end. I stayed with what I knew best and washed it down at intervals with a few Qing Dao beers. What Hong Wei ordered was a little strange to me, but I didn't even ask her. She was eating it, not me. It was a nice meal you could say, where both of our tastes gelled. As the clock was ticking down on my first visit to Anshan city, it would soon be time to go. Would I be back? That depended on a number of factors. We returned to our hotel around 21:30 and the words rest and sleep came into play.

We woke late the next morning. It was Saturday. My time was coming to an end and decisions had to be made within myself. This was where I was at, but also it was where I wanted to be, which helped me in my later decision making.

After breakfast, which was finished around 09:30, Hong Wei said to me in her broken English, "Billy, we will take it easy and just stroll around the city. All of my family want us to have dinner with them tonight."

"That's okay by me," I said.

I just went with the flow as we had a relaxing walk through the shopping malls first and after a light lunch, through one of the several parks there. I didn't know which one it was, as I had other things on my mind. The weather was still cold, but the light snow had stopped, and the temperature had dropped. We chatted about several things, particularly about our own family backgrounds and the circumstances that led us to where we were then. Two divorced people, one from China and one from Ireland. How ironic, that fate had played its part with both of our lives to this point.

In the midst of it all Hong Wei asked me would I keep in touch with her and return to Anshan City soon. To which I replied, "Of course I will."

We eventually returned to our hotel and grabbed a short rest, before Mr. Lee and Mr. Liu arrived on time, as always. It was back again to the beautiful hotel called Shen Li. This was where arrangements had been made for our arrival party a few days earlier, as was the norm. Everything was the same as before. The staff as usual were courteous and extremely friendly, not only to me, but to everyone in our group. Hong Wei's mum, sisters, son, brother and brothers-in-law, nephews and nieces were all there. When all of the hugging, kissing and handshaking was done by me, the food was ordered. I went with the tried and trusted, which was chicken wings, slices of beef and pork. I also had slices of duck and some mixed vegetables. Of course, this meal had to be washed down with Qing Dao beer.

Seeing that it was my last night in Anshan city for the moment, I said to myself, why not have a few extra beers. There was nobody going to question my decision in that area anyway, not even Hong Wei. She didn't even blink an eyelid, while I sank a few extra beers. The rest of the group ate all that was on view and sank a few beers too. The sight and sound of them all talking in Chinese was great to witness. Amazingly, what I was only slightly aware of then and am fully aware of now, is that they all have practically the same taste in food. There was no food they didn't eat. Mr. Liu said a few words about how delighted Hong Wei's family were in welcoming me to Anshan City and being a guest of her family for my stay there.

I also said a few words with Mr. Lee interpreting for me. I told them how pleased I was to have been made very welcome and to be in Hong Wei's company again. During and after our meal lots of photographs were taken, by just about everyone. I suppose it would be safe to say, I was in a lot of them with Hong Wei. I said my goodbyes to them all and I especially gave her mum a longer than usual hug and short kiss on the cheek. I had so much respect for that woman because I knew what her family meant to her and how much she loved all of them equally.

We finished and as they say in Ireland, a great night was had by all. On dropping us back to our hotel around 22:00, Mr. Lee said it was important to get to the airport early the next morning. My homeward bound flight was at 13:00. But as I have said earlier on my travelling arrangements, both coming and going, I always believe in being at the airport early. In whatever part of the world you might be in. Is that just me, or is everyone else the same, I wondered. Hong Wei and I had a pleasant and deep sleep.

Eventually, Sunday morning came after the sunshine had found its way in through the half-opened curtains on the bedroom window of our fifth-floor room. My watch was showing me 07:00, as the alarm went off.

After having a shave and a shower, I was ready for breakfast. My choice of food was the same as the previous few days. Why change now, was my answer to that! Mr. Liu and Mr. Lee arrived on time and all four of us left for Shenyang Airport. Hong Wei held me closely for the duration of our journey. My feelings for her were getting stronger and the vibes I was getting back from her were the same, I felt.

We arrived at Shenyang Airport with three hours to spare. I checked in and sent my two suitcases on their way, which meant I only had hand luggage. All four of us then relaxed and took it easy. After a while, we had something to eat and drink and then it was time for me to say goodbye to all three. The clock was striking noon as the announcement was made for me to head to my departure gate. This was the part I didn't like and still don't like to this day. Saying goodbye for me is always hard. It was then and has always been the case. I thanked Mr. Lee and Mr. Liu for all their help. Now the hardest part was to follow, as I approached Hong Wei and held her tightly, like never before. Tears were beginning to flow as she said to me in her improving English, "Billy, will you come back to see me again? I will miss you."

To which I replied, "Hong Wei, we will keep in touch and I will be back to see you again, as soon as possible. I promise. Do trust me, as I will miss you also," I said.

With that, we hugged and kissed each other. I could feel her thoughts and feelings coming straight through me. The chemistry was starting to mix strongly, and I felt it. Her tears were now in full flow. Mr. Liu and Mr. Lee comforted her as I left her go and the distance between us grew. Within a few seconds I was beyond the point of the no return barrier and had little choice but to keep going. I looked back and saw the three figures, that were becoming smaller and smaller with every step I took. As I was going around the next corner and looked back, they were gone. I had to stay strong, as they were now just a memory. My plane took off at 13:15 and we were airborne within seconds, bound for Beijing. I was naturally left with a lot of memories of my first ever few days with Hong Wei in Anshan city.

Alone again naturally, but only temporarily

These thoughts were to be constantly in my mind for most of the two long flights which would eventually take me back to European soil. We eventually arrived back in London and after a short stop-over. I was continuing on to Cork Airport in Ireland. After landing and collecting my luggage and with my clearance completed at customs, it was homeward bound for me. Eventually, with just under one hundred miles completed, it was great to be back in my home city of Waterford. It was early on Monday evening, as I opened the door to my residence and took in my luggage.

With a tired body, I headed straight to bed. Tiredness ruled unmercifully on my body again. I was not going to argue as I was due back in work on the Tuesday. As my head lay on the pillow and my eyes were about to close for a marathon sleep, Hong Wei and the whole Chinese experience was staying in my mind. Little did I know then, that this whole Chinese experience was now about to seriously enter my life forever! That was where I was at and I didn't feel like changing it. It was about making a huge decision and something that luckily for me, I wasn't going to regret. Getting a second chance was something I was going to give serious consideration to and also, I was going to be most grateful for. The feelings were there, and I knew it.

Fengqin had been a lucky omen for me, but I felt fate had played its part too. I managed to get up for work the following morning and get through the day. When work was finished, I called into Fengqin on my way home. She was delighted to see me, and we had a long chat about Hong Wei over a plate of chow mien that she cooked for me. I also discussed with her what I thought of Anshan city, Hong Wei's family and friends.

The most important question was to follow when she asked me, "How did you get on with Hong Wei?"

"Excellent. We had a great time while I was there."

"Will you be going back there to see Hong Wei again?"

"Yes, I most certainly will," I said.

"You sound very positive about that, Billy," she said.

"Oh yes, I'm very serious about going back to see Hong Wei." I said.

Our conversation lasted one hour, during which time I could see Fengqin was pleased that my relationship with Hong Wei was developing in a positive and meaningful way.

I returned to my abode and shortly afterwards got a real night's sleep. I kept in touch with Hong Wei through emails mostly, when I returned from work in the evening time. She would reply in her own time, to which I was extremely grateful for.

That weekend, I was informed in a phone call from Fengqin that Hong Wei wanted to see me on Skype. This was all new to me, but I got a friend of mine to set it up on my computer. It's a great idea really, whoever thought of it. Being able to see and talk to someone on the far side of the world on your computer. Who would have thought of that a few years ago? Modern technology and the age of science, I guess. But to me, it was such a big bonus to see Hong Wei on my desktop computer screen.

We had set the time for early on a Sunday morning. Due to the time difference, Hong Wei would be seated at a computer mid-afternoon in one of her sister's houses. That historical screening took place on time and what a pleasant surprise it was for me, when Hong Wei's face flashed before my eyes. Her English was improving all the time and our conversation was private. Her main question during our thirty-minute Skype call was, whether I would go back to see her. I told her my mind was made up and yes, I will be back.

My life and everyone else's lives are about making decisions. This was my decision and I was making it, with no apologies! As I said earlier, who gave a damn about me, my personal life, when it really boiled down to it? The desktop screen did go blank when the allocated time was up and in a second, Hong Wei was gone. It was great for me to have been able to talk to her and see her on a screen for some thirty minutes. What a great idea it was and so satisfying.

The next few weeks flew past and I continued working, emailing and talking to Hong Wei on Skype when time permitted. My life and outlook on life was changing and all because of one woman living in a city called Anshan in northern China. How strange was that, was the thought that crossed my mind often in those following weeks. But I was positive this was where I wanted to be! My next free time in that year was in the month of May. I had two weeks off and I made arrangements to stay for the fortnight.

As regards getting my visa, the same arrangements were put in place, with Fengqin's helping hand. The few months passed and much to my delight, my departure date of Friday May 5th arrived. This time I was going to go Dublin – London – Beijing and on to Shenyang. Another long trip was in store, but I was prepared with my usual two books at the ready. I would read one while going to China and the other when returning to Ireland. But I would still have to say, it's twenty-four hours travelling time. Be prepared is my motto – I was!

It was Saturday midday, when I eventually arrived at Shenyang Airport after three flights. When I went through customs and security, Hong Wei was waiting there for me with the widest smile you ever saw. Lots of hugs and kisses were the order of the day. Then Mr. Lee and Mr. Liu emerged from the crowd to say hello. When I saw and greeted the two of them, I thought of the name of the song by my favourite band of all time, Thin Lizzy, *The Boys Are Back in Town*. I suppose the title of the song could also apply to me, as regards my circumstances, by changing it slightly and fittingly into 'The Boy is Back in Town Again'.

Whilst travelling to Anshan city on the motorway in Mr. Liu's car, also in the company of Mr. Lee. Hong Wei was snuggled up to me in the back seat. She was happy and I was happy too. That was all that mattered.

The month of May in China is usually good and getting warmer as June approaches. It was no different on this occasion. The sun was waiting on my arrival in China and didn't let me down. It was another beautiful day in this beautiful country.

Hong Wei whispered to me in her ever improving English and gentle voice, "Billy, we are going to go someplace very nice tomorrow."

"I'm sure that will be interesting, Hong Wei," I said. "You can tell me about it later. But for now, I will have to get some sleep when we get to Anshan city."

When we arrived at one of her sisters' houses and after being introduced to all present, it was then straight to bed for me.

Several hours had passed when I awoke from my sleep and found myself back in the land of the living. There was a lot of introductions to members of Hong Wei's family, who had gathered while I slept. Her mother Wei Qui Wen was the first to get a hug and a kiss from me and the rest of the females I hugged in turn. All the males that were there just got the regular good old Irish handshake. They were all friendly and falling over backwards to please me. I do remember hurriedly having some fruit, as arrangements had been made for dinner at around 19:30 in the Sheng Li Hotel.

Hong Wei had pre-booked us in again just for one night to the highly popular hotel called Huan Qiu, and that was our next stop. Her son Jin Yang dropped us off at the hotel, where we checked in. We laid our heads down for forty winks and then freshened up before my two reliable friends, Mr. Liu and Mr. Lee arrived on the scene shortly before 19:00. Within minutes we were at our destination and went to the same private room as before.

All of Hong Wei's excited family were there waiting again. The waitresses were busy bringing in all the various dishes that had been ordered. I went for the chicken wings, roast duck, strips of beef and a few other small pieces of food that caught my eye. The inevitable bottles of Qing Dao beer were ordered and arrived in time to wash it all down. It tasted delicious, because I knew what I was eating. Hong Wei just ate whatever she fancied; it didn't matter to her. I had to make a few speeches; Mr. Lee interpreted for me to the waiting audience.

As we were nearing the end of our meal, Hong Wei turned to me and said, in her ever-improving English, "Billy, tomorrow we are going away for a few days with Jin Yang. You will be quite surprised, when you see this place."

"Oh," I said, "that's okay by me."

We said our goodbyes to all present and got a taxi back to our hotel. We got a good night's sleep.

The following morning was Sunday. After awakening around 07:00 and having a shower to freshen up, we made our way to the restaurant where we had breakfast. As regards eating, I stayed with what I knew best, but for a change, I drank cold water. As arranged, it was around 08:30 when Hong Wei's son Jin Yang arrived at the front of the hotel. It was a beautiful day, with the sun shining and throwing down its magic rays on those below.

"Where are we going, Hong Wei?" I asked.

"We are going to a place called Bingyu Valley Four Seasons. It is on the way to a coastal city called Dalian. We will be visiting that city later," she said.

Bingyu Valley Four Seasons is about one hundred and twenty-five miles south of Anshan city and north of Dalian city in Liaoning Province. It is a well secluded hidden resort and a well-known tourist attraction, with a difference. It's about three hours driving time from Anshan city, but we were in no hurry, as we had all day to get there. The countryside on the way had to be seen to be believed. There were lot of forests, mountain ranges and green fields.

We finally arrived at this opening which brought us off the main motorway and down a slip road into a wide area, which was a mooring place for boats. There were a few long boats there waiting for tourists or visitors. As a matter of fact, we were their next passengers. Jin Yang parked the car. We got our small compact luggage and placed them into one of the boats, as directed by the boat crews. The three of us sat up at the front of the boat, as I didn't want to miss a thing here.

A few other people arrived, and they did the same as us. After a few minutes we pulled out onto this wide river and the pilot of our boat pointed it northwards. The river was so wide, that I actually thought it was a lake, but in actual fact it was the Yingna River that intersects with the Xiaoyu River further upstream. With the engine at full throttle on the powerful outboard motor, we took off. I had a funny feeling that by boat was actually the only way you could get access to this hideaway resort. This was like going up into a valley, with just high cliffs shooting up to the clouds and the calm smooth water for company. It was just beautiful, serene, but you could hear that there was life all around us from the noise of various birds that were nestling in the crevices of the cliffs. Others were hidden amongst the odd tree or giant plants that showed their heads above the calm still water, broken only by our approaching boat.

It really was in beautiful settings and like nothing I had ever seen before, certainly not in Ireland would you have seen this type of landscape. It was so quiet, only for nature's birds to keep us company. The sound of the outboard motor on the back was all that the pilot had to listen to. We did see other boats away in the distance on their return journey to the jetty with a few people. They just waved, and we did too when our paths crossed. The water was just crystal clear, and I could feel the freshness of it from my dipped hand as we glided along. It was so clear that I could actually see the reflection of the surrounding cliffs in it. That were only broken by the ripples of our boat.

I returned to my thoughts and asked Hong Wei, "Is this place only accessible by boat?"

To which she replied, "Yes Billy, this is a famous resort where people and tourists come to get away from the city life for a few days." She repeated, what she had said earlier. "It's called Bingyu Valley Four Seasons."

"Oh," I said, "it's really beautiful, so quiet and peaceful."

Just then, I wondered would I ever be back here again. Your guess was as good as mine. While looking further up the river I could see another jetty approaching on our right. Yes, this was our stop-off point, as I noticed the pilot reducing the throttle revs and changing the direction of the rudder. We disembarked and the other people on the other boat did too. We boarded two small golf buggies that were waiting there to transfer us to the main reception area.

Our driver drove us around this narrow stretch of road that brought us into an opening, where I was astonished with what I saw. Here was a large number of houses, almost a hideaway village, tucked away in this forest area. They were on both sides of a shallow river. It was just unreal in terms of beauty and regarding where it was situated. We made our way across a paved area and followed the path towards the reception building. This pathway had a series of Chinese lanterns along our path.

I said to Hong Wei, "This place is unreal and such a hideaway. I'm shocked with its beauty."

"Yes Billy, this place here is a most famous hideaway resort," she said.

"Yes, I can see why, and we didn't even look around the grounds yet," was my reply.

As things happened, it was in the late afternoon when the three of us checked in at reception and then went to our rooms to unpack and freshen up. The chalets were made of wood. They were neat, tidy, spotless and cosy on the inside. The rooms were neat and tidy with just basic furniture in them. We had made arrangements to meet in an hour at the reception area. This we did and some fruit was produced by Hong Wei, where we all had our share, to keep the wolves (hunger) from the door.

Next up was a short walk around the grounds to familiarise ourselves with the place. We were going to be here for another three days, just to relax. On that particular day, there weren't too many tourists about. Let's just say it wasn't overcrowded! We had a look around at the scenery, which was spectacular in itself. The Longhua Mountain was beautiful to see, as well as the rugged terrain and forests that surround it. After about another hour, it was getting dusk when we returned to the main restaurant.

We ordered dinner, which was cooked on the open grill, which was my favourite way of cooking food in China. I had a lot of beef, pork and lamb to get through. We ordered a few Tiger Beers. Jin Yang and I drank them. Hong Wei stuck with the hot water to drink and ordered some other types of strange food for herself and Jin Yang. After about two hours of eating our meal, we moved outside where they had some entertainment laid on – a Chinese band in a bar. This Chinese band played their own traditional music with their own instruments. Jin Yang and I further indulged in some more beers and then I was left to go it alone. This was different for me, but Jin Yang had enough, and I went it alone on the drinking front.

The whole area was transformed when darkness fell. All the lanterns we had seen on our arrival were now lighting up the place and all the main buildings were a mass of coloured lights. They were even stretched out around the surrounding hills. Unbelievable, I thought to see this amount of colour. It was around 23:00 when we retired from the bar. Jin Yang said goodnight and we departed to our room, with Hong Wei leading the way, as I definitely had a few extra drinks.

The Monday morning sun was shining through, which started our first full day. It was an easy breakfast for me. I don't even know what I ate;

I think it was some fruit. The other two got stuck into their breakfast and left me for dead.

It was around 10:00 when we set out to see some more of this amazing place. There were loads of separate walks all going in different directions. We went down under the Double Dragon dam, which has a viewing area. You are in behind the water as it flows down through the outside of the dam. Then we went walking to another part of the resort and we found ourselves on a path, scaling a cliff area where there was a platform. We were looking from one gorge to another across the river. The idea, if you were interested, was to climb the platform and get strapped into this harness and to go from one side to the other. It had a makeshift seat, with a place to hold your hands above your head on the steel cable that carried a double wheel above you. Hong Wei and Jin Yang stood and waited in anticipation of what was about to happen. I wasn't too happy about being the guinea pig either, but I just said to myself, 'Just have a go, Billy. What can go wrong.' Easier said than done, was the answer. There were a few people there waiting their turn, and I had to wait for my turn too. When my turn came, I got hitched up to this harness and waited for the moment of truth, when I would have to launch myself off of the platform and then hold on for dear life. There was no turning back now, I had to be brave.

It was a fair distance across the river, but my fear was would I be stuck in the middle. You couldn't fall off, but you were going fairly close to the surface of the water. Then when all was well and ready, the Chinese guy gave me the sign to go. I jumped off the platform and within a few seconds I was hurtling towards the water and moving fast. But the operators had how far you would be from the surface measured to a few feet or so. They also had the elevation right to be propelled from one side to the other. This had taken a lot of planning, as there were no room for error. As I was reaching the other side, I thought of how I was going to stop this thing, especially when there was no getting off until the end of the spin. But I needn't have worried, the Chinese had thought of everything. I looked in the distance and saw a platform standing there, the platform for you to come back on. Alongside it was a huge mattress serving as a stopping point.

This was where I was heading, with no escape clause. I braced myself for the impact. How hard I was going to hit it, I didn't know. With my time only seconds away, I raised my feet and hit the mattress with a fair thud. The assistants were on to me in seconds and expertly freed me from the harness. I was shaken, but it's just the thought of it, I guess. I waved back to the other two on the far side and got a few waves in return.

Trust this Irishman to fall into the trap of having a go on this contraption. No one had forced me to find myself in this situation. I took my time to climb the tower again which would bring me back on my return trip. I said to myself, I'd better get this thrill-seeking episode out of the way fast, without dwelling on it. I was dreading the return trip, but what choice did I have? I got rigged up to the harness again and said to myself, let's get this thing over and done with. I gave Hong Wei and Jin Yang a wave before I departed. They hadn't a clue how I felt and what was going through my head. The next minute I was gone on the return journey. It's a harrowing experience, but the adrenalin is also going at full tilt. I saw the mattress arriving on the departure side and braced myself for round two. Then a thud and it was all over in seconds. It was kind of funny, thinking about it now, but the experience was fantastic and to know that I had done it was even better. Hong Wei and Jin Yang fell about the place with the laughing as I hit the giant mattress. Of course, I had to put on a brave face when I disembarked and got back down off the platform.

Hong Wei said to me, "Billy, did you enjoy that?"

With a shrug of my shoulders I said, "It was nothing really, child's play." If only they'd known!

Although, shortly after and in private, I did say to Hong Wei, "Never again will I be up on that thing." That sentence made her laugh even more! The scenery all around us was breath-taking, with the sun, the river

(It still looked like a lake!), the mountains and the green forests all playing their part.

We ventured over to where they had a few gaming exercises, both outdoor and indoor facilities. One of them was an indoor shooting gallery. I said to the other two, "Let's go in there and see what it looks like." We ventured into this long building. They had a number of long lanes with targets of cardboard cut-out men hanging down from an overhead pulley line. At the top end the rifles were placed on a long counter for support and height. There were two or three attendants there and obviously they looked at me a little curiously. A westerner is a westerner in any man's language, from their point of view. We would be the same, if it was reversed in Ireland, I guess!

We would be curious to know could these guys fire a rifle. I'm sure that's the way the attendants were when they saw me. Jin Yang and I got ready to have a go. The guns were loaded and both of us took aim at our respective targets as the sound of gunfire rang out in the hollow building. We took our time with our aim and when squeezing off our rounds. After a few minutes of being trigger happy, our supply of ammunition ran out. It was good fun and I enjoyed it immensely. Hong Wei found the whole thing amusing to say the least.

The target cut-outs were returned to us via the long pulley cable that ran from the end of the shooting gallery to our shooting counter. The results were good, as the head shots on both of our targets were littered with hits.

"Oh Billy, that was excellent shooting!" said Hong Wei.

"It was nothing really – and that was even with one eye closed." I joked. When in a foreign land, anything for a laugh I thought. Even the attendants were looking at me with surprise. We were both given back our cardboard cut-outs. When I looked at my one, I had done a fair bit of damage to the upper torso. It wasn't bad for a novice, even Jin Yang was impressed.

It was now nearing lunchtime and time for food. We made a quick return to the main area and had some lunch. No beer for me, just water, as the sun was out in force. I genuinely forgot what any of us ate. But after an hour the food gap was filled, and it was back to a surprising invite for me and Hong Wei. Jin Yang told his mother he had arranged for the two of us to go on a horse trek. This should be some fun I thought! We walked over to the designated area which took a few minutes. There were a group of horses all lined up in readiness for anyone who fancied a ride up into the dense forest that was staring us in the face. The handlers had saddles and bridles at the ready for us aspiring jockeys. You could take your pick of any horse you like. Ah, I said I would pick a white horse and Hong Wei picked a black one.

The handlers got the horses ready and gave them a further drink of water and another fistful of food. I pitied them as they stood there in the intense heat that was now generated by the powerful rays of the sun that shone down on this part of the world. It was now around 16:00 and at its peak. When I say it was hot, in actual fact, it was boiling. It must have been easily around thirty-five degrees. And my riding career was about to start, if only for a short period.

Hong Wei was first up on a beautiful black horse after she got a leg up from one of the handlers. I followed suit and found myself perched on the back of a white horse. While all this was going on, Jin Yang was paying the handler. I remember it well, as Hong Wei and I had Brazilian football jerseys on us. They were jerseys with short sleeves. We had no hats on either. We were the perfect candidates for a roasting from the fireball in the sky.

We had a guide who led the way up through the rough terrain that was on our path. He had told Hong Wei to make sure not to go off the beaten track. Jin Yang was going to meet us at the same spot, on our return and at a certain time. The trek began and it was through an opening in the forest. Within a few minutes, we were in dense green lush foliage and surrounded by trees on all sides. Surprisingly there were a lot of small stones under the horse's hooves, but these animals were able to cope. Hong

Wei was ahead of me and she turned around a few times and gave me a big smile and a friendly wave.

The horses just went along with the well-worn path that we found ourselves on. We then went further up into the thicker part of the forest. We stopped at a certain spot, as there was a clearing there. We were able to look back down on the whole of this secluded resort. It was a magnificent view I was sure no Irishman had seen before. While we were there for a few minutes, the horses took a well-earned rest. Soon we were back up on our horses, as we continued on an up and down path. It was certainly different to all other aspects of our travel. This was a throwback to yesterdays in China where the skilful Mongolian horsemen ruled the plains in their thousands.

These thoughts went through my head, as our journey continued. We actually went up one way and came back down another way. Obviously, you would still end up back where you began. The experience and uniqueness of being on a horse in those settings were most unusual, for both of us I suppose. I would say the trek took a little over an hour, but it was fun. Although I did encounter insects and all kinds of flies, feasting on my open arms at different intervals, such was the heat. Jin Yang as promised was there waiting for us on our return. He had been sitting in the shade while we had gone trekking under the blazing sun. It was more like blazing saddles for Hong Wei and me!

It was now time to let the body thaw out and recover. We slowly returned to our dwelling. It was now 18:00, as we opened the doors of our respective accommodation. We would meet again at 20:00 and go for food in the eating area.

After resting and showering, I noticed small bites on my arms, where the unexpected small winged creatures had attacked me. I brought this to Hong Wei's attention, but she was clean and then I realised it was just me. Did the attackers sense that there was a foreigner in their midst? I blamed myself to a degree, as the short-sleeved jersey gave me no protection against them. After all, I was on their patch! We went to the reception and told them of our predicament. Special cream was purchased by Hong Wei for me and that certainly eased the soreness. I applied it for a few days after and just got on with things.

At 20:00 we were on our way to one of the several restaurants. Like the previous night, we followed the same routine. A few beers washed it all down, which brought our closing time to around 23:30. On our return to our accommodation, I again took in the splendid views of this magnificent hideaway resort under darkness. It was transformed with many lanterns and lights all over the place. Early to bed and early to rise is the principle rule applied by most Chinese people. In this exceptional case, for us it was late to bed and late to rise.

It was Tuesday and with breakfast finished at around 10:00, we took it easy. In actual fact, we took it easy for the whole of that day under the glorious rays of the sun in the blue sky and just went for a few different walks and took in the scenery and, of course, we took lots of photographs. We had a midday meal and later that night, we had dinner, where we basically ate the same as the previous night. Why change your choice of food, when you enjoyed what you had eaten before?

Wednesday was our departure day and it was timed for around 13:00. We had breakfast finished around 09:00 and just relaxed. The sun was out early and playing its part too. There were scenic spots all around where one could throw their body down and just relax. This we did, as other patrons went about doing whatever they fancied with their relaxing time in this wonderful place. The clock ticked by and one hour became two, two became three. Then we were in departure mode. For me it was a case of where to next and would I ever see any place like this again.

Hong Wei did ask me, "Billy, did you like this place?"

I replied, "Yes, it's beautiful. Such a unique and peaceful place with only the sound of the different birds for company."

After Jin Yang payed our bill, the golf buggies were in action again, as they brought us back down to where our arrival had been three days earlier. As we were returning back down the river, two other boats passed us and they were going to their arrival point from which we had just left, and so the process continues. The water was just as blue and clear in these serene surroundings as before. When we arrived at our jetty, I took one last look upriver at the scenery. Yes, that is Bingyu Valley Four Seasons. I said to myself, I certainly won't forget it. I would recommend this wonderful place to anyone. There were only two words to describe it: Just beautiful.

We transferred our small luggage into Jin Yang's car and started the road to the coastal city of Dalian, which was about one hundred and forty miles further south. The weather was still beautiful, as Hong Wei and I took in the views that were on offer.

After about an hour's driving on this secondary road, hunger kicked in and Hong Wei asked her son Jin Yang to pull in somewhere. I remember it well, like it was only yesterday. Shortly afterwards, we pulled up to this fish restaurant on the side of the road. Obviously, they don't have any big signage over their doors as these are just small stop-off eating places. Still it's fascinating to see how they operate though, compared to us in the west. They had all different kinds of menus, but all relating to fish. Fish this, fish that, fish everything. I'm afraid I was outnumbered by two to one.

When I saw the dishes that arrived, I was not for bending and just told Hong Wei and Jin Yang to enjoy their food and I would make do with a few beers and a selection of fruit. Don't get me wrong, the food they were eating was all good and healthy, but it was just its appearance that put me off. They were things on their plates relating to fish that I never even knew existed. I couldn't even describe some of them to you, but my two eating partners wolfed into their dishes. They did finally finish theirs after about a good hour and I finished mine too. I was full of beer and fruit, while they were full of fish dishes and hot water. What a contrast that was! I said to myself, this could only be in China. Go with the flow is the motto, as this is the way things are here and everybody is happy with their food choices. They have unbelievable food tastes, but then again you look at their skin and how young most of them look for their age. There is an answer there somewhere... I wish I knew it!

In her wisdom, Hong Wei did ask me on exiting this little roadside restaurant, "Billy, are you sure you're not hungry?"

To which my reply was, "No Hong Wei, don't worry about me. I'm okay, the few beers and fruit will do me fine until we get to Dalian city. I can't wait to see what this city looks like."

To which her reply was, "Oh Billy, you will love this coastal city. It's only beautiful."

With these words spoken, my expectations were on the high side. I wasn't to be disappointed, when the time came. We continued on this secondary road for a little while longer, which eventually brought us out onto the motorway.

This well-kept and well-swept road stretched out for miles ahead of us. At times I'm sure the view from the sky, was like a large anaconda snake finding its way along this dense mountainous path and winding countryside. The views were only beautiful as we continued on our way to the coastal city that is Dalian. The weather was just fantastic for the time of the year.

At one point and just for a fleeting moment, I thought to myself, who from Waterford city back in the Republic of Ireland had ever been on this road before? I was fairly sure the answer to that question was nobody!

As the census showed in 2010, Dalian city then had a population of about seven million people. There were a lot of interesting sights and places to visit, and I wanted to make the most of our three-day stay there. We continued on our way at a leisurely pace. There was no reason for Jin Yang to break any speed limits. Eventually the outskirts of Dalian city were in our sights. I was excited at seeing another city and wondered what it held for the visitor, particularly someone from the west. Dalian stands on the tip of China's Liao Ding Peninsula, south of Liaoning Province. Its history goes back over one hundred years, with a Russian background. That was because it began as a Russian town and port. Then it became part of Japan's mainland Colony from 1905 to 1945. After 1945 when Japan was defeated, it was then back under Chinese rule and it still is today.

This city is now one of China's busiest ports for shipping and cargo. Its location is close to Russia, Japan and Korea and surrounded by The Bohai and Yellow seas. This very clean city also has several well-known beaches, which explains why they are visited regularly by Koreans, Russians, and Japanese tourists. It is now a major city and financial centre for business in the North East of China which is why it's called The Hong Kong of Northern China. It is also known as the Northern Pearl. Plus, it is also famous for its football club called Dalian Shide who since 1994 has won the domestic football league eight times, making it one of the most successful clubs in China's history. They certainly like their football. Such was the demand on football; another club was formed in 2009 called Dalian Yifang FC. The city is also known as The Fashion City. The Dalian International Fashion Festival is held there every September.

We made our way to our hotel called The Holiday Inn Express City Centre. It is located on Tianjin Street and in the Zhongshan District. It was now around 18:00, so we said we would freshen up and take it easy in our rooms. There was no need to rush to try and see this city all at once. We met in the lobby at around 19:30 and Hong Wei got some information from the receptionist about a few places to eat in.

The taxis here were just as efficient as anywhere else, as regards waiting time. Within ten minutes we were at a restaurant, which again, would you believe it – I never even looked at its name. Hong Wei and Jin Yang consumed whatever and I went for chicken wings, roast duck and slices of beef from the open grill – which as you know by now, is my favourite way of cooking food in China! I stuck with the Tiger beer to wash it all down. Two hours later and we were saying goodnight to Jin Yang back at the hotel with the time for breakfast our parting words. We both slept soundly that night in a new city and for me, a new experience. It would be a bright day tomorrow and expectations of what this city held for the tourist would be interesting from my point of view.

Through all of this time, I was well aware of my thoughts and feelings for Hong Wei. Nothing was changing in that regard for me. I was here in a positive frame of mind, on this, my third trip to China, because of her and only her. Thursday morning arrived and on waking I thought to myself, yes, this could be an interesting day.

After our early breakfast was finished around 09:00, we were ready to tackle this new and exciting city. Hong Wei got a few brochures in the lobby of the hotel. Then we emerged out into the bright sunshine that was making its way through the disappearing clouds. The nearby streets too, were slowly filling up with tourists and locals alike. An excited Hong Wei was holding my hand as all three of us wandered along at a leisurely pace. We were in no rush; after all, we had all day and the next! We went to see Zhongshan Square, as it was within walking distance from our hotel on Tianjin Street. Do you know that Dalian city has more public city squares than any other city in China?

When we got there, I was taken aback by the sheer magnitude of this huge public square. From the air, it's shaped like a big round wheel laid flat, right in the middle of the city. The main traffic circles the square, but you can still get access to it. In one area of the square there is a huge statue of the former Chinese leader Mao Zedong, with his outstretched hand, pointing the way.

He is on a plinth with carvings of workers, peasants and soldiers beneath him. It really is huge. It's been said that this was the biggest statue of him in China then. Today in the month of June and in the year of 2017, I know there is a statue of the late leader under construction in the village of Zhushigang in Tongxu County in Henan Province. It is built on farmland and is reported to have cost in the region of three million Yuan. The money was collected by a group of Chinese entrepreneurs. He is in a sitting position, although I don't know if it's finished yet, but it is thirty-seven metres high and covered in gold paint. I have seen the photograph of it and it's huge.

As I'm writing this part now on 27/06/2017, I'm getting reports that this statue has been broken up due to its features. Other reports suggesting that there was no direct authorisation or approval from the relevant authorities regards who directed it to be demolished. I feel that is a shame, after all the hard work that went into making it. It also took nearly a year to build it! I thought it was a terrific piece of work and the likeness was good.

We took a few photographs there, while I also looked up at Mao Zedong and wondered how the statue was created. All around there is lovely flowerbeds neatly done and with all different varieties of flowers on show. There were other tourists there too, of all nationalities. We spent a good hour there relaxing and taking in the views.

Next stop was Tiger Beach. We hailed a taxi and were there in a few minutes. There were people on the beach as you would expect, but we just took in the magnificent view and strolled along it. Holding Hong Wei's hand, we talked about things regarding our relationship.

"Billy, will you come back to see me again, when this trip is over?" she said.

"Oh yeah, I will come back to see you, Hong Wei. Don't worry about that," I said. "Why do you think I'm here in the first place?"

"Okay. Thank you, Billy," she said.

The three of us spent a relaxing two hours there, but the water didn't tempt me in, even though it looked beautiful. I'm afraid, cold water or even lukewarm and me don't mix. Around 13:00, the hunger arrived, as I knew it would. So, it was time for a snack in one of the many restaurants scattered along the coastline. A big bowl of noodles with beef and mushrooms in it and one bottle of beer was enough for me. The two of them had something like beef dumplings in sauce and hot water to drink. With that finished, I wondered where our travels would take us next.

Jin Yang spoke to his mother in Chinese and then Hong Wei turned to me and said, "Billy, are you frightened of heights?"

"No, I'm not and never have been," I said.

Hong Wei pointed in a certain direction and I could see a cable car operating in the distance. "We are going up on that," she said.

"That should be a nice view then, looking down on the bay," I said.

We made our way over to the starting area. I could see this whole operation at close quarters. It was true what Hong Wei said, if you were scared of heights, this wasn't the place for you. We took our turn in the queue and waited patiently as the small cable cars went over on their outward journey to the landing area. This was on the other side of the bay, a wide bay I might add.

The other cable cars returned repeatedly to start and began the process all over again. I was in other cable car systems in China on my other visits and I often wondered how they get the steel cables across from one side to the other. Then get the tightness on the cables that are the key to the safety element of this whole system and operation. I would love to know the answer to that! The three of us jumped into a cable car and began our outward journey. It moved quite slowly as we took in the magnificent view of the bay and the surrounding areas. We did hit the halfway point and I remember looking down and saying to myself, if the cable snaps we're dead! There was a drop of about one hundred and fifty feet – straight down. There was nothing to hang onto. Jokingly I thought a parachute here was no good either. Then again how unlucky would you want to be! But that negative thought only lasted a few seconds and our journey continued to the other side. You had a choice to go on a single trip which would take you to the other side of the bay, from where you could go sightseeing elsewhere and come back when it suited or return there and then. We decided to go one way and have a look at the other side. We made our way down to another beach and enjoyed another hour or so there.

With the clock ticking away and us deciding to hail down a taxi, Hong Wei said to me, "You like museums, don't you, Billy?"

To which I replied, "Hong Wei, you know I love museums."

"We are going to the Dalian Modern Museum," she said. That was okay by me, as I was open to any suggestions.

The museum is on the west side of Xinshai Square, on a street called Huizhan Road. It took us a while to get there, but we found our way there eventually. It's a funny looking building from the outside at a distance. It has stone pillars like a frame around it and on the inside it has a dome-like roof.

As we approached the entrance, there was an old steam engine from yester-years on display. Looking at it and examining it, I thought back to when it was in use and what it must have been like all those years ago. I wondered when it was operational in the transport system and how many people would have used it. We then entered the main building and the usual things greeted us. There were paintings, sculptures, statues, photographs and other artefacts there of every description. An hour disappeared in minutes. But, like all museums in China, I found it very interesting and well worth a visit. It was still early, and I was happy to get to see what we could.

"What's in close proximity to this museum?" I asked Hong Wei.

"Let me see where we'll go next, Billy."

"We'll go to the Olympic Square and just have a look as the time is moving on," she said.

We arrived there a few minutes later by taxi. The first thing you see is the five Olympic rings. These are massive and are bolted into the ground. A photograph had to be taken of myself and Hong Wei. Her son Jin Yang obliged us and took it. Then we reversed the situation for him. A few feet away was a huge bronze figure of a man called Liu Changchun in a mid-sprint pose. He was the first Chinese athlete to compete at the Summer Olympic Games in the year of 1932 when they were held in Los Angeles in the USA. It was then time for food as the clock struck 17:30. We sought out the nearest restaurant and found ourselves a seat in the corner. They had all the usual foods that I liked, and I stuck with them.

As you would expect in a coastal city, there was a large fish menu. So, a large fish appeared to accompany Hong Wei and Jin Yang's order too. They drank hot water with their meal while I downed a few bottles of Tiger beer and watched how a fish is eaten with chopsticks. It never ceases to amaze me how they can strip it down in their own time. I ordered beef, chicken wings and a few slices of duck. When our meal was finished, it was time to go. At 20:30 we were re-entering the hotel foyer. How the time had flew.

After a good night's sleep and rising early, our breakfast was finished around 09:00. We were ready to take on our second day in this city. It was Friday and I remember thinking to myself that this could be another interesting day. I was also aware that the days were disappearing fast.

While making the most of our time, we took in a lot of other interesting sights around this fabulous city. Firstly, we went to see Dalian National History Museum. This place is a must for all tourists to see. It's on Xicun Street and easy to get there by taxi. It's basically a two-tier museum, consisting of two main areas. In one you enter a large area where there are huge exhibits of whales, dolphins, sharks and lesser known sea mammals of all description to see. Then you can go to another area where you pass through a see-through tunnel and you can see live sharks and other species of all kinds of fish swimming over your head and in full view of you. This is quite amazing to see, and you would wonder how they built that. I did think like everyone else does, I hope the glass walls don't break or crack while we are in here!

After seeing these two amazing places and being in no rush, we ventured out into another wide-open area where there was rows of tiered seating and a huge pool for the public to watch dolphins, sea lions and seals do tricks through hoops, slides and other obstacles for their handlers. It's like a circus except it's all got to do with the sea. The handlers got them to do all sorts of tricks and stunts. The children and their parents got tremendous enjoyment out of all this and it was great to see.

Circuses, whether they be on land or sea, never fail to impress the younger generation. I looked at all that was going on around me and felt the firm grip Hong Wei had on me as she laughed. Jin Yang found some of the stunts amazing too. We spent about three hours in there and then got something to eat in a nearby restaurant.

What's next?" Was the question I put to Hong Wei.

"Would you like to see another place with a sea theme?" she asked.

"Yeah, I'm easy and will go anywhere you like."

"Right then let's go and see Sunasia Ocean World on Zhongshan Road," she said.

Again, this was another fabulous place to see. It was divided into different areas. In one area you had a glass tunnel and we could actually see divers feeding all kinds of tropical fish that are on show there. The colours of some of these tropical fish were just amazing. They were orange, purple, yellow, green and red. Some I didn't even know what they were. Then we moved into another area where it was like a cold storage zoo. There were live penguins, seals, walruses' and other small animals in huge see-through enclosures with their own habitat temperatures and surroundings there. A little like the National History Museum but different in their own right. Two fabulous places to see and as predicted, it had been an interesting day. We had spent up to five or six hours of our time visiting them.

We returned to our hotel and had a real rest which consisted of a two-hour sleep for Hong Wei and me. We freshened up and were ready to go out for dinner. It was another restaurant, which again, I didn't bother to look for the name of. But they had a nice selection of food and drink, so I stuck to something similar to my usual choices. Hong Wei and Jin Yang ate whatever tickled their fancy. Their choices and taste amazed me and how they all looked healthy. We arrived back at our hotel at around 22:00. A good day was had by all. The chemistry between Hong Wei and I was growing strong. A lot of thoughts passed through my mind that night about my future. Of where it was leading me and of where I wanted to be.

Saturday morning arrived and after breakfast at 09:00 it was off to see something new and interesting. Hong Wei asked me was I scared of heights and I reminded her of the cable cars experience – no, I was not!

"Firstly, we will go and see the Yinggeshi Botanical Gardens, Billy. Is that okay?"

"That's okay by me," I said.

"Then we have a surprise in store for you afterwards," she said. Jin Yang went with the flow and never queried our itinerary over the course of the few days. What a wonderful son he truly is, and he loves his mother very much. We arrived at the address on Lyshun Middle Road and entered through very impressive settings. There were wide-open areas with monstrous flower beds where one could walk to see unlimited types of flowers and plants. There were rows and rows of every description and a lot of the plants and flowers were in full bloom.

Nature is a beautiful thing and the way the seasons come and go with different climates the world over. It would make you think about it all. I studied a lot of the plants (not that I know anything about them) and was intrigued by their shapes and sizes. The sun was out in force and the settings in which we found ourselves were ideal.

After spending some time there, Hong Wei said to me, "Are you ready for your surprise, Billy? Our next stop will be the Dalian Sightseeing Tower?'

Again I said, "Okay let's go and see it then."

This was easily the most recognisable landmark in Dalian City. We made our way over to Mt. Liu, in Lvshan Alley where it sat proudly by taxi. What a magnificent sight this was to see from close quarters.

It's mainly made up of steel frames that surround its core structure. It was built at a cost of ten million dollars. It took three years to build and has 3,000 metric tonnes of steel in its structure. The height of it is a colossal 190 metres or 623 feet. There are two lifts and two restaurants (one revolving) which can cater for around eighty people. It takes one hour to revolve, which gives you plenty of time to look out over this magnificent city. There are three hundred and sixty windows in it and a viewing stand at the top. They estimate they get 200,000 visitors per year and have had around four to five million visitors since its opening in 1987. Lastly, and not forgetting the water tank that has a capacity to hold three hundred and thirty tons. Would you believe that? All this information we received on entering the foyer.

Then we took one of the lifts, which took us all the way to the top and the viewing stand. What a sight to see when you get there. The cameras flashed, as the three of us rotated our positions in different sequences. I wanted to spend a little extra time up here, taking in all the views. A half hour passed doing this and then I said to Hong Wei, "Why don't we get dinner in the revolving restaurant? We won't be here again and it's so unique."

"Okay Billy, if that's what you want. Let's go," she said.

We made our way back down to that restaurant and got ourselves a table with a nice view. The surroundings inside the restaurant were exquisite and had a lot of Chinese artefacts on view as well. The menu was a little different and I just went for basic chicken, strips of beef, duck and pork.

The restaurant had a mixed variety of foods which satisfied Hong Wei and Jin Yang's needs. It was beer for me and water for them. Two hours had passed while we consumed the beautiful food. Then it was time to leave. I had one last look back at this impressive structure from the ground, as we left. I said to myself, this truly is a structure to marvel. Hong Wei or her son Jin Yang always paid the bill, which I continually noticed. On my other visits, I did give Hong Wei Euro currency to change when it was appropriate.

We then went by taxi to an area which is called Russian Street, which was previously known as Engineer Street, referring to its past history. These are two places combining an Old Russian district called Jinjiang Inn Russian style in Juanjiehu Street and Home Inn Russian style in Xigang District, which is a more modern Russian area. We just strolled around at our ease and looked at the architecture of this part of Dalian city first. They were all Old Russian-style buildings and they still had loads of antique stalls, souvenir stalls and tourist shops scattered along the streets. A lot of these buildings were soon to be demolished by the demolition ball of the construction companies with the government's approval. This was still a huge area; we spent over an hour there. Then we flagged another taxi and went to the more modern Russian district. This was another vast area, but we took our time and had a look in the shops, countless stalls and a lot of the other Russian-style buildings. We spent over another hour here too. That too was most unusual but still fascinating to see the contrast between the two. Everything moves on, it's inevitable I suppose. The new takes over the old, that's life. Nothing lasts forever.

The same routine prevailed as regards going back to the hotel, getting a rest and then freshening up before we went out for dinner. After ordering our efficient taxi, we went to a restaurant called Da Lian Huang Cheng. I stuck to my usual choices and as regards the drink – anything in a bottle was okay by me. Hong Wei and Jin Yang ordered whatever; they just ate it and drank water. Yes, we spent at least two hours there having the last supper, before we returned to our hotel at around 22:00. This was the end of our last day in Dalian and I had enjoyed this city.

The following morning, Sunday arrived as it always did. Freshening up was followed by breakfast, as it always was! We now had a long drive back north to Anshan city. It would be tedious, but with three people in the car and conversation going, even at times if I was only listening, the trip would be over some time. We would eventually get there, you just don't think about it. Jin Yang turned the key in the ignition of the car as the clock showed 10:00 and away we went. There were other tourist's attractions to see in Dalian city, but with our time limited, they got missed. Perhaps on the next visit, if there was ever to be a return for me to this city.

On our return trip, the scenery we encountered along the way was breath-taking in parts. Jin Yang kept his foot on the accelerator as we continued on the motorway. We did stop for a quick snack around the half-way point, as our schedule was tight. But with conversation in Chinese and English between the three of us, the time and the miles passed. Hong Wei was snuggled up to me in the back seat and I could see she was happy. Her English was getting better by the day and our relationship was developing, getting stronger.

It was late in the afternoon as eventually the city of Anshan beckoned to us away in the distance. This was to be my home, until the following Sunday, my departure date. We were dropped off at the Huan Qiu Hotel, the same as before. Dinner was planned for us and Hong Wei's family around 19:30. We were tired, but a long rest followed by a shower worked wonders for the body. It's amazing!

They all came to our hotel around the same time. We arrived in the private large room that was booked, and we all took our seats. Her family kept asking Hong Wei the same one question, "Did Billy enjoy the few days away with you?" I sank a few beers that night with Mr. Liu and I ate a lot of the foods that I knew were edible. Through Mr. Lee, her family asked me to make a speech about where I had been, what I had seen and what I thought of the Bingyu Valley Four Seasons resort and Dalian City. Mr. Lee conveyed my answers to them, to which they clapped and showed their appreciation.

A great night was had by all and it ended with a load of photographs being taken where Hong Wei and I were the main participants. By 22:30 they had all departed the hotel. It was just me and Hong Wei back in our room, where we were left to dwell on the past few days' events. I expressed to her how much I enjoyed the time and the places I went to with her and she in turn told me how much she enjoyed my company too. The few days passed and our relationship grew stronger.

Most of that week was spent visiting family, relatives and friends all over Anshan City and sharing meals with them. It was right and proper to be respectful to their hospitality. We had spent some of the days just strolling around the city centre and walking through the three public parks that are there.

On one visit in the 219 Park which contains a manmade lake, I noticed a group of older men all swimming in a certain area. We made our way over to them and I just observed them at close quarters. It looked to me like it was common practice for them to be here every day swimming. They all looked fit and healthy for their ages. Hong Wei told me they all swim there most of the year. I managed through Hong Wei to say hello to them and even got a few photographs taken with them. They were all very friendly and asked Hong Wei who I was and what I was doing in Anshan city and, of course, was I going to join them for a swim. There was only one answer to that and that was a firm no! It was like a regular swimming club and I suppose another social outlet for them to enjoy. It was nice to see that kind of friendship. I have seen them on subsequent visits since and they are all happy in each other's company. These guys are seasoned campaigners, when it comes to swimming.

On the Thursday of that week we were to take a short trip to the city of Benxi, which is north of Anshan city and about forty-five-minute drive from Shenyang. Jin Yang said he would drive us, as we could go early in the morning and return the same day. We set off after breakfast around 09:00 for our destination, which was Benxi Shuidong National Park about twenty miles outside of the city. This place was declared a National Park in 1994. Firstly, we went to the Geological Museum, which was a very impressive building. This museum had lots of relics and rare specimens of all kinds of things and is well worth a visit. There is a monument outside the entrance on a wide slabbed area. We spent an hour in there.

The real purpose of our visit was to see the spectacular Benxi Water Caves. These are a series of partially submerged caverns which are nearly four miles long under this mountain. The roofs contain a forest of stalactites and stalagmites in this five-million-year-old cave. Now this was worth making the trip for. We made our way to the entrance of this amazing place. It is what it says – a huge wide-open cave you just walk through. The first part of these caves is dry and has twists and turns in them. This brings you into an area where there are loads of boats which can be hired to travel for about two miles under the mountain.

I think it is the longest underwater river cave in the world and is only accessible by boat. We jumped into a waiting boat and our boatman turned on the outboard engine. There was no rush to see this underworld of water. The stalactites were hanging down from the roof like daggers and the stalagmites were sticking up like spears.

To see all of their different lengths was phenomenal. You keep going where you think you can't go because the cave narrows as you proceed, but our pilot knew his way. The water was illuminated in certain sections and there were lights shining down from the roofs. How they got electricity in there was beyond me. The water was crystal clear, and the temperature was cool. Hong Wei was holding me closely, as we pushed on. I too was wondering whether we were ever going to turn back. We met other boats on their return trip and just gave their passengers a friendly wave. As I said earlier, you can go nearly two miles under the mountain. But we did get to our return point and started on our return trip.

This was all done at a slow speed to allow you take it all in. What an experience this was and to see what I saw. Again, I wondered had anyone from my home city of Waterford in Ireland ever been on this boat ride. I doubted it. We docked at the departure area, as other tourists were about to begin their boat ride. We were met by the beautiful sunlight, in comparison to the darkened amazing world we had been in for the previous hour. What a contrast, when you compare the two worlds. What an experience that was and how privileged was I to have seen it! We got something to eat nearby, before we made our return trip to Anshan city. We got takeaway food when we got back and relaxed. I thanked Jin Yang, as I would have hated to have missed what I had seen!

On the Friday night, all of Hong Wei's family gathered in the same hotel again for a last meal and to say their goodbyes. I had to make another speech (with Mr. Lee interpreting) to thank them for all their kindness that was shown to me and also for making me feel so welcome. One of Mr. Liu's friends, a Mr. E gave me a present of a beautiful watch. A few other presents were also given to me, which was totally unexpected. I thanked Mr. E and the others most sincerely for their generous gifts. With drink drank, food eaten, photographs taken, and everybody was gone by 22:30. It was time for a good sleep. This we did, as we went off to the land of nod.

On the Saturday morning and with breakfast over by 08:00, our instructions were to be in the lobby for 08:30. We were there on time and I wore my Newcastle United jersey and matching Newcastle United windbreaker and was proud of it. I heard the honking of traffic outside the hotel reception area. Hong Wei said, "Let's go. Your surprise is here now."

As we went out into the daylight, the sun was shining brightly in the sky and waiting to do damage on us poor souls below. The first thing I saw when I went outside the hotel was Mr. Liu and Mr. Lee at the side of two minibuses and a group of Chinese men all waiting. I noticed they were all wearing red jerseys and had flags attached to the vehicles. I was pleasantly surprised to be told by Hong Wei that we were going to a football match. I needn't tell you I was delighted to be getting this opportunity to go and see a live league game in China.

Mr. Liu excitingly introduced us to the others individually. I must say they were all very friendly, as I expected. He also told Mr. Lee to tell me where we were going. Mr. Lee said, "Billy, we're going to take you to a football match in Shenyang. It's at the Shenyang Olympic Sports Centre Stadium. There is a league game there and we want you to see it, as Liaoning (Whowin) Football Club are playing against the league leaders Shandong Luneng Taishan." They are commonly referred to as Shandong FC. I knew this was going to be a quality side.

"All of these people here know that you are a football scout in Ireland for Newcastle United Football Club in England," he said. "A few journalists and television people will want to talk to you when we get there."

"Okay, Mr. Lee that sounds interesting and I'll oblige them."

We piled into the two minibuses with Mr. Liu and Mr. Lee accompanying us. Hong Wei was by my side and refused to budge, but I knew she was happy, that I was happy. With flags flying from the windows, away we went on the road north to Shenyang city. Remember, I had only seen Shenyang Airport before, but never the city. Hong Wei and I sat together amid the Chinese conversations around us. The time passed, until I noticed the traffic getting fairly intense on the road to our destination.

The closer we got to the stadium, the heavier the traffic got, which is common practice the world over on match days. China was no different in that respect. We had plenty of time to spare, as we were directed by the stewards into one of the massive car parks. My travel companions had plenty of food and non-alcoholic drinks onboard the bus. Having time on our side, we all tucked into what was on offer. Hong Wei picked what food suited me from the selection that was available. Her choice was good, as I ate most of it and washed it down with a cold drink from a large picnic cool box. These guys thought of everything and I sensed that they were regular travellers to away fixtures.

They were real fanatical fans in supporting their city's football team. I was in good company. I could see the adrenalin was starting to kick in with this bunch of supporters. I knew they couldn't wait to get out amongst their own fans and let their vocal support be heard.

There were loads of buses, cars, trucks, motorbikes and even bicycles to be seen all around this huge stadium. It had a 30,000 person capacity. Now that's a lot of people, you'll agree! Liaoning FC had massive support and over the years had been fairly successful in winning leagues and cups. The club were also known as The Northeast Tigers. We joined the fans on our way to the many turnstiles and access gates that greeted you.

There were stalls selling jerseys and other sporting memorabilia, like flags, photographs and pennants for both clubs. There was a large police presence around the grounds and observing the fans going through the turnstiles, showing their tickets. We had ours and we took our place in the long queues. They just scan them, so the process moves quickly. In no time we were inside the grounds and going to take our seats in one of the main stands. The stadium was never going to be full. They left the opposition fans on the opposite side of the grounds. It worked a treat and there is never any trouble. On both ends of the grounds there was a huge military security presence. Some sat in designated seating area, others lined the running track that surrounded the pitch.

I must stress that this game and the other two games I attended over time were totally non-violent. I didn't see one incident over the course of the three games. The banter and singing were great and added to the atmosphere. A media man had joined our company as we took our seats in the stand. When everyone in our party were seated, he conveyed to Mr. Liu that the media wanted me to go down pitch-side and do an interview for China Sport live. Two security personnel and the media man escorted myself, Mr. Liu, Mr. Lee and Hong Wei to the back of the main stand.

They brought us down through several doors and corridors that eventually led us out into the players' tunnel and across the running track, between the stand and the pitch. This area was totally off limits to the ordinary fans. I looked back and behind us I could see all the Liaoning fans singing and waving flags as they waited for kick-off, which was about a half an hour away. When I looked ahead, I could identify the photographers and media reporters by the bibs they wore in a designated section at the side of the pitch near the half-way line. Camera crews and television crews from the various sports channels were getting ready. How I was going to handle this, I thought. But I had done it before back in Ireland and with Mr. Lee as my interpreter, I was relaxed, believe me! Mr. Liu did all of the introductions to whoever wanted to talk to me.

The two teams were warming up at either end of the pitch, but they were still in close proximity to where we were. I could hear the coaches and players talking, as the drills and instructions were being carried out.

Mr. Lee said to me, "Are you ready, Billy? They want to start now."

"Yeah, I'm as ready now as I'll ever be. Let's go."

The cameras were rolling as the lights lit up our immediate area and the microphones were switched on. Mr. Lee took the questions from them, one at a time and gave them to me to answer. He then translated my replies to the waiting television reporters and newspaper journalists.

The questions were straightforward, such as:

Which club today are you supporting and why?

What is the premiership football like in England?

What kind of crowds do they get at the games there?

What is the standard like, compared to Chinese football?

Is there ever any trouble at the matches?

Is this your first game and do you think you will enjoy it?

What do you think of the Stadium and the fans?

How long have you worked in a scouting capacity for Newcastle United Football Club?

Do you know Alan Shearer, or have you ever met him?

On that question alone, I didn't have enough time to tell them about the great man. Where would I start with telling them about Newcastle United's greatest ever player, in my opinion. But they certainly had heard of him and that was good enough for me.

A few other questions were thrown in, with Mr. Lee taking them and giving back my replies. He informed me, that this was going out live on China Sport and there would be a feature in the newspaper tomorrow. That was interesting, I thought. All in all, it was a satisfying experience for me and not for the first time, I might add. With all of that finished and being thanked by the media, for facilitating them, we retreated back up to the stand via the same route we had come down. We took our seats and waited for kick-off, which wasn't too far away.

At the appropriate time the two teams entered the arena and the fans went wild, as they do in most grounds around the world. Liaoning FC in their all-red strip and Shandong FC in their all-white strip with an orange stripe across the middle of the jerseys. It was all singing, blowing horns and good banter in a friendly atmosphere. I would say the attendance was somewhere in the region of about ten thousand. The two captains were called together as the referee tossed the coin into the air. This was to decide which way the toss-winning captain's call would play. Then the game commenced amidst the vocal noise from both sets of supporters.

I studied the style of play from both teams and some of the individual players caught my experienced eye. Most were fast, some were skilful, and others played the game with an attacking frame of mind. They certainly weren't set up defensively, which pleased me. I compared it with the pace of the Premiership in England and in my opinion, I found it would be the equivalent of the Championship, which is the tier below. But Shandong FC were the fancied side and showed that little bit extra, by coming out the eventual winners on a 5-0 score line. There were no complaints from me as they were the quality team on show that day.

Some of the Chinese teams then might have had one or two westerners playing for them. I know there was one or two on both teams that day. Our group were naturally disappointed and that was understandable. But they didn't let it dampen their spirits and were just as vocal leaving the grounds as they were entering it. Hong Wei didn't show any emotion after the game, but she did get excited several times during it when Liaoning FC had the ball. Football is all about having the ball and what you do with it.

When we were finished, we joined the exit queue, which was whittling down by the minute at this stage and left the stadium before getting back onto one of the main roads. There was loads of activity outside the grounds as fans from both teams were loading onto buses, trucks, cars, motorbikes and anything else that moved, in order to get home at their earliest convenience. We got to our parked bus in the designated area and proceeded to have some food. There was no rush, as we wouldn't have been going anywhere anyway with the intense traffic.

Looking back, it was a great experience for me to see the professional game in China and to judge it by my own standards. As this was my last day, the timing was perfect.

We eventually got back to Anshan city, as darkness was falling all around us. The bus driver dropped off some of the fans at various points around the city. Mr. Liu and Mr. Lee said their goodbyes at a bus stop and gave us our departure time for the following morning after our breakfast. Hong Wei made a mental note of that, as I said to her "Hong Wei, whatever happens, we must be up in the morning at the appropriate time."

"Don't worry, Billy. I have it all taken down."

Our turn came to be dropped off at the hotel, where we thanked the bus driver and headed straight for our room. Within a few minutes we were asleep, but I with the thoughts of my two-week stay floating around somewhere in my head.

Mr. Liu and Mr. Lee arrived early on the Sunday morning, after Hong Wei and I had finished our breakfast and packed my cases and her bag. Her son Jin Yang was going to meet us at Shenyang Airport. It was now time for us to go to the airport too. This was to be the first of three flights that were ahead of me. Then a one-hundred-and-ten-mile journey by car back to Waterford city. I wasn't looking forward to it, I tell you. I had a long way to go, but I knew deep down, this was not the end of my travelling. In actual fact, it was only the beginning of a new chapter in my life.

We arrived at the airport and went through all the usual proceedings with baggage and paperwork. All was in order and we then moved to a seating area.

Hong Wei and I talked, with her asking me repeatedly, "Billy, will you come back to see me?"

I repeatedly replied, "Of course, I will be back to see you, Hong Wei."

Mr. Liu, Mr. Lee, and Jin Yang were also present as we walked to the first security area in departures at the scheduled time. I said goodbye to the other three and left Hong Wei until last. It wasn't any easier than before. I hugged and kissed her, holding her tightly with the assurance that I would return, and we would keep in touch through email and Skype.

The security guard waved at me to move on – I wasn't going to argue with him! As I walked away towards the checkpoint and looked back. They all continued to wave. I could visibly see the tears flow from Hong Wei's eyes, because the tissues were out in force. Within seconds, I was gone and so were they. Saying goodbye, I felt it too, as I did before on my other visits. Hong Wei was beginning to leave an impression on me now; to such an extent that I knew things were beginning to move between us in a more serious direction. My plane took me to Beijing, then to London and finally to Dublin, Ireland.

On the car journey home to Waterford city a lot of thoughts went through my tired mind. One thing was certain; I was going back to China to see Hong Wei. When was immaterial. It was going to happen, that was for sure. Of that I was certain. This was now for real. When I got home, my head hit the pillow and within minutes, and I was in the land of nod. I slept like a baby for about ten hours.

My grip was tightening on both

～∞～

On Tuesday morning I was back in the land of the living, and I went to see Fengqin in her flat, as I was due in work on the Wednesday morning. Luckily enough she was at home and she was delighted to see me, as I was her. We talked about my third trip and she asked me were my feelings for Hong Wei as strong as ever.

To which I replied, "Yes Fengqin, my feelings are as strong as ever, if not stronger," I said.

"That's good to know, Billy. Are you going to go back and see Hong Wei again?" she asked.

"Yes, I am. As soon as possible," I replied. I stayed for about an hour at Fengqin's place and then left. That night I went out with a few of my close friends for a few drinks and chatted with them about my travels. They all knew my circumstances and never interfered or passed judgement on me. That's what friends are for, never being judgemental. That's why they were my close friends. I picked them carefully and still do to this day!

The weeks passed and my work continued, as did my football scouting job for Newcastle United Football Club on the weekends. I kept in touch with Hong Wei through emails and with Skype on my desktop. Getting more time off work was an issue for the moment. The next holidays I had off was in October of that same year. I would have around fourteen days in total. That worked out at a day to go there and a day to get back, leaving me with about ten days with Hong Wei. The weeks passed and the months passed too! I continued with my usual routine.

My visa was gotten by the usual means and my flight was also booked well in advance. This was to be my third trip to China in 2006. Who would have guessed it, not me! Life has its ups and downs and I felt mine was now going up and not down, as I had once feared, like the waves on the ocean's surface. But not once did I feel sorry for myself. That wasn't the answer for me, and I knew it! The sad reality was that nobody cared, nobody that I could think of. I stayed positive in my relationship with Hong Wei, in my job and keeping my life on track.

My fourth trip to China was scheduled for Friday October 13th in 2006, would you believe it. I was going to travel Dublin to Paris, on to Beijing and then to Shenyang, where Hong Wei would be waiting for me. My departure from Ireland happened on that date. Eventually after the three separate flights, I arrived in Shenyang Airport. Hong Wei, her sister Pan Pan and the reliable Mr. Liu were there to greet me at arrivals.

Meeting Hong Wei was emotional for me, a great feeling of being lovingly greeted. We kissed and I gave her a strong hug. I knew she was delighted to see me, after a lapse of around four months. Her English was a lot better, than on any of my three previous visits, so I knew she had been busy learning English, as she said she would. Pan Pan got a light hug and a short peck on the cheek. Mr. Liu even got a hug and a firm handshake. It was great to see all of them again even though a lot of time had passed in between. But the friendliness and warm welcome was still to be seen, as I knew it would be.

It was straight to Anshan city for the four of us, in Mr. Liu's car. Mr. Lee was nowhere to be seen, as Hong Wei was confident she could communicate with me now on her own. Hong Wei and I had made plans to get away by ourselves for a few days. When I was back in Ireland, I suggested going to see The Terra-Cotta Army in the city of Xi'an. So, in her wisdom Hong Wei had pre-booked a flight for the two of us for early on the Monday morning.

When we got to Anshan city, a rest was called for in one of Hong Wei's sister's houses. Later, around 20:00 on that Saturday evening Hong Wei's family joined us for dinner. It was in a hotel room that they had privately booked. It was great to see them all again. I received the same friendliness and warm welcome by everyone. A great night was had by all and a few beers were sunk by all the men present. We stayed with Hong Wei's sister Pan Pan, as she had a spare room at her house. We retired around 22:30.

We took it easy on the Sunday, relaxed and gathered our strength back for the few important days that lay ahead. The plan was to fly south from Shenyang Airport straight to Xi'an in Shaanxi province. It's a fair distance on the map, but by plane, not too far. I think it was about three hours flying time. In the early hours of Monday, Mr. Liu drove us to Shenyang Airport for our early flight to the city of Xi'an. Going to see the famous Terra-Cotta Army spectacle is not something you do every day. This was to be another milestone in my Chinese experience itinerary. We thanked Mr. Liu for getting us there and said goodbye. He had been so helpful and obliging over the years he has become my best friend in China.

We got our flight around 09:30 and arrived in Xi'an after midday. It was close to an hour's drive by taxi to the city centre. We admired some of the eye-catching sights on our journey in from the airport. The driver dropped us off at our hotel called Xi'an Xingzhengyuan and after checking in and being shown to our room, we said we would put our heads down for a quiet rest. This we did and awoke some two hours later. It was now the late afternoon. We decided to take a quick walk around part of the city centre to have a look at the shops. We got one or two small presents, but what I noticed they had in abundance in all the gift shops were little groups of figurines of the Terra-Cotta Army and that was quite understandable, I suppose, considering what city we were in.

With the little bit of shopping done, we flagged down a taxi and I suggested to Hong Wei that we just have a look at a section of the old city walls. The taxi dropped us off at a certain section and we got out. I was aware that daylight was disappearing fast, so it really was just for a quick look. What amazed me about the old city wall was the height of it. We spent a few minutes looking up at it and I reminisced on what it must have been like all those years ago. The same as I did on The Great Wall some months earlier. We were in Xi'an for three days, and we intended to have a better look at it in more detail, when more time was on our side, but for now it was just a quick look at one section.

With regard to food, our best option was to go somewhere for dinner and then have an early night, as tomorrow had only one purpose for me and that was to see the Terra-Cotta Army in reality. I was excited at that prospect and marvelled at the idea of being so close to seeing it. With that thought, I wondered would I get a proper night's sleep!

There was one restaurant Hong Wei knew about, and we said why not try it. It was called First Noodles under the Sun. I thought what a funny name that was, but who cared! I remember it well, because its speciality was, you guessed it – noodles. They had noodles with everything, noodles with this, noodles with that, but my choice was noodles with beef. I forget what Hong Wei ordered, although I knew it was noodles with something but I know she ate it. She drank hot water and I drank a few cool beers. After spending two hours there, when leaving the premises darkness had fallen. We hailed a taxi and were back in our hotel shortly after I had gotten a few brochures from the hotel reception earlier just to read a bit of the history on this city, and before I went to bed, I read them. Hong Wei had still beaten me to bed!

Here are just a few little facts for you to ponder on, as I did later that night when thinking about the city of Xi'an. It is the capital of Shaanxi Province in Southern China. It's a sub-provincial city and one of the four great ancient capitals. It's also known as the City of Everlasting Peace. I didn't know what the population of the city was in 2006, but in 2015 it was close to nine million. Nowadays it is noted for its culture, its industries and its educational facilities. The city is also the starting point of the famous Silk Road. I'm sure you've heard of it at some stage! In years gone by, the city was home to some thirteen dynasties, including the first Emperor of China, Qin Shi Huang. There were others like Han, Zhou, Sui and Tang. It housed the largest palace ever built on earth, which was actually seven times bigger than The Forbidden City and eleven times the size of The Vatican City in Rome in Italy. The walls were built around the city in 1370 and as you know, can still be seen today. The city of Xi'an was also the training base for the Chinese National Boxing team at the time.

Both of use slept well and rose early around 07:00 on the Tuesday morning. After freshening up and getting a quick breakfast, we got some information from one of the reception staff at the hotel regard the transport to get to the site of the Terra-Cotta Army. This famous place is about twenty-five miles east of Xi'an city. I think Hong Wei and I were equally excited at the prospect of seeing what will one day be the eighth wonder of the world, I'm sure.

The taxi man arrived to pick us up at our hotel entrance around 08:30 and dropped us off at our departure point where the tourist buses leave from in the city. As we waited our turn in the queue and the waiting buses were filling up with the many tourists that were there, I wondered how many people from my home city of Waterford back in Ireland were an hour away from seeing the sight of the Terra-Cotta Army, as I was about to do now.

Hong Wei and I took our seats on the next bus when our turn came. The adrenalin inside me was building with every mile our four-wheeled vehicle took us. I could see it on the faces of our other passengers too. Hong Wei was cuddled up to me and making herself as comfortable as she could, for the ensuing hour. We eventually got to the drop off point and disembarked like everyone else. It was out in the countryside and my initial impression of where we were was of a wide-open space. There were groups of tourists there who had individual guides with them and their identification flag giving them an informative history of the place.

Hong Wei and I were on our own as we walked at our own pace to the huge shed-like building that is called Pit 1. I had Hong Wei's hand caught as we entered the main entrance. Back then in the month of October in 2006, there were other outlets and tourist attractions like souvenir shops and eating places in the vicinity. I knew it would only be a matter of time though, before the outlying areas that surround the mausoleum would be commercialised and grow to enormous potential, as is the practice the world over in other famous places. This world-famous site has been gathering momentum ever since we were there. I do remember as we made our final approach on foot to this huge entrance, which was now in full view, that there were various steps leading up to it. Finally, it was there in front of us.

There in front of us, was the Terra-Cotta Army. It was in a wide-open space, but you were on a level, looking down into a pit at them. You could see all the life-like figures in their battle dress, each one individual, different. I was gobsmacked at seeing this sight. I couldn't believe what I was seeing. When you see it in reality, you really don't believe it!

There were other groups of tourists looking on with the same transfixed stare as us. You do ask yourself the obvious questions. How did this happen? How did the whole Terra-Cotta Army survive, buried beneath the earth's surface in the countryside and for many years, undetected? These and a few other questions were at the forefront of my mind while looking at this whole scene.

There are railings around this huge open area so tourists won't fall down into the pit and also to keep people away from the figures themselves. I noticed that there were several people with white coats and some with face masks on (I think they were archaeologists) scattered around down in this huge pit and I could see them from a distance attending to some of the figures with their hands and instruments. A lot of the clay soldiers were broken on discovery and these had to be painstakingly put back together piece by piece from the thousands of other broken, individual pieces. This could take weeks, even months and possibly years to find the right piece; like a jigsaw, I suppose. How much patience would you want for that job? You would want to love your job and the challenges that go with it. It is an extremely slow labour of love, in my book. But these are wonderful people who do a fantastic job, in saving and restoring treasures from their countries' historical past.

We stood there for several minutes and I for one was amazed at what I was looking at. I was speechless to see the detail in the figures that were closest to us. It was true, this was an army, but made of clay soldiers.... It was unreal! You can see the drills in the ground and the formation that the soldiers are in, with banks of clay in between the rows. This was where the support for the artificial roof came from. There are actually three Pits there, all with roofs. The soldiers are all lined up in separate rows, as if they were on sentry duty. In actual fact, when you think about it, they were.

Hong Wei turned and said to me, 'Billy what do you think'?"

"Unreal. I just cannot believe what I'm seeing," I said. "I can't believe I'm here in person, looking at this," I added.

In 1987, UNESCO deemed the place a world-class cultural heritage site. It receives two million tourists annually and they reckon close on fifty million visitors have visited this place over the last twenty years.

The first Emperor Qin Shi Huang's tomb is in another separate area, away from the three pits. His tomb had remained hidden for more than 2,200 years after his death. The famous Chinese's historian Sima Qian believed there were mercury streams running through Qin's burial chamber. In 2005 the famous archaeologist Duan Chingbo tested four thousand samples of earth from the tomb. To protect the people working there and for fear of damaging the corpse and its contents, only 1% of the tomb has been excavated then. What the story is presently, I don't know!

The story goes that on the 29th of March in 1974 a group of farmers from the nearby Xi Yang village were digging wells in search of water, when they stumbled upon a section of Pit 1. There were upwards of 6,000 to 7,000 soldiers there, but historians since believed that there are another thousand or two soldiers elsewhere in the vicinity. Another statistic the historians now believe is that some 7,000,000 workers worked here for close on three decades. This was to build the mausoleum in order to protect the emperor after his death and into the next life. Numerous workers also died during its construction and nearing the end of its completion, others were killed to protect its secrecy. That's the way it was then, all those years ago. It's frightening really, when you think about it!

Of course, this Irishman was not content with staying in the one spot. You were allowed to wander around the perimeter of this huge rectangular sight. We wandered up the left-hand side of the giant pit. We were now seeing the length of the Terra-Cotta Army from a side view. This was really impressing me no end. Coming around at the back of the pit there are singular items to be seen in show glass cases. Also, there was a restoration area where there were lots of broken soldiers and all of these had pieces missing. These then had to be reconstructed to be full figures. We went right around the whole viewing area of the rectangular site in Pit 1.

After Pit 1, we came outside and went to Pit 2 where there were more things to see. There was excavation work going on there, meaning public walking space was a lot more restricted than in Pit 1. Archaeologists were there a plenty excavating in between loads of clay and moving from different areas. The whole place had a different appearance than in Pit 1. There were actually chariots, horses, weaponry and a lot of other artefacts to be seen in certain sections.

There were even archery soldiers there, some standing and some kneeling with bows and arrows. Other things like pottery of all shapes and sizes were on view. There were also new findings there from Qin's Mausoleum. Exhibits that had been found, were all relating to the Qin's period before and after his death. There were huge craters in other sites with loads of broken soldiers to be seen and other artefacts.

But as I said, this was a work in progress. It was hard to keep track of all that was on view, but we persevered and spent some time walking around. We then made our way to pit 3 which was a lot smaller from the outside, but it had more of the same, of what we had seen in Pit 1 and Pit 2. I don't know what it's like now in 2020, compared to 2006.

After spending less time in there than we would like, and as the hours were passing, we were understandably getting hungry. It was time for food. We made our way over to the multiple service halls. Here they have shops, restaurants and toilet facilities. We got a table in one and I kept it simple and just ate some salad with eggs and fruit and drank some Coca-Cola. Hong Wei ate something that looked like noodles with a whole load of other things thrown in for good measure. That woman's constitution amazed me then and even more so now, some fourteen years on. She had her usual hot water to wash it down. We stayed there and rested our tired limbs. After a good hour we took to our feet. We decided to go over to have a look at the souvenir shops and exhibits in the multiple exhibition halls.

In one area there were a lot of souvenirs, books and photographs on view. While we were in there, we noticed a constant crowd gathered in a certain spot, a short distance away. We had purchased a few small novelty items from one of the shops and I had bought a book called *The Qin Dynasty Terra-Cotta Army of Dreams.* It cost one hundred and twenty Yuan which was about twelve euros then. It was published by Xi'an Press and first released in August of 2005.

I said to Hong Wei, "There is something going on over there. Let's go over and have a look."

We made our way over to the waiting crowd. These were all visitors of every nationality, and Chinese visitors too. When we got an opening in the controlled crowd, I saw an older tall thin man sitting in a large rocking chair. He was wearing a black Chinese traditional suit (not like the western suit) and wearing a black peaked cap. He was in a cordoned off area, that had one opening for one person at a time to meet him. He was smoking a long pipe and was relaxed, as cool as a cucumber. He was signing a lot of individual books for people, as they approached him one at a time with one continuous stroke of a thin black-coloured marking pen.

Hong Wei said to me, "Billy that man there that you see in front of you is the farmer who discovered the initial sighting of the Terra-Cotta Army, while drilling a hole in the ground in search of water."

"Ah damn it, (terminology) your joking Hong Wei!" I said.

"No seriously. Billy, that's him," she said.

I said to myself, this is going to be my lucky day, I can feel it. I said to Hong Wei, "Wait here while I get him to sign the book for me."

As you know by now, I believe in fate. This was all meant to happen and I for one was not going to let this opportunity pass me by. This was no time to be shy about grabbing the bull by the horns, (old English saying) not on this occasion. This was about to be history in the making for me.

I took my place in the queue and waited like everybody else, until it was my turn.

When my turn came, I approached him and just opened the front inside cover of the book and held it out for him. He looked at me and then duly signed it with one continuous stroke of his marking pen. For a further few seconds, I just stood there and gazed at him. Boy, I said to myself, I bet he could tell you a story or two. Everyone else there getting something signed, following the same procedure as me and in an orderly fashion. Here he was, initially being a poor farmer in search of water and now he was being catapulted into the world limelight in front of visitors from all over the world. I knew he was able to handle it by his body language, as I think he didn't see it like that. He was a national treasure and a celebrity, but not in his own eyes, I don't think. I shook his hand and thanked him and then with the book, returned to Hong Wei, who had a smile as wide as a Cheshire cat.

I felt honoured, privileged and so, so lucky to have been there at this time and to have met him in person. What he wrote on the book, Hong Wei couldn't even make it out, when she tried to read it. But I was very lucky and happy. I didn't know then, afterwards or even now to this present day what the Chinese's man's name was. I believe that the same man was alive up to the summer of 2016; reported by someone who visited the Terra-Cotta Army tourist centre at that time. With respect, I suppose that's irrelevant, but that really was the bonus for me regarding my visit to the Terra-Cotta Army. Whoever thought I would meet the farmer that actually discovered the Terra-Cotta Army in person. Certainly not me! It really was a privilege.

Looking back on things, I think these two landmarks (the other being the Great Wall) in particular don't really sink in initially when you see them in person. The sheer magnitude of what you are looking at is immense. I think that is a natural feeling, whoever you may be. We are all human after all, aren't we? Of course, there is one way to solve all that – go and see them twice.

There was one more building for us to visit. We said we would do it and we did, even though the time was slipping by. The Circle Vision Hall was close to the information centre, which was close to the official entrance. There is a short continuous film there showing the history of Emperor Qin and the construction and subsequent destruction of his Terra-Cotta Army 2,200 years ago.

That was it then, over and out, but what an experience! Hong Wei was happy too as we made our way to the bus for our return trip to Xi'an city. It was teatime when we finally got back to our hotel. The usual routine followed, a rest and a freshen up, then out for dinner somewhere. We said we would try the First Noodles under the Sun restaurant again. As the old saying goes, the devil you know, is better than the devil you don't.

Between going there and returning to the hotel after dinner, a further three hours had passed. Again, we slept well that night until Wednesday morning arrived. The weather for the time of year was surprisingly mild.

There were a few places in the city that I especially wanted to see. With that in mind, once breakfast was over our taxi arrived at 09:00. First it was to the Shaanxi History Museum on Xiaozhai Dong Road. This museum is basically divided into four big exhibit halls. They give out a certain amount of free tickets early in the day – our luck was in, as we got two.

We went in and wandered around in this very interesting place at our leisure. There was a huge big stone lion standing in one of the halls. As I looked up at it, I wondered how someone could have made that. I marvelled at the size of it and wondered what it must have weighed as well. As we went from hall to hall, taking a few photographs along the way, there were loads of statues, paintings, cultural artefacts and a history about the Qin dynasty and of course the Terra-Cotta Army. It was all there to see and I took it all in. Hong Wei was enjoying it too and I was happy.

Next up was the Giant Wild Goose Pagoda, as it was not too far away. We got there eventually. I looked up at its structure with amazement. It is a most holy place and one of the most famous Buddhists pagodas in all of

China. It was first built in 652 during the Tang Dynasty. It originally had five storeys, then they built it up to ten and later it was reduced to seven, all through different dynasties. This all happened over the course of time.

We went in and saw it all for what it was worth. Amazingly it was built with layers of bricks and without cement. I think there were brackets used in its construction. Priceless, was my verdict as we saw all the different Buddha's and sacred artefacts from way back in the different eras. We spent a bit of time in there and took things at our ease.

After a while, we ventured outside onto the north side of the Pagoda. Here there was a large square, where the largest fountain in Asia is. It is a musical fountain phenomenon as it projects water high into the air by jets to the sound of music. This is done daily at noon and after sunset. Our luck was in as it was nearing noon.

I said to Hong Wei, "Let's wait and see what this is all about then."

At noon on the button, the music started playing and the jets started firing the water high into the air. It was amazing to see the water spurting up and down to the music. Again, I wondered as I stared at this and asked the question to myself, 'How could somebody make this work?'. It was beautiful to see. What must it be like in the evening time, I thought.

Then it was time for a snack in any one of the small restaurants around the place. I stuck to the basics and Hong Wei made her choice too. She had water, I had Coca-Cola. When we were finished, I wanted to visit one other museum, which was the Xi'an Museum. It's actually not too far from the Shaanxi History Museum.

This museum was the jewel in the crown for me, even before we entered it. Its shape, design, neatness and its dome like mushroom top appearance, all appealed to me. At the entrance outside on the Xi'an Museum sign, there is a lady on a horse, with Chinese writing below her which says Xi'an Museum. I later saw a miniature replica figure of this same lady inside the museum in a glass case. The museum has four entrances, but we entered though the main one. The usual sights greeted us. There were loads of small statues and other artefacts in individual glass cases all around us. There were paintings, Chinese art, Buddha statues, decorative stonework, carvings and other exhibits relating to the different dynasties, as you would expect, but especially to the Qin dynasty. The history of Xi'an city is there for you to read on a giant informative and impressive sign.

We finished up by going out onto the top balcony, on one of the four sides and taking in a view of the city. In summer it must be a fabulous sight with all the gardens below us, as they would be in full bloom. After taking a few photographs, it was time to move on and Hong Wei was by my side every step of the way. All this takes time, of course, and the clock moves on also.

Next up for us was a taxi to the old city walls, where we had briefly been on the Monday evening. We arrived at the South Gate, which is most tourists' choice. The first thing that struck me again was the height of the wall. I learned that it was forty feet in height. We then walked up the side steps to get to the top of the wall, where I was met with a most amazing sight. The stonework on the surface (where you walk) was just unreal. It is eleven meters wide at the top and when you look over the wall, you can see that the base is wider, by a few feet. The stonework in the walls was impressive too. There are six thousand openings in the block work around the outer wall, just like The Great Wall. There are also eighteen gates at different intervals along the wall.

We saw people on bicycles cycling around on it. In the good weather, I'm sure there would have been a lot more. They also have battery operated buggies that take people around the four sides of the wall. It would take you around three to four hours to walk around the full rectangle shape of it. Going forwards, in 2013 a bicycle sharing network was set up and there are now fifty thousand bikes serving thousands of tourists and locals alike and saves them from having to walk around it.

I said to Hong Wei, "Have a look at the width of the wall on both sides and the amount of stones that are in it. Have a look at the length of it."

I was blown away, looking at this magnificent structure. I know Hong Wei, like me was just as surprised and impressed too. My God I said to myself, what a sight to see. The wall was erected in the 14th century by the Ming Dynasty, under the regime of Emperor Zhu Yuanzhang. It is the most complete wall that has survived in China today. We got on a battery buggy with a few other people and took in the sights eventually from the four sides. There are four watch towers on each corner. There are also gate towers, main towers and shop outlets there too. I would say, we were around two and a half hours in there.

Scattered outside the walls are stallholders selling the usual stuff, like souvenirs, ornaments, flags and photographs. We had a look around them at our leisure, which took another hour. Then it was a taxi back to our hotel, as teatime was approaching fast. The usual routine followed, and we were soon ready to go out for dinner.

"Hong Wei, will we go back to the First Noodles Under the Sun restaurant, as I thought the food there was nice," I said.

"Yes, if you like, Billy," was her reply.

We arrived there in a few minutes by taxi and we had more of the same food, except it was beer for me, instead of Coca-Cola. The beef noodle dinner was just as nice as before. Two hours after that we were back at our hotel and planning for tomorrow, which was to be our last day in the city of Xi'an.

Hong Wei and I were getting on like a house on fire (old saying, meaning getting on great). A good night's sleep followed, as the nightlife in the city continued around us. Our itinerary was more important than dancing the night away. After all we were on a time schedule, with no room for complacency and I was about to do something the next day, that was to have a big bearing on my future. Or so I hoped.

We were up out of the feathers (expression back in Waterford city, meaning get out of the bed) early on the Thursday morning.

With breakfast finished, our taxi arrived on the stroke of 09:00. The Drum Tower and the Bell Tower were two more places I particularly wanted to see in Xi'an. They are both fairly close to each other in the Belling district of the city centre. They are actually called The Sister Buildings, so that helped regards time. I had every intention of making the most of the last day as it was also going to be special. Away we went, and it was straight to the Bell Tower. It didn't take long to get there.

What an impressive sight to see at first. It was built in the Ming Dynasty in 1380 and now stands on a roundabout. Entry could only be accessed through an underground passage, due to the high volume of traffic. It's actually where the four roads join the roundabout, coming from north, south, east and west. Hong Wei had bought double tickets at the entrance at a special discount price to take in the Drum Tower later. Amazingly, the structure of the Bell Tower building is made of wood and has three tiers in its thirty-six meters of height. There are no nails used in its construction, only grooves and spikes. We made our way in and had a look around and then made our way up the spiral staircase that leads to the second tier. In ancient times the huge bell was rung every morning to tell the time for over four hundred years. That bell was changed in time, moved elsewhere and a new smaller bell was made to replace it.

We made our way out to the balcony and took in the excellent view of the city. We took a few photographs there and even got one of us together with the help of a tourist who obliged us, by clicking our camera. After spending a while there and further admiring the view from the four sides of the building, we made our way back down to where the bell was.

I said to Hong Wei, "I want to have a go at ringing that bell."

"Oh, alright then," she said. You only pay a small fee there and you can ring the bell. One of the attendants there came over and gave me a big wooden stick, (like a gong) where I then proceeded to give the bell a huge bang. Hong Wei saw the funny side of it, but then followed up with her having a go too, at my request. With that finished and the echo sound of the bell after dying down, I called Hong Wei closer to me.

"Hong Wei, this is my fourth visit to China and the only reason I'm here is because of you." The big question was coming next and little did she know what the question was, but only she could answer it. I said to her, "Will you marry me if I come back to China again?"

"Yes Billy, I will marry you, because I love you," she said without hesitation, which I was delighted to hear.

"Are you sure about that Hong Wei?" I said.

"Yes, I'm sure about what you are asking me," she said.

I also added that I had put divorce proceedings in place sometime earlier and I was expecting these to be accepted in November, as there were no counter objections. We kissed under the frame of the bell support and I could feel the sincerity in it. I never thought this would happen to me! But this was where I was now, and I felt positive about my words and actions from a few minutes earlier.

"Right Hong Wei, let's make our way over to the Drum Tower and see what that is all about," I said. It took us a few minutes to reach the Drum Tower, but we got there. Hong Wei was now sticking to me like glue. Was it because I had popped the inevitable question to her a few minutes earlier over at the Bell Tower, I wondered.

The main thing for me was, she said yes, instead of no and I was very happy about that. The Drum Tower is a more rectangular structure and only has two stories and stands thirty-four meters high. It was built in 1384, four years after the Bell Tower. The main drum was banged at dusk everyday over the same period. We entered the main building and Hong Wei showed the attendant our second separate ticket for entry here. There was a drum museum there with every kind of drum from the past that you could imagine, with the story line behind them. I found it all very interesting. There are drum performances daily, on the hour. As it was now nearing midday, we said we would hang around and see one.

While we were waiting, we ventured up onto the second floor and made our way out onto the balcony, from where we got another bird's eye view of Xi'an city. We took a few worthwhile photographs and pondered there for a while with our thoughts. Hong Wei took me by surprise when she said to me out of the blue, "Billy, I'm very happy that you asked me to marry you."

"Oh, Hong Wei," I said, "I'm very happy that you said yes too."

"We will set the wedding day for some time in January, is that okay?" I asked.

"Yes, that's okay by me. I will look after and organise everything," she said.

She was then and still is now, a very cool woman.

With that and with the time approaching midday, we made our way back down to see and hear the drum performance. A group of Chinese people dressed in traditional costumes all sit behind different drums and play away to a certain beat. It sounds boring probably to you the reader, but not when you see it live. That lasted a while for us to study the timing and the different sounds that were made.

With that finished, we went outside and took in the drum collection. There are twenty-eight red drums around the building and are divided into twenty-four small ones and four big ones. In 1996 a new big drum was added to the collection. This is the biggest drum in China today. It is six feet tall and weighs one and a half ton. What I found truly amazing, as I looked at the surrounds of the big drum is that it had studs in it. 1,996 studs in fact. This number depicted the year in which it was made. Quite amazing to see it really! You are not allowed to touch the drums, except the big one. We took a photograph or two in front of this big, big drum. We had seen what we had come for and it was time to go!

"Where to next?" I said to Hong Wei.

"Billy, are you hungry?" she asked.

"Yeah, we could do with a little snack now, I suppose," was my answer.

Hong Wei, while holding my hand, guided me to the North of the Drum Tower and under a huge arched exit. That brought us out into a wide market area, where I noticed the Chinese stall holders, shop assistants and other retail outlets there were a little different in that most of the men were wearing round hats and the women wearing head scarves.

"Who are these people?" I asked Hong Wei.

"They are all Hui Muslims and they dominate this whole market area and surrounding region in Xi'an city," she said.

"Oh, how interesting that is. They have their own identity, within this city?" I asked.

"Correct," Hong Wei said.

What an intriguing place this was, I thought to myself, looking at all the different sights that greeted my eyes. "What a place this is!" I said to Hong Wei. This was fascinating and such a huge market with shops, restaurants, eating outlets with unlimited amounts of food on display and stalls of every description. Thousands of people were walking all around this marketplace.

The main street is called Beiyuanmen Muslim Street or Huimin Street in the Muslim Quarter. Around twenty thousand Muslims operate the whole market area and around half a million Muslims live in the region. Hong Wei asked me will we get some food in one of the many restaurants that litter this place. "Hong Wei, pick out a restaurant anywhere and we will go there," I said. We were spoilt for choice, but we did go into one, but funnily enough, I never did look at the name. Anyone can forget, especially in a foreign land, so I hope you will forgive me.

One of the main dishes they serve is marinated meat in a baked bun and they do various dumplings with different fillings. I tried a little of both and they were nice, plus I had two bottles of beer. Hong Wei ate the same and it looked like she enjoyed it more than me, or perhaps that was just my imagination! Apart from the food, it was great to take the weight off our tired feet. In the course of our conversation, I did say to Hong Wei that I wondered where all of these Muslims pray. She said to me, "Billy, we will go to a place called The Great Mosque after we finish our food here, okay?" "Yes. Let's relax now for the moment and enjoy this food," was my reply.

Eventually we finished our meal and taking a good rest, we got our walking appetite back. After Hong Wei had gotten some directions from a Chinese man to The Great Mosque, we decided to get a taxi.

Within minutes we were at the entrance to this strange complex. The Great Mosque is in Huajue Lane in Xi'an city. It is one of the oldest and most famous mosques in China. It was built in 742 in the time of the Tang Dynasty. There are also about ten other mosques scattered around the area to accommodate the Muslim population. You go into a series of court yards and arches, until you get to the big hall. This mosque can hold up to a thousand people, in one sitting. But with several prayer meetings during the day, there are smaller groups of around a hundred present.

We had a look at the interior, and I found it very colourful and decorative with paintings and carpets all around the place. There were no prayer meetings at the time we were there. But I found it interesting and a place I never even knew existed. Yes, it was good to see it and what it represented. We then got a taxi in around the main shopping areas and spent a period of time there, getting a few small souvenirs for the folks back home. Eventually, tiredness was creeping up on our bodies and the clock was also moving on, towards the late afternoon. So, it was back to our hotel, for a rest, before we went out for dinner. The last supper was coming up fast, to coincide with our last night in the magical city of Xi'an.

We were at the hotel entrance and ready to go out at 19:30. Our taxi pulled up one minute after, and we got in. Our destination was the world-famous Tong Sheng Xiang restaurant on the Keji Road in the Gaoxin District near Zhonggulou Square. This restaurant has four floors, all serving different menus on each. As we entered and made our way to the stairs, I could see photographs of a lot of famous people and celebrities on the wall. These people had obviously dined there and praised its service, surroundings and food.

After scouring the menu with Hong Wei's assistance, I went for cruded pancake in beef soup and roasted lamb chops. Hong Wei went for cruded pancake in mutton soup and some other strange dish. I never even asked, as I was much too hungry. A few bottles of Qingdao beer were ordered to put me in the mood. Coincidently, I must say it was the best food we had in Xi'an City, during our stay. We were back at the hotel entrance at 22:00, satisfied! Our eyes closed shortly after hitting our pillows as Friday approached in the passing of the night.

It would be an early start on Friday morning. An idea that fitted into our schedule, but it would not have been everyone's cup of tea. There was to be a change of plan from the customary plane journey. Instead of us travelling by air, it was now a case of travelling on tracks. We were going to travel from Xi'an city to Beijing on a train called a slow sleeper. Basically, it's a train with long carriages that have bunk beds in sixes per open compartment. Three on either side; top, middle and bottom. They are mostly used for overnight journeys, but for daytime travel also. Back in 2006, there were no bullet trains (that I knew of) from Xian to the capital.

The travelling times varied, but back then it was around ten or eleven hours. That's a long time, you might say and I agree, but I wanted to see the countryside and towns and villages that we would pass through in the daylight. Plus, you could still go for a sleep anytime during the journey. So, while it didn't sound exciting being on a train for that length of time, (it wasn't the Orient Express) we were prepared to go with it.

We got to the train station by taxi from our hotel, having been picked up around 06:30. Breakfast would have to come later! Our departure time was around 07:50, if I can recall. Luckily for us, we got a compartment and were the sole occupants. We took the bottom one each, not that I was scared of heights. I must say, from the previous journey, the beds had been changed with clean sheets and the surroundings were spotless. Their standards were high, which were welcome. It was plain to see there were no short cuts here as regards efficiency and promptness. The journey began on time, with a lot of mileage to be clocked up by this Iron Horse (train), with its final destination being Beijing. The weather was crisp and dry, which made visibility good.

We got our food early and talked and laughed in the early part of this unique journey. I took in all the sights that greeted my excited eyes and wondered about this vast country and its resilient people. On the journey, the train stopped at several small towns, just for a minute, to leave off and pick up passengers. The hours passed, as did the mileage. This Iron Horse was clocking it up at a fair speed. We took a nap for an hour or two in the early afternoon after finishing our lunch.

Eventually the finishing line was drawing to a close; we were informed by the train conductor that our journey's end was an hour away. Other passengers along the corridor were getting their belongings together and freshening themselves up in the respective bathrooms. Hong Wei and I followed this procedure too when it was convenient for us to do so. Eventually the time did come when we arrived into Beijing Grand Central Station, and on time, I might add. I asked myself the question, Would I do that journey again? The answer would be no, unless I was pushed. I would certainly not do it on a regular basis. It was a long and tedious trip, but it was worth it to do it. I had no regrets as it was different and also was a change of scenery. If you ever want to see a large crowd of people in a train station, this is one place on earth (Beijing Grand Central Train Station) where you are guaranteed to witness it. There are thousands of people going here, there and everywhere. They were either arriving, waiting or departing. All of them I'd imagine with one objective -- to get to their destinations.

After gathering up our belongings and exiting the train station, we took a taxi back to the Jade International Youth Hostel. We booked in, the same procedure as before. Hong Wei did everything. What would I have done without her! One or two of the receptionists remembered us from being there previously. Hong Wei and I were tired, but we were hungry too. When we got to our room, we freshened up. In my case, it was a wash, a shower and a shave.

I said to Hong Wei, "Let's go somewhere special to celebrate our future."

"Okay Billy, I know one such restaurant," she said.

We left our residency at 19:30 by taxi and a very popular place called Quanjude Roast Duck Restaurant was our destination. It was a well-established restaurant situated in the Dongcheng District of Beijing and came with a great reputation. An impressive frontage to this eating establishment greeted us on our arrival. We got a warm welcome from the front door staff and were guided to a small little table in a corner of this fine restaurant. Obviously, I had roast duck and vegetables with French fries. Hong Wei had roast duck with dumplings, accompanied by hot water. A few beers were my choice of drink. One of the chef's actually came out and cut the duck in strips straight in front of our eyes. I can only say that the food there was delicious, and the drink was satisfying too. After a two-hour stay, it was back to our abode.

Friday was coming to a close and so were my eyes, as were Hong Wei's. It had been a long day, but an enjoyable and unique one at that. Sleep, boy, did we get some sleep that night. But Saturday morning did come around and after pulling back the curtains, brightness descended on our room. Which was now telling us it was late. We were late.

We just made it to breakfast, with minutes to spare. I wasn't too fussy about what I ate, although I do remember it was a few boiled eggs with boiled rice. This was my last day on this my fourth trip to China and I was in Beijing. Out of all the things I had done and the historical sites that I had seen previously, I wanted to go back and see Mao Zedong lying in state again. I just felt the need to do it and I wasn't taking no for an answer. Hong Wei with her good sense of humour, laughed respectfully when I told her of my wish.

"Again?" she asked.

"Yes again," I said.

"Oh alright, let's do that first then," she said.

We made our way to Tiananmen Square on foot. It was the same as when we had left it the last time. It still looked the same as the tourists and Chinese people wandered around it and marvelled at the sights there. I said to myself, as we made our way to the starting point in the queue to see Mao Zedong again. The protocol was the same, as regards the queue, patience, time and the adrenalin. We got there eventually after following the ritual and I had another look at the former Chinese leader lying in state. To me it was still a unique and privileged sight to see. I treated it with respect, as I had done previously too. I was glad I had done it and made no apology for doing so.

We spent the rest of the day just relaxing and browsing around the shops. There are shops of every description to be seen in Beijing. We had a bit of food in the early afternoon and continued until it was time for the lowering of the Chinese National flag in that ceremony that takes place every day on Tiananmen Square. I wanted to see it again. We waited for the appropriate time and got a good vantage point. It was just as spectacular as before and I was glad I done that again too.

There are some sights or things that you can see twice, and they don't lose their appeal. Believe me, I did two that day that needed to be done. They were fulfilled and I was happy. Hong Wei in her wisdom, went with the flow. Shortly after that, it was back to the hostel for a rest. We decided to go to a different restaurant again. This time it would be a restaurant called Jing Yaa Tang in a hotel called The Opposite House in the Chaoyang District. That certainly sounds a little strange, doesn't it? But it's true. This place was also famous for its Peking duck. We got there by taxi. It was impressive from the outside and even more impressive inside. It was spotless, neat and tidy and was a beautifully coloured interior. Hong Wei ordered a Tofu Dish with noodles, rice and water. I tried the roast duck with vegetables and steamed potatoes and a few bottles of Qingdao beer.

Everything went down a treat and our conversation was excellent. The service, the quality of our food and the efficiency in which it was served, was all first class. Hong Wei's English was improving every day and I could feel it. We returned to the hostel around 21:00 and got a good night's sleep. The next morning was Sunday, Beijing Airport beckoned! I found saying goodbye then and now has always been the same, heartbreaking for me!

After breakfast it was all about getting ready for my return flight to Ireland. We made our way to the airport early and followed the same procedure as before. My flight was booked for 13:00. Hong Wei and I chatted, having a snack in between. We discussed my return in January and getting married. I reassured her that I would be back, and the wedding would go ahead. My conscience was totally clear. I was not answerably to anyone, only myself. As I have said before and make no apology for it, who gave a damn about my life? Nobody, that I can recall or if there were, they certainly didn't tell me at the time. But it was time to go to the security gate with Hong Wei holding my hand tightly. It felt like she didn't want to let go, but deep down she knew she had to.

Soon it was a case of letting her go. The tissues were out in force once again and she even gave me some too. But when you've got to go, you've got to go! I looked back and saw her thin figure getting smaller and smaller as the distance between us grew. Then when I turned the corner, she was gone. I felt leaving her go this time was harder than before. Hong Wei would get a later flight back to Shenyang and be picked up by Mr. Liu, my faithful friend. I had my book to read, my films to watch and food to eat. I just got on with it. It is a long trip home to Ireland. But I did miss Hong Wei's company that was for sure. After take-off, I was over Beijing in minutes and looking down on this monstrous city that is full of excitement, intrigue, mystery and for me on this occasion, sadness.

Me, meeting Pele in the Waxworks in Beijing. I saw him playing live. I can die happy.

Hong Wei and I in the "Forbidden city" in 2005

Hong Wei and I at the Great wall of China

Tired, but going nowhere in Beijing.

Here I am outside the Shenyang Olympic Sports Centre Stadium with a group of Liaoning (Whowin) football club supporters fromAnshan City

Hong Wei and I in Beijing in 2005, with Tiananmen Square in the background.

A family photo on one of my earlier visits to Anshan City.

Pictured with Hong Wei's late mum Wei Qui Wen. a great lady with a kind heart.

Hong Wei and I pictured in the famous "Bingyu Valley Four Seasons" Retreat Holiday Complex Resort.

Hong Wei pictured early in the evening before the rush, on the famous "Wang Fujing Street" in Beijing.

Pictured prior to going down the Yalu River, which separates North Korea from China. Quite an experience that was.

Pictured at the end of the famous Yalu River Broken bridge, which was bombed by the Americans in the 1951 Korean war. Situated beside the city of Dandong.

We had to change transport at this barrier, on our way to the Red Sea Beach outside of Panjin City.

A section of the famous Red Sea Beach outside of Panjin City.

Pictured at the entrance to the unique underground Benxi Water Cave in Liaoning Province.

Pictured at a private moment after the wedding of Hong Wei's son Jin Yang to Wang Hao.

Arriving at the hotel for Hong wei's niece's wedding. Mr Liu and Hong Yan 2's daughter Liu Jin Chi was marrying Zhang Guo XI.

The end of an enjoyable night out in Ashan City with some of the gang of twelve.

The National Art Museum of China in Beijing.

One of several suspension bridges that we crossed on our travels in 2019.

Looking down on the Double Decker Bridge over the Qiantang river from the 7th floor of the Six Harmonies Cultural Relic Pagoda.

It was nice to see somebody doing their bit for the environment.

The female Buddhist, Guan Yin (Goddess of Mercy) on Mount Putuo, Putuoshan Island.

The Martyrs Memorial Monument in Anshan City.

The Castle in Disneyland, Shangai. I walked around this fascinating place for ten hours and came out on my knees.

Looking down on Shangai by night from the Shangai Tower.

The Terracotta Army near Lishan in Shaanxi Province, central China.

No shortage of plates in this restaurant.

Hong Wei's grandson Hao Yang, pictured on his third birthday.

Hong Wei pictured with her granddaughter Yue Yue in May 2019.

On my last visit to China when I was leaving in May 2019. Hong Wei stayed on a little longer.

Time for serious thinking now!

This was my fourth visit to China finished. Who would have guessed it? Certainly not me! I got back to Ireland on time and following the same routine, I got back to the Crystal City that is Waterford, also on time. After getting sufficient rest on my return home and it being Monday evening now, I made my way to Fengqin's flat. She was delighted to see me, as I was her. I spent some time there, telling her all about the trip and what was in store when I returned in January. She seemed happy for my future. She was and is the most relaxed and coolest woman I have ever known.

I kept in touch with Hong Wei through the media means (phone, e-mail and Skype) as she told me about the plans for our wedding. I was discreet about the same plans here and kept things to myself. I didn't feel the need to have to tell anyone or having to explain myself to others. This was the way it was and so be it. I certainly didn't want to offend anyone either.

My divorce came through in late November of 2006. The weeks passed and late December was approaching. There was not much excitement in that month for me, as I was waiting for January 2007. The hierarchy in my job at Bus Eireann were more than obliging in giving me the time off. I needed about two weeks off, but they were flexible. The usual arrangements for my flight and visa were put in place. My bus driving job continued, as before with the same level of professionalism, as I had always shown from day one. I also had thoughts and reflections on my life and where it had led me to now. I was happy with what I saw when I looked into it and my conscience was totally clear.

My departure date in January 2007 came. This was to be my fifth visit to China, though I never thought it would be to get married! Yet this was to be the case in my life.

A Chinese wedding was going to be all new to me, but I was prepared for and positive about my forthcoming actions in a foreign country, on foreign soil. This was about two people making a decision about their future lives together. It was obvious to the onlooker Hong Wei was going to come back to Ireland with me. She had informed the Chinese authorities of her intentions. In the meantime, for my part, I had sent all the relevant paperwork that the Chinese Government had requested, to the various departments to satisfy their criteria and get their stamp of approval. Everything was legal, approved and above board – it had to be!

My flight took off on Friday January 19th. Irrespective of which way I travelled, I still ended up in Shenyang on time. The same level of tiredness hit me after my three flights. An excited Hong Wei and an equally excited me met in the arrivals area and duly exchanged kisses and hugs. I was so pleased to see her, as she was to see me. My good friend Mr. Liu, her son Jin Yang and her sister Pan Pan also greeted me warmly. They had two cars ready for the journey back to Anshan city. I was getting used to it by now, you might say. Hong Wei spoke to me in an excitedly manner of what the preparations were and when everything was happening. I just went with the flow and said, yes that's okay by me. The day, the time or the hour didn't make much difference to me either. I was here now and ready to take the plunge (get married) for the second time in my life.

The rest of her excited and immediate family greeted us on our arrival in Anshan city. It was mutual, as I was glad to see them also. It was now Saturday afternoon and Hong Wei informed me that plans were in hand for a family meal that evening in some hotel. The obvious thing to do was to not disagree with my body and to get sleep quickly. Hong Wei's sister Pan Pan obliged us with immediate accommodation, and it was welcomed and appreciated.

After a few hours' sleep and at the appropriate time, I freshened up and we went with her son Jin Yang to the designated hotel called Sheng Li. Everybody from her family were there and they all greeted us warmly again. As on my previous visits to Anshan city, I was well aware of how popular Hong Wei was with her family, close friends and still is today. I always insisted Mr. Liu sat next to me then and on my other visits also. I always made a habit of making sure of that.

I have found over the years that this Chinese family and their friends have always made me feel very welcome. Which I appreciated and welcomed so much. There was nothing spared as regards ordering food. It came by the plateful and the choices were plentiful. I ate several choices and ignored several others, with respect. As I said to Hong Wei then and even now, without being offensive, if I don't like it, I just won't eat it, simple as! That has been my policy then and has remained so since. The Anshan beer was the same too. All I could drink was ordered for me and the rest of those present.

A good three hours passed and with pleasantries, gifts and conversation passed around, the family photos rounded off the evening, as they always do. A family friend had given us the use of their house for the few days. The wedding was scheduled for the Thursday. The following few days understandably were spent meeting various people and having a dress rehearsal on the Tuesday in the Xin Fu Xing Hai Hotel, where we were to be married.

Like I said earlier, I went with the flow and stayed positive. Hong Wei and I spent the few days leading up to the wedding at various hotels and restaurants eating out, at other people's insistent invitations. This was also with her family and friends, as she made last-minute preparations. This was her big day and I wanted it to be a happy occasion, especially for her. My biggest fear, believe it or not, was preparing my speech. What was I going to say, but I stuck to rehearsing it and finally got there.

Mr. Lee was recalled for the wedding, as he was to be my interpreter for the day. There would be a lot of Chinese people to meet and greet. Most of them would have no English at all. Surprisingly, most Chinese weddings are held in the morning time, as ours was. The weddings are completely different to that as in Ireland. I can only tell you about my experience.

The big day came, Thursday morning and I took all of the prior proceedings in my stride. Hong Wei had to go off early and get her hair done. I just had a wash, a shower and a shave, then I relaxed. When she arrived back at the house, her son, Jin Yang, her sisters, her brother and mother had called earlier and were waiting for her. I got myself ready and her sisters helped her. At the appropriate time of 10:30 a fleet of ten glittering limousines arrived outside the house. I noticed all of them had a special array of purple coloured balloons on the roof of the limousine. This was the custom here and it was a sight to see. It was similar to being treated like royalty. A few photos were taken, as Hong Wei and I made our way to the lead car. Then the cortege moved off for the hotel. They do a wide circuit of the city and mainly use the major inner-city roads.

We arrived at the hotel, where the customary balloon arch across the entrance is visible and small fireworks are lit in conjunction with us entering the hotel's front doors. It can be a little bit scary, when you don't know what is coming next. But in my case it was so far, so good. What was next on the agenda, I wondered.

Going inside there were a lot more people there than I would have expected. At a rough count, anything up to around two hundred people were present. Obviously, Hong Wei's immediate family, distant relatives and friends were all there. Even her ex-husband Mr. He was there and he wished us well. There was and never is any animosity there when we meet, which is great to see. As I say in a marriage break-up situations, why should there be? It's all about acceptance and getting on with your life! I was certainly outnumbered by two hundred to one. Hong Wei had the task of introducing most of them to me before the wedding and the rest after.

Proceedings got under way with a Mr. Chen Tong, who was to be the Master of Ceremonies. There was music and photographers there, which coincided with the ceremony. All of the questions that were asked and answered during the ceremony were dealt with. Mr. Lee played a blinder with his interpreting when needed.

We finished with a toast, in a lot of champagne glasses being filled in a pyramid style. The last time I saw that trick was the late, great, but much loved and sadly missed Manchester United and Northern Ireland football idol, George Best. It was in a Manchester nightclub and that was only on one night out, for him! He truly was a football genius.

I keep using the phrase 'I went with the flow', but I did, because this was all new to me. We got through it and lastly it was my speech. Surprisingly, I got through that too – by keeping it simple and meaning what I said. Then it was time for food in two big banqueting rooms. Believe you me, there was no expense spared here, with drink and food in abundance. I did have my fill of food and definitely quenched my thirst with a lot of beers. Lots of different family members made speeches and wished us well, which both of us appreciated and knew how sincere they were in making them. I do remember one custom I had to do after the wedding when Hong Wei was introducing me to loads of guests, particularly the males. You shook their hands and offered them a cigarette, which you then had to light for them. I never really got the reason why, from Hong Wei. I presumed it was to do with good luck and wishing us well.

Weddings in China don't last all day, only for a few hours, but it's enough time for all that is needed to be done. In the late afternoon, proceedings slowly came to a halt. There was no rush to be gone from the hotel, but there were guests (some elderly) there who had travelled from outside of Anshan city to be there for our special day, and it was understandable they had to leave at a reasonable hour. When the whole affair was over, it was back to Mr. Liu's house where most of Hong Wei's immediate family continued celebrating our wedding. There was singing, talking, eating and drinking. But like all good things, the end did come. Unfortunately, the end of Hong Wei living in Anshan city was coming to an end too. This was something we had discussed, but she was adamant and positive about moving back to Ireland with me.

Through a lot of the paperwork leading up to the wedding, Hong Wei could only enter Ireland on a temporary visa, even though she was now legally married to an Irish citizen. But this wasn't a problem and after a few months in Ireland the appropriate channels and criteria were went through to the satisfaction of the Irish authorities. We spent a further three days socialising and slowly coming to the realisation that we would be leaving soon, and she would be saying goodbye to her family and friends. On one of those days though, there was something that I wanted to do and we both agreed to do it. We had an invite from Mr. E (remember him) to visit the famous Anshan Iron and Steel Works factory in the Tie Xi part of Anshan city. With our departure looming, there was no time like the present.

We had a pre-arranged time to meet Mr. E (he was one of the top bosses) at the main entrance. I was really looking forward to this, as I had heard a lot about this factory and its history. We met him and went inside this huge factory and put on our red safety helmets. Even then, the first thing I felt was the heat and we weren't even after starting! He then brought us up several flights of steel stairs to a viewing platform which ran the length of the production line. The whole working of this iconic workplace is based on a conveyor belt system. Everything starts at one end and you follow the steel through its life from the start to the finish. The viewing platform is way up and practically under the roof, and you are at the furthest point away from where the real heat kicks in. Boy, was I in for a surprise when he pointed where we should look, as the noise was deafening.

We started at the start and saw all the raw steel going in to be smelted down. Then we saw this huge oven door open upwards and a huge length of white-hot steel literally poured out in sheets onto a horizontal conveyor system. The heat was intense at that precise moment, that even though we were up about sixty feet in height, the heat literally attacked us. The steel was so hot it was like jelly as it rolled down the conveyor tracking and continued its journey to where it was cut to the appropriate size with a giant guillotine, with the ease of a knife going through butter. This came down and cut it into precise sizes and from there it went on to where it is then flattened with a giant hammer into the proper thickness. To see the pounding on the hot steel and it slowly losing its furnace heat as the seconds ticked away was just amazing and unreal.

While this fantastic process was going on, Mr. E was busy talking to Hong Wei, pointing out and describing the different stages it was going through. The steel continued on its way, as different giant hammers pounded it continuously. Then we lost it as it went through different cooler systems causing the steel to become different lengths and thickness as it came to the finishing line. It arrived at the point where it automatically started to coil itself into huge steel rolls of the finished product. We ended up looking at new huge rolls of pure glistening shiny steel. It was quite amazing to see where it started and what it looked like at the finish. You would never believe it unless you saw it. What an experience it was for me to have seen it! I told Hong Wei to tell Mr. E how impressed and privileged I was with what I had just seen. We thanked Mr. E and he said goodbye as he understandably had to get back to his very responsible job.

We only saw a handful of workers during this whole process, in between the working machinery. Modern technology I suppose would be the word for it, and the age of the machine. We emerged out into the welcome sunlight as I shook my head and said to Hong Wei, "What an experience that was and to know that we saw it first-hand!". I looked back at the factory outline and realised then what went on under that roof. We got a taxi back into Anshan city and told our tale in great detail to Mr. Liu and others.

Saying goodbye is always hard and this was no different, because Hong Wei did not know when she would be returning to her home city of Anshan again. It was a tough ordeal for her, but she handled it surprisingly better than I thought she would, when the time came. She is a very strong and positive woman, which I learned then and I certainly know that now after being together for the past thirteen years.

The departure day did arrive and the hugs and kisses went around her family and friends in abundance. We asked that just Mr. Liu and Mr. Lee accompanied us to Shenyang, as we had to go a day earlier. It was where we would be departing from, but it was also where we had to go to get our final departing papers checked and stamped by the authorities and show proof of our marriage certificate, as regards dates, times and places. We departed for Shenyang and went straight to the appropriate Government office block. Everything was checked and checked again. A lot of questions were asked, until finally we got the go ahead to leave the country.

It was a bit harrowing for both of us, in case there had been a mistake along the way. But all our fears were to be allayed when the lady attending us said to Hong Wei in Chinese, with Mr. Lee interpreting for me at the same time.

"All is in order. You can leave China and travel to Ireland. Do have a good journey, to you both," she said. Getting up from the counter, I breathed a big sigh of relief, as did Hong Wei also. Did you ever have that feeling that something might have gone wrong, even though we knew everything with the paperwork was in order? With our clearance to travel assured, we were to fly out from Shenyang and then to Beijing, the following day.

All four of us then went for a few beers and had a relaxing meal somewhere in Shenyang that evening. I don't even know where we went for the meal, and even now I couldn't tell you the hotel where we stayed that night. As you can imagine, my mind was elsewhere earlier in the day, but it was now beginning to relax, and I was beginning to unwind. We all had a good night with a few cold beers and a nice meal with plenty of choice when it came to food, but I only ate what I wanted and enjoyed my choices.

Mr. Liu and Mr. Lee dropped us off at the airport the following morning and said their final goodbyes, before they began their journey back to Anshan city. I thanked them for all their help, as they had played their part in their own way. Their help had been invaluable when it came to it and was greatly appreciated by me.

We got our flight to Beijing, arriving around teatime. Hong Wei and I had plans to stay in Beijing for about four days. We actually went back to the Jade International Hostel again. We spent our time in a relaxing manner over the course of the four days and looked around at some of the familiar sights again. On one day alone, we spent the entire time in The Forbidden City. On another day, we went back to have a look at another section of The Great Wall.

We followed the same routine as regards transport to The Great Wall. Even with the weather being a little cold, the crowds weren't any smaller. We landed at a different part of the Wall, which pleased me. Looking at this section of the Wall, the terrain with its ups and downs were the same. The starting point was different though, from a visual point of view. When we started, we got on a kind of a conveyor belt bucket-seat system. This took the weight off our feet and brought us so far up to our starting point on the Wall. Like Mao Zedong and The Forbidden City, I wanted to have another look at this phenomenal sight. After spending another three hours there, we came back to the conveyor belt bucket-seat system and it took us back down to the start again. We got a meal there, before we departed for Beijing. We took it easy and relaxed on the last day and I could plainly see that Hong Wei was happy. We took lots of photographs over certain parts of this fabulous city.

When the morning of our flight came, we got to the airport early, checking in our luggage and waited for our flight. The time arrived for us to go to our departure gate and we boarded the big bird (plane). As we took off and looking out from our side window, I said to Hong Wei, "Have a look down at Beijing. God knows when we will be back again."

"That's okay with me, Billy. As long as I have you and we are together, I'm happy," she said. With that, the huge city of Beijing below us disappeared in a matter of seconds. We were left with our thoughts of the previous days and I was also left with the thoughts of my previous four visits, as this was now ending my fifth. Whoever would have thought of it? Not me, for sure! Whoever said life is just a lucky dip, I was beginning to agree with them, when I looked back on mine. But I was not forgetting another word called fate!

With one stop-over in Amsterdam, we finally boarded our plane and found ourselves arriving into Dublin Airport in Ireland on time. Hong Wei got through the emigration officials when they checked our papers and saw that everything was in order. With our luggage collected and finding my parked car, we set off for home. Just under three hours later we were entering Waterford city – Hong Wei's new home, and going across Rice Bridge, then down the famous quays of the oldest city in Ireland, to our city address. It was bed straight away, as sleep needed to be recouped as early as possible.

Hong Wei's new dwellings were completely different than that of her former home in Anshan city in China. The following day we paid a visit to an anxious Fengqin, who was very glad to see Hong Wei. It had been a few years since they last saw each other. She made some food for us and we all had an enjoyable few hours together. They got up to date with current affairs and past events from their home city of Anshan and China itself. We stayed in touch with Fengqin. At times she visited our house for a meal and a chat. She was always made welcome by us. After all, only for Fengqin, Hong Wei wouldn't have been here in Ireland. Where that would have left me was anybody's guess! I owed that woman so much, when independently I had been going through such a dark period in my life.

Within a short space of time Hong Wei set about joining an English learning class at night, because I knew she was determined to learn English as quickly as possible. She spent every available minute with her head in translation books. When she wasn't at classes, she was asking me continuous questions and looking for answers.

Hong Wei was only here a few weeks when my mother died on May 2nd in 2007. She had met my mother on several occasions, and they were getting on great in each other's company. It was a bad blow for all our family, as she was a wonderful woman. As we say in Ireland especially, 'she was the salt of the earth'. Meaning she had good nature and was thoughtful in every way. She was always there to lend an ear, if needed. Money or material things meant nothing to my mother, except the well-being of her family. But life goes on, as it has to when you lose a loved one. Unfortunately, that's one of the harsh realities of life.

The weeks passed as did the months and then it was years, before we returned to China. In actual fact it was to be two and a half years, from late January 2007 to September 2009.

I got Hong Wei a part-time job, when she was here about a year and her English had improved. My work continued with my bus driving duties and the responsibilities that went with it. I also kept up with my writing ambition of self-publishing my long awaited first book *The Flight of a Magpie.* My scouting job with Newcastle United in Ireland continued and the exciting challenge that presented on a weekly basis.

Fengqin kept in touch and at times visited our house, as we did her flat. She was good company for Hong Wei, which I was pleased about. She still did her own thing though and as I said earlier, she was a very independent woman. Hong Wei also kept in touch with members of her family, through email and on Skype.

Early in 2009 we decided that it was time to go back to China. Looking ahead, we knew around the 15th of September would be the designated date, as it suited us both with regard to holidays from work. The weather was still going to be a little warm; it was all about bringing light clothing with us. We would be there for around three weeks and had planned to visit a few cities. This was to be my sixth visit to China after an absence of two and a half years. Who would have thought that, as the same answer followed, certainly not me! I was just as excited about this trip, as I was about the previous five. As usual, we made all of the necessary arrangements regarding my visa and travel tickets.

The weeks and months rolled by and slowly as it seemed, our departure date arrived. I knew Hong Wei was looking forward so much to going back to see her family. I was looking forward to seeing them too and especially my great friend Mr. Liu.

On this trip we went from Dublin to Paris to Beijing to Shenyang. The usual travelling time scale elapsed before we eventually got to

Shenyang Airport. What a tiring trip this is, with no short cuts. But in my position, I was now married to Hong Wei and she was the most important person in the world to me.

Mr. Liu and Pan Pan were waiting at the arrivals area, with broad smiles on their faces, which I knew would be the case. They were very glad to see Hong Wei, as we were to see them. The weather was still warm and sunny, which was welcomed. The next stop was Anshan city and the usual greetings applied from Hong Wei's family and friends.

The next few days we took it easy while visiting other relations and friends across the city. Between drink and food, I had to throw caution to the wind. I thought to myself, what difference was three weeks going to make to the shape of my body?

On one of the nights there, we were invited again by one of Mr. Liu's friends, a Mr. E to dinner. When we got there with Mr. Liu, five other male friends were there, with their wives and partners. Their sum total of males in their overall circle was eleven. I would always refer them to Hong Wei as the gang of eleven. They all had good jobs and were from all walks of life. They were engineers, hotel and restaurant managers, others worked for multi-national companies, a doctor and factory bosses. We had met some of them several times before for meals and drinks, but never all together. There was no limit to the amount of good food they would order, most of it on my behalf! Each of them would foot the bill in turns and they wouldn't dream of having it any other way. They enjoyed our company and I certainly enjoyed theirs!

As I mentioned earlier, it's amazing how many Chinese people are thin. Most of them were thin, as were their wives and partners, which didn't go unnoticed by me. There must be some message there, there's got to be! I just wish I knew the secret. The first thing we did when we gathered, was to thank Mr. E for showing us the steel factory in operation and what was involved. We all had a good night and the beer flowed.

After them relaxing few days in Anshan city, Hong Wei's sister Pan Pan asked me would I like to go and see a city called Dandong. It is a city south east of Anshan city and it straddles the North Korean border. It is quite famous for the two bridges that spans over its river and for one in particular which represents China's past history. We decided to go, as did her mother, her brother Hong Yue Bin, three of her sisters, Mr. Liu and her grand-nephew Yang Ren. I wondered what was in store for me.

We set out the next morning after a good breakfast. We used two cars for the long journey that it entails. When I say long, the infrastructure is so good that the distance is not a problem, as you don't really feel it. Somewhere along the way, we stopped at a little roadside cafe to have a snack. I can't remember what I ate on that particular day, but I ate something. We got there late in the afternoon of the day we travelled. This was just going to be a two-day stay, as there were only three things we wanted to do. See the two bridges, see the Museum of American Aggression and take the boat ride down the Yalu River which separates China from North Korea.

We booked into a hotel called the Home Inn Hotel, as it was reasonably cheap. It was just to put our heads down and freshen up in the morning. We all went for a walk around the city centre of Dandong. After a while, someone picked out a nice restaurant and we ventured in to see what was on offer. Hong Wei knew my taste for food by now. What I would and wouldn't eat. I can't remember now, but I think it was chicken wings and slices of beef. We definitely had a few extra beers, as we stayed a little longer. My good friend Mr. Liu always sat next to me with Hong Wei to my left. Her family have been so friendly to me over the years and could not have done enough for me. This was something I appreciated very much in this far off land, such a distance from Waterford city.

I presumed this was going to be another exciting experience for me in China. We were all up at a reasonable hour the following morning.

After breakfast, which wasn't much for me, we made our way by car down to the quayside of the famous Yalu River. It was in the early morning sunshine, which also refreshed me and Mr. Liu, as I thought he looked a little seedy too.

When we got to the quayside, there were two impressive sights that greeted us. The new bridge is called, The Sino – Korean Friendly Bridge or The China – Korean Friendship Bridge. This bridge goes fully across the river to the city of Sinuiju, which is in North Korea. This bridge is crucial to both countries as it is used every day for transporting goods, vehicles and workers. It links China to North Korea, believe it or not. There on the quayside, we encountered some Korean women with loads of men's and women's traditional Korean clothing on stalls. You could put on some of the clothing stuff and they would take photographs of you with North Korea across the river in the background. I wasn't too pushed, as I was more interested in seeing what I came for – the Bridges.

We looked at it and took a few photographs before moving the short distance to have a look at the second and most interesting bridge. It's called The Yalu River Broken Bridge. What a contrast we had here, between the two.

This was a bridge that was bombed by the Americans to cut off supplies to North Korea in 1951 during the Korean War. Only half of this famous bridge remains, and it is now a major tourist attraction to the city of Dandong. There is this impressive steel monument of soldiers in battle at the start of the walkway out onto the bridge. There is also a large plaque telling the history of the bridge. After paying a small fee, we began our walking journey. Tourists are allowed to walk the length of it, except that it only spans half the river. When you get to the middle part, it is railed off, but you can actually see where the steel girders were melted from the impact of the American bombs on that fateful day. There is a large specially cut stone there which has some red writing on it. I actually forgot to ask Hong Wei what it said, but I'm sure it represents something relating to what happened with the bombing in 1951. While holding Hong Wei's hand, I studied all of the damaged structure close to me. I wondered what the intensity of the heat from the blasts must have been like for those on the bridge on that day. For those in close proximity, it mustn't have been a pretty sight to see – war never is.

We took more photographs of this historical place, with North Korea in the background. The rest of the concrete support pillars are continuing on, only there is no bridge there. On the way back and at intervals on both sides of the bridge, there are large photographs showing different phases of the attack on this bridge. These are quite impressive to see and give the tourist or visitor a valued history in pictures and writing. When that was over, we took a short walk to a place called The Museum of American Aggression. It was a tall, huge, wide and very impressive stone like building. On entering the front of this impressive looking museum, we paid our small entrance fee. We entered the lower part of the museum and saw lots of artefacts mostly relating to the Korean War and other interesting war memorabilia stuff. There were all types of machine guns, rifles, grenades, bombs in glass cases. They were maps, clothing, medals, photographs and a huge selection of other memorabilia to see.

Adjacent to this section on the outside was a wide-open area where there were tanks, planes and armoured personnel carriers to be seen – all left over from the war. A lot of these were still intact, but as regards whether they were in good working order, I don't know nor did I ask. We spent a little time going around this area and observing all that was to be seen. We then went back inside and ventured up the long winding stairs to the top floor where I was greeted with an unbelievable sight. I never thought I'd see what I saw here.

It was a wide circular open space with a dome roof on it, but it had a round viewing space with re-enactment of periods in the Koreans war battle. It was like a huge model of the war zone, but it was done in sequence and all around in a circular fashion. It was an incredible sight to see and very impressive in the detail. It showed the land and river all around. It had hills and valleys with model tanks, planes, armoured personnel and soldiers. They even had the noise of the planes when they were coming in to attack. There was a continuous mural of the battlefield, all around this wide round room. It was done so professionally that it blew me away. I certainly took my time looking at all of these sights with Hong Wei by my side, as did the rest of the group.

Then you were able to get dressed in military clothes with a hat or helmet and a rifle or short arm (pistol) or machine gun. For the occasion that was in it, we all got dressed up in different uniforms depicting different ranks and sections of the Chinese Army. There are people there that will capture the moment in nicely coloured glossy photographs for you.

I couldn't believe the detail in the whole construction of what I was seeing. How someone thought up of the idea and then how they put it into practice, was beyond me. It really was amazing to see this and what an impression it left on me.

"Did you enjoy those sights, Billy?" said Hong Wei.

"I sure did. It was unbelievable how they constructed that whole story," I said. That was two out of the three things we wanted to see. But if I thought the museum and the bridges were a sight to behold, I was in for a rather big surprise with our third destination. This was to knock me for a big six – in a big way!

We had a small hurried snack in a nearby cafe, which kept the hunger at bay. It was still early as we set out on this next adventure. We got back into the two cars and headed up the coastline for a few miles, until we came to a small pier. It was in from the road and I could see that it was used for ferry cruising sightseeing trips on the Yalu River.

Hong Wei said to me, "Billy, we are taking you for a spin on this famous river. Do you want to go, or are you frightened of the water?" she said.

"You must be joking! You think I'm going to miss this experience? Not for the world!" said I.

But there was another twist in this never to be forgotten experience. They also had some speed boats that were moored there as well. I don't know anything about boats, but I could see that these were long high-powered vessels, by the engines on the backs of them. After Hong Wei negotiated a price with one of the attendants, we donned our orange lifejackets. I knew these vessels were powerful – they needed to be for what was about to follow! Following instructions from our pilot, we were scattered throughout this long boat – balance being one of the reasons, I guessed. As a guest, Hong Wei and I were up at the head of the boat, where she held me tightly. This was a very wide river at the point where we embarked. I wondered who, if anyone, from Waterford city had ever been on this river. I bet the answer to that would have been an emphatic 'No!'.

Then we set off at high speed under the guidance of this very alert pilot. He steered the longboat straight out into the middle of the Yalu River. The ferry cruisers present, going at their leisurely pace were left for dead, with this machine at full throttle. Hong Wei informed me that the land opposite was North Korea. You could have knocked me with a feather! Where would you see it – China on the right-hand side of the river and North Korea on the left? On the Korean side we could see a lot of forestry and hills, but very little houses only a few small isolated huts near the riverbank. The place looked really isolated, but I was informed that we were being watched by the border guards. Then the pilot detoured us in the direction of the Korean side, where we could see a few watching soldiers amongst the scattered trees. We had to look closely amongst the greenery and wooded areas as their brown uniforms blended in very well with the background.

The pilot brought us to within about ten to twelve feet of the shoreline. He then idled the boat there for two minutes, where we observed a few of the watching soldiers and just gave them a wave. We got no response from them, which didn't surprise me. I thought, if by an act of God our engines had cut out here (which was highly unlikely) and we drifted to the shoreline, I guess we would have been history. You wouldn't be reading this story now, I'd imagine. It was some feeling and experience to be sitting there. They were undoubtedly the longest two minutes of my life. The experience and expertise of the pilot reversing back was a welcomed relief to everyone on board, I would imagine. It certainly was for me, although I don't know what way Hong Wei thought. She was still holding me tightly throughout.

We continued down the Korean side of the river. When we looked again, we saw some Korean fishermen with their small boats and nets working away. We waved at them and a few waved back. We went a fair distance down the river until the turning point came and our pilot swung into action again. This boat was powerful, as I said at the start. On our return journey North Korea was on our right. I was still shaking my head at what we had just done. The pilot had remained cool throughout, as he had probably done it a thousand times. We arrived safely back at our starting point and discarded the lifejackets for the next unsuspecting visitors. But it was a great and unique experience to have done it and I would definitely do it again. Who knows if we'll ever be back there?

But it was a thrill a minute while it lasted, as they say. I would imagine from the start to the finish, the trip was certainly around the half hour mark. Don't forget we had a high-powered speed boat! Was it value for money? I would say it was good value for what the pilot charged after Hong Wei had bargained with him. But think of the historical attachment to such a boat trip. You cannot buy that part of that unique experience for any money.

After all of that excitement, it was back in the cars and back to the city of Dandong. When we got to our hotel it was time for a rest for everyone, this would be followed by a short walk to a nearby restaurant. Two hours later we left the hotel for a restaurant that we had seen and had ear-marked earlier in the day on our way down to the quayside, as where we would go for our dinner that evening.

We had a lot to talk about when we were seated at a full-length table and our orders were taken. Hong Wei did all of the ordering for me, which I was getting used to by now. I had something like chicken wings, rice, slices of beef and dumplings and the Tsingtao beer was not forgotten about either. The rest of our party had a cross-section of everything you could think of from the Chinese food selection. God bless their appetites, as they are such great eaters, with their food tastes. I did then and do now on my trips to China, salute them, when it comes to food.

Mr. Liu was seated on my right and as his English was not great, he was the first to ask Hong Wei, what I thought of the three things we had done during the day. The rest all joined in at intervals when Hong

Wei caught her breath in between answering the previous question from someone. But it was a most pleasurable day and I thanked Pan Pan through Hong Wei for suggesting it. When our dinner was finished and a few beers drunk, we returned to our hotel and bedded down.

It was just after 08:00 when we awoke the following morning and our bodies were refreshed. It's amazing what a good night's sleep can do for a person. After breakfast, it was a long, but satisfying drive back to Anshan city, for all of us. We arrived back in Anshan city in the early afternoon, having taken a short break earlier in the day for a snack along the road somewhere.

Arrangements had been made for when we got back to have dinner with Mr. E from the gang of eleven. As usual a private room was booked in one of the hotels and a large selection of food was ordered. There were normally five or six of the gang there, with their wives or partners and they always made me feel most welcome. A good night was had by all, which was brought to a halt around 22:30. It was easy to get sleep that night, as tiredness ruled both of our bodies.

The following few days were spent visiting Hong Wei's family and friends. I knew she wanted to spend as much time with them as possible and that was understandable. At one of the family gatherings, Pan Pan again asked me through Hong Wei did I want to see another city that was not too far away? I said I would love to, any city you like. The name of the city was Panjin and it was south west of Anshan city. After another day or two relaxing, we set out to see the city of Panjin. It was only going to be for two days, with time being tight, as regards our remaining schedule.

It was early the following morning after breakfast when Hong Wei, Pan Pan, her husband Dong Bin (who was driving) and their son Tiger and I left Anshan city and headed south. The infrastructure in the road system was as good as you would get anywhere. It was not a case of driving all day. On that day, the weather was cold, crisp and calm, but dry. We got to Panjin and continued on to a place called Red Sea Beach in Dawa County, about twenty miles away. It has the largest wetlands in the world (fifty-one square miles) and is close to the Liaohe River which also accompanies the Shuangtaizi River estuary.

Being a little hungry we first stopped at a small beach area and entered a restaurant that was in the middle of a chain of similar eating places. I remember eating chicken wings, a little bread, all washed down with a bottle of Pepsi-Cola. They all ate something with fish, crab and chicken wings, which they thoroughly enjoyed, as I enjoyed my choice. It was around midday when we were finished, and it was then on to the main purpose of our visit, to Panjin.

There are roughly three main tourists' areas to see. They are all in close proximity of each other and easy to find. We went to this place called Broad Reed fields first. Of course, I did not know what to expect in this place. Another case of going into the unknown, but I was getting used to it now as regards surprises. We parked the car and set off on this path, walking through a wide-open field of reeds. I could see in the distance one or two elevated coverings like viewing areas. There were a few other tourists in the area. They crossed our paths as we walked, although none of them were westerners. These fields were like a giant maze, with walking paths everywhere, but you couldn't get lost really, because from any point you could still see the viewing buildings. We got to the viewing area and spent a few minutes there, where you could see the wide-open area of these reeds covering several fields and a lot of walking paths in between. We spent a few minutes there and then made our way back to where we started and got into Pan Pan's car and drove for a while along the seafront and headed inland where we observed the views from there. There were a lot of wetlands all around us, which made this place most unusual to see.

After a period, we stopped at a certain barrier point where we had to change to other transport, which was like a big golf buggy as it was now a privately zoned area. There were other people waiting there as well. We got on one of these buggies that held around a dozen people and headed off on this wide-open stretch of private road. I remember the weather had changed to a slight drizzle and we were given these poncho rain macs before we started.

After a few minutes, I noticed the colour of the scenery had changed from green to red on both sides of the road. This was continuing all around us and I could see as we came to our drop off point, that the red was now redder than ever. There was a sea of red all around us. This was the famous Red Sea Beach outside of Panjin city. This is a special place in China where this grass only grows in the saline and alkaline soil. To the ordinary person with the naked eye, it's like grass growing on mud. It's actually called seep weed and it changes its colour three times through its life every season, from green to red and finally to purple. Where we were dropped off, there were two of these wooden walking jetties with railings that go out a fair distance into this sea of red grass. It is also nicknamed Red Carpet Beach. It is home to the famous Red Crowned Crane. There are around two hundred and sixty varieties of birds there and around four hundred species of wildlife. For the tourist there is also a souvenir shop building at the end.

I remember buying two beautiful photographs of this Red Sea-like area. When we were out at the souvenir shop, I was told by someone, that to fall into this gooey substance would have been fatal, as it is deadly poisonous. We spent a relaxing twenty minutes or so there and took a few photographs amongst ourselves with the background of a sea of red. A funny thing caught my eye which I pointed out to Hong Wei on our return journey. As we were coming back on the jetty, I looked across into one of the nearby fields and saw these two giant turtles perched on a huge slab of stone. It was such a rare thing to see and I asked myself, were they real or false. I still don't know, even to this day. Because I never asked the question, I never got an answer. They must have been false, but they looked nice and real. It was a most unique and fascinating place to see, and yet another wonderful experience for me!

We backtracked our steps and returned to Panjin city, arriving a short time later. We had pre-booked into a hotel called Jinjiang Inn Panjin Shiyou. It was cheap and only for us just to put our head down for the night, as we would be starting out early the following morning. We had two rooms between us and after freshening up we went out for dinner to a restaurant called Neijia Lao Yuan Zi. I can't recall what we ate, the four of them did their own thing. I, as always, was careful with my selections. But what I selected, I ate and washed down with a few bottles of Tsingtao beer. We retired to our rooms shortly after, where Hong Wei and I got a nice relaxing sleep.

After breakfast the next morning, we set out on the road back to Anshan city. We didn't see anything else in Panjin city, as Hong Wei and I had plans made for our remaining few days in the city of Beijing. Dong Bin was a very good driver and knew his way around these roads, although I must say the signage is excellent. We got back to Anshan city in the afternoon and took it easy, before going out to dinner with her family that night. The conversation, food and drink were okay. As always, time moves on and so did the night. The next day arrived and we relaxed in each other's company. Hong Wei and I said our farewells to her family and friends when we had dinner with most of them early that evening.

We retired again for another good night's sleep. Our departure was for early the following morning on Tuesday 29th of September in 2009. That date mightn't look much to you the reader but add two days onto it and you have October 1st. It just so happened, that it was the 60th anniversary of the Chinese revolution in 1949 in 2009. I was aware of this period and had said it to Hong Wei previously that I want to be in Beijing on that date. I wanted to see how China would celebrate and honour their dead on this historical date in their calendar. Little did I know I was in for a real eye-opener. Hong Wei had arranged and booked for us to take the bullet train from Anshan City to Beijing. A journey of just under six hours, that leaves on the minute and arrives on the minute, as I was soon to experience on this journey.

It was an early start for us when the alarm clock struck 06:30. Opening the closed curtains in our room, showed the darkness covering our view of Anshan city, except for the lights of the early morning traffic, on the roads close by. There was no time for breakfast, as we had to be in the train station by 07:30 for our 09:00 departure. Sleep and food would come later, as we had to get our priorities right. You only get one throw of the dice here and you have to make the most of it. Mr. Liu, Pan Pan and Jin Yang accompanied us to the train station in two cars. We had a few minutes to say farewell to them and we told them we would be back, when an opportunity arose. It was goodbye and a final wave again as we went through security and then took our place in the correct waiting area.

When the time came to board our train, we went to the appropriate platform. As we made our way to it, we saw the other trains were waiting in their lines too. It was like looking at a miniature railway station from a high, such was the neatness and organised layout. We waited at a certain point on the platform, to coincide with our corresponding train ticket seat. This was pure genius of an idea, as everyone knows where they are sitting and in what carriage they enter. There is no big mad rush and free-for-all like you see in a lot of places. The spacings on the platform are done in such a way that the train and the door to your carriage stops at your feet. The platform is dead level with the carriage door, so it makes it easier to lift in your suitcase and lift it out when you reach your destination. The shape and length of this silent train makes for an impressive sight. The front of it is like a plane, but you know this is modern technology at its best.

We took our pre booked seats in this very impressive carriage that was spotless. The interior was all modern fittings: lights, tables, armrests, leg rests and headrests. It was luxurious in every sense of the word. With Hong Wei snuggled up to me and in a relaxed mood, the bullet train pulled out on time, to the second in fact. There was no time for latecomers here, you just waited for the next one! Daylight had arrived to greet us on our departure from Anshan city. The train picked up speed fairly fast and was soon travelling flat out, in between cities.

We got something from the snack trolley early on for to make up for the missing breakfast. I think it was something in a bun and some chocolate, if memory serves me. Plus a few cokes for me and water for Hong Wei to quench our thirst. The scenery coming into the wintertime is obviously not the same as in the wonderful hot summers that China gets. Winter was setting in and the farmers were battening down the hatches on their farms and preparing the surroundings shelters for when they would have to bring in their livestock.

They have a system on the train service in China, which is worth mentioning, as I found it excellently designed. The way it works is any passengers getting off at a pickup or drop-off point along the journey, does so normally. But some passengers getting on at that point and are travelling to the final destination (in this case Beijing) are booked into the same seat as the passenger who has just left it. That way there is no waste of seats and it continues with full quotas. Whereas in Ireland how many times have you seen trains arriving from other main cities into Dublin with lots of spare seats, because when passengers leave their seat at their destination point prior to Dublin, it becomes a waste, an empty seat. Granted the population is bigger in China than in Ireland. But it's the principle and economics of how simple the system works through modern communication and organisation that made me think about this method. I thought it was brilliant to see it in operation first-hand.

As I said earlier, winter was approaching and the scenery was different, to that of the summer. But that didn't change the mountains, forests and landscapes that we saw. There were lots of small villages that we passed through, but they were gone in the blink of an eye. Another thing I noticed after a few hours into our journey and while Hong Wei was sleeping on my shoulder, was the smoothness of the train. There wasn't a budge in movement and as I have said to people several times over the course of time back in Ireland, you could balance an egg on the palm of your hand at the start of your journey and it wouldn't have moved by the end of it. That's true. Such was the level of aerodynamics in the system on this train and in the journey, believe it or not! You'd have to admit there has to be some technology involved there.

They were other small cities also en route to Beijing, where the train stopped for a short few minutes. We did manage to get some more food nearing the end of our journey. The experience of travelling on the Bullet Train was great. We got to the city of Beijing, precisely at the designated arrival time. It was now the afternoon. We got a taxi, which then dropped us off at a hotel called Zhi-De. After booking in and relaxing, we went out for dinner and returned around 22:00.

Tomorrow was another day, with another surprise or two in store for me.

Hong Wei said to me, "Billy, you saw the Olympic Games last year from Beijing, isn't that right?"

"That is correct Hong Wei and it was a terrific spectacle and a tremendous event!"

"How would you like to see the National Stadium, where the Olympic Games were held? As tomorrow will be a total lockdown in Beijing with the parade and celebrations," she said.

"Oh, it would be super to say I was there and saw it," I said. We made our way through a few streets and got to a certain bus stop from where we waited for our bus. The bus arrived and dropped us off at a location, from where we got a taxi straight to the National Stadium. It earned the name of 'The Crow's Nest' because of its shape and appearance from a distance. Its location is just outside of Beijing and as we approached it, I could see its shape in the skyline. When we got there, other sightseers were there too. Not too many I might add on the morning we were there. They arrived by car, bus or taxi. There are huge wide-open spaces and it was just a case of walking to our entry point. There were still security barriers there in certain spots and we had to pass through one of them and showed our ID. This stadium is still a major tourist attraction for visitors to Beijing and rightly so. The National Swimming Centre is adjacent to it too and it was called 'The Water Cube'. When we got close to 'The Crow's Nest', I could see all the curved and interlocking huge steel like lengths at close quarters. On feeling one of them, I realised that this was some spectacle. This was some piece of engineering and architectural work by the Chinese authorities. On entering the stadium and looking around at all that was in front of us, we immediately took a few photographs. It was a case of having to really. After all, without a photo, who would have believed that I was back here.

We saw where the athletics entered the stadium to compete in their various events. I said to Hong Wei, "We'll start here and work our way right around to this point again."

"Okay," she said. I wanted to take all of this in, step by step and not miss a thing.

As we walked between the first rows of seats, we saw the press and media areas. We saw where all the competing National Flags were flying. I saw the blue lined running track all around and as we got to the finishing line, I thought of the great Jamaican superstar, Usain Bolt and pictured him in full flight in the 100m, the 200m and on the 4x100m relay team. All of which he won gold medals in. Not that I know anything about athletics, but I know about him. At that time and at that point too, a lot of tourists had gathered to take photographs. It was like the main area where they congregated after their tour. To coincide with that, there were five figures dressed in costume representing the five pandas that were the symbols for the Olympics. They had five different names and were in different colours. They did a short dancing routine, which all added to the occasion. The memories came back to the forefront of my mind in a visual context. When we got back to where we had started, we took a final photograph of the stadium, pointing the camera in four directions.

We then made our way over to the National Swimming Centre. This was impressive too. We entered through an area where we took up positions high up on the spectators viewing area, which was close to the roof. All around the roof circumference there were the flags of the competing nations still all hanging down in an orderly fashion. I did obviously look for the Irish flag first and found it – even though we never got near the medals podium. It was quite a view, from where we were. We saw the main pool and the main diving pool area, with all the different levels of diving boards. Believe it or not, it was empty at the time, as workmen were there, doing some work. We spent a while in there and when we were finished thinking about the past Olympics, we went to a few souvenirs shops and bought a few things for those back home.

Seeing was believing, as they say, and I had seen. With those two sightseeing tours finished, we exited the area and waited for a bus that did come along and eventually we did find ourselves back in the hustle and bustle of the fabulous city that is Beijing. It was now in the early afternoon and hunger raised its head again. We had lunch in the nearest restaurant from where we exited the bus.

With our stomachs full of food and beer, we went for a walk around one of the main shopping areas. This took up the rest of the afternoon, but we were in a relaxed frame of mind and Hong Wei was happy. During the course of our walk at certain points and being a little observant, I did notice a lot of armed soldiers and police around the shopping areas. Then we hit a few hastily made checkpoints on a few streets and then saw a few SWAT vans with armed personal on board. These were at certain street locations around where we were moving.

I said to Hong Wei, "There is a lot of activity starting to happen. You do know, Billy, tomorrow is the day when all of China will be celebrating its 60th anniversary of Independence Day. Security is tight and Beijing will go into lockdown, starting now. We will just go with the flow and obey any orders that are given to us. You understand?" she asked.

"Oh, I understand completely," I replied to Hong Wei. I do agree, as when you are in any foreign country, you obey their laws. I don't, or never did have any problem with that. After all, it's their country.

We casually made our way back to our hotel and relaxed. Later that evening we went out to a nearby restaurant and had a nice meal. Another occasion where I even forgot what I was eating as my mind was elsewhere. Tomorrow was the day when I wondered how China was going to celebrate their special day, particularly as it was the 60th anniversary. There had been a bitter civil war in China from 1945 to 1949. Shortly after it ended on October 1st in 1949, Mao Zedong (Chairman Mao) proclaimed the establishment of The Peoples Republic of China. You can see how important this date is to the Chinese people. How lucky was I to be in Beijing.

The night passed and morning arrived on Thursday October 1st, 2009. Beijing was now in total lockdown, as the Chinese government and its people were about to celebrate this milestone occasion in their unique history. The massive parade was going to take place in front of the Forbidden City, where the portrait of Mao Zedong hangs proudly. On this occasion, it was to be in the presence of the whole Chinese government. They were going to oversee this whole military parade from the main balcony, from the main building at the front of The Forbidden City that looks down on the famous Chang'An Avenue in front of Tiananmen Square.

Hong Wei and I had breakfast at the usual time and returned to our room to watch the television, waiting for the proceedings to get under way. I remember it well. We were lying on the bed, with extra pillows behind our heads for support. As it happened, October 1st of that all-important year, threw up a beautiful and glorious sunny day. The occasion was made for it and was I in for a surprise. Tiananmen Square was bedecked in coloured floral arrangements with invited guests and dignitaries from all over China present. There had been months of preparation put in from all of the participants from every section of the military. There were ten thousand people ready to march. There were another one hundred thousand civilians from various organisations and groups to follow. So, you see this just wasn't like a St. Patrick's Day parade in Ireland. This was to be an impressive international spectacle.

We were not to be disappointed when it happened! The Chinese President Hu Jintao emerged from the main entrance of The Forbidden City in a specially adapted open-top limousine. He stood to attention in the car as it drove in front of the watching thousands. The vehicle cruised at a moderate speed and headed to its intended location. The car made its way to the end of the starting designated area and then made a wide swing and returned at the same moderate speed to its starting point where it re-entered The Forbidden City. Hu Jintao returned to the viewing area and in due course, a signal was given for the parade to start.

Hong Wei and I were glued to the television, with the volume raised. I was not going to miss a second of this parade that was about to start. I'm sure all of China did likewise. We all waited, in anticipation of what we were about to see and for the signal to be given. The signal was given from one high-ranking military official and the parade began!

What a sight it was to see, as the parade commenced. All the different sections from the Chinese forces were marching with pride and honour. They all gave a salute to the reviewing stand, at the appropriate time, as they passed. The length and width of the sections were unreal. The military precision with which they marched together, took my breath away. There was music coming from military bands in front of Tiananmen Square to accompany them by keeping the beat in the parade. As I lay on the bed, I remember saying to Hong Wei, "This is what you call a parade! Boy, do the Chinese know how to put on a showpiece!" As it went on, the more impressed I was, even with the different colours representing their various sections within the Chinese forces. I could see the pride in the participants' faces and how honoured they were to be the chosen to take part. It really was breath-taking, and I marvelled at every minute of what I was seeing.

You couldn't but be impressed at this spectacle. Section by section, with rows and rows of personnel within them, they just kept on coming. The straightness of the lines was so precise you could have run a ruler over them, they were that straight. We could hear all the proceedings live from our open window in our hotel room. We were only a few streets away from where it was all happening. At one point during the parade, there was an air salute from a squadron of fighter jets. On the television, we could see them in the sky as they flew over the parade and within seconds, as we rushed and looked out from our window, we saw the same planes above our hotel.

The parade continued in full march and with military precision. From back on our bed again, I was spellbound looking at it. Knowing I had been in that area on a few occasions previously and the way it had been transformed into what I was looking at now. Eventually the marching military ended, and it was the turn of the military vehicles to take their place in the parade. Hundreds of tanks, missile carriers, anti-aircraft defence carriers and other vehicles passed by, some of which I didn't even know what they were. The drivers and occupants of these vehicles, all saluted the viewing stand under the watchful eye of Mao Zedong. When all of that was finished, the other one hundred thousand civilian participants with their own sections took their turn in the parade, feeling honoured to be there. I could see this by their body language. Certainly a few hours passed by. I lost all track of time. I had just seen the greatest ever national parade in Beijing, China, to remember Independence Day on October 1st in 1949. What an occasion it was in 2009 and to know we were only a few streets away from it was happening live. It truly was an amazing feeling to be there and seeing it.

We took it easy for the rest of the afternoon and waited until evening time to freshen up and venture out for dinner. We went to a nearby restaurant and I tucked into slices of roast duck, beef and chicken wings. As this was to be our last night in China, I tried a new beer called Yanjing. Tomorrow it was going to be an early start to Beijing Airport and back to the Emerald Isle (Republic of Ireland). As they say, all good things come to an end, as did our stay in Beijing in China for the year of 2009.

My experiences to date had been unique and they weren't finished yet.

The next morning after breakfast Hong Wei and I took a taxi from the hotel to the airport and checked in. Everything was in order and with three hours to spare, we just relaxed in one of the seated areas. Around 11:00 we had something to eat and then moved to our departure gate, where we waited for our outbound flight. It was just after 13:00 when we took off in this giant plane, which would take us back to Paris first and then to Dublin.

As we rose into the sky and looked out from our side window at Beijing disappearing below us, I turned to Hong Wei and I do remember saying to her, "Hong Wei, you do know it will be a while before we are back in China again?"

"Yes Billy, I am aware of all that. But I'm your wife now and this is where I want to be."

In actual fact it was to be over three years, before we were to set foot on Chinese soil again. My six trips and experiences to date for me had been unreal. What would this one hold, I wondered, as the sound of silence fell silently throughout the plane. I think sleep was on most peoples' minds, knowing the flying time involved between Beijing to Paris. After the usual flying time, we got to Paris, waited and then got our connecting flight back to Dublin in Ireland. The winter weather had arrived in Ireland, what was new? Another three hours passed, and we were back in my birthplace of Waterford city and Hong Wei's new-found home.

The following day after a good night's sleep and breakfast, we paid a visit to Fengqin in her flat. After saying hello and me briefly speaking to her in English, Hong Wei and Fengqin spent the next two hours in continuous conversation in Chinese. If only I knew what they were saying, but I was happy reading the local and national papers and catching up with what was happening in the football world. Fengqin made us some lunch, which we accepted and were always grateful for, while also never wanting to offend her with a refusal. One thing she did tell us was that she was going back to England in the New Year. Hong Wei and I returned home later in the afternoon. The next day it was back to work as usual for me and as usual the following weekend came and my scouting job with Newcastle United Football Club continued. Hong Wei was working away when called upon and also kept in touch with her family and friends by e-mail and Skype.

The end of 2009 arrived and the New Year of 2010 loomed in. I never thought I would be where I was, but these were the cards I was dealt! The weeks and the months passed in 2010 and I continued with my routine and writing my book, *The Flight of a Magpie* when time permitted. I kept my other interests alive also. Hong Wei met a few Chinese friends through English classes in night school and I was pleased about that. They are still her friends today and they keep in touch.

The only thing that changed in that year was that Fengqin returned to England in June to be close to her two children, who lived with their father. I was sad to see her go, but it was her choice and she was happy making it.

The end of 2010 came to a close, which coincided with my scouting job with Newcastle United Football Club also coming to an end. It was outside of my control, but nothing to do with my record during the previous ten years. A new owner came in and things were changed within the scouting system in the club. I got two offers from two other Premiership clubs, but I declined. My heart and commitment would not have been in it, as it had been when I was scouting for Newcastle United Football Club and supporting them for a lifetime, since I was aged eight. There is a big difference when you do it for the club you love. That's life. I just got on with it, as I did with all the other ups and downs that arrived in my life.

2011 came and there was a date in the calendar which was monumental to me. It was in that year in which my book *The Flight of a Magpie* was launched on April 28th. It was a great success and even surprised a lot of my close friends, when they read it. The year 2012 arrived and passed also. Hong Wei's english was after improving no end, but I knew about all of the continuous hard work she had put in. My work continued with the National Bus Company (Bus Eireann), but I had discontinued my run on the daily Euro Lines service, as the company had withdrawn their involvement.

Before the end of that year, Hong Wei had got word that her son, Jin Yang, was going to be married in May 2013. We set plans in motion that we would be going back to China and Anshan city again. Hong Wei was excited at the prospect of returning home and of her one and only son getting married. I was looking forward to it for other reasons too. This was going to be my seventh trip to China! Who would have thought of it, let alone believed it, not me! I certainly knew this trip was going to be different. As you have read to-date, my previous six trips to China all had a purpose and a reason. Was I going to have a few new experiences on this one?

The year 2012 ended, obviously the start of 2013 arrived. The early weeks of January went very slowly by as anticipation grew within us for our forthcoming trip. But funnily enough the weeks of February and March passed a little quicker. As April arrived, so too did our departure date which was set for Friday 19th. With our tickets got and my visa collected, our stay was to be for just under a month.

The day arrived and we got to Dublin Airport early for our 09:40 flight. To be brief, two of our four suitcases were overweight, as I knew they would be, after watching Hong Wei packing earlier in the week. When you keep throwing things into what she thought were bottomless suitcases, what do you expect happens when you put them on the scales at the airport? We had to withdraw from the check-in desk, then empty their contents onto the tiled floor and decide what we would leave and what we would carry. This was all done in full view of the waiting queues and the watching eyes in the ceiling above us.

While all of this was in progress, Hong Wei and I exchanged words and understandably, due to the circumstances, at times they were heated. Quoting the words of the name of the film *Nightmare on Elm Street,* well this was it. The nightmare did end, when we left certain items behind and the weight showed a correct reading on our suitcases. Never again, were my thoughts, as we came away from the check-in desk. It was a bad experience, but little did I know, a further one awaited us in Amsterdam airport...

It's been too long to be away

The plane left Dublin on time and as we were flying with KLM, we were bound for Amsterdam in Holland. On arrival, we had to change flights, with a break in between. To be brief, I forgot to get our new boarding passes at the KLM transfer desk. Then we went to the wrong departure gate, which when the penny dropped, reality kicked in. Fifteen minutes before our scheduled flight was due to depart, we were a mile away, on the other side of the airport. I know what you are thinking, how could you let that happen! But after the Dublin experience, forgetfulness was the only excuse I could find. Oh, I accepted full responsibility for this mess, have no doubt about that. Hong Wei was totally blameless, and I held my hand up.

When we hurriedly got back to the main customer service desk and telling the understanding lady of our plight, she informed us that we would not make our original flight now as the departure gate was closed and the plane was already on the runway. "What about our suitcases? They are on that flight." "There is no need to worry about them, sir. They will be waiting in Beijing for you, when you get there." I did throw my eyes up to the man above and ask what we did to deserve this. The lady informed us that the best she could do was to see if we could get on the evening flight, but that would depend on one or two passengers not showing up. I cast my eyes up to heaven again and said, 'Lord give us a break and I'll make it up to you in due course!'. I wondered was he listening, or even looking down. How many times in the course of my life, have I said that to him? Too many if I was truthful with myself.

After getting some food, we waited anxiously in the nearby departure lounge for a few hours, to see what fate had in store for us.

As the intending passengers arrived in dribs and drabs, I turned to Hong Wei and said, "I think we're in trouble." They are all turning up to board the evening flight.

Then as the departure gate closing time was approaching, surprisingly one of the check-in attendants approached us and said, "Mr. and Mrs. Costine, we have two seats available, but they are not together. Will that be okay? Do you want them?"

He didn't have to ask us twice, as I replied, "I will gladly take them, who cares where we're sitting." As long as we are on that plane, that's all that matters now, I said to myself, beggars can't be choosers here! I then turned my eyes up to the man above again and said, 'I owe you big time!'. Mind you, in payback terms I still owe him for more than one divine intervention! I was unlucky to get a middle seat of three on the side aisle. But that was the least of my worries now, as I was so grateful. Hong Wei was a few seats behind me. It's always a long and tedious flight, but after the previous six trips, I was getting used to it by now. Hong Wei would still be the same – relaxed as ever.

We eventually arrived in Beijing early in the morning time and on time, thanks to the wonderful airline and staff that is KLM.

We made inquiries at the lost and found luggage department and they were holding our suitcases for us. Pan Pan was also in Beijing at that time, as her son Tiger was resident there in his first year in college studying art. Pan Pan had been staying there for a few weeks with him, as Tiger was still very young. She collected us at the airport about one hour after our arrival. Both of them were obviously delighted to see each other, after all it had been over three years since they had seen each other. The airport itself is a few miles from Beijing and as you can imagine, it's one of the biggest and busiest in the world. We got into the city and found a restaurant where we had some food to eat. They had a lot to talk about, while I just relaxed and thought about what the next twenty-eight days would bring.

Our plan was just to stay overnight in Beijing and continue on to Anshan city the next evening, but by a different schedule. We were booked into The Jade International Youth Hostel again, just for the one night. Otherwise Hong Wei would not have seen her sister until the wedding. We were in no rush anyway. Everything fell into place for once. We booked in and just took it easy during the day. I could see all the same sights were still there and the tourists were just as excited as I had been on my first visit. Some things never change in the wonderful city that is Beijing. All four of us had dinner that night and it was great to see Pan Pan's son, Tiger. He had grown up since I last saw him. After our meal we returned to where they were staying.

He showed me some of his artwork, which was impressive, to the naked eye – even to me. We found our way back to our accommodation and got a good night's sleep. The following day after breakfast, Tiger went to college with his mother for company and we took it easy until Pan Pan returned at a pre-arranged time and designated spot. She spent most of the day with us and we had some food in the early afternoon.

For the first time our connection from Beijing to Anshan city was to be different. Hong Wei's son Jin Yang had pre-booked our train tickets. It was the iron horse (train) again. When the time was right, Pan Pan took us to the train station. We said goodbye and thanked her for giving us the use of their apartment for a period of our stay when we would get to Anshan city. At this stage, all I wanted to do was sleep. Our open cabin of six bunk beds was occupied by three males and a female. One middle one and one top bunk was free. Hong Wei took the middle one and I took the top one. We were in the company of four strangers, who were all friendly and looked in their twenties, facing a three-hundred-mile journey to Anshan city in Liaoning Province.

We all introduced ourselves to each other at the start. This was no time to be shy, as our two bodies were tired. Don't forget, I had worked all day on the Friday. I finished work at 23:30 and having had very little sleep on the plane and then having the fiasco with waiting in Amsterdam. I had the middle seat on the plane from Amsterdam to Beijing. Add it all up and you can imagine where I was at that point. As regards the bunk beds, it was a case of first come, first served. The other four Chinese people had boarded the train a few minutes before us. I really didn't care, as long as I got some sleep. Hong Wei would sleep on a bed of nails. What a sleeper she is, as I've mentioned earlier.

On time and being punctual, the train pulled out of Beijing Grand Central Station in the early evening. My eyes closed immediately as fatigue kicked in. The wonderful scenery would have to wait until I was ready. There was plenty of it out there, miles and miles of it. About two hours into the journey, and with everyone asleep, my kidneys were giving me a message, 'It's the time to go!'. It might have looked funny, but you try and get out of a top bunk bed on a three-tier system without looking stupid, when everyone else is asleep and you'll know what I mean.

There was a fixed narrow steel ladder with room only for one foot at the end of each three bunks but serving six as the bunks were back to back with the adjoining compartment next door. Not easy I tell you. A few minutes later having given my kidneys the all clear, it was time to re-enter my top bunk bed with the same difficulties as I had getting out of it. What a sight - you would have to had seen it and I did it without waking the other sleeping bodies. Fossett's Circus would have taken me on as a trapeze artist.

My good sleep resumed immediately, as my body was still searching for lost sleep. The steady pace of the train continued on its long journey to Anshan city, but not for a few hours yet. I did wake from my sleep eventually and quietly woke Hong Wei as we went in search of food. When we got back, with no luck, the other bodies were waking up from their slumber. Hong Wei spoke to them in Chinese. The darkness was disappearing fast and the sunlight was taking over for a new day. I viewed the passing countryside and scenery with great interest. Summer was coming and the crops had been sown a few months earlier. It was field after field, all coming to life. A good hour later as our journey was nearing its destination, passengers were making their way to the toilets and wash up areas to freshen up in rotation. Hong Wei and I waited our turn too and did likewise. Some passengers were returning home from having spent a few days in Beijing or further afield. The train's steady pace finally slowed down as it neared Anshan city's main train station and finally came to a standstill. It was early in the morning; I can still remember it. Before I go any further, I would have to say I had a great sleep. All this meant was that my body was now recharged and ready to go again. What a sight that greeted us on alighting from our carriage – the place was thronged big time with people.

As we were going through the ticket exit area, Hong Wei's son, Jin Yang, and his bride-to-be, Wang Hao, came into view. He greeted his mother as any son would do, with a big hug. I just shook his hand and gave him a hug. Wang Hao did likewise, and I could see she was glad to see her future mother-in-law. After all, it had been over three years since mother had met son. Wang Hao got a small kiss on the cheek and a light welcoming hug from me. Mr. Liu (my great friend) had arrived also, as they had taken the three suitcases and three carrier bags into account. He got the usual handshake and hug from me. Mr. Liu was always courteous, obliging, friendly and helpful. He is still my very best friend in China.

Jin Yang's job was a professional driver, as mine was, but he needed to be able to get out of this heavy morning train station traffic, followed by Mr. Liu. This was Anshan city with a population of three and a half million, not just any train station. There were hundreds of people going somewhere and everywhere in a hurry. Then you throw the taxies, cars and buses in on top of all that and you might have a picture of it all.

Jin Yang brought us to Pan Pan's new family residence in a high-rise apartment block. This new tower block was thirty-two storeys in height and their floor was on the twentieth. Her husband Dong Bin was there. He welcomed us, showing us to the spare bedroom. His wife, Pan Pan and son Tiger would be back from Beijing for the wedding. I have always found the Chinese people sincere in their welcome. The planning and layout of these new modern apartments is magnificent. They include furniture, electronics, the flat television screens and the tiled floors, all new. Then you have the bonus of the magnificent views over Anshan city which are breath-taking.

After first unpacking some of the contents from some of the suitcases, Dong Bin informed us that there was a family gathering planned at 18:30 in a nearby restaurant. There was plenty of time to relax and take it easy. Later there would be time to freshen up. Dong Bin would bring us to the gathering later. When we arrived at a private room in the restaurant all of her family were there. Hong Wei hugged them all in turn. The obvious question being put to her by just about everyone was to tell them all about Ireland and how life there was treating her.

The food arrived without delay and in abundance. It still tasted the same, as I stuck to my usual choices and the drink hadn't changed either. Mr. Liu was on my right and Hong Wei was on my left. Understandably a lot of photographs were taking in the course of the meal, with the two of us being the main participants. The night ended with a load of goodbyes, hugs and kisses and the parting words from us of, "We'll see you all at the wedding!".

Visiting Hong Wei's extended family takes time, because of the distance and Anshan is not a small city. On the Tuesday morning we visited her mother's oldest sister and her husband in their apartment. Her mother and another aunt just happened to be there when we called. As you would expect, they were all happy to see her, as she was them. I was happy just making up the numbers. All of us had a small meal around midday and finished with a few photographs. There was plenty of fruit and nuts on offer too, as there is in nearly every house in China. Why do most Chinese people love photographs? I don't know the answer to that one! We parted with the words, "We'll see you all at the wedding!".

We had another engagement that evening in one of the up-market hotels. Mr. E who was No. 3 in the gang of eleven had sent us an invite. Mr. Liu who was No. 5 in the gang collected us from Pan Pan's apartment shortly after 18:30. On arrival, Mr. E and the rest of those present, No. 1, No. 2, No. 8, No. 9 and their wife's or partners, greeted us with such open friendless and warmth as before. Likewise, it was so nice to see them again. They too wanted to know all about Ireland, and Hong Wei was kept busy relaying their many questions in Chinese. The meal was excellent, with the selection of food that was ordered, as has always been the case in this company. Generosity was to the forefront. You might ask why they are called the gang of eleven. There just lifelong friends that have kept in touch with each other. There isn't a twelfth man yet, but I have got an invitation to fill that position, when I feel the time is right. Glad to say, it was never a position that I had to fill on the football field. These guys don't suffer fools gladly! The meal finished with photographs all around.

A good night's sleep followed that kind invitation from true friends. Wednesday morning arrived bright and early. After breakfast Hong Wei informed me that we had to go and see another uncle and aunt, who lived in another city. Pan Pan's husband, Dong Bin, obliged us again by being our driver for the few hours it would take us to get there and back. The usual sights greeted us on our travels from the back of Dong Bin's 4x4 vehicle. As regards a motor vehicle, it was a beautiful piece of work and only a year old.

There were people selling anything and everything from stalls on the side of the road. The road sweepers could be seen with their distinctive orange coloured overalls and their long palm brushes keeping the highways free of discarded litter. There were long cargo trucks, vans, buses, cars and motor bikes all heading north in the same direction as us and similar vehicles passing us going south to Anshan city. They were all on a mission. The infrastructure is first class, as regards the layout and the thinking that went into its construction and direction.

Just over an hour later, the three of us arrived at Hong Wei's uncle's and aunt's house. They were a very elderly couple. Again, the welcome was sincere as I could see it in their eyes the minute they opened their door. They were very happy to see Hong Wei, but they would have known Dong Bin as well. I did remember them from our wedding in January of 2007. Our arrival had brightened up their day, as they excitedly held conversations with Hong Wei and Dong Bin. I just relaxed with an offer of some fruit, some nuts of every description and Coca-Cola to wash it down. They had good hearts, but I knew they had seen hard times too. Hong Wei had a gift for each of them, as she had for all her other relatives that we visited. What a thoughtful woman she is and always has been.

When there was a break in the conversation, Hong Wei's uncle brought me to their bedroom, where there was a large framed photograph of him in uniform at the age of twenty. He was a veteran of the 1949 war, and he showed me his commemorative boxed medal showing the years 1945–1949. I could see it in his eyes; he was totally committed to the cause. Who was I to judge, it was their country, their beliefs and their decisions? After two hours in this gentle couple's house and after persuading them to get in front of the lens of the digital camera for a few photographs, it was time to leave. Handshakes and hugs were exchanged in the beautiful summer sun on the path outside their modest house. We waved them goodbye, as they did likewise and then we departed down the steps and into Dong Bin's 4x4 vehicle. It was in the late afternoon when we got back to Anshan city and then arrived at Dong Bin and Pan Pan's high rise ultra-modern apartment. It was time to rest, which we did. We had some food later that evening. I was given the freedom of the television channels, where eventually I managed to find a Chinese Super League game.

The following day was Thursday, not just any Thursday – it was a Thursday with a difference. It was Hong Wei's birthday, which falls on April 25th. On awakening, I gave Hong Wei her card and present, all the way from Ireland. That was followed by a kiss, a hug and a smile.

We took it easy during the day, with just a visit to one of her sisters, where we spent most of the day. We had arrangements made just to go out with her son, Jin Yang and his future wife Wang Hao for a quiet meal around 18:00 that evening. Hong Wei didn't want a full-scale party, as that could have been arranged easily too. But I respected her wishes, as it was her decision and her day in the sun. When it was time to go to the hotel for our meal, unknown to the two of us, a surprise was waiting. Going upstairs and behind a closed door were all her family. She was surprised and shocked with the attention and well wishes from all of them in turn. Now I knew how hard it was to keep a secret in China.

The presents came shortly after the food was ordered. As regards food, there were all kinds of everything on the two large round tables, which were to cater for everyone. Again, choices had to be made by me, as regards what I would eat and what not to eat. But there were always one or two dishes that would catch my eye and they would get the benefit of the doubt. Everything was trial and error in my experiences when it came to food in China. There were a few boxes of Qing Dao bottled beer ordered too. Mr. Liu and I availed of it without going slack on our elbows, from the bottle to the glass and finally our mouths. It was time to celebrate and why not! When the time arrived to sing during the night, 'Happy Birthday' in Chinese got a full airing from the lungs of all that were present. Hong Wei treated those present to a song or two from her unique voice, which as always got a fantastic response from those present.

Then there was the birthday cake, which had to make its entrance at the appropriate time. When the time was right, her son Jin Yang made an appearance from a separate room, pushing this rather large birthday cake with lit candles. With her family members watching, Hong Wei made the effort to blow them all out. There is no need to tell you how many candles were on the cake. She did eventually blow them all out, to rapturous applause. It was a huge cake, and one of her sisters divided the cake equally into moderate slices for the would-be takers. I was not giving up my slice for anybody, particularly when I saw the strawberries and the cream oozing on top of the light sponge beneath. It was a beautiful piece of work from master bakers. I did say at the time, with Hong Wei translating, that we sent compliments to the bakers. They certainly knew how to bake a birthday cake here. I was going to forget about the calories for one night.

The evening wasn't over yet, as her son, Jin Yang, had also ordered a Karaoke session. When our bellies were full, we just had to move to another large room in the hotel where a Karaoke music box and large screen were set up with microphones. Karaoke sessions in China are very popular with the people in cities, as most of them love to sing at any time of the day. Well, the people I met on my travels did lots of singing! Loads of songs were sung by those present, obviously in Chinese, which was understandable.

Her mum, Wei Qui Wen, gave me a rendition of an old Chinese song, to which I warmly thanked her, with a kiss and a hug. She was such an alert lady for her good age. She also knew about hard times; rearing her six children with her late husband, back in the late 1950's. I learned a lot about the qualities in this woman, not just on this visit, but on the other visits as well. Her body language told me all I needed to know about her. It wasn't just reserved for the football field in my scouting job for Newcastle United. I would be confident of studying body language on anybody over a period of time and not be far wrong! I suppose the night wouldn't have been the night without my participation in Karaoke. I sang two or three songs, but I would have been lost without the microphone, large screen and voice over. I genuinely can't even sing in the bathroom. But I didn't disappoint anyone there either, as I naturally sang in English.

Again, a great night was had by all that were there. The younger children with guardians had departed earlier. The end did come, with the clock beating us to it, as it struck 23:30 sharp. We accompanied Dong Bin back to the apartment. How ironic and true, that the clock was striking midnight as we entered our bedroom. It had been such a long day and night, our eyes closed almost immediately on hitting our pillows. That was Hong Wei's birthday over for another year. Did I ever think one day I would be celebrating it in China? How appropriately it fitted into the occasion. The Eurovision winning song for Ireland one year and sung so excellently by the talented Johnny Logan was called, 'What's another Year'? We'll leave it at that and remember the happy occasion!

Boy, was I tired on the Friday morning. I knew I had sunk a few extra beers… We had made arrangements to go early to a local park, named 219, where Hong Wei was to meet a cousin of hers.

With no breakfast of any description got, we reached the perimeter of the park, where her cousin was waiting patiently. On greeting her and introducing me, we went to a nearby little small roadside cafe. A lady emerged from the back, as we entered the front door.

I knew from her appearance that she had been busy serving people earlier before we arrived. The cafe had three tables and twelve chairs. This was as basic as it got and with the small display of food on offer, I could see why. It was mainly used for workers rushing to work and grabbing a hurried quick bite to eat on the way. Hong Wei and her cousin ordered, but I declined. No disrespect to the lady that ran it, I'm sure she was a good honest hard-working person. But my body didn't feel good. She even sat and conversed with us, while I just listened to the three Chinese ladies talking. This was around 09:00 and I was reliably informed by Hong Wei that this little eating house opens its doors to the passing public from 05:00. I wondered, at what time did this lady really start preparing the food. These four hours were the peak time for her and after 09:00 it was just the passing trade. But whatever she earned on a daily basis, she deserved it. This was hard work, but then again as I have said earlier in the book, the Chinese people do know how to work hard. I have seen enough to convince me over the years. I stand by that judgement and statement.

After saying goodbye to her cousin one hour later, we then had to meet her other sister Hong Wei 1 (whose husband was Sun Guang) in the nearby park, as their son Niu Niu was on a school outing and picnic. There was a huge amusement area in a section of this park, where the different schools could bring their classes at different times for a treat. There were other schools there on that morning, as we could see as we approached. There were different coloured tracksuits from the various schools. Niu Niu was like any child of his age, he was full of energy. His mixed class were under the strict supervision of two young female teachers. I could see they handled their positions with authority, discipline and responsibility. The age group was around five.

The parents were allowed to be there, as a picnic was scheduled for all the children afterwards. This was a wide-open grass-covered area. The parents all had food with them, and they pooled it all together. Niu Niu and the other children also had food which they took from their lunch boxes. They wasted no time in quenching their thirst and feeding their hunger. By the parents sharing the food, it meant the children all had unlimited choices of food. This was a big plus for them. This for me was an eye opener and it was great to see. It showed me a fine example of togetherness. All for one and one for all. I was sure that this togetherness and sharing would stand to these children in the future. All of the teachers were there with their own classes and gave the children plenty of time to play and enjoy the sun as it shone down on the future of China. The end of the picnic eventually came, and all of the children dispersed and made their way to their waiting parents.

There was a huge amusement playground nearby, which had not been on the itinerary for Niu Niu's class as far as I knew. He was all excited at the sight of the big wheel and to my surprise, asked his mum Hong Wei 1 could he go up on it. She and Hong Wei were a little scared of heights, so I gladly obliged. It was all about the excitement on his face, as we made our way to the big wheel. We got into the bucket seat, pulled across the safety bar and it took off upwards. We got to the top point where we had a great view over the park and looked down on his mum and Hong Wei below. They looked up and got big waves from the two of us.

The chair-o-planes were next, then the merry-go-round and finished with the water boat conveyor drop. This was where you went on a narrow tube-like boat on a track conveyor belt in a man-made pool and ended climbing to a dropping point. It was then straight down on the tracks, where a big splash brought it to an end. Through all these things, I could see the excitement on his face, it was priceless. It brought my mind back to my own two children when they were young a long time ago. I suppose we had to finish with an ice cream and Niu Niu's wide smile appeared again, when I mentioned this treat. After spending another hour in their company, we said goodbye to her sister Hong Wei 1 and nephew Niu Niu.

Hong Wei and I wandered off along a path at the side of the lake. I noticed a group of men fishing together. This lake has a lot of small different species of fish swimming in its waters. You can see them swimming just under the surface. The extraordinary thing I noticed about this group of men was their fishing rods did not have any reels attached. They were just long fibreglass rods with just a limited piece of line and a hook on the top. That was it. How they would have reeled in the small fish, I just don't know. Perhaps it was the bait or spinners they were using. Did they eat them? I doubt it. Perhaps it was just for the thrill of catching them. They more than likely would return them to their natural habitat. I did not wait around long enough to see. Having given them ten minutes, I didn't see any fish biting. Perhaps it was the presence of an Irishman there.

We returned to our temporary accommodation in the tower block and took it easy for the afternoon. Hong Wei made a nice meal that evening, which Dong Bin and I took full advantage of. We washed it down with a few beers, of course. We retired early after watching football on the giant television screen. I slept with thoughts of this fascinating country where I was now visiting on my seventh trip. Tomorrow was another day. I wondered what would it hold for me.

Hong Wei and I rose early, around 08:00 and said we would have a nice leisurely day. No arrangements were made; it was just a case of doing whatever came next. I wanted to take a few photos around the city, and this was as good a time as any to avail of the free day and use the opportunity.

Weather-wise, it was the best day so far as we set off from the tower block around 10:30. The sun was shining, but I knew it was not at its glorious best yet. I thought to myself how good it was to be alive and have my health on a day like this. I cast my mind back to several friends of mine, who had passed on to their eternal reward in the later months of 2012 and the earlier months of 2013. It just goes to show you how precious life is and the things we take for granted. There were sick people in hospitals in Anshan city on this beautiful morning and back home in Waterford city, Ireland too. I don't know why these thoughts came into my mind at that particular time, but they did. It's true, as the saying goes, 'Your health is your wealth'. We just don't think about it as often as we should.

Only when it visits us in person, do we get things into perspective. These were just my thoughts on the matter, on that particular day. I looked up to the clear blue sky and thought of the man above. Why, I don't know. We took in a few everyday sights with Hong Wei's directions, we achieved our objectives. The time for lunch arrived and after looking at the menu in some restaurant, I was willing to try a few new foods that I had not tried before. Not saying I liked them, but I had a go. Some were going to be tried again, when my hungry stomach called. The other foods would not be getting a second chance!

The clock was striking 14:00 as we finished our meal. The day was now extremely hot and beautiful. The sun had kept its promise and not reneged on us, which was great.

"Do you fancy doing a bit of shopping, Billy?" Hong Wei said.

"Of course, if it makes you happy," was my reply. It was just her way really of saying: can I do a bit of shopping. I viewed it as a day less that we had to plan for. What was to come, reminds me of the opening line to an old classic song, 'There may be trouble ahead'. I suppose I'm like most men when your wife wants to go shopping. I can go to a department store, but me personally, I would just prefer to sit on a seat and let them off to their hearts content.

Emerging from her first store, Hong Wei's phone rang. It was her future daughter-in-law, Wang Hao. She wanted to meet up with us and do some shopping too. When we met her a few minutes later, the expedition was on when it came to shops. The main city centre shopping area in Anshan has hundreds of shops and department stores. You can buy just about anything and the choices are endless. The prices compared to Europe, are a giveaway. The next four hours were spent looking, searching and going up and down elevators in various stores.

I made the conscious decision after one or two shops that I was opting out. I said to Hong Wei, "Ye look around and take your time. No rush. I will be here on your return." As it was such a hot day, I perched myself outside the main doors of the stores at street level. I didn't care how long they took, but sometimes I did ask myself, 'How long is long?'. As regards people, I just watched this part of the world go by.

I saw poverty at its lowest ebb over the course of my visits. I must stress, it is no different than in other countries. On this occasion, my eyes scanned the nearest street or open space. There were individuals begging for no more than the throwaway change from the passing hundreds. These sights saddened me, as I said to myself, 'How have their lives took them to this point? Where was their next meal coming from? Where would they be spending the night?' Most of them were dressed in rags and didn't have any baggage except the clothes they stood in.

Some people got into their expensive cars and didn't even give them a glance, let alone money. They looked expendable. I thought that was very sad. The imbalance in the world today is wrong. It shouldn't be like this, but it is the world over. The well off want more, the middle class strive to keep their heads above water and the poor just want to survive and don't even think about tomorrow. I don't know where the answer lies. I think the governments and politicians are the only people with the answers. But in some cases, greed and power rule. I have seen it all over Ireland too; the poor are forgotten by most. These sad sights ruled my mind while I sat idly by, waiting for Hong Wei and Wang Hao to emerge from their shopping trip. Sadly, I could not change things, or peoples' circumstances.

Both of them did eventually see daylight, when they emerged from the last department store on their itinerary. The time was 18:00 on the dot, but there was no sound of the Angelus bells ringing anywhere. Wang Hao insisted on getting us dinner. We went to the nearest restaurant, which was just across the road. The usual choice of food was there and a few new ones, but I stuck with the tried and trusted. We exited that particular restaurant around 20:30 and summoned a taxi. Again, with so many taxies continuously spinning around this city, a minutes waiting time was all it took. On this, my seventh trip, I did not see the same taxi driver twice. What does that say?

We dropped Wang Hao at her designated stop, and we got to the apartment block a few minutes later. As I mentioned earlier, most Chinese people go to bed early, but get up early too. Hong Wei followed suit, but as it was Saturday, I decided to watch the television and see some foreign football. It just so happened that Newcastle United's game versus Liverpool in the Premiership was scheduled on the fixture list for that day. I knew it would be late when I got the result, but I had all night. It was after midnight when the results were coming in. In hindsight, I too, really should have gone to bed early, like the rest of them. I was shocked, as Liverpool had won 6–0. This was our worst home defeat since 1925, which upset me no end. The manager, Alan Pardew, was not my favourite person at that time, on hearing that result. Unacceptable! I thought to myself, 'Mr. Pardew, I think it's time for you to go!'. I didn't think I was alone with those sentiments. The texts on my phone from Ireland started to come in from fellow Geordie fans at an alarming rate. They were all giving me their views and comments, most of which I agreed with.

Mr. Liu had rung Hong Wei during the day to tell her that arrangements had been made for me to attend my second league game the following day, which was a Sunday. These were the thoughts I slept on, as I somehow had to blot out Newcastle United's result as best I could and as soon as possible. The hours passed and then I awoke from a torturous sleep. The only consolation was that the sun was shining brightly.

Mr. Liu was a big football fan, like me, and a Liaoning FC fanatic. Liaoning were playing Quindao, in the city of Shenyang. Hong Wei and I hurriedly ate our breakfast. Mr. Liu arrived on time driving a minibus. Like me he was always punctual, and he was always in good humour too. We joined the other five occupants as Mr. Liu introduced me to them. Some of them I knew as I had met them before. As always, they were all friendly and Hong Wei was enjoying their company too. The conversation between them all was great for me to hear. If only I knew what they were saying!

On the way to the match, as always, the adrenaline starts to flow in anticipation of what the game might bring. The game of football in China was slowly getting more popular in 2013. We had a supply of food and water on board, in anticipation of the long hot day that lay ahead. The traffic on the motorway was heavy and we did pass some other fans on the way to the game too. We acknowledged them by the tooting the horn when we saw the Liaoning flag being displayed by its occupants. But as the time rolled on, so too did the mileage on the clock. Mr. Liu was a good driver, which I knew as I had observed him in his car numerous times. He knew when we were approaching Shenyang city and how to get to the stadium.

As you have read earlier, I had been there before. We found our way to the parking area and dug into the food and drink first. Surprisingly, there was no alcohol to be seen. For me I would have declined if there was anyway, as I never indulge in alcohol before any game. Hong Wei had a lot of fruit, which I devoured. The Liaoning fans were out in force, with their red replica jerseys and flags in abundance. We had ours too, which looked impressive. Mr. Liu had the tickets, which he gave to us all.

It was a welcome sight, as we took some group photographs and then approached the correct entrance. The banter and singing from the opposing fans all added to the atmosphere. There is always a huge security presence around the entrances, where police and stewards are to be seen. All bags are searched; as mine was and a bottle of water was confiscated. The army were present inside the stadium at various points. I had no problem with that. I think it's still a good policy to enforce, as prevention is better than cure. Plastic bottles with water in them can do damage if thrown as a weapon. I want to state quite categorically, that I did not see one incident of any description, during this match or the previous one. I had my sunglasses, my camera, hat and a scarf that Hong Wei had bought for me outside the grounds from one of the many stalls that were present selling their wares.

We took up our good seats with a great view (thanks to Mr. Liu) and waited for kick off. It was only about a half hour away and the time passed quickly, as I continually looked around the stadium at the fans from both sides. The atmosphere was good and boisterous, as you would expect. Everybody loves their own team and that will never change. No matter what league they are playing in. That's life and who would want to change it! The two teams made their entrance to rapturous applause and had a short kick-about to get a feel of things.

The referee tossed the coin between the two captains and within seconds the game was on. The to-ing and fro-ing of the game added to the excitement of all that were present. Even Hong Wei was joining in with the singing, which I was pleased to see. Liaoning were holding their own against a good team and were rewarded with a penalty from a generous referee midway through the first half. They held the lead to the break, but I knew Quindao were still a real threat. Mr. Liu asked Hong Wei was I enjoying the game and she assured him that I was.

The second half commenced, and I could see that Quindao were after upping the pace and were fully intent on equalizing. This resulted in Liaoning being on the back foot, as the mounting pressure started to show. A few chances went abegging on Quindao. Liaoning FC rarely threatened. The clock was ticking away, as the finish line approached. But as I have said on numerous occasions, it's all about putting the ball in the net. I was continually looking across at the giant clock to see what it had left to go. Liaoning's defence were holding firm, but they conceded a free kick on the edge of the area. I remember what happened next quite well, like it was only yesterday. The striker struck it sweetly around the wall and into the top corner. The Quindao players celebrated wildly on gaining a point, as well they might. It was inevitable that they were going to score at some point. Most good teams score late in some of their games.

It's all got to do with self-belief, I suppose, and considering the amount of possession they had in the second half. Jubilation from the Quindao fans and quietness from the Liaoning fans followed. The game finished on time, with a score line of 1-1. It would have been a big scalp for Liaoning, had they pulled it off, but it was not to be. I always say this – my views are well documented on this, as regards football: If your team is winning, the closer you get to the finishing line, the more concentration is needed, from a defensive point of view. Why surrender, what you have worked so hard for (in this case the previous 85 minutes) throughout the game? But that's football in my opinion, one of the most unpredictable sports in the world. As they say, it's never over until the fat lady sings. It was not the end of the world, considering the 6-0 defeat to my team that I had to live with the previous day. We left the stadium and returned to the minibus, where the lads were showing the signs of disappointment on their faces. Jokingly, I told Hong Wei to tell Mr. Liu to start up this bus and let's get out of here. It was difficult to get away early as the volume of traffic was as you would expect – heavy! But I had enjoyed the occasion and the experience.

We eventually reached Anshan city where Mr. Liu dropped off the gang at various addresses and then delivered the minibus back to the owners' premises. We then went for a meal, all three of us. The various foods of one's own choice went down well, and the Yanjing beer went down even better. We finished the night with two taxies and went our separate ways. Sunday April 28th was fully down, over and out.

Monday arrived (everybody's favourite day) and unlike Bob Geldof naming one of his songs, I don't like Mondays. I did like this Monday, because I had no work. I was in a foreign land and had no idea how the day would end or what it would bring.

As things happened, Hong Wei informed me that she and one of her sisters had to go to one of the hospitals to check on a few things concerning women. She assured me that everything was okay and that Mr. Liu would be calling me, as she knew I wanted to go to the city centre and get a map of China in English. Mr. Liu had very little English, but I was always able to read his body language. He picked me up and brought me to the main bookstore in downtown Anshan city. What an impressive store it was, with its four floors of books and stationary goods. Mr. Liu insisted on buying the map for me, which I thanked him for. His daughter Liu Jin Chi worked in a bank across the road and he suggested we drop in and say hello to her. It had been a while since I had seen her.

We entered the bank and she was surprised, when two unexpected and uninvited guests arrived at her desk. She is a very intelligent, beautiful and outgoing girl with a great personality. She had some English, but a lot more than her father. The clock was striking 11:30 and coincidently she was starting a lunch break. Without hesitation she suggested we have lunch in a nearby restaurant. Entering, I notice this restaurant to be a little different than the rest. It looked a popular place as I noticed a lot of people eating what looked like European food. I saw steak, chips, mushrooms and noodles were all being served around the place.

We got a table and she said, "What would you like, Billy?"

I replied, "I'll try the steak, if that's okay with you?"

I was about to eat my first ever steak in China, with all the trimmings and with a knife and fork. I must say it was beautiful and even nicer when it was washed down with two cold Tsingtao beers. I returned an empty plate to the waitress on her arrival after a half hour. Mr. Liu and his daughter had a noodles dish.

"Billy, I insist on you having dessert here," said Liu Jin Chi.

"Okay then, why not?" was my reply.

The arrival of a square sponge cake with toppings of cream, chocolate, fruit and ice cream was irresistible. It was amazing to see how the baker had managed to do it. Ah to hell with it, I thought, what are a few more calories going to do? When am I going to have something like this again? This was going to be a rare treat for me, as I got ready to take the plunge with a fork at the ready. They abstained and just looked on with smiles on their faces. I wanted to pay, but Liu Jin Chi insisted on paying for it. Finally, with the desert eaten, she had to return to work. She is a daughter that any parents would be proud of. After escorting her back to the bank, Mr. Liu and I returned to the hustle and bustle of the main streets and reality.

People were going in all directions and I presumed all with a particular shop or store in mind. As we were walking at our leisure, I happened to look in one direction and saw a small crowd of people. What's this, I thought as I ventured in that direction. There was no need to be shy here, as this was basically downtown in a city in China. Mr. Liu was hot on my heels and intrigue was etched on his face. Finding my way to the top of the crowd, the sight that greeted me was an eye-opener. There was a man with no arms sitting on the ground painting with a brush in his mouth. What a sight to see! He had a blank square of paper sectioned off in square segments on the ground. Opposite it he had a book with all the Chinese symbols in it. He was painting copies of these onto the blank squares in front of him. There was a jar of black paint in front of him, as he continually dipped the brush into the jar, holding it between his teeth. What an extraordinary feat this was when you saw it live. He had one chance to get it right with every stroke of the thin brush from his mouth. If it slipped, the sign was ruined, as there were no room for error. He had people waiting for their own signs.

There were several things crossed my mind as I saw this unfortunate figure in front of me. One was the way he was fighting against the odds. To me, this was a case of survival of the bravest, not the fittest. I wondered how he opened the jar? How did he close it again? How did he get dressed or even undressed? How did he feed himself? How did he even go to the toilet? This man wore only a coat over his shoulders, T-shirt and shredded trousers. A pair of shoes that were nearby and looked like their life was coming to an end. You could practically see through them and no socks to accompany them. After all his feet were his hands and fingers. Again, I thought what a cross to bear and did this poor individual deserve this. These were the cards he was dealt but was it fair? The people that were witnessing this amazing feat, like me were spellbound. Mr. Liu witnessed this too but remained calm.

The man only had a collection of coins in front of him and an odd note in money. For every person that gave him something, he stopped painting and thanked them personally. This was indicating to me how grateful he was. Remember, they were only coins. The smallest paper money was only one Yuan, just ten cents. For the time I was there, I didn't see any other paper money being given to him. I thought again, who but for the grace of God go I.

As Mr. Liu and I retreated from this scene, the man turned the pages of the Chinese symbols book and he got a new sheet of paper with the blank squares on it to start afresh. All this was done with his feet – what a feat. It was quite amazing how many people passed without even giving him a glance. I thought about him long after I had left the scene with Mr. Liu and again the next day and the day after, such was the impression he left on me. I thought I might see him in and around the city centre on my occasional return visits with Hong Wei, but it was not to be. As time passed and on occasion, I did think about him and where he was now. Mr. Liu and I returned to the apartment in the early afternoon. He stayed a while, as we watched football. He said goodbye when Hong Wei returned later.

We had some food and took it easy for the evening. Hong Wei went to bed early and I watched some snooker on the telly. As luck would have it Ding Junhui, the Chinese man, was playing at the World Championships in Sheffield, England. He was playing against Mark King, and I was in Ding's corner. Why not? He was Chinese, and I was in China. I thought that made sense and I'm a fan of his since. Ding Junhui is from a city called Yixing in China. After the snooker, I went to bed and chased my lost sleep.

Jin Yang and Wang Hao's wedding was approaching fast, as Sunday May 5th was the big day. The last day of April arrived, Tuesday 30th. Jin Yang and Wang Hao did call over around lunchtime and the four of us went for lunch to a small little hideaway restaurant. After that we went to one of Hong Wei's sister's house to play the Chinese game of *Ma Jiang*. It's usually played by around four people and they play it for a few Yuan. Nothing like Las Vegas now, the stakes are far lower. It's purely to generate a little bit of interest in the game. For us, when I looked at it for the first time, it would be like Monopoly. I worked away on the desktop in the bedroom catching up on the world news. The football news was also at the forefront of my mind. It's always important for me to know what is going on at Newcastle United, the local football scene in my own native city of Waterford and football nationally also.

We returned home to Pan Pan and Dong Bin's apartment that evening and took it easy, until the hands of time took us to Wednesday May 1st. After breakfast, which consisted of two eggs, two bananas and I tried a glass of milk, what a combination that was. Hong Wei and I said we would go for a walk and see where things took us. I remember this day quite clearly, because of what happened next. Walking on this wide footpath outside of our tower block, the sun was again shining. There were very few pedestrians in view, although I did notice a man walking his two poodles a far distance away, coming towards us. Nothing too strange about that you might say, from where we were. But I didn't look too closely, as Hong Wei and I were talking. As the man drew closer, I wasn't surprised to see that both dogs had little jackets on their bodies, one red and one blue. But I was more than surprised to see that they both had matching shoes, one set of red and one set of blue on their four paws. I thought to myself, I'm after seeing it all now! I really thought I was seeing things. I couldn't but stare, much to the amusement of their owner. Hong Wei just laughed at the sight of this. I had never seen that before, shoes on a dog! Have you? You'll have to admit, it is a strange sight to see – even in China.

Shortly after, we got on a bus, which took us to the far side of the older part of the city. These old houses are surrounded by modern tower blocks where there is an old temple-like building built on a hill. We said we'd have a look at it. When you reach the top, there is a view to be seen as you can see across Anshan city from four angles. We did this and took a few photographs at our leisure. With no time limit on us, we retreated back down the hundred or so stone steps that had taken us to this magnificent viewing point. It led us to an old back road in between the older houses. As things happened, Hong Wei got a phone call, which stopped her in her tracks. I drifted ahead, but still had her in view.

I found myself in an area where I could see these long gardens but I didn't know whether they were at the front or the back of the houses. All I know is that most of them had a little vegetable patch where a few things were growing. As it was close to midday, the sun was waving down at me. There was an old woman in her garden as I approached from the roadside. She was washing down the garden path, which was made up of marble slabs. Her vegetable patch was close by and I could see it was coming into full bloom. I knew she took a lot of pride in this garden because of its layout, which was neat and tidy. There was a small shed in the corner of the garden, and I could see it was being used as a hen house. A few hens were clucking away and running around its entrance. I laughed at her and pointed at them, where she beckoned me to stay.

I approached the old lady and said hello to her in Chinese. She answered me back and smiled, while possibly questioning where I had come from. She then entered the hen house and searched around in the straw in a certain area and found two eggs. She brought them out into the sunlight and proceeded to wash them with her garden hose which she had been using a few moments earlier. She gave them to me and nodded her head as if to say, I want you to have them. I accepted them and thanked her. Here was a total stranger and a foreigner at her gate, yet she was generously prepared to give me two eggs. How thoughtful and Christian that was, I thought to myself. I thanked her and insisted on a photograph of this gracious old lady in her treasured garden. She obliged, but still looked a little puzzled at my request. Coincidently, Hong Wei was just finishing her phone call and came into view, as I was retreating and waving goodbye to the old lady's piece of heaven. Such an event is rare and worth recalling, when one is in a foreign land.

Hong Wei's phone call was from her son, Jin Yang, asking her to go to a certain address from where we were presently. This we did by taxi and arrived at Wang Hao's parent's house. They lived on the third floor of another high-rise apartment block and were there to meet us when we arrived. They warmly greeted us in typical Chinese fashion. Jin Yang and Wang Hao were already there. All six of us sat down to a well-prepared meal. There were ten dishes on display of meats, chicken and fish. The chicken and meat passed my lips, but the fish was a no-go area.

A box of Budweiser beer was open, and I made my presence felt with the bottle opener. My camera was taken from its hiding place in my bag and a few further photographs were taken. After spending around three hours there, it was time to go. Thanking Wang Hao's parents for their hospitality, with a handshake for him and a hug for her while saying through Hong Wei that we would see them for the wedding on Sunday.

There was now only three days to the wedding, and I felt the time was flying. Pan Pan and Tiger had returned from Beijing. We spent the evening relaxing back at their apartment, where after a period, Pan Pan, Dong Bin, Tiger and Hong Wei all retired early. I stayed up watching snooker and football on the telly, for a while. There was the offer of a few beers to keep me company, but I declined. My body needed a break from beer before the wedding. I retired too just before the midnight hour, but I was no Cinderella.

May 2nd is a date all of my family remember very well. It was the day on which my mother died in 2007. We all still miss her, even to this day, as she was such a wonderful person. Hong Wei had only been in the country three months and had met her on a few occasions. But life goes on and it did, but she is always in our family's thoughts.

On Thursday morning, Hong Wei had an appointment for a minor complaint in another hospital. We had to be there for 09:30. I wrote these notes while waiting for her in the outpatient's department. She emerged some two hours later. We took it easy during the day, as a lot of Hong Wei's school friends knew she was back in her native city and she was in touch with a few of them by phone.

Mr. Liu had also been in touch with Hong Wei during the day, to inform us that No. 6 of the gang of eleven had been in touch with him and wanted to invite us to dinner that night. It was nice to be thought of by the gang of eleven with invites from all of them in turn. The time was set for 18:30 and Mr. Liu would pick us up at the apartment block. The time arrived and Mr. Liu and his wife, Hong Yan 2 (Hong Wei's sister), duly picked us up on time. Arriving to a different hotel and going to a private room upstairs as was customary for the gang of eleven when entertaining. There to meet us on this occasion was, as usual No. 3 Mr. E and his wife, No. 5 and his wife, No. 2, No. 6 Mr. Muller and his wife, No. 1 and of course, No. 4 Mr. Liu and his wife. I remembered them all, having met them on different occasions previously. They weren't all always available for every gathering! No expense was spared in the sharing of this generous hospitality that was bestowed on us. The selection of foods that were ordered by No. 6 Mr. Muller, had to be seen to be believed. This was always the case, when anyone from the gang of eleven was present. Three boxes of Yanjing beer were ordered to wash it down. The conversation was about everything, especially Hong Wei's new home in Ireland and the country itself.

The current economic climate and the weather were the more fashionable questions that were directed at me and answered by Hong Wei. My camera made an appearance as did their phones cameras and they were all put to good use, with flashes continually in action. With the delicious food from my usual choices and one or two new ones to accompany them gone, things were winding down. The beer boxes had nothing but empty returns in them and satisfaction was on the faces of all that were present. I thanked No. 6, Mr. Muller and his wife for the hospitality shown to us. No. 3, Mr. E and his wife dropped us home by taxi. It was now two days to go to Jin Yang and Wang Hao's wedding. I could feel the excitement building within both families as the days were counting down to their special day. I was looking forward to it and I knew Hong Wei was excited at the thought of it too. Friday May 3rd was another beautiful day, with the sun out early and waiting to greet us all.

When I wake up in the mornings now I say, 'It's good to be above ground!'. That wasn't always the case with me, as in my earlier life, I always took a lot of things for granted. But not anymore, I now look at things from a different perspective.

The date of November 5th in the year of 2013 was to be the year of my 60th birthday. I now treat every day as if it was my last and treasure every minute of every day. You cannot do any better than that in today's world at my age, I suppose.

Hong Wei's future daughter-in-law, Wang Hao, had an appointment at 08:00 to see a doctor about a medical matter. Hong Wei said she would go with her for a bit of support. Afterwards they wanted to go to their apartment and give it a good cleaning before the wedding on Sunday. I knew the apartment was clean, when I last saw it, but if they wanted to do it again, so be it. Who was I to tell them otherwise?

On reaching the medical centre (which was near the 219 park), I left both of them go in, as Hong Wei said they would be at least an hour.

On previous early morning visits to the 219 park, I had seen a street-market on a road outside of the medical centre. I had never previously taken much notice of it, but now was as good a time as any. Of course, Hong Wei in her wisdom, would have preferred me to have stayed in the waiting room. I said to her on this occasion, "I'll be okay. You must trust me. I know where both of you are."

I was reliably informed that this market opens at 05:00 every morning and takes over the whole road, from top to bottom. Everything from fish to fruit and veg, meat, clothes, shoes, souvenirs and jewellery are all there to sell and be bought. But this was to be no ordinary marketplace, as I would soon learn. I started on the left-hand side of this long road and started walking my way slowly up that side. It was an education in itself to see these stall holders selling their goods and at such an alarming rate. Being a foreigner, I was naturally taking my time and observing all these stalls, which I found fascinating. Obviously, my presence caught the eye of a lot of the local people there. But I was oblivious to what they were saying, so it didn't matter. Hong Wei had told me previously, that people mainly get their fruit and veg there. This is a very popular early morning marketplace, compared to others. This was the scene here every morning, hail, rain or snow.

There was one scene that did catch my eye though, when I had gone about fifty feet up this crowded road. I noticed this man in front of me as I approached him from behind. He was sitting on the road by one of these stalls and I could clearly hear Chinese music coming from the square box that he had in front of him. It was like a portable juke box, which had a small set of wheels on it. The man had no shirt and just a rag for trousers. The music he was playing was quite popular, as I had heard Hong Wei singing the same song regularly back in Ireland.

Although I felt there was something strange going on as I approached, by now was only a foot away from him. The man was straight in front of me, as I looked down on him. Then I noticed to my horror the full extent of this man's disabilities. It was a sight that would bring a tear to most people's eyes. The man was tying two pieces of motor bike tyres cut in half with just ordinary twine to the ends of his shins, as he had no feet! One of his hands had two fingers and a thumb. My God, I thought why someone should have to suffer like that. I wondered what he did to deserve all of this. To think of all the murderers, rapists, robbers and child molesters alive in jails all over the world – I bet very few of them have limbs missing or have a disability of some sort.

I asked myself the question, 'Where is the justice in this?'. I looked up to the sky and asked the same question to the man above for a different reason and looking for a different answer. Some people were giving him some paper and coinage money for playing the music. When the man was finished tying the tyres, he got himself ready to push the square music box up the road as the market was winding down. Obviously, he must have been living in the nearby vicinity. It was sad to watch this poor individual pushing his music box on wheels along the road. Here he was shuffling along on the tyres that were covering his knees and shins to protect him from wear and tear. He couldn't even stand up. He was grounded with no supporting limbs. All he had was a trousers', or what was left of it.

Think about it and try and visualise the scene. Ask yourself these questions: How far was he going? How did he manage for the rest of the day? Where and what conditions was he living in? Did he deserve this card in life to be thrown at him? Did he deserve this existence, if you could call it that? These were the questions and thoughts (with no answers) that were going through my mind after witnessing such a sad, sad sight. As I got to the top of the street and crossed over to begin my return journey, I could see that a lot of the stall holders were gathering up their unsold wares.

The time was approaching 08:30, the time to pack up the stalls. I was later informed of this by Hong Wei when I asked her why they were gathering up their stuff so early. Practically all of them had these little small truck-like vehicles, where they carefully packed everything. She told me that there was a strict law in place, where they started at 05:00 and finished at 08:30. It was quite amazing to see the road being cleared by degrees as the time was approaching 08:30. On finishing my walk, the market scenery was all but gone. At 08:30 exactly there was no sign of any stalls in operation. The road was on a busy route and a minute after the time, it opened up to a lot of traffic. The street was full of cars, trucks, vans and buses. It was like there had never been a market there in the first place. The transformation in the road was amazing.

The stall holders with goods left to sell go to other parts of the city and continue as normal. I suppose you could say that this market was an early morning bonus for them. This is the scene here every morning. It was quite an experience for me to see it all happening. I went back and sat on the steps of the medical centre and waited. Hong Wei and Wang Hao appeared from the door of the medical centre shortly after. All Wang Hao's tests were clear and that was good news. Hong Wei was glad to see me, as I was her.

"Are you okay, Billy?" she asked.

"Of course, I am. I just went for a walk up the road," I said.

"I was worried about you," she said.

"No need to worry about me Hong Wei," I said. Then I was informed of our next port of call, which was to give Jin Yang and Wang Hao's apartment a thorough going over (good cleaning) before the wedding on Sunday. Now that was a story in itself. We walked to the apartment and got there around 09:30. Wang Hao's mum arrived shortly after, and then it was all hands on deck. I shifted a lot of the furniture around for them and moved other things that were too heavy. But I'm afraid when it comes to washing windows or hovering floors, I hold my hand up and say, I'm not into that. Call it what you will, but please don't use the terminology 'male chauvinist'. I just wouldn't have the patience.

At around 13:30 the work was finished, to the girls' satisfaction. The place was glittering, from top to bottom. Now it was time for lunch in a nearby restaurant. Not too much, were my thoughts, as we were going out for dinner that evening. Just something to fill the gap or to keep the wolves from the door, as they say in Ireland.

After the light lunch, Wang Hao's mother said her goodbye to us. I must say here and now, Wang Hao's mother and father, who I met later, are two wonderful people. The afternoon rolled on and evening time approached. Hong Wei, Jin Yang, Wang Hao and I went out to another nearby restaurant that we had been to a few days earlier. It was just the four of us for a relaxing meal. It had a good name, so as expected, the meal was terrific. It had the open charcoal fire, which as you know by now, is my favourite way of cooking food in China. Not saying I ate all that was before me, but what I did eat, I enjoyed. When the meal was over and the taxi had made its second stop, we were at our apartment block. We took it easy and relaxed. As usual, Hong Wei went to bed early. I watched some Italian football on the telly for a change and enjoyed it. I also touched up my notes for this book. Dong Bin, Pan Pan and Tiger had been out and returned earlier and went straight to bed. Bed beckoned to me around 23:00 and I obliged.

Saturday 4th May was only around the corner, just one hour away. Another early morning rise was the order of the day. The sun was keeping its promise to shine on us. It was two weeks to date now and it had not disappointed us so far. Finishing breakfast at around 09:00, I thought if I eat anymore eggs, I will be a hen. As the day goes on and being outside with so many eating establishments and with the prices of meals as they are, your choices for lunch and dinner are abundant.

Hong Wei had arrangements for us to go to her sister Hong Wei 1's house. This was to finalise things with her for the wedding, which was less than twenty-four hours away. Understandably I was expecting to take a back seat for most of the day. I went to the spare room where the computer was and checked my emails. I was also about to start reading an excellent book by an English author called Garry Jenkins, relating to the Brazilian footballing side of 1970.

They won the World Cup Final in Mexico for the third time in their history on that never to be forgotten day in the glorious heat against Italy, on a score line of 4-1. Which meant they were allowed to keep the trophy for good. In my opinion and I reckon in the opinion of a great many others, they were the greatest international side of all time. There was so much chemistry, skill, vision, craft, flair and finishing in their game.

Defensively they were suspect, but once they got the ball over the halfway line, they were magic.

For any football fan reading this book, I would recommend they read that book sometime. It's called The Beautiful Team in search of Pele and the 1970 Brazilians. Garry Jenkins went back to Brazil to track them down, one by one. A fascinating read, with such unique interviews and quotes, one of which I will leave you with from that midfield maestro Gerson who said, "Those who saw it will never forget. Those who didn't will never see it again." I couldn't have agreed more with those words. I was lucky to have seen them play. I can die happy in the knowledge and belief that they were the best team we saw. Of that, I have no doubt. Globally, that's the general view of most football fans.

As I was in the privacy of the spare bedroom relaxing on the desktop computer, Hong Wei and her sister Hong Wei 1 were out of sight for a few hours. The time flew past and it was around 14:00 when Hong Wei called me for a bit of lunch, or so I thought! On entering the dining area, I noticed a rather nice smell coming from the kitchen. Hong Wei surprised me with of all things, an Irish stew. Yes, you are reading it right, an Irish stew in China. The one meal which back in Ireland, she makes to perfection. Hong Wei and her sister were not spectators, as they got in on the act too. Have no doubt, my plate was empty after two helpings and there was still some more left. The rest of Saturday was spent with various members of her family calling to the house at different stages of the day and checking on last minute arrangements, for the big occasion the following day.

The remainder of the stew was finished before we left Hong Wei 1's house that evening. Think of an old Chinese saying, 'waste not, wants not'.

We got back to the apartment at the reasonable hour of 22:00 and hit the sack (bed). The other occupants were not to be seen, as they had retired already. The scene was set as Hong Wei and I closed our eyes – the darkness of our room inside the apartment and the bright lights of Anshan city on the outside.

For better or for worse

S unday May 5th was finally here. The wedding day Hong Wei had been waiting for over a year and a half had finally arrived. Her son Jin Yang was getting married to the girl of his dreams, Wang Hao. My plan was just to go with the flow and see where it took me. Weddings are big events in China and taken very seriously by the families involved. Everyone was up early; 07:00 in my case and 05:00 in Hong Wei's case. She and Pan Pan left around 06:00 to get their hair done and the rest. I was washed, showered and shaved by the time Mr. Liu arrived to take me to the hotel.

After a quick breakfast, we still had an hour to kill. I checked my emails to see if there was any news of importance and watched a bit of television as well. Dong Bin and Tiger had left to pick up other people; shortly before Mr. Liu arrived. The sun continued its role in brightening up what I'm sure was going to be a wonderful day, for all concerned, especially for Jin Yang and Wang Hao. To be fair I suppose, it really was to be their day in the sun!

On the way to the hotel with Mr. Liu around 09:30, I did think back to my own wedding in January of 2007. It was all still fairly vivid in my mind. I can recall it passing very fast. I suppose most of the reason was I didn't know what to expect or what was coming next. Regrets? No, I have none whatsoever! Fate and Fengqin played their part in matching me to Hong Wei! Seven years had certainly flown by, all for the better, I might add. In 2013, I studied events with interest.

There was a hive of activity when we arrived at the hotel, as expected. So much so, that we had to go to a nearby street to get a parking space. It's customary for the hotel to put up a big arched balloon decoration in the front of the entrance. It's normally bearing love hearts or some other emblem, something significant to a marriage taking place.

On entering the front foyer, there was a huge gathering of people, all deep in conversation and getting acquainted with each other. Some were casting their eyes in the direction of Mr. Liu and me, after we had made our entrance through the main door. Hong Wei appeared from the gathering and was delighted to see me, as I her. She introduced me to several people, in the relaxed atmosphere. Proceedings were due to get underway at 10:00.

She had to take the official line with her ex-husband and join in with the parents of the couple. There was a guy there hosting the event. Boy, could he talk and make his presence felt. On time at 10:00 the bride and groom arrived under a canopy in this large function room of the hotel.

The guy introduced them and talked about their marriage. Then he introduced a guy to do the official exchanging of the wedding rings. Then the bride and groom shared a toast, amid a huge round of applause from those gathered. I had the cine camera on and managed to get a good shot amongst the other photographers present at the proceedings. They had one designated guy there who videoed the whole ceremony from start to finish. Then the guy introduced the two fathers separately. They both spoke about the happy couple and wished them well in their future lives together. I must say Jin Yang and Wang Hao looked the perfect couple and were cool out. The ceremony eventually closed with the MC guy winding it all down in customary fashion. The happy couple were then showered with well-wishers from all angles. Hong Wei had to stay with the official party of Jin Yang's father Mr. He and Wong Hao's father Wang Yi and mother Zhang Zhong Hua and the newlyweds. They had dinner in a special room reserved for the occasion. I stayed with Mr. Liu as we joined the celebratory dinner in another function room. The selection of food on display was immense.

I had noticed something earlier before proceedings got under way; as we waited in the foyer of the hotel a sight had caught my eye. I had noticed two chefs coming through the lobby and making their way over to a large fish glass tank that contained a lot of live fish. They caught a few of them with a special net and dropped them into rather large buckets that they had with them. As they passed on their return journey, I could see these fish were hale and hearty and they were all splashing around. Then I realised they were on their way to the chef's table. Their number was up, and it was time for them to be served for dinner. The chef's sharpened machetes were waiting to greet them in the kitchen. Sad in a way, but I suppose you could use the same argument as regards the killing of cows, pigs, sheep, horses, goats. They were, here one minute and dead the next. When these fish made their entrance (one for each table) while the other foods were being served, they were quickly eaten by those present, but not by me. You know my views on fish by now!

On each table, there were around twenty-five dishes served. I would say I made my presence felt on around twelve to fifteen of them. Budweiser beer was the host beer. It's not my favourite, but the Chinese seem to like it. Nevertheless, I made my presence felt with that too and with Mr. Liu as my drinking companion.

For any of you readers out there who in the future ever get a chance to visit China, my advice would be, if you don't like what you see, don't eat it, simple as that. Admittedly you will have to try and eat something. You cannot go on holiday and hunger strike at the same time. That's why I would highly recommend you go to Beijing first, as the choice of food is greater and you can gradually ease yourself into your preferred preference. Everything is worth a try, don't get me wrong. It's purely down to the individual, as we are all different.

Hong Wei joined us and her many friends and relatives when she had finished the official meal with the wedding party. Mr. Liu and I sank quite a few bottles of Budweiser. We were there for a pleasant occasion and it turned out to be exactly that. The newly married couple made an appearance after a while and they went around to every table and greeted everyone. Plenty of photographs were taken of everyone present from just about everyone's cameras – mine included. A short while after the wonderful meal was finished. A lot of the invited guests were winding down and saying their goodbyes to friends and relatives they had not seen for a while. A good time was had by all, were my observations of the event. The hotel staff was slowly starting to clear the tables in the function room.

Mr. Liu and I were in the company of a selection of individuals who wanted the party to last a little longer. I'll put it this way, we were the last to leave and that was long after the rest had gone. There was a lot of Budweiser drank between us. If we had been promoting the drink, the company would have owed us a fortune. There were a lot of empty bottles at the finish.

Mr. Liu and I were still standing, but I would admit that we were a little shaky on our feet. Not to be going home early, as it was now only around 15:30 in the afternoon, one cousin of Hong Wei suggested we go to a karaoke, as there was a reservation made somewhere else in the city. Okay was the vote from a show of hands from the last table. We were all still standing (drinking terminology) and in agreement. There were four or five taxies ordered to take this travelling party to the karaoke venue across the city. When we got there, we were shown to a large room upstairs in this establishment. The party got back on track within a few minutes. The labels on the beer changed from Budweiser to Tsingtao, my favourite drink in China.

There was no need for me to be shy here when it came to singing. After all, look how far away I was from Waterford city back in Southern Ireland. Who was going to tell me that I was out of key when it was karaoke? The karaoke is there to be enjoyed by all who participate. Hong Wei's family are not shy either when it comes to singing. Hong Wei herself is a terrific singer, although she never admits it when I tell her. She doesn't need to improvise with the karaoke machine. Mr. Liu and I kept our drinking elbows in constant use and it was nice to think you sounded like Frank Sinatra (who I think was the best singer of all time), Elvis Presley or any other famous singers when your turn came to sing any of your favourite songs.

The time was moving on and so too was the alcohol through the system of Mr. Liu and me. The karaoke was a good laugh, and everybody present enjoyed the session. Before it ended, someone suggested we finish with some barbecued food. Some of the party dropped out and a few more were up for it. Mr. Liu, his wife and Hong Wei were staying the distance with me. Two taxies were ordered, as it was now around 19:30. We then went to another restaurant, somewhere – I can't remember where, with what alcohol I had consumed!

I thought barbeque meant outside, but in actual fact it meant cooking the food on the open grill. The label changed on the beer bottles again, to one which I did not recognise. I said to myself, 'Billy, be careful now as you are on the home run. Don't mess it up by mixing your drink.' I just sipped away on the one beer and ate the delicious food. Mr. Liu was a little tipsy too, but it was relaxing and the craic was good.

Around 21:00 the charcoals from the two fires had slowly come to the end of their lives. I for one was now at the end of the road in the food and drink's department. Taxies were ordered for all that was left. I said goodbye to Mr. Liu and his wife and the rest of those present. Photographs were exchanged, as were kisses and hugs. A good day and night was had by all. The celebrations were great while they lasted but had now run their course. It was now time for bed and my body was telling me so big time! On our arrival at the apartment, Pan Pan, her husband Dong Bin and son Tiger were about to retire too. My thoughts were of going to sleep on the great day we had. Hong Wei always dozed off to sleep easily. My eyes closed in the darkness, within seconds.

What a glorious day we awoke to, as the sun was keeping up its promise. The body's recovery was slow, considering what I had put it through the previous day, although it was for a good reason. What I didn't know was that Pan Pan had organised a gathering in their apartment for the Monday afternoon. All of the family that were available turned up at the appropriate time. An Irish stew was on the menu again, which I gladly welcomed. But what a surprise that was, as Hong Wei had knocked me for six again! A meal is their way of communicating and often serves a double purpose. The meal started at 12:30 and finished at around 14:30. One beer was all my body would take, as I had to be fair to that too.

Feeling a little better after the meal and while those that were present played the popular Ma Jiang game again; I caught up on my notes for an hour or two. What was coming next was anybody's guess. Nothing is planned too far in advance here, as most of it is spontaneous. That was my experience in this department. As things turned out, nothing happened. It was the first day since we arrived that we didn't stir outside the door. There was football on in the late afternoon and while those present continued with their Ma Jiang game, I settled down to watch a match. Believe it or not, when that game was over, I settled down to watch another game in the league. I was interested in studying the Chinese football game and have been on my other travels also. As early evening arrived, I treated myself to the last bowl of the left-over stew. That's the secret of it, as it tastes the same as when it's first cooked.

After the football, there was snooker on the telly. The world championships were on in Sheffield in England and had now reached the final stage. The Ma Jiang game was still in progress with the group that was left. Hong Wei was enjoying herself. Whether she was winning or not I didn't know. In her case it was purely for the fun of it. I can assure you, there was no sign of the Las Vegas betting stakes here.

I must admit that I had not shown too much interest in snooker since my hero on the green blaze gave up playing professionally through bad health and loss of form. I speak of the late great and legendary Alex (Hurricane) Higgins. At his peak, there was no more exciting player in the game than the Hurricane. With Alex, you just never knew what was going to happen next. He brought much excitement, skill and flair to the game. Controversy did not escape him either, especially when he had his demons. Quite simply, he was a genius that you either loved or hated! It's sad that he is no longer around. RIP. I also think the game is all the poorer for his passing. For me the only other player that I would watch back then was Jimmy (The Whirlwind) White.

Of the present-day players, only Ronnie O'Sullivan would keep me interested. Incidentally Ronnie was due to play Barry Hawkins in the final. He had beaten China's Ding Junhui a few days earlier at the quarter final stage. I watched the snooker until late, as Ronnie O'Sullivan was winning and keeping me interested. Ronnie eventually crossed the finishing line. I was pleased.

The game of Ma Jiang had long finished, and Hong Wei had retired a little earlier. But now sleep was kicking in on me too and the body was telling me to go to bed now.

I had heard a whisper during the day, that my great friend Mr. Liu had something on the football front arranged for me the following day.

Tuesday came and it was a far busier day than I thought. The weather hadn't changed, in fact it was even warmer. Following breakfast, Hong Wei's nephew, Tiger wanted me to go for a walk with him, as he wanted to show me some place close to his mum and dad's apartment block. He had a few days off from his art studies in Beijing and was taking it easy. This place happened to be right under my nose for the previous two weeks, but I had not checked it out. Where these new high-rise apartment towers were situated was called The Whistlers. Don't ask me why or where they got this name from. There are other small private ground level apartments in this complex as well.

It was around 10:30 when Tiger showed me the start of what turned out to be an amazing area – I would go further and describe it as a sanctuary in the middle of this apartment area. It started with a constant fall of water flowing under a little footbridge in amongst specially selected large stones that were strategically placed in different spots, but they were all still connected to each other. This allowed a natural walking path to be formed in the middle, surrounded by hundreds of exotic plants and numerous small young trees that were scattered all over. The water, the path, the big and small stones, plus the trees were all spread out in a downward continuation. We followed it until we came to another footbridge that brought us to the lower part of these apartments. It then broke into a clearing, where to my surprise a man-made lake appeared.

Tiger said to me in his broken English, "Billy, let's have a look at the fish." Looking closely, I could see there were fish swimming around in this tranquil setting of every colour fish you could imagine. There were red, blue, yellow, green, black and even multi-coloured ones. Don't ask me what kind of fish they were, except some were big and some were small. There was nicely constructed decking outside in various places with tables and chairs provided for residents, tourists or visitors. You could completely switch off here from the pressures of the day, just relax and take in the views.

Tiger and I did relax at one of the tables for a few minutes. The sun was beating down on us and I just thought there and then, this could be heaven. No noise with very few people around and the beautiful scenery that surrounded us. After a few minutes there, we proceeded along the decking to the far end of this narrow lake. This was the last area of this sanctuary and it provided us with a fountain artistry display. I said to myself, this looks impressive indeed. There were all different pipes set in a pattern. They were facing in different directions, different angles and some horizontally. It was a beautiful arrangement and then at different intervals water shot up and out from every angle and in different sequences.

It was just a wonderful sight and I remember saying to Tiger, "Where was this whole place hiding out?" Tiger laughed and was as amused as I was looking at this fountain sight and the wonderful water display it was producing. A classic example to compare it with would be in Las Vegas, America. There you have huge fountain displays outside some hotels and they come on and off to the rhythm of music. I just looked around at what was on view here and the man above came into my mind okay. I turned to Tiger and said, "Tiger, thank you so much for showing me this wonderful place. I can only describe it as a sanctuary!"

It was then time for Tiger and I to return to the apartment block. I was full of praise to Hong Wei and Pan Pan in describing my views and experiences of the wonderful walk, the scenery and tranquillity of the place where I had been for the last hour. To think it was just three minutes' walk from the apartment blocks. I kept asking myself, how did I miss it in the first place?

Hong Wei wanted to do a little shopping downtown. We left immediately, with instructions from Mr. Liu to meet him at a certain shop at a certain time. After the shopping, Hong Wei and I met Mr. Liu at 13:30. He had made arrangements for me through a coach to go and see some school kids of all ages playing in a school. This school's main sport was football. There were seven-a-side games scheduled for 14:00, as we got there at 13:50.

There is strict security at all schools during school hours. The gates are like a musical accordion, only on wheels. They retract when you open them and expand when you're closing them. The coach had the school security guard under instructions to be expecting the three of us before 14:00. After gaining entry, we were warmly greeted by the coach, a Mr. Jiang. Mr. Liu had known Mr. Jiang for over twenty years, and he had already told him of my position in Newcastle United Football Club.

The games were for three twenty-minute periods and consisted of four teams. The age group was from nine to about thirteen and two girls were allowed on each team. The first team we saw all had Barcelona jerseys on them. Their opponents also had Barcelona's away jerseys on them. This I had to ask the coach about. I knew they couldn't all be Lionel Messi, but he had a good answer. "Barcelona is the best passing club team in the world, so we make the kids feel good," he said. I couldn't have agreed with him more with his answer.

They played three twenty-minute sessions, which I enjoyed watching. The next match started around 15:00. One of the teams had Barcelona's third strip, which I found amazing. Their opponents had a royal blue strip and the crest was showing me Chelsea. I inquired to the coach again, where he informed me that they were from another school and had been invited in to even up the teams from three to four. As the second game was coming to an end, the coach made his way over to our vantage point and asked Hong Wei, was I enjoying what I was seeing and was there anyone that had impressed me? Hong Wei passed on the message, to which I replied, "There was a boy in the first game that was technically the best that was there." He was only ten, but I knew he had potential. The same boy was in the area watching the other game with his teammates, when the coach called him over. The coach introduced him to me. I shook his hand. Through Hong Wei, I asked him did he like football, to which he replied, "Yes." Another question I asked him was, "Who is the best player in the world at present?" His reply was simple, "It's Lionel Messi, sir." Surprisingly he then said to Hong Wei to tell me thank you for watching me. "I love football very much," he said.

Mr. Jiang called all his teammates over and they all stood in for a photograph with us. I knew had it been in England, there was every chance that one of the clubs would have taken this boy into their academy in the under-ten age bracket. I knew from my experience in being at the Newcastle United academy, he had potential. The second game finished. We chatted with Mr. Jiang for a few minutes. He thanked me for coming and said, the last two hours were his pleasure. We shook hands and said our goodbyes to the four teams, to which they acknowledged.

Mr. Liu went back to work and Hong Wei and I strolled around the city. We met Mr. Liu around 18:00 and had something to eat. We arrived home around 20:30, a few beers the worse. Hong Wei did say to me, before our tired limbs relaxed, "Billy, tomorrow you will enjoy where we will be going." The days were slipping by, as sure as morning follows night.

Wednesday morning came, as it always does. After breakfast, Hong Wei and I had to meet her two cousins at a designated spot, for 10:00. We got there on time and waited. For me it was in anticipation. Her two female cousins arrived with a man who was the driver of this rather large car. When I say big car, I mean big car. I was directed to the front seat of this high-powered vehicle, as I was a guest. I would say if you were to buy this car in Ireland then it would have set you back about twenty-five grand. The driver was a little quiet when he introduced himself to me. Our destination was a special mountain a few miles outside of Anshan city.

After leaving the city and we had travelled for over an hour, the road got rougher, narrower and quieter with less people on it. We were now in the thick of the open countryside. They pointed out the range of mountains away in the distance, which was our target. While travelling, I had noticed the driver at times had his hand on a walkie-talkie. He was getting continuous messages but answering none of them. Ah yes, I said to myself, I bet he's a policeman. When I asked Hong Wei later in the day, she confirmed what my hunch was. He couldn't have been any nicer, except he was a little quiet. We eventually arrived at this very isolated spot, deep in this mountain range. This was called the mountain of a thousand mountains. The sun was hammering its rays down on us with no mercy. This was a beautiful, quiet and scenic spot. We had gone as far as the car had been allowed, and it was shanks mare (walk) from here.

We started our accent at the rough terrain that started at the foot of this mountain. It was all uphill on the manmade paved pathway. Yes, straight up with no exceptions, even for a fifty-nine-year-old, like me. The steepness of this pathway was taking its toll on this very unfit human being, I didn't know about the other four. After a good half hour of walking, we eventually came to the last hundred steps, which were straight up to the top. My body was now out of breath and I would have gladly sunk a pint of my favourite lager Carlsberg. That was my drink in Tom Maher's, my local pub in my home city of Waterford. There was a clearing there and we were able to look all the way back to Anshan city and the surrounding areas. What a magical view it was, and all for free. A short distance away, there were three small Buddhists Temples to be seen.

Like the other stories you have read, how did they ever get the materials up here to build these temples was beyond me. There was a monk there in attendance, although there was no one else there on that day and at that time, only the five of us. The first thing he informed us, was that there were to be no photographs taken in the temples. He was small in stature, (just over five feet) thin and age wise I couldn't tell you.

Hong Wei asked him the following questions for me:

How long have you been here? He replied, "I have lived here for ten years."

How many monks live here? He replied, "There are fourteen other monks living here."

Where do they get their food from? He replied, "Yes, we grow most of our own food up here and get occasional deliveries of other things."

You look very happy and contented in yourself. He replied, "Yes, I'm very happy here, content and at peace with God."

Going on his appearance, I would say he only weighed around seven or eight stone. He wouldn't have been out of place, if he was a jockey at Aintree in the Grand National or at any other racecourse around the world. The three girls prayed at two of the shrines, and then the monk took us to the third upper shrine, where he had to open the locked gates. This had a cave-like appearance and a Buddha statue like the other two. The girls prayed here also and made a free donation. While this was going on, the monk was gently banging a drumstick at different intervals off a copper bowl. The monk then directed us to a small opening in the back of the cave which was dark, except for a small bit of natural light that came in through the roof. There was a huge boulder which stood guard on its own. It was about twelve feet in height and about five feet in width. I wouldn't like to think what weight it was! There were three equally large tall silver basins in different positions underneath this boulder.

There was no noise only the dripping of water from the ceiling in different parts, which were covered by the two feet in depth basins. The monk invited us to drink from any of the basins with a silver mug. Don't forget it was a very warm day outside! The basins were overflowing at this stage, obviously after building up continuously over recent times. I drank a mugful of the water first and I would have to say, it was the coolest (ice cold) and purest water that I had ever tasted. It was like in the film about the fountain of eternal youth. The clearness of the water was such that I could see right down to the bottom of my chosen basin. I could have seen an ant crawling down there. Seeing this amazing sight and to taste that water, was something else.

We thanked the monk and said goodbye, before retreated from this most holy place, even though it was in the wilderness. The scenery looking back again over Anshan city when an opening presented itself through the wooded area was only breath-taking. It was a lot easier going down than coming up, that was for sure. When we reached the car, it was straight back to Anshan city, leaving this special place behind, with its magical serenity feeling.

Eventually, the hustle and bustle of everyday China greeted us on the outskirts of Anshan city. It was now time for dinner and boy, was I hungry.

A huge new experience greeted me here. The five of us went to a local hotel where the layout was completely different than what I had encountered before. It was like a buffet, where everyone went to a food display area. Meats of every description were to be seen. Chicken and fish dishes were in abundance also. Some of the food was already cooked, but the majority of it was raw. Even the smallest pieces of food to be cooked were all on separate plates. Hundreds of them wrapped and individually displayed. You just picked what you wanted and gave it to a member of staff.

The charcoal idea was gone for the moment. The food was cooked elsewhere and returned to your table. I kept my choices plain and simple. A few bottles of Tsingtao beer were ordered which went down well with the hot food. With that finished, it was time for dessert. What a treat that turned out to be. Ice cream and jelly first, a slice of light sponge with a ton of fresh cream emerging halfway down, accompanied by a chocolate éclair. That was it, over and out, enough was enough! The calories didn't come into the equation on this occasion either.

Karaoke was then on the itinerary upstairs in this hotel at 15:00 in the afternoon. Where else would you see it? Only in China, I thought. All five of us got our voices warmed up for the singing. We enjoyed the next three hours of relaxed singing and eating loads of fruit. Hong Wei didn't need the karaoke; she is an excellent singer anyway.

At 18:00 the singing stopped, as the karaoke came to an abrupt halt. When the time is up, that's the strict rule with karaoke. It didn't matter who passed the grade here, there were no prizes. It was all fun and the five of us enjoyed it. We said our goodbyes and parted. Not before I told Hong Wei to tell them I appreciated their company and to thank them for the hospitality that was bestowed on me for the day.

Hong Wei's son, Jin Yang had a treat in store for us on the Thursday. An early night was called for. Following a good night's sleep, the body was ready for the next experience. What an experience this turned out to be!

Jin Yang and Wang Hao called us at 07:30 after our breakfast. The sun stayed with us on our long journey to a city called Jinzhou (south east) of Anshan city in Liaoning Province. Some three hours later, we arrived in this city of over three million people. I wore one of my Newcastle United jerseys for this journey. We went directly to a war museum just on the outskirts of the city.

This turned out to be a very interesting place to visit, as I was to find out over the following three hours. A lot of it was related to the war back in 1945. It resulted in the deaths of 470,000 soldiers. These fallen soldiers were highly praised as heroes, having fought so gallantly. Their names are enlisted on massive walls outside the main complex. In the Panoramic Picture Hall there is a war scene which reproduces the battle of Jinzhou on a rotating circular screen. Similar to what I spoke about before in the city of Dandong on our visit there. All the history is there to see and read about. I would truly recommend this museum if anyone ever gets the chance to visit the city of Jinzhou. After that it was time for early lunch. We visited a restaurant at random and found the food okay. Plain and simple was the key, as it has always been with me.

The other patrons there always find a westerner amusing to look at. Then again, I can understand why, as they don't get too many other nationalities passing through. It's not strange or surprising when you think about it. After that it was back in the car and a visit to the countryside again. This was to another famous mountain on the tourist trail. It was like other visits to Buddhists temples, as regards access. You can go so far by car and then it's a case of walking further up the mountain. On this occasion the same applied here, as Jin Yang parked the car.

After climbing for a while through a narrow walkway, we came to a vantage point. There we could see two temples close by and a church-like building further on in the distance. There were a group of monks in their red robes, heading in our direction. As we passed the two temples, they were approaching them too. They just looked at us and said nothing, as they weren't in the talking mood. I just thought they were going for food or prayer. We made our way to the main church like building and found access through the main door that is usually open for visitors. We were met with a group of monks all singing and chanting like a mantra. We observed and said nothing, as this went on for several minutes and then there was silence. Then it started up again and continued for a further few minutes. I observed this and wondered how a person could live like this. There were no pretenders here, looking or waiting for a free lunch. These monks like the rest I have encountered on my other visits, are totally focused in their views on life and how they want to live it, with God.

'How come they all have the same look of contentment on their faces?' was the question that kept coming back to me. Why should any of us judge them, for whatever reason? After about ten minutes we exited the building and saw six monks in a group talking outside. One of then saw me in my Newcastle United jersey and said, "Hello."

I was taken aback by this gesture. I doubted if he was a fan or was ever in St James' Park. I approached him and said, "Hello." He asked me through Hong Wei where I was from. She told him Ireland, to which he smiled.

"How long have you been here?" I asked.

He answered through Hong Wei, "Three years."

They were all different ages in this six-man group. After a further few minutes in conversation and as hard as I tried, I didn't manage to convert him into being a Magpie fan. We said goodbye to them. They shook our hands as we left the area. I wondered when the last westerner had paid them a visit. As we were returning, the first group of Monks that we had encountered on the way up had emerged from a building that had very few windows and even less doors.

My appearance caught their eye once more (was it the Black & White jersey, I wondered) as we passed them. On looking back at the larger temple, we could see in a clearing that there was another temple in the process of being built, further up the mountain. We could see the outline of the building and even the stone steps around it. Again, I asked myself the question, how they managed to get building materials up there. It was the same question that intrigued me as before on seeing all of these temples on various mountains. I still haven't got an answer, I'm still waiting.

Further down the trail, Hong Wei pointed out to me a cable car system which was in operation away in another valley. From our vantage point, I could see it was deep in the surrounding green forest and practically camouflaged. On closer inspection, I could see where its journey ended, which was at a smaller and completely separate shrine. I marvelled at this achievement. Steel cables, pylons at intervals buried deep into concrete basses and cable cars. Then to top it all, I asked myself the question again, 'How did they manage to get the tension on the steel cables, in that environment?' I stopped torturing my mind for an answer and just said, "What's the point, sure I can see it all in front of me!" I still shook my head with the wonder of it all though. I was happy to leave them with their secret of how it was done. The answer was safe with me, as I didn't know it. But, I sure as hell would love to know someday! When we got back to Jin Yang's car the clock was striking 17:00.

Just over an hour later, we were booking into our city centre hotel. Our itinerary was forty winks (quick nap), a quick wash and a shave. We were going for dinner at 19:00. Hong Wei told me this was going to be different. I wondered how. We hit the pavement on time and followed the cobbled stones that took us into the darkness of a few side streets.

A warm occasion

Shortly afterwards, we arrived at our intended four-storey restaurant on the main lit up street. It looked like all the rest, but how wrong I was. The four of us entered the restaurant and were greeted warmly by some staff. Jin Yang spoke to one of them and then we were directed to a cool fridge counter. On display was a large a selection of big and small raw legs of lamb. Jin Yang directed me to pick one, which I did and then it was given to a waitress to weigh. Seemingly this was one of the city of Jinzhou's claims to fame, when it came to cooking. No other city around to my knowledge had this tradition of cooking raw legs of lamb from scratch. Boy, was I in for a warm time. If only I had known...

We went upstairs onto the third floor and picked a table in a private cubicle. Jin Yang ordered a few Tsingtao beers, while the two girls ordered a teapot full of hot water. We waited for the unexpected and when the unexpected in the form of the leg of lamb did arrive, it had a different appearance. There was a steel bar running straight through it. The guys that usually put the small buckets of charcoal sticks into the hole in the table arrived, and did the usual, except adding some extra. This is a very delicate job in itself, as you are dealing with real fire and with people in a confined space.

One of them gave Jin Yang instructions on how to cook this thick leg of lamb over the charcoal fire, which had a double steel basin in the table opening. Protruding from the fires was a steel casing, like three steel rungs on a cooking ladder. The lowest one obviously, being the hottest for cooking. I looked at this strange sight and said to myself, we could be here until midnight. This thing will never cook that leg of lamb. The normal heat is warm, from the ordinary charcoal set up. But this was operating out of an outsize steel container, with double the charcoal. I would say it was the closest I was ever going to get to Hell's Kitchen. This really was Hell's Kitchen in a hole in a table.

The heat that was spitting out at us was unreal, as the leg of lamb was in the thrones of hell itself. I wondered what the world-famous chef Gordon Ramsey would have thought of this, if he had been present. Would he have approved of this cooking method, I wondered grinning to myself. I was and always have been aware of cooking food and wondering was it done enough. This was my fear here as the leg of lamb was pure raw going in. I waited in anticipation of the final outcome, plus I was hungry.

This might have been a tradition in the city of Jinzhou, Liaoning Province, China, but I was worried about the outcome to Billy Costine. Where would I be in the morning or would I ever see it? The charcoals were red hot in their pursuit of the leg of lamb. There was no other food for us to cook that night, but the two girls did order some pre-cooked food, to mix things up a bit. The heat was building by the minute. The Tsingtao beer off the cooler was even starting to get a little warm. After a good twenty minutes, the moment of truth arrived. How would this soul have survived the fires of hell for twenty minutes? I felt I was there already, such was the heat. Jin Yang cut off a few of the outer slices with a special long steel knife and a giant fork as well. He then put them on a special wire tray which you can finish off cooking on their own. While this is happening, the main leg of lamb continued to roast in hell, or so it seemed.

Jin Yang took the plunge and sampled it first. Then it was my turn to try this, but I thought it would be raw. No to my surprise it was beautiful and tender. It tasted a little different, but it was cooked right through. I continued to indulge in the slices with Jin Yang's approval. Why not! The two girls ate away on their separate dishes. The fires of hell still burned, with the slowly shrinking leg of lamb being their present victim. After about two hours of cutting and slicing the lamb, the bone was beginning to show. Good, I said to myself, we are coming to the end of this horror show. How wrong I was! Jin Yang beckoned to a waitress for attention. She arrived and took the bones of the lamb away on a tray.

"That was nice, Jin," I said. "A little unusual, but it tasted okay." Considering it was the closest thing to being burned alive.

"Oh no, we are not finished yet," Hong Wei said.

Seemingly they take away the bones with little bits of meat attached and chop them into little pieces, which are then returned to the table for the final incineration on the wire trays. Like a delicacy, if you wanted another word for it. This was duly done and passed around amongst us. We were nearly on the verge of taking off our clothes, such was the heat. But I knew it had to cool down sometime. There were other tables in private cubicles around us with their different sizes of lamb ebbing away slowly too. On completing this rather strange eating practice, it was time to go. Yes, it was quite an experience and one that I will not forget in a while. By the time we got back to the hotel, we had cooled down. A good few Tsingtao beers had passed our lips, in response to our thirst, which was a lot. Hong Wei told me, that we would have a long and interesting day tomorrow.

On Friday 10th of May, all four of us were up early after the night before. It was a lot cooler, which I for one wasn't complaining about. We checked out around an hour later, at 08:30 and headed out of the city of Jinzhou. I didn't know which way we were going, and I didn't care either. Like in all such cases, I just went with the flow. After driving for about an hour, I noticed a lot of police activity at different intervals along the motorway. I knew that there had to be a reason and wondered why. Hong Wei informed me that the city of Jinzhou had recently opened one of the biggest garden exhibitions centres in the world. It had been opened only a few days earlier. By the end of this day, I knew why.

After another short few miles, I noticed that the police presence was getting more frequent. The traffic was slowing down, so I knew queues were building up ahead of us. Away in the distance we could see huge signs displaying their messages, all relating to this monstrous exhibition. On reaching a certain point on the road, we were directed into one of the giant fields being used as car parks.

The stewards used every available space to them. It was all done in a controlled, military style way. There were separate parking areas alone for the hundreds of buses that were converging on this world exhibition.

It was quite a distance from the parking areas to the main entrance, but I was excited at what this prospect might hold. With Hong Wei by my side, I was happy. The wide-open road was lined with police and army personal. Hong Wei informed me that this was a huge daily operation. We bought our tickets and gained entry amid strict security. It would be impossible to give you an estimate of the number of police, army, undercover personal and employees in this massive spectacle. I would say there were hundreds.

There were huge entertainment areas for children and parents. There were acres and acres of planted flowers, shrubs, trees, exotic plants and rare sights within the green world. There were live open-air shows in different locations. There were two giant aquariums, with every fish you could imagine. Ah, this place was just huge and blew me away. There were thousands of people there, all enjoying their particular interest in what they had come to see. The sun of course played its part too, with its downward rays of heat, from its relentless presence.

The most fascinating sight for me to see was a sand area that borders on the beach coastline of this magnificent place. The sealed off inner sand area has been made into permanent sand sculptures based on Chinese history. There was a train, an athlete, a politician and other famous people. Plus, there were several replica places portrayed of historical interest. It really was incredible to see this. The detail in each exhibit was unreal. To think that all of this was made of sand, by talented individuals, I can say no more! Coming away from that extraordinary spectacle, hunger pains made their way to the forefront. It was time for food; we had to choose from the hundreds of food outlets that were distributing their wares to hungry patrons. I kept it basic with just two burgers, chips and Coca-Cola. Hong Wei, Jin Yang and Wang Hao had rice and a few other things, which I can't really describe, because I don't know what they were!

This definitely was the biggest flower exhibition I had seen to date and was ever likely to see. The famous Chelsea Flower Show would have fitted into one corner alone. We spent about five hours there. It could have been ten, although it felt like twenty. Really, to sum it up, this place was simply too big for human consumption. We must have walked about ten miles, such was the magnitude of this location and where it was ideally situated. As we were leaving in the early afternoon, buses, cars and vans were still arriving to this fabulous site.

Hong Wei and I had an appointment for dinner with the gang of eleven, set for 19:00 in a hotel back in Anshan city. Jin Yang knew where the accelerator was, and he used it when it was appropriate and safe to do so. Considering it was Friday afternoon and the volume of traffic heading back into Anshan city, Jin Yang did well. I would have given him ten out of ten. Then again he was a professional driver like me. Believe it or not, we arrived at the city hotel at exactly 18:55.

This time No. 9 was hosting the meal; being late was not an option. He was the first to welcome us, as soon as we entered the private room. No. 3, Mr. E, was there with his wife and was delighted to see us, as he always was. My great friend, No. 4, Mr. Liu, was there and also delighted to see us. No. 5 was there. Pleasantries were exchanged. No. 6, Mr. Muller and his wife were there also. No. 1 arrived a minute after us and was introduced. Apologies were accepted from No.2, No.7, No.8, No.10 and No.11.

Their work dictated where they were at any given time, but it was never an issue with those that were present. On this occasion Mr. Liu informed me, much to my surprise, that I had been accepted into the group as No. 12. Approval votes had been given from the absentees. What a surprise that was and left me a little speechless, for a change! Even Hong Wei was taken aback, as she did not know. That called for a bit of a speech from me, where I conveyed to those present that I was honoured and humbled to be accepted. It was a great night, as usual, when you were in this company. We said our goodbyes and took numerous photographs. I knew this was the last time I would see any of them for another year or two. I said to myself, if my weekly lotto numbers were ever to come up, I would be back here earlier. No. 3, Mr. E and his wife insisted on giving us a lift back to The Whistlers apartment complex. I have always had great time for him and Mr. Liu respectively.

The angels slept with me that night, as I had a few nightmares and pleasant dreams combined, until I woke up. Where they came from, I don't really know! Saturday was to be our second last day in Anshan city, but our last full day. We took it easy after breakfast and waited for Hong Wei's family to arrive in one's and two's, as we knew they would.

After 12:00, it all started to happen as we predicted. Pan Pan, her husband Dong Bin and son Tiger were hosting this going away party for us. Hong Wei's son Jin Yang and Wang Hao arrived with her parents. Hong Wei's mother, her sisters and brother arrived shortly after and then all of their offspring arrived sporadically. You could say the place was kind of full alright.

The pots, pans and other cooking utensils were out in force and about to go to work. It was a kind of mixed emotions really, as all of us waited for the meal. The meal did arrive and was laid out in various bowls of all shapes and sizes. You just took your pick. The meal was accompanied by two boxes of Yanjing beer. There were no full plates at the finish, which pleased Pan Pan. Lots of photographs were taken by family members with Hong Wei and me. They all stayed until late afternoon and then left in dribs and drabs. Pan Pan is very close to Hong Wei and they spoke for a lengthy period. The evening entered the equation and as our departure was the following morning, an early night was called for. My tired eyes obliged my body and closed.

As I have said previously, going away is hard and saying goodbye to your family and friends is even harder. Sunday morning came and that was the case when we got to one of the three railway stations in Anshan city. This had been my longest continuous stay in China of twenty-eight days. This is still a long time in another country, but for Hong Wei, it was a case of leaving her country of birth. All of her family were there and chatted with her until the clock told us it was time to go. Hugs and tears were evident as we entered through the departure doors of which there is no return. The farewell waves from her family became distant and then a blur. Yes, it was the bullet train again and the magic it portrays when you are a passenger on it, never changes. You have to experience it to feel it. As

I spoke about the aerodynamics of the train, there is no need to tell you twice. The train left Anshan city at 09:15 and arrived in Beijing at exactly 15:15. After a journey of five hours, it arrived on the minute. What more can I say about this marvellous feat on tracks? This was just for two days to get a break.

During the journey this time the views had been somewhat different. It looked to me like it was the sowing season, as I saw numerous farmers in the endless fields digging the soil. I'm presuming they were planting seeds, but I stand to be corrected. These farmers who live in this wilderness are amazing people. Their houses are just small shacks in the middle of nowhere. Talking about survival, this was resilience to the core, as I mentioned in my opening lines at the start of the book. How they could cultivate this dry barren land and produce different crops was just unreal. I also noticed that most of the soil is like an orange type of clay.

Eventually, our amazing train ride was over, but prior contact had been made with a cousin of Hong Wei's to meet us. She was originally from Anshan city, but had been living in Beijing for the past eleven years. Sure enough, we had only been on the arrivals platform a minute when Wei Chong arrived. She was delighted to see Hong Wei, as she had known her since their school days. I was introduced to her and she came across as being very friendly and courteous. I was delighted to see her for another reason. We now had someone who knew Beijing like the back of their hand. Even if it was only for a few hours, Wei Chong's knowledge would be invaluable.

We offloaded our luggage after booking into our hotel and we were back on the street, literally within minutes. We made our way to the nearest subway station, at Wei Chong's request, as she wanted to show us how to use it. We had never ventured there before on any of our previous visits to Beijing. It's such an incredibly busy place, that if you were on your own, you would get lost in seconds. Even with Hong Wei, you would need to know the system. As we walked on the wide footpath, on the way to the subway station, one sight amazed and saddened me. I saw a young man around thirty-five with just a rag for trousers. He had no shirt, no shoes and was on his hands and knees or, as it's more commonly known, down on all fours. He was actually barking and moving around through passing people, while pretending to be a dog. Yes, you heard it right, pretending to be a dog. I thought I was seeing things, but he was there in front of me. I stood there and watched this sad spectacle and asked myself the question, 'How low does one's dignity have to go, to resort to this?'. Hong Wei and Wei Chong stood there with me, but I think they saw it in a different light than me.

In that minute or two while we were there, a well-dressed Chinese man approached this individual. He produced a monetary paper note, which could have been one Yuan, five Yuan or even ten Yuan, who knows. Before he gave it to him, (Hong Wei was translating for me) he told him to get up off his hands and knees and not to lower himself to that degree again. He then gave him the paper note, to which the man thanked him. He looked up to the sky, kissed the note and then disappeared into the passing crowd. It was like he had won the lotto, such were his actions. I shook my head and walked on with the two girls.

There is now a lot of security in screening hand luggage in some subways and in the entrances to most of the underground rail lines. The amount of people travelling on the tube system is frightening. The stations are literally packed with commuters of all ages. The trains that I saw were running about two minutes after each other, in both directions. The communication and control centres that run this system as efficiently as I saw it was unreal. Just imagine one mistake and the catastrophe that would have followed. It's the same on all the underground systems scattered across the world, I suppose.

Wei Chong showed us the different routes and how the different time schedules operated. I certainly wouldn't venture down there alone, as with the language barrier, I would be lost in seconds. We took a train somewhere across the city and surfaced in another part of the wonderful city that is Beijing. The three of us then went for food at a restaurant of Wei Chong's choosing. The waitresses were working flat out in this busy food establishment. The food went down a treat and the beers accompanied them likewise. Hong Wei and Wei Chong spoke at length, as they had not seen each other for such a long time, and she was working the following day.

I was content in listening to them talking and checking to see if there was any new food that I was prepared to try. After our meal, Wei Chong showed us a few other buildings of interest even though they were all shutting up for the day by that time. But I took note of them to see if they would be on our itinerary for the following last day in Beijing. Wei Chong had work the following day, so she said her goodbyes to us and disappeared from view. We thanked her and Hong Wei left her know how much we appreciated her help. Hong Wei and I returned to our hotel and ventured out later in the night to the nearest eating place and had a quick snack before retiring and sleeping on the day's activities.

Our last day arrived in Beijing and having been up early and with breakfast finished, we needed to go to the railway station to check something. When we were in close proximity to the railway station and in the midst of hundreds of people in the vicinity getting trains, using the subway and going to work elsewhere, the time on my watch showed it to be around 08:30. The wide footpaths cater for the volume of people that put shoe leather on it every day. It just so happened that another tragic sight met my eyes. There was a man on the footpath coming towards us. He had no legs from the waist down and would you believe it, he was shunting himself along on two smoothing plastering trowels that plasterers use when they are finishing a job. I thought I was seeing things, with this sad sight. Here he was, just imagine, two trowels in place of his legs. How strong must his arms have been? Think of it, every day to be faced with a handicap like that. He wasn't begging, he was just going somewhere. The world was just passing him by as he made his way along the crowded footpath. Such people amaze me, but I respect their courage so much.

Hong Wei done her message and then we needed to go to our next destination. We took a bus, because this was also a new experience for me. This city would wear down our Lord. The bus system is different to that in other cities in as much as you enter by a middle door. Then you exit at the front door or the back door. When you enter the bus, there is a conductor sitting in a box like seat that checks your ticket or sells you one. That's her job all day, in one door and out any of the other two. The National History Museum of China was our destination. For anyone who has not seen this, when and if you ever go to Beijing, this has to be seen to be believed. I had visited other museums in other cities on my visits, but this was the ultimate. This museum was upgraded a year or two earlier, which explained why we had not visited it on our last visit to Beijing. So, it was overdue a visit. It's literally at the side of Tiananmen Square. When we got there, I knew this was worth seeing. I just had a feeling from looking at it. There was a huge impressive entrance with steps leading up to it, which all had been upgraded. Security was at its highest, as we entered the main building. Our small carrier bags were searched and screened. Then you had a row of about ten security people doing a body search on you. In situations like this I always go with the flow. We soon found ourselves clear of any further security and were free to roam anywhere within the confines of the buildings.

I'm sure we went to three levels and there were security personnel all over the place at different points. This museum is huge and houses so much treasure that it's frightening. The architecture of the buildings alone is very impressive, with the marble floors and marble support pillars. Everything that you could think of regarding China's history, culture and political past is housed there. There were rooms of huge paintings, treasures and artefacts of a historical nature. War exhibits from the past and China's historical background. All of these items were accompanied by huge notices in Chinese and mostly English, telling you of what you were looking at.

We wandered around through the three floors at our ease and just took in this massive array of history. There were impressive signs up all over the place, telling the visiting tourists, *NO FLASH PHOTOGRAPHY PLEASE.* You could easily spend the day in there, but as it was, we spent about four hours in there.

One room I must mention was exhibiting presents that were given to the former Chinese leader Mao Zedong from visiting heads of state from all over the world during his reign. On close inspection of the glass cases that most of these presents were housed in, I noticed a Waterford Crystal vase that was given to Mao Zedong by a past President of Ireland, Patrick Hillary. I found that amazing but having worked in Waterford Crystal for twenty-three years as a cutter, it was easy for me to identify it.

Going back out onto the street outside, the bright sunlight was there waiting for us. Hong Wei and I were hungry. We went to the nearest food outlet. I wasn't choosey, I just wanted something to eat and drink. One hour later we were on our way back to our hotel for a rest. It was nice to take a break when it presented itself to our tired limbs. We went out to a small restaurant that night and just had a light meal. This was to be our last night in Beijing for a while. With that finished, we just went for a small walk just to burn off the calories. The nightlife in Beijing is exciting to see and it seems like it never ends, amidst the bright flashing neon signs and continuous traffic. When we got to our hotel entrance, I took one look around and said to Hong Wei, "What a city this is! Where could you compare it to?"

With our cases packed and at the ready for the next day's flight back to the Emerald Isle (Ireland), a good night's sleep was needed.

Wednesday morning's breakfast was short and sweet, as regards what I ate. I kept it simple, as I always did, with two eggs, rice, bread and some fruit. Orange juice provided the thirst quencher. Hong Wei had her usual self – anything goes! Beijing Airport is outside the city and as you can imagine, it's as busy as a beehive. We booked in on time and took a break, while the clock moved on to our departure time. Then, as before on my previous six visits, it was up like a bird and away. It's always a time of mixed emotions, but you have to leave them to one side and think positively about the future and what might lie ahead. The journey can be quite tiresome. I try not to think about it these days. After several hours flying and a changeover in Amsterdam, it was on to Dublin. Then the boring three-hour drive to Waterford city. We arrived back home worse for wear, but after several hours of sleep, normality resumed.

That was my seventh trip to China and what an experience it had been.

The next day arrived and as my work was paramount, I went in and worked my shift. That was the kind of make-up I have. If I told someone I would do something, I would do it. Saturday came and a visit to Fengqin was called for, just to bring her up to speed about her family and friends. This Hong Wei did, much to the satisfaction of Fengqin. The months rolled by and the end of 2013 arrived and went.

The year of 2014 was no different than 2013 in the sense that nothing extraordinary happened for the first nine months. Hong Wei was getting on okay and had a part-time job which kept her ticking over and gave her a form of independence. Her English was improving no end as every spare minute she had, saw her head stuck in a book. I knew she was one determined woman when it came to wanting to learn English.

During the month of October in 2014, word reached Hong Wei through Pan Pan that her mother Wei Qui Wen was not well and was showing signs for concern. Obviously, it was a situation where we had to stay in touch. This Hong Wei did, by telephone every few days. A few weeks passed and her mum's condition was not improving. I said to Hong Wei, "I think you should go to China in case your mum's condition deteriorates, as it will take you too long to get there at short notice."

Hong Wei booked a flight and reluctantly went without me. In mid-November, Hong Wei made the long and arduous trip back to her native city of Anshan in China. She was there for five weeks, where surprisingly her mother's condition stayed stable. She was in touch with me every few days and kept me up to speed. The five weeks passed, and Hong Wei returned to her adopted home in Waterford city. Surprisingly, her mother's condition remained the same. But I knew deep down that the inevitable sad day was coming. The question was going to be, when. To lose any parent at any time is a harrowing experience. It is a defining moment and a time which comes to us all. Such is life amidst the highs and lows.

The new year of 2015 kicked in and understandably Hong Wei's main concern was still her mother's health.

A bad blow for all concerned

Everything was going okay until one bright sunny day in February. The news arrived that Hong Wei's mother had taken a turn for the worse. Immediately contact was made with Hong Wei's travel agent in Dublin. They did their utmost to facilitate her with a travel date, but things were proving difficult. It was fast approaching the Chinese New Year, which is in February. This meant that Chinese people living across Europe and elsewhere were returning home for the festivities. This made things a lot tighter in the availability of seats on flights. But through persistence, her travel agent got Hong Wei a flight.

On the travel date in question, I brought Hong Wei to Dublin Airport and saw her off at the departure gate. Her stay was to be for a month, and I was to go out two weeks after her for two weeks. A week earlier I had applied for my Chinese visa at the Chinese Embassy. Once Hong Wei had departed the Emerald Isle (Ireland) on that morning, I made my way to the Chinese Embassy in Ballsbridge in Dublin to collect my approved visa. I felt lonely on my return to Waterford city without Hong Wei. The one question that kept coming back to me on the journey home was, will she make it in time. We had been told two days earlier that her mum had slipped into a coma. It had been a long day when I finally got home.

I was due to fly out on 4th of March, but in the intervening days, Hong Wei's mother died. Hong Wei rang me to give me the sad news. I knew she was heartbroken over the death of her mother, as anyone would be. I was saddened to hear this, as I had taken to her on my first visit and subsequent visits to Anshan city. She was a small woman in stature, but a woman who had seen hard times, with her husband dying so young in 2000. She had a strong personality, a kind heart and a resilient nature. It wasn't easy to bring up five daughters and one son, but she had.

My plane departed from Dublin to the far-off land where the flag with the five yellow stars on the red background reigns. The usual route was taken – Dublin, Amsterdam Beijing and lastly, was Shenyang Airport. Hong Wei was there to greet me with Pan Pan and the reliable Mr. Liu, my best friend which he still is, when we go back to China. She was delighted to see me, as I was her.

I sympathised with the two of them on the death of their mother and then the bombshell exploded. Hong Wei broke down as she told me her brother Hong Yao Bin had died a few days before his mother. You could have knocked me for six, such was the impact of this shocking news. She explained to me, that her four sisters decided not to tell her this news when she was in Ireland and wanted to wait until she got to China. They felt it was the right thing to do, under the circumstances. I had met Hong Wei's brother several times on my previous visits and found him a very quiet and inoffensive guy.

With respect, what a double whammy that was for the rest of the family. They are a very proud and close-knit family, believe you me. Think about it, your brother and mother to pass away in the space of a few days. With taking in all that sad news, I had to think positively with regards the rest of our stay. The drive to Anshan city was somewhat different to previously as a sorrowful atmosphere understandably hung over the occupants of Mr. Liu's car.

When we got there, Anshan city still looked the same. Some of the main streets I recognised, as we made our way to a restaurant called He-He for a welcome home meal. All the family were there and greeted us accordingly. As before, with a kiss, a hug and a handshake. Their friendliness was very evident and sincere. The food still tasted the same as long as I ate the same.

My opinion is to never, at any time, try to be a hero and eat something just to impress the onlookers. Some three hours later our meal was finished and washed down with several bottles of Tsingtao beer. But tiredness was kicking in fast, with all the time without sleep taking its toll.

Jin Yang, Wang Hao and the addition of their baby son, Hao Yang were not at the meal. Afterwards we dropped over to their place and we gave them presents that I had brought for all three of them. As usual Hong Wei was delighted to see them, as they were likewise. We spent an hour with them, but we had to get to our accommodation, which was lent to us by a family friend. It was 20:00 when we both put our heads down. Tiredness was after passing me out at that stage. I had the longest sleep ever in my life, from 20:00 to 08:00.

When my eyes opened it was Friday 6th. It was a new day calling. What the end of this day would bring, I wondered, not for the first time. But it was breakfast first, as always. I kept it simple, food wise, with no heroics attached.

I said to Hong Wei, "What will we do today?"

She said, "Do you want to go for a massage and sauna, Billy?"

Being a little cautious and curious, having never experienced anything like this before, I said, "Okay, I will give it a go." I still had a few aches and pains from the previous day.

An hour later Mr. Liu and her sisters, Pan Pan and Hong Yan 2, arrived and collected us en route to this whole new experience for me. I stood in a tracksuit and t-shirt. As regards what to expect, that was anybody's guess. Hong Wei reassured me not to be embarrassed. We arrived at this modern day and very impressive building called David Hot Spring Hotel on the outskirts of Anshan city.

We were greeted at the reception in customary fashion, as was the case in all the other hotels that we were in over the course of time. As expected Mr. Liu and I broke ranks with the three girls, as we headed in different directions. We went to the spa area, within the men's area. Here I was going into the unexpected, though not for the first time in my life. As we say in Ireland – in for a penny, in for a pound. What lay behind the entrance doors was going to be all new to me. Going through them led Mr. Liu and myself into a very beautiful, spacious tiled area with dressing rooms, which had no doors. It was just open plan, but still looked private. Boy this was impressive. And it was spotless.

Two male attendants escorted us to our designated individual lockers. Embarrassment and modesty disappeared as Mr. Liu told me to take off all of my clothing. Okay, I said to myself and just did it. Then we were directed into another spacious area by the same two attendants. If I thought the open dressing rooms were impressive, well this just blew me away. This whole floor area was tiled and there was marble seating around and on the edge of these five specially heated pools.

There was an individual clock showing the different temperatures in each of them. They were from thirty degrees to forty-five degrees. You had a choice to enter any of them and stay there for as long as you wanted in each. There was a row of showers where we went first and had a nice relaxing wash. There were a few other Chinese men there as you would expect, using the facilities, which were now impressing me big time.

Everyone sitting around the pools or in the pools was totally naked. No one gave anyone else a second glance, even though I was the only westerner there. After using the shower, I popped into the thirty degrees pool first and spent about ten minutes there. Relaxing and thinking about the world going by and what might have been happening in my country of Ireland and in city of Waterford. I also doubted if anyone from Waterford had been here before me. Then I tried the next pool and the next until I reached the final forty-five-degree pool. On feeling the water with my finger, I said to Mr. Liu, this one is just too hot. I felt if I had jumped in, it would have scorched the skin off my back (in joking terms), such was the heat.

By the way, these hot springs are not manmade, as I had thought. Natural hot springs are the background to these facilities scattered around Anshan city. We then went to the sauna room and boy, was this impressive too. This was a huge open-plan room, capable of holding around fifty people, not like the small sauna rooms in the spa facilities back in Ireland.

After around twenty minutes in there with Mr. Liu I could feel the extreme temperatures. It was time to get out and cool off again. Another half hour passed and then it was time for the inevitable massage. Mr. Liu directed me into another tiled and spotless open area, where there were half a dozen leather bench couches.

Masseurs were in attendance there and warmly welcomed us in. Mr. Liu explained where I was from and that this was my first time being in such a place. One of the masseurs directed me to get on the bench and face downwards. The hot water he poured over me was perfect temperature-wise and felt very relaxing before he even started. He then rubbed down every inch of my body slowly and very professionally, I might add.

This took several minutes, where time was not his priority. It was about him giving his professionalism and expertise. Then he directed me to turn over, which meant I was facing upward. Where, he proceeded with the second half of his routine. I did as he asked and just thought of my favourite football team Newcastle United, which I had supported for fifty-four years then. When he had finished some fifteen minutes later, there was not an inch of my body that had not been rubbed down, but in a very professional way. I rolled off the bench and felt good, somewhat like jumping out of my skin.

Then it was back out to the showers, where I washed again and probably had the best shave I ever had. Then back into the four pools again in rotation with the forty-five degrees one still not capturing this victim. Then it was back into the sauna again, where a further fifteen minutes were spent relaxing. Then it was out for the final thawing out in the forty degrees pool. My mind had definitely not changed about the forty-five degrees pool on this maiden voyage.

They even had a tall and special machine for drying the body from head to toe. I had a go in that too, just to try it out. The spa facilities in this equally impressive hotel were second to none. I couldn't imagine one better than what I had experienced with Mr. Liu over the previous two and a half hours. If there was one better, perhaps it was in heaven!

Ask me did I feel good and recharged after that experience – I was a little tired, but certainly all of my pains and aches had disappeared without trace. We got back to the lobby before the girls re-emerged back on planet earth, some fifteen minutes later. Without delay it was lunch that beckoned.

That meant another restaurant, another menu for the five of us. Over the course of all of my visits to China, I basically stuck to the same food choices, except for the odd change. Again and as always, it was washed down with whatever lager was available. Two hours later when our hungry bellies were full and our thirst quenched, Mr. Liu dropped us off at Jin Yang's house. Wang Hao was there with her baby son, Hao Yang. Jin Yang arrived home from work and was delighted to see his mum, as always.

Jin Yang's father Mr. He arrived shortly afterwards and we chatted. We got on okay and there was never any hint of a dislike between us. They don't entertain bitterness (not like in other countries). Sad as it seems, people here end their relationships and just get on with their lives.

Around 19:30, we went for dinner, where we were met by Mr. Liu. He informed the attendees of our activities and where we went earlier that morning. When the meal was finished, it was back to our accommodation for a night's sleep. As was always the case with me, it was just get through the night and see where the next day takes you. This adventure for me was always open to the unexpected and unexplained.

When Saturday morning arrived, it was another new day dawning. We had a week to go and I knew the loss of Hong Wei's mum and brother was still a big blow to her and the rest of the family. But, as I have learned over the course of time, she is a tough woman.

After breakfast, Hong Wei and I went downtown – as title of Petula Clarke's great classical hit song of the sixties goes. You should see the people, going here there and everywhere and all with a purpose. There were no sad sights for me to see, on this excursion. But of the few I had seen previously, where were they now I wondered?

We arrived back in Jin Yang's house a few hours later and took it easy. We had changed accommodation and were now staying there. We had an appointment for dinner with the gang of eleven around teatime. Mr. Liu led the charge by collecting us promptly at 18:30. There were to be two firsts on this trip for me. Firstly, the spa experience from the previous day and now wait for it – going to a cowboy restaurant in Anshan city for dinner. Think about it. Wouldn't it make you wonder?

We arrived at this cowboy restaurant called whatever – I never looked up at it going in. All of the staff had cowboy hats, check shirts and dungarees with braces. I thought I was seeing things when we walked through the door. All that was missing was their guns.

No. 3 Mr. E, No. 4 Mr. Liu, No. 5, No. 7, No. 10 and No. 11 were all present. They were all delighted to see us again. The menu was a little different and I varied my eating choices accordingly. We drank the Yanjing beer from tin mugs, like being out on the range (wasteland), listening to the coyote dogs howl. There was no sheriff, no arrests were made, and Clint Eastwood was nowhere to be seen. The time passed and eventually our quota of food and drink was reached. We said our goodbyes and exchanged pleasantries and as usual in this company a great night was had by all.

Within a few hours it was Sunday, where we took it easy and just relaxed. Monday was the same, with the weather being the same too. There was a blanket of snow across the city, but for most of those few days, surprisingly the sun shone brightly during the mornings.

Tuesday 10th of March was an unusual day, as it entailed going back to Beijing by bullet train. There was another reason, why we should have checked the date more closely. I wanted to see Tiananmen Square and The Forbidden city again. I needed two days there to satisfy my conscience and check out a few things such as dates and some historical facts in relation to writing this book. I could have spent another week there alone.

Hong Wei's ex-husband Mr. He dropped us outside the main railway station in Anshan city early on the Tuesday morning. I got the sense that things were different than on previous occasions around and in the railway station. Security had hit the station by storm. There were police, army and swat teams all over the place. Baggage and personal were being checked vigorously. An ant wouldn't have been overlooked at these checkpoints. Then the penny dropped with Hong Wei, the Chinese government were meeting in Beijing.

So, security started with everyone all over China that was Beijing-bound. Eventually, we got through a checkpoint and onto our departure platform. The train arrived to the second and we boarded it. Our train departed Anshan city at 10:30 and arrived in Beijing at exactly one minute to 15:30.

If you ever want to see masses of people, check out Beijing Grand Central Station. Incredible sights await you, believe you me. There were security checks inside and outside the station and randomly on the streets. The city of Beijing was in lockdown, literally. We made our way to our hotel, which was called the Jinjiang Inn. We had a shower and relaxed until teatime. We then looked for a nice restaurant amongst thousands. Finding one, I ordered chicken wings, beef slices and green peas, all washed down with Yan Jing beer. Surprisingly, they didn't have any Tsingtao beer. Hong Wei ordered her own food, as was the norm. We took our time and just relaxed, until it was time to go. Then it was back to the hotel, for a good night's sleep.

Breakfast for us was at 08:00 the following morning in the hotel restaurant. A combination of pastry rolls and eggs were washed down with a cool glass of milk. When we ventured out onto the street around 09:00, Beijing was alive and well. The usual sights greeted us as they had on our other visits. Traffic vehicles of all sizes going everywhere and people going to their place of work or wherever. They were all going somewhere in a hurry, but only they knew where. I knew where I wanted to go, with the enormous help of Hong Wei. She was invaluable to me, getting directions and enquiring about public transport, when needed.

The streets are long and wide, you wouldn't walk them in a month of Sundays. We got a bus which dropped us close to Tiananmen Square, which meant we only had to walk a short distance. As we approached from one direction, I noticed a crowd on the footpath up ahead. It was security meltdown again with another checkpoint. The police, army and swat teams were out in force again, checking everybody.

We waited in the long queue that had formed and showed our papers and moved on. A few minutes later as we continued our journey, it was more of the same. Again, I didn't get overexcited or agitated about this procedure, as I understood why it was happening. The story is that once a year, the Chinese Government meets in Beijing for fifteen days in the Great Hall. Everything is discussed, from health, education, the economy, the finances to the state of the country. They also meet in other cities at different times, one being Chongqing, where we were to visit on our next trip. We made our way to see the National Flag on Tiananmen Square. I walked to the flag and observed the activity surrounding it from the roadside.

It is such a majestic sight, blowing in the wind. Like all national flags, especially here. It is respected by everyone who has the privilege to see it, as I did on a few occasions. I was left with my thoughts, as Hong Wei waited patiently. It was strange to see Tiananmen Square with not a single civilian on it, except for patrols of soldiers in their green uniforms crossing over and back on duty. We then crossed the ten-lane road, using the subway, where more security was in force. I was becoming accustomed to them by now. Surfacing on the other side of the street leaves you in front of The Forbidden City. I stood in front of Mao Zedong's large photograph that confronts every visitor to this magical place and thought about the past. Hundreds of people (Chinese and Westerners) filed past me, while I silently stood there. This is what Chinese history is all about, once you enter these gates. As you know, I was here on my first trip and the rest. The intrigue and mystery of this place just grips you again and again. Of course, most people only see it once in their lifetime. I wanted to double-check dates and events from inside this place. Three hours later, we emerged from this magical place where it hadn't lost any of its mystic. We had planned to see *The National History Museum* again, but that too was closed for security purposes. The flag lowering ceremony was not due until 18:15 and as it was now around 16:30 so we said we would go for food.

Chow Mein is a food I never ate previously in China, except in Waterford city when Hong Wei would make it at home for me. But this menu in this restaurant had Chow Mein on it. I tried it with bits of beef and chopped up chicken. Hong Wei ordered it too. It was piping hot and delicious. Whatever brand of beer was available, I drank a few of. We got back to the flag lowering ceremony around 18:00 and found ourselves a vantage point. At 18:05 the sun was just starting to drop and disappear. The lowering of the flag took place, amid all the flashing of cameras, particularly from the first-time visitors to this gripping ceremony. With that much-awaited request having been fulfilled, I was very happy to have seen it all again.

Hong Wei then hit me with an idea, "Billy, with every place that we were going to visit tomorrow being closed and our remaining time limited, why don't we get the late overnight train back to Anshan city?" On reflection and giving it a bit of thought and as we had done it before, it did make sense.

"We would be back in Anshan city on Thursday morning instead of Thursday night," she said. That would give us nearly an extra day to be with the family.

"Okay, let's check the train station and see if we can change the tickets," I said. We made a beeline for the station and when we got there, Hong Wei's gentle persuasion in explaining our situation to the ticket office employee worked. She cancelled our two tickets and issued us with two others. She was very helpful and accommodated us for the 23:00 train. I love and appreciate it when people understand, are obliging and not awkward. After all, as they say, fair exchange is no robbery, as she would have been able to re-issue them the following day. On returning to the hotel and explaining our story to them, they understood and accommodated us too. They refunded us the money for half the bill for that night which I thought was fair enough. I didn't think our room would have been vacant for too long anyway.

As you have read earlier about our previous overnight train ride and what it entailed, you know the score. It was still a good experience and didn't lose any of its uniqueness. We arrived in Anshan city around 08:00 the following morning.

Hong Wei's son, Jin Yang picked us up at the station and brought us to his house. It was Thursday. This also meant that Hong Wei would have another precious day with her cherished family. I knew that was important, under the circumstances. After all, we only had three days left before departure. I remember getting a few more hours sleep and taking it easy in the afternoon. We watched a bit of television that night and took it easy.

Friday morning came and we got an invite from the gang of eleven for dinner at 18:30. We did a little shopping during the day and spent some time with different members of her family, and it passed away the intervening hours.

Teatime arrived and the reliable Mr. Liu picked us up at 18:00 from Jin Yang's house and drove us to this market restaurant. I actually forgot to check the name again, believe it not! From the gang of twelve, including me, those present were, No. 1, No. 3, No. 4, No. 6, No. 7, No. 8 and No.11. As usual they were all delighted to see us. The food was ordered from this varied menu and a few boxes of beer were ordered too. These people just kill you with kindness and hospitality. After several bottles of Yanjing beer were consumed by me and a few new tastes of food sampled, the night was passing. Eventually, the night came to a slow close at around 21:30. Not like in Ireland, where its common practice to hear the midnight bell chime.

Photos were taken and pleasantries were exchanged in this terrific company. Although the question I get asked the most is, "Billy, when are you coming back to Anshan city."

My usual reply is, "As soon as possible. First chance I get!"

The night finished. We said our goodbyes, regretfully.

Saturday 14th arrived and as is customary, it's a family get together on the day before departure. A room in one of the hotels was booked and a time set. It's not a night-time affair, but usually around 13:00. Mr. Liu usually looks after all of the arrangements. This man was and has been invaluable to me on my ten trips to China.

When Hong Wei and I got to the hotel, most of her family were there. We waited for the rest of them to come, which they did shortly afterwards. Tsingtao beer was the main drink for me on this occasion. Two bottles of Chinese wine were produced from somewhere, with an offer to me of trying a sup of it. "Okay, I'll give it a go and see what happens," I said. I just put a touch in a glass, which was all I needed, on this pioneer run. While toasting at the start of the meal, I cautiously emptied the measure of wine, straight down the hatch (throat). It went down okay, but the heat from the inside awakened my body. This was a whole new experience for me. What a message I got, and the kick that followed! Boy, this stuff was deadly strong.

I said to myself, I'll leave this particular brand of wine to the Chinese – I'll stick to the Tsingtao beer. As usual, it came to the part where I would have to say a few words. Firstly, telling the family how sorry I was to hear of the death of their mother and even more shocked to hear of the passing of their brother, all within the space of fifteen days. It was a big blow to the family on both counts. I know most Chinese people get cremated, when they die.

I thanked them for accepting me into their family some eight years ago and what Hong Wei had brought into my life, in the form of stability. I reassured them that I would look after her wellbeing on our return to Ireland. They in turn, through Pan Pan thanked me for coming and respecting their sad loss. We all finished our meal some two hours later and said our goodbyes to certain members of Hong Wei's extended family, who we would not see again until we returned in the future to Anshan city.

The rest of the day was spent in Jin Yang and Wang Hao's house with their son, Hao Yang. He was a source of great joy for Hong Wei at that sad time and I was pleased about that. Like most grandsons, he was bright, beautiful, intelligent and as clever as they come. Hong Wei and I took it easy for the rest of the evening. I watched the television, particularly the news when it came on and covered an update from the Chinese congress meeting in Beijing. This was still the main news of the day and I was interested in viewing it and trying to understand it, even though it was in Chinese.

The last day came. It was Sunday March 15th, 2015. From early morning Hong Wei's sisters, nephews and nieces and Mr. Liu all arrived at different intervals. They had gifts and presents. Their kindness to me and their love for their departing sister was most evident. We all sat down in the house for an arranged meal. A large selection of food was on offer. What else could you drink only more beer, although I was offered a glass of the Chinese wine, but I sensibly and rightly refused it on this occasion. Our meal was finished at 14:30 and our departure time from Shenyang Airport was at 19:00 that night. This meant we had to be on the road for 15:00.

We had close on one hundred miles by road to travel. We departed promptly, followed by a cavalcade of two more cars. Hong Wei's family just don't know how to say goodbye. We got to the airport in Shenyang and checked in immediately. As we had about two hours to kill, we found a seating area. Their conversation was in Chinese. I just listened and left them at it. I rambled off for a short walk and surprisingly saw a shop selling ice cream. I treated myself to a 99-ice-cream cone with raspberry. Amazing. All the time I was conscious that the hands on the clock were moving on.

At 18:30 it was time to say goodbye for real. An occasion I was dreading from when first we arrived. It really does hit you like a ton of bricks. Hugs and tears engulfed us both at the final departure gate, as we said goodbye. You would want to have skin like a rhinoceros not to feel it. We went through the departure gate and looked back at the waving hands until they were out of sight. Then it was just the two of us showing our tickets to the cabin staff and boarding our plane. We chatted while we waited, like everyone else until the engines started up. It was only minutes to take off. The captain guided the plane out onto the runway and in a matter of seconds, we were away and up like a bird. The city of Shenyang was now below us and disappeared fast.

We returned to Ireland and Waterford city by the usual route, which took the about twenty-four hours travelling. The usual practice applied when we got indoors – sleep. It was badly needed. That was the end of my eighth visit to China.

Little did I know there would shortly be another one in the offing.

It was Monday night when normality prevailed. I had work on the Tuesday evening, so we said we would see Fengqin in the morning and bring her up to speed on everything. Tuesday morning came and after breakfast we visited Fengqin in her small apartment. She was delighted to see us and welcomed us in with open arms. She and Hong Wei had a long chat and I joined in occasionally. I had and still have a lot of respect for this woman, particularly in the way she viewed life. Material things meant nothing to her. She was content in her humble surroundings.

Fengqin did give us a bit of disappointing news while we were there though. She informed us that she was going back to London before the end of the year. We were sad to hear this, as she was always there when needed and she was someone we could relate to on any subject. This woman was highly intelligent, had good English and was educated to a high standard. I went back to work and Hong Wei got on with things. She kept in touch with her family and friends back in Anshan city, on a regular basis.

The weeks and months rolled by and around the end of November, Fengqin departed for England. We were sad to see her go, but that was her choice and she was happy making it. We saw her off one evening on the daily Euro Lines service which was still operating between Ireland and England. That was it, with the click of your finger, she was gone, the woman who had found Hong Wei for me in China. How lucky was I and how could I ever repay her for that!

The year of 2015 ended and 2016 arrived on our doorstep. Time goes by so quickly and crystal balls are not given out freely to see into the future. Around the middle of the year, Hong Wei told me that Mr. Liu's daughter Liu Jin Chi was getting married in September and her mother (Hong Wei's sister, Hong Yan 2) wanted us to be there. Also, it was the same month that her grandson Hao Yang would be celebrating his third birthday. I said to Hong Wei, "We'll go and kill two birds with the one stone. Why not!" We said we would go for a month, as we were also going to take an internal flight to two other cities.

This was to be my ninth trip to China. Who would have believed it? I had come a long way since that faithful first day I landed in China, when my personal path in life was to change forever.

The day finally arrived and with all our prior arrangements made, it was all systems go.

Our travel route was the same and eventually we ended up at Shenyang Airport in China. Going through the arrivals area, I could see Hong Wei's family with Mr. Liu, Jin Yang and his wife Wang Hao and their son Hao Yang, her sisters (Pan Pan, Hong Yan 1, Hong Yan 2, Hong Wei 1) and her niece Hong Hong were all there waiting excitedly to greet us. I could see the joy Hong Wei brought to them by her presence. For those initial few moments, the thrill is always there.

After the one-hundred-mile trip to Anshan city, we arrived at a city centre restaurant called Mei Yan, where the rest of the family members were waiting to greet us. The food was eaten, and the drink was drunk. Toast after toast followed, for whatever reason. But tiredness was setting in fast, as we finished our meal around 15:00. We were staying at Jin Yang and Wang Hao's apartment again; they didn't mind. Back at their place we chatted. I could see how pleased Hong Wei was to see her grandson, Hao Yang. I gave him some of my time. I watched for signs of genius from this three-year-old, as he kicked and headed a football back to me. He took to me warmly and without hesitation.

At approximately 16:00 my body ceased to function with tiredness. I hit the bed with the welcome response of sleep. Four hours later, my body said, let's continue this journey. Hong Wei made me some chow mien and I had two bottles of Tsingtao beer to wash it down. They were delicious and cool; they went down smoothly, as always. I took up where I had left off with Hao Yang, as regards football. Would he ever make it into the big time – it was too early to say.

We all retired to bed at 22:00. One down and only twenty-nine days to go. Tomorrow was another day, but not for earning another dollar. I thought to myself as my eyes were just about to close, 'You have come a long way on this journey!'.

Our wakeup call came at 08:00 the following morning, by the strong rays of the bright sunshine that entered uninvited through the open-curtained window.

It was Monday, but my body still ached from twenty-four hours of travelling. We had breakfast of pastry rolls and slices of chicken, which I followed up with a large glass of Pepsi Cola to quench my thirst. After that, Hong Wei said to me, "Billy, I need to see someone in the city. Do you want to come with me?" "Of course, I'll go with you," I said. Well this certainly was going to be a new experience for me!

After a short drive through the afternoon traffic with her son Jin Yang (before he went to work) we arrived at a block of flats in the older part of Anshan city. After climbing several flights of stairs and knocking on a darkened door, it was opened by an elderly lady. Hong Wei spoke to her and we entered the darkened hallway and made our way into a bright sitting room. Hong Wei had come to see a nerve specialist who had been recommended to her. Back in Ireland for the previous six months, she had been complaining of pains in her neck, shoulders and back. The lady's husband appeared from another room and introduced himself to her. He was a small man in stature but looked to me as if he could handle himself if he needed too. There were a few stools adjacent to a treatment table and I could see some surrounding cupboards with scattered medicines.

There were some plastic containers with an unknown liquid on the floor. He asked her to sit on a stool and lift her top up at the back, up to her neck. He then proceeded to feel all the exposed area with his fingers. He looked very professional in what he was doing, even though I was just looking. He spoke to Hong Wei in Chinese of course and pointed out on her back and neck about what the problem was. I was going on his body language and his motions with his hands. After a further few minutes he filled a glass full of this liquid from one of the plastic containers that were on the floor.

Then he took a big gulp of the liquid and didn't swallow it but held it in his mouth from where he proceeded to pick a spot on Hong Wei's neck and then spat it out powerfully at the intended area. This was indeed strange treatment; you might say and it was! He repeated this spitting action in several other areas, between her neck and her whole back area. Then he left it for a minute or two, to dry naturally. Each time he kept the bottom of his spit and spat it out onto a towelled surface.

There was a strong smell from this liquid. As the exercise went on, the more powerful the smell became. You can imagine what I thought when I saw this treatment being spat out, literally. This whole unique experience took about thirty minutes from start to finish. When he was finished, I asked Hong Wei to ask him one question, had he ever treated anybody famous, to which his reply was, a few. One was a high-profile person who paid him a visit. All he would say was this man was very wealthy and money was not the problem, it was the relief of pain that mattered most to him. He did not reveal the identity of the person, to any of us.

With that episode finished, we returned to the apartment and waited for Hong Wei's son, Jin Yang, to return from work, which was at 18:00. At 19:00 we went for dinner to a restaurant that I had never been to in Anshan city before. It was called *Jiang-Hu-Xin-Pai* and it was particularly known for its beef dishes. Never before did I go for a meal where I only ate beef. There was a full menu on offer, which Hong Wei, Jin Yang, Wang Hao and their son, Hao Yang, all availed of. But I stayed with the all-beef choice. I picked three different choices of beef and tried them all on the open charcoal grill in the middle of the table affair. The three of them were graded and I was asked by the proprietor to taste all three.

After a few minutes under this heat, believe you me, they are cooked. They were like three steaks and all placed on the grill together. To my surprise they were cut with a scissors first into strips. My first choice was their no. 2 rating. My second choice was their no. 1 rating and my third choice was there no. 3 rating. My no. 1 beef was just supreme in flavour and taste. I remember telling the proprietor that it was the best beef I had ever eaten. This two-hour meal was washed down with satisfaction by a few bottles of Anshan beer. At 21:00, with our meal finished, it was straight back to the apartment. Everyone was asleep as usual for around 22:00. Tomorrow was going to be a long day, as my body was recovering slowly but surely.

It was Tuesday 20th; a long day was to be an understatement. We were up at 07:00 and breakfast for me just consisted of two bananas and a bowl of Weetabix. Hong Wei had something that resembled a war zone on her plate. The horn from Mr. Liu's car sounded at preciously 08:00 as arranged.

As we headed out of Anshan city, the glorious sunshine continued to shine as if it owed us something. Hong Wei informed me that we were going to see her late mum's grave. This was going to be the first time I had ever been to a Chinese graveyard. I didn't know what to expect.

Another trip into the unknown and left me wondering, what would this experience be like.

We continued for a few miles and finally arrived at our destination. We were met by Hong Wei's four sisters. The setting was high on the side of a mountain, where we could see Anshan city a long way away in the distance. All the graves there were laid out neatly and as tidy as you could get. They each had a head stone with a marble surround. They were about half the size of a normal grave. They brought fruit and cigarettes and said individual prayers in turn to their departed parents. I just looked on and studied all the other graves in close proximity. It got a bit emotional for them as this was happening, which was understandable. The neatness of the graves surprised me and the order in which they were kept. By being cremated, I wondered was that the custom. I suppose it meant that there was more ground there to accommodate the new arrivals. With that moving tribute over, our two cars convey went back down the road where we stopped at a site and left our vehicles. There was a large smouldering chimney, with a big fire grate and a series of individual square openings in an adjacent one storey long red bricked building. In all of these openings there were an animal sign above them.

These were a pig, a rabbit, a horse, a sheep, a dog, a rooster and so on. The family then got four or five yellow bundles of packed paper, like serviettes from the boot of one of the cars and brought it to two of the openings. Families burn these papers at their departed one's signs. In Hong Wei's family's case, it was the pig for their mother and the rooster for their father. I just watched at this ritual as the bundle of yellow papers, were burned in their two designated burning vaults.

We then got back into the cars and proceeded to another designated burial site which was a few miles away. This was for their late brother and it was further into the mountains. When we got there, the setting was different, as it was a Buddhist temple. Once we parked the two cars, Hong Wei told me and Mr. Liu not to go any further. This was another ritual that they had to do themselves. We obeyed their wishes.

They disappeared behind the temple building and into a wooded area. They carried more bundles of blue paper to burn. Mr. Liu and I relaxed in these picturesque settings high up on this mountain. The sun shone down mercifully on the two of us. While they were gone, I noticed a few monks going in and out of a few outbuildings. I got the attention of one of them and called him over. An Irishman is never shy about asking a question or two. The obvious question was how long have you been here? To which he replied with his fingers, fifteen years. The same line of questions followed about food and the isolation of this temple. As I said previously with my other visits to other temples and monasteries, contentment seems to dwell within all who are resident in these most holy of places.

He pointed us in the direction of a tree that my alert eye had seen from a distance a few minutes earlier. This was in an inner garden away from where we stood. We made our way over to it and looked. On further inspection, I could see that its long branches reaching outwards in all directions had man-made steel supports of all heights under them. These were all placed in strategic areas and in different places. They were there to support the expanding limbs. This tree was like an Octopus turned upside down, such was its shape. It was then that Mr. Liu informed me that this historic tree was in actual fact one thousand three hundred years old. He could have knocked me with a feather. What an incredible sight for me to see and it was right before my transfixed eyes. I gazed at it and gently touched its flowering branches. This was all under the watchful eye of the monk. I knew with confidence that nobody back in Ireland had been to this place. There and then, I felt very privileged at what I was looking at in that moment. It truly was a magnificent and rare sight that was bestowed on me.

Shortly after, Hong Wei and her four sisters returned, having paid their respects to their recently departed and much-loved brother. We returned to Anshan city where we had dinner at a restaurant called Jia Xin. Again, there was no shortage of food choices. No charcoal fire, just all pre-cooked for our arrival time. I stuck with the Anshan beer and sank a few with Mr. Liu. The four girls drank tea or hot water with their meal. It never ceases to amaze me how disciplined Chinese people are. When our enjoyable meal was finished, there was another trip to be taken. The time was around 14:30 when we set off on this trip. It was to the city of Liaoyang in Liaoning province, about forty miles away.

Only three of us went to see Hong Wei's aunt, because her husband who we had met previously (remember the old war veteran man) had died the previous year. Hong Wei had phoned the previous day and made arrangements. She wanted to pay her respects to his family. Why not, were my thoughts on this, as it was another sightseeing tour for me. Pan Pan did the driving and what a good driver she is.

This woman was an elderly lady from the old Chinese tradition. I knew when I met her the first time that she had a kind heart and was gentle by nature. When we got to her house, she was in the company of her three sons, two daughters and her grandchildren. They had all gathered there to meet us. The conversation between them all was lively, open and friendly. Her late husband's photograph was still hanging on the bedroom wall, where I had seen it previously.

I just listened to them all talking Chinese and marvelled at the pronunciations and speed at which they talked on occasions. I certainly wasn't bored as Hong Wei told them about my background too. After two hours and when I thought it was time to go, Hong Wei informed me that her aunt's family insisted on taking us for a meal. It was 17:30 when we left her house and drove a short distance across the city to a restaurant called Mu Zi Mei Chu. It was around 18:00 when the food arrived on the circular glass rotating table. There was no charcoal fire grill here, but the food was piping hot. Again, you just picked what you wanted as the glass table rotates. The golden rule with me was, eat what you know and be careful with the rest. I did sample one or two other choices but left them to others. The drink was ordered too. It was called Liaoyang beer. It was a dry lager, which I hadn't tasted before. But we had a few and there was more if I had wanted them. As usual photographs were taken. Another two hours passed before proceedings came to a close.

Finally, I requested one family photograph to be taken and a waitress obliged us. Hugs, handshakes and kisses were plentiful at the final parting. It was an enjoyable and reminiscent gathering. We arrived back in Anshan city around 22:00. I was tired but not hungry or thirsty. After a little telly, lights were out just after 23:00, as the sound of silence ran through the apartment. It was another day down and different for other reasons.

Wednesday was a day of rest, but there was one thing Hong Wei had to do. Jin Yang's wife, Wang Hao, had to bring Hong Wei and me back to the medicine man. The same unusual procedure followed. I just sat there and gasped. We then went to visit her eldest sister Hang Yan 1. Pan Pan was there, and they all played the popular game of Ma Jiang. After about three hours there, we had some food and as my choices we limited, I played it safe without offending. We returned home after 18:00 and took it easy. While Hong Wei chatted to Jin Yang, Wang Hao and their son Hao Yang, I switched my attention to the reading from a brilliant book I had brought with me, called *Crossing the line*. The autobiography of Bruce Reynolds, better known to everyone as the man who masterminded the Great Train Robbery in England in August of 1963. What a read and what a story, without glorifying his past actions. Bruce Reynolds died in 2013, but I would have liked to have met him.

Hong Wei went to bed early and I followed before midnight. Switching off the lights last, as it was the end of another day.

When we awoke, Thursday had arrived and so had the sun. The weather had been good for the previous five days. I wondered how long more it would last or would I speak too soon. After breakfast we went for a little walk around the park close to the apartment and Hong Wei did a little shopping too.

Around 15:00 in the afternoon Mr. Liu arrived and we went back to the same spa facilities where we had been on my last visit. The hotel was called David Hot Spring Hotel. The scene was the same and the pools of water were just as hot. We went through the same routine as before, although, I still avoided the forty-five-degree pool! It was refreshing. When we were finished that I felt about ten years younger.

When we got back to the city, it was time for dinner. It was back to the restaurant called Jiang-Hu-Xin-Pai, with a few members of her family. Once again I went for the all-beef choice on the charcoal grill fire. The owner was delighted to see me and our party entering his premises. The taste of the beef was just the same as before, simply delicious. The rest of our party had other food, which they enjoyed also. Some two hours later our meal was finished, and it was time to go. We were all satisfied customers as we left this popular restaurant. Believe you me, generosity knows no bounds when you are in these people's company. I was very much family to them, and they treated me as such. It was very nice for me to feel welcome in their company.

I awoke on Friday morning a little later than usual; it was around 09:00. Hong Wei always got up earlier than me and still does. I could hear the sound of heavy rain against the windowpanes in our room. Pulling back the curtains, I could see it for myself. I suppose on reflection, it was too good to be true with the weather we were after getting up to then. I thought this change in weather could only happen in Ireland. How wrong I was. We took it easy, except Hong Wei had to go back to the medicine man for the last visit. I watched in amazement as this strange man set about his strange routine. But I was sure Hong Wei felt better after the treatment rather than worse for the experience.

That afternoon around 17:00 we had to go to a dress rehearsal for Hong Wei's niece, Liu Jin Chi's wedding to Zhang Guo Xi that was scheduled for the Sunday. I had to give an introductory speech, which was nerve-racking in itself. This involved learning a few lines of Chinese. What an ordeal this was for me and this was only a dummy run. How would I fare on Sunday when this exercise was for real? It would be in front of both families, relations, invited guests and friends amounting to around three hundred people. So you can see, this was going to be no small wedding. When the rehearsal was over, Zhang Guo Xi parents who were in attendance insisted on us going for a meal. It was to a restaurant called Lao – Beijing. Hong Wei, Mr. Liu and his wife Hong Yan 2, Jin Yang, Wang Hao and their son, Hao Yang and I all went to this upmarket establishment.

This restaurant had a new way of cooking food which I had never seen before. This was a whole new ball game to me. Another new experience was about to confront me in the cooking field.

When we entered the private room there were two tables there, one for each family. Both families mixed well, and everybody got on fine in each other's company. Each of the tables had a hole in the middle, like the charcoal method only there was a difference. It was like a basin with charcoal inside a funnel placed into the hole. This was filled with water and a cone like object was placed over the funnel, which resulted in the set amount of water coming to the boil quickly. You then threw your portions of beef, mushrooms, fish, chicken, noodles and lamb into the circular channel which held the water. This still water could reach temperatures of around 100 degrees. As the water would slowly start evaporating, you just keep adding more to it. You really wouldn't want to dip your finger into this water. Chopsticks were used at all times to put in the raw food and to take it out when it was cooked. I stuck with the beef, the chicken and the lamb. The rest I left to the others.

Anshan beer was the choice of Mr. Liu at our table, I didn't argue. There were several toasts made (wishing the young couple well) by both families during the course of the meal. As always, a great meal was consumed. We left a dent in the boxes of beer that were ordered. We finished our meal at around 21:30 and were back at the apartment by 22:00. For me, it was another day down in this country, with its wonderful people.

One thing Saturday always represents to me is football. No matter where you are in the world. In China there was football, mostly on a Saturday. Mr. Liu had made arrangements for me to go to Sian to see Liaoning Football Club play in the league again. Mr. Liu had too much to do, with his daughter's wedding the following day. This meant it was just Hong Wei and I who were to experience this trip. He had arranged the tickets and we were to travel on a supporter's bus to the game. Jin Yang dropped us at our pickup point, just as a few of the fans were putting a flag on the front of the bus. We introduced ourselves and they did likewise. We got a photograph taken with the group both inside and outside the bus. They presented us with two jerseys, which I thought was a fabulous gesture.

The trip was to take about two hours on the motorway. We got to the ground and both sets of fans were out in force. The banter was vocal but friendly as we occupied our seats with our newfound friends from the bus. Liaoning lined out in their home colours of red, while their opponents Yan Bian lined out in white. It really was one-way traffic from the off, as Liaoning dominated the opening minutes and duly went ahead after ten minutes with a good goal. This was the pattern up to within two minutes of the break when they added to their one goal advantage. The level of enthusiasm from the fans was an eye opener, the same as I had seen a few years earlier in a previous game.

They were as one in voice, and the banter was great to hear. There was no nastiness evident, not like in other countries. This rivalry was friendly, but boisterous, the way it should be.

The second half was a repeat of the first, such was the dominance of Liaoning. The score remained the same until the closing stages, when Liaoning added to their two-goal advantage by adding a third. They had an Australian player in their ranks, and he was the best player on the park. His name was Michael Thwaite and he was worth the admission fee alone. I just loved the way he read the game and distributed the ball.

Our group of fans were happy as they were leaving the ground and making our way to our bus. Hong Wei was happy too, as I was. The two-hour journey home was in good spirits. I have said and preached to teammates when I played and to players when I managed, "There is no better feeling than winning!". Any drink tastes like champagne when you win and like pee when you lose. That was my feelings on things during my career. When we got to the drop off point, Jin Yang was waiting. We thanked the lads for making it such an enjoyable experience for us and they acknowledged it!

Jin Yang saw the smiles on our faces, as we approached his car. We got some takeaway food at a roadside market and were back in the apartment in minutes. When the food was eaten and a beer or two drank, it was time for bed. The sitting room clock chimed as the hand struck 22:00. It's quite amazing but the time of 22:00 seemed to be the magic time we went to bed every night. What a coincidence that was as it was never planned, it just happened like that.

In at the deep end

When we opened our eyes, it was the day of Mr. Liu and Hong Yan 2's daughter's wedding. Sunday had arrived and the anticipation on Hong Wei, her son, Jin Yang and his wife Wang Hao's faces was most visible to me. The one main thought that was on my mind was of giving my speech and not making a balls of it. It was another obstacle to be cleared by me. There had been a few obstacles in my life, and I cleared them. One more wasn't going to get the better of me. I stayed positive, remained calm and stayed focused. All five of us left the apartment at 09:00 and took a taxi to the hotel. This was a very impressive affair with lots of people I knew, including members of the gang of twelve. Don't forget, I was now the 12th man.

I didn't know how much this wedding was costing, nor did I ask, but I could see from the surroundings, that there was no expense spared for this special occasion. When it is your son or daughter, naturally you would want to give them the best and really celebrate their marriage day.

Both sets of parents greeted everyone as they arrived at the main door of this impressive hotel. There was lots of activity by the staff and it showed as they waited for the wedding party to arrive. While we were waiting outside the main entrance of the hotel, I was approached by a few different Chinese people who asked me would I stand into a photograph with them. Hong Wei didn't mind, so I obliged with their requests, when asked. Fireworks always indicated that the wedding party had arrived. The young couple were cool out and took it all in their stride.

Everybody then moved into the main reception hall which was a very impressive sight. There were arrangements of flowers on every table. There were lights set up for photographers and video people also in attendance. The introductory speeches were made by the MC and the married couple made their appearance to rapturous applause. My introduction was coming fast, and I knew it. There was no turning back now, as the MC announced my name to the guests. It was the moment of truth in front of the watching three hundred. Here they were looking at a stranger in their midst and wondering what I was going to say. But I stayed calm and with Hong Wei by my side, I said what I had to say in Chinese, and it went down okay. I was pleased I did not let anybody down, for the occasion that was in it.

When the rest of the wedding proceedings was finished, the dinner was served. Along with both families and personal friends, we retired upstairs to the VIP suite. Around thirty people sat down around the biggest round glass rotating table I had ever seen. Budweiser was the chosen drink, and I just went with the flow. There was China's best wine on offer for the opening toast, so refusing was not an option. I just sampled a small drop in the end of the glass. Taking a sip led me into the unknown. What a blast from this stuff as it went down to the lower regions of my body. The next quick full glass of Budweiser got there before the heat from the previous liquid's arrival, became a fire on the inside. There were lots of speeches made from both families and the married couple when they arrived from their private meal thanked us all individually for being there.

The proceedings all came to an end around about 15:00. It was a great occasion and everyone there enjoyed themselves. The five of us returned to the apartment and took it easy. Hong Wei's four sisters arrived, and they all played the Chinese board game called Ma Jiang for a few hours. While they were doing that, I got stuck into reading the final few chapters of Bruce Reynolds' wonderful story. A further three hours and I was finished it. What a read it was, gripping, heart rendering and sad. The man certainly had nerves of steel. He believed in fate, like me, but there was a difference. I don't think I could ever match his record, even if it was for all the wrong reasons.

It's amazing how after a few hours, hunger comes back into the mind. At around 19:00, Hong Wei said to me, "Billy, we're going for food. Is that okay?"

I said to her, "Can we go back to that steak house restaurant again?"

"Okay, that's no problem," she said.

We all went back en masse and were joined by Mr. Liu and his wife, Hong Yan. Mr. Liu and I called for Anshan beer and a few boxes arrived in seconds. The steaks kept coming with other food in bowls, but I remained absent from them. Other food like chicken wings and sausages I had off the charcoal fire. We got through a good few of the beers. Everyone is entitled to get drunk, even if it was in China. It's not a crime, but it happens. We finished around 21:30 and the food was enjoyed by all. While we were there, again a few people came over to our tables and asked me for a photograph taken with them. Why not, I was on their patch and it cost nothing to be nice. On that night, our two heads hit our separate pillows at 22:30.

I wondered how Waterford city in Ireland was doing in our absence. I'm sure it was fine, patiently awaiting our return, no doubt. We had a good day and great memories to sleep on, I know I did. This was and always has been a case of two different worlds. One was about existing and the other was about survival. At times I didn't know which was which, with the economic crash in Ireland and the damage it done.

One week was gone and it was three to go. There were a few more experiences waiting around the corner for me!

Monday was an easy day for us, as I had to recover from the extra few beers with Mr. Liu. After a little breakfast, a short walk in the nearby park was the remedy that I needed. Then there was some shopping in the afternoon, where Hong Wei was at her happiest. I didn't mind sitting outside the shopping centres and relaxing watching the world go by, until Hong Wei re-emerged with her hands full.

That night we were not stirring out. While Hong Wei watched telly with Jin Yang, Wang Hao and Hao Yang, I started on a second book ahead of schedule. It was called *The Life and Times of a Sporting Hero*. It was written by Jeff Powel about the great West Ham and England football defender, Bobby Moore. He was a true legend in football. I was keeping it for the return journey to Ireland, but the Bruce Reynold's book changed all that, as I couldn't close it when I opened it! Hong Wei went to bed before me, as was always the case and still is. For a change, my eyes closed at midnight.

The next day was Tuesday. Breakfast was running along the lines on a regular basis of two egg sandwiches or fruit. In the afternoon, Hong Wei had an arrangement to meet a few old school friends for a karaoke session. They met at around 15:00 in a club and they were delighted to see her. After the introductions, I was just there as an onlooker in these situations. They conversed, reminisced and sang songs. This musical reunion was winding down around 18:00. Then her friends insisted on us going for food. We made our way to a restaurant called Hai Yan Feng. Once again their conversation ruled, with me being a good listener. They chatted and we ate until 21:00. With everything ended her friends insisted on a few photographs being taken. This we did and everyone was happy. We said our goodbyes and were back in Jin Yang's apartment at 21:30. At 22:00 we were in the land of nod! Amazingly, the Bruce Reynolds story still crossed my mind.

Wednesday arrived and I wondered what Hong Wei had in store for me today. It started with the continuous sun except for that one day. It was a bonus for this month, and we were grateful for it. Hong Wei did tell me that the gang of eleven plus me wanted us to go for dinner that evening, which was a nice thought for the start of any day, I suppose. Hong Wei's ex-husband, I called him Mr. He, called over to the apartment around 10:00 and we exchanged pleasantries.

Jin Yang was gone to work and we brought Hao Yang for a walk in the park for about two hours. It was a hive of activity with old and young all enjoying the public facilities that are provided there. There were groups of old people exercising, singing, dancing and walking. There were kids' playgrounds scattered within the park and a boating lake there too. There was no sign of vandalism like we might see in Ireland, because the deterrent is there. A public park is supposed to be there for everyone's enjoyment, so why should a few morons ruin and deprive the general public of the enjoyment that can be got from these facilities. I say punish them hard, with no sympathy to be shown.

Mr. He invited us for lunch at 12:30. While the other restaurant Jiang-Hu-Xin-Pai was the best for beef, this restaurant was called Come Barbecue a most unusual name, you'll agree, and it had a reputation for lamb. I ordered lamb over the charcoal fire and it turned out the flavour from it was only delicious. The rest of the party had a bit of everything to eat.

Pan Pan arrived around 13:30 as we had an appointment at a tea house for 14:00. We thanked Mr. He for his hospitality and left with Pan Pan. In my eight visits to Anshan city, this was my first time here. I had never heard or seen this place before. It was called Shi He and it was like a little retreat, where they ran classes, near the Anshan city museum. It was also a place where groups of people would go to have food and drink tea. We had a special invite for this 14:00 class. There were about sixteen other people there and two or three leaders from the house.

They explained about different flavoured teas in showing you how to pour it, shake it and drink it. I found some aspects of it very interesting – if you drank tea. But I must admit I also found it a little boring and a slow process to observe. It was hard to sit there from 14:00 until 16:00. When it was over, Pan Pan and Hong Wei wanted photographs taken in the beautiful gardens, which on request one of the leaders obliged us by using the camera. The manageress arrived and introduced herself. She was a little surprised of how much interest I was taking in the garden. Then again, it was a nice peaceful and private place.

I also explained to her that I had never drank tea or coffee in my entire life. Both the manageress and the other leader were astonished to hear this coming from an Irishman, of all people. The manageress then asked the leader to go and get something, while she continued with our conversation. A few minutes later the leader returned with three little presentation tea bowls in little velvet pouches. She presented them to us, and we thanked her. I thought it was a wonderful gesture from a stranger in our midst.

Pan Pan dropped us back to Jin Yang's apartment, where we took it easy, waiting to see when we would get the usual phone call from Mr. Liu.

315

It was the practice that No 3. Mr. E always decided where and at what time we would go for dinner. The big guns were going out on the town. These were big players and personalities in the everyday happenings of Anshan city. The expected phone call did come around 18:00 and it was from Mr. Liu with instructions of which eating establishment was going to be our hosts for the evening.

By sheer coincidence and against the law of averages and as luck would have it. Hong Wei told me, "Billy, we are going to the Come Barbecue restaurant. It's the same restaurant, where we had been with Mr. He earlier today," she said. "Mr. Liu will pick us up here at 18:15." Now I ask you, how much of a coincidence that was!

Both of us were ready when Mr. Liu called as punctual as ever on the dot at 18:15. We got there by 18:30, on time. Finding our way upstairs on arrival, we were directed to a private room, as always. Everybody there was glad to see us, as we were them. The attendance included No. 1, No. 3, No. 4, No. 6, No. 9, No. 10 and yours truly at No. 12. Some had wives and others had partners. The selection of food was, as it always is, with unlimited choices. Top class with no expense spared. A few boxes of Tsingtao beer were ordered too. There was no Chinese wine on view, which I was happy about, as the last experience was breath-taking and hot. Great conversation and laughter was had by all, in between the excellent food and drink. It's easy in this company, as they are all laid back and friendly.

But they were getting used to me by now. Hong Wei, as usual, played her part in translating everything from me to them and vice versa. What would I have done without her? She truly was worth her weight in gold. The gathering finished with a few songs, which Hong Wei obliged them with her voice. What a singer she is, but she just won't admit it. That's not the view of those that hear her sing though. It was all over after three hours, including our goodbyes and photographs. What a genuine bunch of people these are. Mr. Liu shared our taxi home, which arrived at Jin Yang's apartment as the clock struck 22:30. We were asleep before 23:00, waiting for Thursday to arrive. It was only a matter of a few hours really, when you think about it.

But Thursday morning did arrive and after breakfast Hong Wei informed me that we were going swimming at 11:00. It was in a complex that I was not in before. This building was outside the city. There was strict security in the reception area, but Jin Yang had the tickets pre-booked. I could see that this was a very impressive complex and run with strict guidelines. The main pool was massive, with two lifeguards on either side. We got changed and enjoyed swimming in this giant pool. It was really about getting Hao Yang to not be afraid of the water. With his arm floats and being coaxed by Jin Yang and Wang Hao, he got over the fear and threw himself into the water. His fear disappeared and his confidence grew.

After a while there we moved to companion pools that were smaller and adjacent to this massive pool. Each of these four pools were different temperatures. They also had something unreal and that was they all had different scents. One was of roses, one was of raspberry, one was of blackcurrant and the last one was of apple. We sampled them all and moved onto another pool that had live fish in it. You just saw them, but not too many people ventured in there. We observed them and kept our distance. We spent two hours in this swimming complex, and I must say it was spotless.

On our return trip to the city, we stopped at a little roadside cafe. I'm afraid the food here was not for my liking, but the rest of the party wolfed it. I just drank the Anshan beer and watched them enjoy their edible food. We got home that afternoon and just relaxed. We went out for dinner that night and just kept it to the family. They actually had chips on the menu, what a treat that was. We retired that night at our favourite time of 22:00 and waited for the next day. All this time, while we were still in Anshan city, I had not seen a westerner. I found that to be amazing, but it was true.

On Friday's itinerary for Hong Wei and I was a trip with her grandson, Hao Yang, to a professional photographer with his dad, Jin Yang, and mum, Wang Hao. It was his birthday in a few days and the photo shoot was scheduled for 10:30 and it was in downtown Anshan city. When we got to the studio, the photographer decided on account of it being a beautiful day that we should go to a certain location to photograph him. We went down to a beautiful green area with wooden bridges over a stream and huge boulders scattered around in strategic positions.

The photographer knew his stuff when it came to professionalism. He had a whole wardrobe of different clothes and Hao Yang was a natural in all the changes that were required for the different settings. This all took about two hours and I thought they don't do things by halves here. I just sat down on a bench in the glorious sun and took it all in. At the finish they included me in a few family ones. I felt I wasn't worthy, but Hong Wei, Jin Yang and Wang Hao insisted. I was new, but in their eyes, I was still family.

As a treat, we then brought Hao Yang to a McDonald's outlet. He enjoyed himself like any other four-year-old. I did notice that a lot of Chinese people (adults or children) put a lot of red sauce or tomato ketchup on their chips. I'm the complete opposite, as I never use red sauce. But we ate the burgers, onion rings and some chicken wings and drank a few cokes. These were followed by different flavoured ice creams from the menu. Hao Yang was thrilled with the change of food and to see the excitement on his face said it all. We returned to our temporary abode and got a short rest.

Over the course of the last two years, I had a little weakness in my back. Nothing to get overexcited about, but with our bed less a mattress, like most beds in China apart from hotels, I was finding our bed a little hard. This resulted in me, finding it hard to get a proper sleep on my right side. It was like a pinching in my lower back. I thought it might have been a trapped nerve.

Hong Wei had casually said to me a few days previously, would you like to go and see a doctor. So, on this particular day when we got back from the photo shoot, Hong Wei suggested I should go and see a doctor. We went to the hospital, just a stone's throw from where we were staying. We waited in a waiting room for a while. Eventually a very young doctor appeared and introduced himself to me, with Hong Wei translating. He brought us to a private room with a bed. He asked me to get up on it and lie face down. He then proceeded to feel all of my back. The next ten minutes were hell on earth, but there was no escape. He picked a few spots on my right side and addressed them both individually and in a sequence. He used his elbow to apply pressure in certain areas. My Jesus, what pain he put me through. I was waiting for his elbow to come out through my chest, such was the pain. Torture – you name it, boy, was this agony.

He told me my complaint was a weak muscle that never recovered from an injury from a few years ago, when I played squash and football competitively. Through Hong Wei, I thanked him most sincerely for his time. He was a really nice man, but he certainly knew how to give out punishment. If it was in war time and he was interrogating me, I would gladly have told him anything he wanted to know. He left me for dead on the bed and left the room. It felt like a herd of buffalo had run over my back, or I had been harpooned with a whale gun. His parting words to me through Hong Wei were, "You will feel better tomorrow!". I got off the bed and put my body back together again. Never was there a truer word spoken.

We stayed in that night and watched telly, with a sandwich and a few Pepsi-Cola's. My body needed a break from beer, and I knew it.

Saturday 1st of October was another day with a difference. The 1st is the start of a festival week celebrated all over China every year. Hong Wei had made arrangements with a few of her school friends to meet for lunch around midday. The way it was every day, I didn't know where it would start or where it would finish. We met at 12:05 in a restaurant called *Tiexi Lao Jun Lu*. Don't ask me what that name means in English. Your guess is as good as mine. They were delighted to see Hong Wei. I was glad she was happy seeing them. I just joined in the chat occasionally and left them to it. The Yanjing beer kept me occupied, as I sampled a few new foods. We finished the meal around 15:00.

That evening we had an engagement with an aunt of Hong Wei's. We were to meet her at the war memorial monument to the fallen dead at a certain time. It's like the cenotaph in London, only this is five times higher. This is a huge stone structure that overlooks Anshan city from a high vantage point. There are two hundred and fifty-three wide stone steps leading to the top, from the base of it. I know, because I counted them all on the way up and on the way down too!

There were wreaths there which had been laid recently on the four sides of it. I admired the block work of equally size huge granite stones, which were all neatly knitted together. How they built it and where they built it left me scratching my head. It was duskish, but the monument was all lit up to reveal a giant inscription in gold Chinese lettering on the front and back of this gigantic mass of stone. There were war scenes with figures of soldiers in battle cut into the stone on each of the two sides as well. I studied all of this in great detail, as Hong Wei was in deep conversation with her aunt, who was very pleased to see her. Surprisingly, I didn't ask her what the inscriptions meant. I really should have though!

The view from the top of this Plato at evening time was only spectacular as you're looking down on Anshan city and you can see it all lit up. The neon lights look like they were touching the night sky. The red lights on all of the skyscraper's roofs were flashing away. This view also takes in one of the main busy streets. The movement of traffic with their lights on is like a continuous swarm of bees going in and out of their hive. After being there for a while with Hong Wei and her aunt talking and me watching, we made our way back down the two hundred and fifty-three steps again. As we got to the end, I could hear music and then saw about one hundred figures in the dark all dancing to a set pattern and lined up in front of us. Songs were being played from two big giant speakers entertaining these people of all ages. It was like a musical form of exercise, with one leader out in front. This form of exercise is practised every night around different places in Anshan city. You see them outside shopping centres and on the main streets. I already had enough exercise for one night, going up and down those steps!

We said goodbye to her aunt and returned to Jin Yang's apartment. It was lights out by 23:00, as Sunday was another day. Practically every day there were things happening. We did not waste many days. We made the most of our visits, this being my ninth. Earlier that evening, Hong Wei had gotten a phone call from the doctor at the hospital saying he wanted to see me on the Monday. All I could think about was him inflicting more pain. I thought I had told him all the secrets of the war.

When Sunday morning came, we had an appointment to meet Mr. He and a friend, plus three other policewomen for early lunch at 11:30. That meant no breakfast only a glass of Pepsi-Cola for me. We entered the Come Barbecue restaurant on time and met our guests. I was beginning to think that this was Mr. He's favourite eating place. The three policewomen were all classmates of Hong Wei, as well as the other policeman.

They were all delighted to see her, so it was her stage. Mr. He ordered the food and it arrived pronto. Again, the selection and broad choice of food astonishes me every time we sit down for dinner as guests of somebody. I stuck with the tried and trusted, which were chicken wings, prawns and charcoal grilled lamb and some duck. A few Yanjing beers kept me lubricated and cool on the inside. The large selection of other dishes I left to the others. They all had great conversations. I just listened to them speaking. Hong Wei kept me informed of the general topic anyway. Two hours later we said our goodbyes, amid handshakes, hugs, kisses and photographs. We did a little shopping and went home.

We took it easy that evening and Hong Wei's grandson, Hao Yang, kept her occupied. She even made me some Chow Mein and French fries, with a few Pepsi-Cola's. It was like she was cooking at home; such was the flavour. It was two weeks now and I still had not seen any sign of a westerner, amazing when you think about it. With regard to the weather, we still had had only one day's rain.

On Monday breakfast was over by 09:00. A walk in the nearby park with Hong Wei, Wang Hao and her son, Hao Yang, took up most of the morning. He was even getting used to me at this stage and would hold my hand on occasion.

Later that afternoon, we had to go back to the hospital at 16:00 to see the doctor. He wanted to check my back again. I have to say, the harpoon wasn't as sharp, while he was working on me. He said there was an improvement and to take it easy. When her son, Jin Yang, got in from work that evening, Wang Hao and Hong Wei cooked some food, including Chow Mein. What a welcome change it was from fourteen days of the other food and drink.

Jin Yang had some great news for us when we first arrived in September. He told us that on Tuesday 4th of October, we would be going on a five-day break to two cities. In one of which his mum wanted to visit a grave of a very dear friend whom she had lost the previous year. Included was an internal flight to a city called Chongqing in Sichuan Province. This was to be our second time getting an internal flight in China. This was going to be another experience for me, to go with the rest. Chongqing city is famous the world over, reputedly for having the spiciest food on the planet and I don't like spicy food - never have done and never will do! I think you'll admit, my experiences were good up to now. In my opinion, the best was yet to come, as they say. It was fate, that we kept the best wine until last. Amazing! We all retired to bed around 22:00 that night. I knew the next five days would be interesting. With that I closed my eyes in a happy thought of what might follow.

Tuesday was the day. In fact, it was to be the longest day. I skipped breakfast, as we had dinner planned for 11:00, before the one-hundred-mile drive to Shenyang Airport. It was in an eating establishment called *Mother Dumpling Restaurant.* Our flight to Chongqing was later in the afternoon. This city is way south of Anshan and Beijing. That meant the weather was going to be a lot warmer than I thought. I just took it as fate raising its head again. We left for the airport at 14:00. We were there for 15:30 comfortably.

There was a police checkpoint en route and trust our luck, we would get pulled over, but they just check your passport and ID. Jin Yang obliged here, with what needed to be done. The same happened at the airport. After checking in, we had to go through security. You don't mess with these people. You just do as you are told and follow their instructions, simple as that! We made our way to our departure gate and waited to be called. Our departure time was 17:20 and the flight would take six hours. What I didn't know was that this plane made a scheduled stop at a city called Zhengzhou in the Henan province for half an hour. This was about halfway through our journey.

This was to drop off passengers and to take on others, whose destination was the same as ours, Chongqing. The plane was full again, with the vacated seats being filled. It was a kind of funny arrangement, but I, like the rest of the passengers, just accepted it. We finally touched down in Chongqing at 23:10. Security was tight, and nobody escaped the net. We were out of the terminal by 23:35. It was a busy airport and it seemed like the whole world was looking for taxies. It was very humid, even at that time of night. There were fleets of yellow taxies, and I presumed that these were the main colour of the taxies in this city. Eventually we got one after Jin Yang bargained with the driver. The airport was a fair distance outside the city, and we were travelling for a while on our inward journey.

What a unique city

We reached our hotel that was called Shui Zhi En. What an impressive sight it was, even in the dark of night. It was so big that it actually had two parts to it. Jin Yang had made the reservations. We just showed our passports at reception. We then had to walk across the complex to reach our rooms in the other part of the hotel. Our two rooms were forty storeys up, which still took us a few minutes to get there, even in the lift. Do you know that there were 3019 rooms in this hotel? Hong Wei hit the bed straight away, as she was wiped out. What a sight it was to look out over this massive city, from our viewing balcony, even if it was 01:00 in the morning. This city was a hive of activity. The night life and bright lights below made me think so. I gazed at the marvel of it all for a few minutes and wondered.

They say the city of New York in America never sleeps. Well, I think they have a competitor here. Tomorrow was going to be a journey into the unknown, so I had to be ready for the unexpected. Hong Wei had beaten me to her pillow by half-an-hour. My eyes closed on making contact with my pillow and the soft bed. There was still no sign of a westerner in sight. Surely later today in a city of thirty-two million people the surprise would come. It was true that it had been the longest day.

I was up early the following morning and made my way to the balcony. Straight away, I knew this city was energetic from first light. From my viewing point at 08:00 I could see this monstrous city on the move. The early morning traffic was moving along the wide streets in both directions – as the saying goes, as far as the eye could see! Jin Yang had gotten vouchers for our breakfast in a restaurant adjacent to the hotel. It was a strange arrangement and the first time I had encountered this. It didn't make any difference to me, as I was just having some dry Chinese bread and Pepsi Cola. The other four all tucked into dumplings, rice, eggs and bread. I had picked up a head cold and sore throat while travelling

324

on the Tuesday and didn't feel well. But I knew how to handle it. I knew what was needed. After breakfast we paid a visit to the chemist for a cough bottle and some tablets. I knew I would be on the mend in a day or two.

Hong Wei's great friend who had died the previous year was one of the main reasons why we had come to Chongqing. Her ex-husband and his new wife picked up all five of us outside the hotel around 10:00. His name was Mr. Woo and he came across as being very friendly. Hong Wei met him years earlier when he was married and living in Anshan city, before he moved to Chongqing. He only had to drive us a short distance, where he then parked his car. One thought kept rolling around in my mind, 'Twenty-two million people living in Beijing and thirty-two million people living here!'. The mind boggled at that statistic; don't you agree?

The first place Mr. Woo took us was to the underground subway system. I thought 'Was this for real?' as we headed under the main road. Seeing was believing. I saw. There were two tiers of subway lines and one monorail line as well. With Mr. Woo's instructions, we took the middle one first. On most platforms they have stewards who close off the arrival space in the area as the train arrives to allow the passenger to board. This prevents other passengers trying to get on, in the same spot. If you can picture it, passengers are trying to get off and others are trying to get on – all in the one spot. The passengers getting on have to wait. Of course, this is all due to the amount of people that use the subway.

Otherwise this whole operation would lead to chaos and mayhem. You only have seconds to get on the train as the next one is due in another two minutes. The crowds on the trains were jam packed. Talking about peas in a pod or packed in like sardines! There were no end doors on these carriages, it was just like a big long tube you could see straight through. We stayed on for a few stations and then got off and went down to the lower subway to catch another train. It was unreal to see all of this in action and people going in all directions. They have barriers that make you go through them (you can't avoid them), in single file. This also controls large crowds of people from charging the transferring exits. There is also tight security between exiting and entering the different zones. We got off after a few more stations and took an elevator straight up to the street level. After having seen masses of people underground, now it was my turn to see them on the street above as well.

We surfaced right in the middle of the main shopping area and moved onto a main side street called, The Street of Food. There were five or six main streets coming into a centre, where there was a big tall pillar like structure called *The People's Liberation Monument*. I went back with Jin Yang just for a minute to see this piece of history and get a photograph taken. All around us there were thousands of people going everywhere. There were hundreds of small shop outlets, most of them selling food. There were also the big brand names, with their huge neon signs over their premises.

As we were finding our way through the crowds, Hong Wei was holding me tightly, for fear of losing me or somebody grabbing me and making me theirs. Hao Yang was on his father's shoulders observing it all, with Wang Hao in close attendance too.

Mr. Woo had seen it all before and was not overawed by the sheer volume of people. He asked us were we hungry, to which we replied, yes! Hong Wei was translating everything for me, as we moved along. He directed us to follow him downstairs to the biggest eating establishment I had ever seen. This was a floor with hundreds of cooking stalls set out, all around on the perimeter of this massive eating area. There were hundreds of tables and long benches, with people eating all kinds of everything that was edible. There wasn't a table to be got, such was the crowd. It was so busy, that you just couldn't sit down until someone that was finished their meal got up.

You heard the expression 'It was like feeding the 5,000'. This was just a throwaway comment from me. This truly was organised chaos, which had me laughing at where we were going to sit. But there were no seats to be found, which meant we couldn't rest our tired limbs either. Through patience and a watchful eye from Hong Wei and Wang Hao for an available table, we moved at lightning speed when one became free.

You had to order the food, by walking around to the outlets and seeing what was on offer. We men left that in the hands of Hong Wei, Wang Hao and Mr. Woo's wife. We guarded the fort (table) with our lives, while the women departed. While they were gone, I asked Mr. Woo out of curiosity, how many would this place hold at a sitting? He said to me in his limited English, "5,000 Billy, even though it is the festive week.". This is the normal crowd that is here every day. Think of it, 5,000 people underground eating food, all at the one time. Looking around, I could see that the people cooking the food couldn't cook it quickly enough and the people eating it weren't exactly taking their time either. When you were hungry, why would you take your time eating?

The choices of food were enormous and endless. Every second person sitting around us, their plates looked like they all had different food on them. The three girls returned and had their hands full with plates of food. Hong Wei got me boiled potatoes and three cooked pieces of chicken. They all had a cross section of food and we tore into it. I then went up with Jin Yang and got the drinks. They did sell Pepsi-Cola, which was my choice. This was my ninth trip to China and some of the food was recognisable, not by taste but by appearance. The food disappeared off our plates fairly quickly too. There were empty plates being returned by their users to a certain area, as the staff didn't have time to collect them. It was the biggest crowd of people I had ever seen eating and talking in the one place, at the one time. But what a sight it was for me to have seen it. Again, I wondered had there ever been anyone from Ireland in this place. Where I now stood, I doubted it. I had still not seen a westerner in my travels.

Our tired bodies got up from the table and re-entered the thousands on the streets. We then made our way down to the side of the famous Yangtze River. This is the longest river in China and the third longest in the world, after The Nile and The Amazon. There were shops and more food outlets scattered along the bank of it. We looked around there for a while as we went in and out of all these interwoven shopping areas. This was like a shopping maze. But it was interesting to see the amount of people here as well. When we had our fill of that, Mr. Woo then decided to bring us to one of the older parts of this city. It was called Ciqikou Old Town. I immediately thought of the much loved and late departed Philip Lynott of the great Thin Lizzy rock band fame. My favourite band of all time! One of his classic songs was called *Old Town*.

When we got there, you pass under the sign that invites you into this multitude of small narrow streets. It has souvenir shops, food outlets in their hundreds and dozens of cloths shops, shoe shops, furniture shops and anything that you wanted. The salesmen here were so good, they had to be seen to be believed.

There were thousands of people on these narrow streets, as we were moving along shoulder to shoulder. It was an incredible sight to see and easily the most populated group of moving people I was ever in the midst of. But there was a surprise when we turned one of the narrow corners – there were three westerners, straight before my eyes. I actually made my way over to them and asked them where they had come from. They had cockney accents, which could only tell me they were from London in England. I told them how long it had been since I had seen a westerner. We shook hands and kept going in our opposite directions.

Everyone was screaming at you to buy this, buy that. I would go as far and say, anything you wanted was here. To pass through this shopping experience could take you anything up to two to three hours, at the very least. We stopped at a little food outlet near one of the many exits out of this shopping maze and had some food and drink. I had some boiled potatoes, while the rest had noodles and other things that I didn't even know what they were and to make it better, I didn't even ask. I played it safe in this minefield of shops and food. Between entering and exiting this unreal and unique part of this city took us about three hours. It was an incredible journey to have been on and the experience was something you would never forget. This was another place, where organised chaos was the order of the day.

We went from there back to our hotel and took it easy. Hao Yang was unconscious with tiredness and needed sleep, a bit more than the rest of us. Mr. Woo had made arrangements to meet us at an outdoor restaurant called Di Gua Lao Huo Guo (I don't know what that means in English) around 19:00 that evening. There were loads of these restaurants all over this city. This was going to be another new experience for me, as regards the food. We set off on our travels around 18:30 and found the outdoor restaurant, which wasn't too far from our hotel.

There were about thirteen in the party when we sat down. Mr. Woo introduced everyone to us. His wife, son and daughter-in-law, and a few family friends made up the numbers. The system they had for cooking the food was the same as (remember the basin with the water and the funnel) that I mentioned before. There were two areas where the food was cooked. One was the outer channel and the other the inner pot, as we'll call it. The gas was connected through a hose which ran out to your table on the street, from the main bar area. The gas was turned on and the party began. The two compartments of water came to the boil quickly and all the different foods were added to the outer channel and then a load of spices and chillies were added.

I put my slices of beef in the inner pot, which were free of all spices and herbs. I ate the beef and it was okay. The rest of them just piled on the spices and chillies in on top of their cooking food choices. I just shook my head and said to myself, how you could eat that was beyond me. There were also separate plates of fish, noodles, pork, ham, but I just ignored them. Hong Wei, Jin Yang, Wang Hao and even Hao Yang ate everything. My beef was okay, but the rest of the food on display was just too spicy for me. I just could not bring myself to eat it. But they all ate it and even added more spices and chillies!

It was beyond my comprehension, how you could eat this food. Don't get me wrong, the food was quality, but for me it was just too spicy. The waters were now as hot as hell and certainly not for touching with the human hand. To take out your selected piece of food, everything had to be with chopsticks, or you would be missing a finger. But the atmosphere was extremely friendly, and everyone seated at the table got on well amid the sound of laughter. I was never going to be a killjoy, not then and never have been. The company we were in couldn't have been nicer. The last thing I ever or have ever wanted to be was rude or offensive in refusing food. But there is a line in the sand and if you want to cross it, so be it. I didn't. The cold bottles of Tsingtao beer reached where certain foods never got to go. When the meal was finished, we all set off in four cars to see one of the main viewing points in this fabulous city by night.

We drove around this lit up area along the quayside and then finally stopped at a point by the riverside. This led you to an entrance into a big shopping mall with escalators that brought you up onto a plaza, which gave you a sensational view of this part of the city from a great height. All the far side of the river was illuminated and there was an entertainment boat docked there that kept changing colour every minute, from red to green to yellow to blue. We took plenty of photographs amongst our group and against these colourful backgrounds. There were other groups of people there, but no westerners, which didn't surprise me. It was actually close to 23:00 when all this was finishing. Mr. Woo had been very helpful throughout the day and he finished it off by dropping us back to our hotel. Tomorrow was to be a special, but a sad day for Hong Wei. I knew this was the main reason why we had come to Chongqing.

After breakfast we met Mr. Woo and his son, Woo Ting at 10:00. Jin Yang, Wang Hao and Hao Yang didn't come with us, as a lot of Chinese don't bring children to cemeteries. The four of us, moved out of the city by car in the early morning traffic, in the continuous sun that just kept on shining. With Mr. Woo driving, we arrived at a point where I could see the perimeter of the graveyard. There were a few flower sellers outside on the main street corner, selling their wares. Flowers were bought and the mock paper money was sold as well.

We made our way in through the gates in the lower part of this well laid out cemetery, where the dead were recognised with respect. We first entered a holy building with various Buddha's and other statues on view. Bear in mind this was my impression, I didn't ask any questions. I was only there in a support role for Hong Wei when the crunch came. We made our way out the top entrance of the building and found ourselves up a few tiers on paths that led us to separate divisions within the cemetery. All of which were beautifully laid out, I might add, under the warm rays of sunshine. Mr. Woo and his son led the way along the designated path, passing grave after grave until finally the picture of Hong Wei's great friend's face appeared on the headstone. I knew this was going to be an emotional few moments, so I stood back and let them have their privacy.

The three of them lit two candles and three sticks of myrrh and then stuck them in a holder. Then they pulled the petals from the flowers they had brought and scattered them in formation around the headstone. Funnily enough there was continuous low music playing in the background across the whole cemetery. This cemetery was kept in spotless condition, which all added to the serenity of the place and the scene that was unfolding before my eyes.

Mr. Woo and his son stood in silence, and I am presuming said a few prayers. They then stood back and left Hong Wei have her private moment in the sun. They left as this was happening. She said her few special words to her departed late best friend and got emotional, as I knew she would. The radiant photograph of her friend smiling back at her was heart-breaking. Hong Wei cried from the heart and I got a lump in my throat as well. It would bring tears to a stone. She had to say goodbye and learn to let go, which she did. We re-joined Mr. Woo and his son who had moved to the area where there was a big iron stove-like barrel. As is customary, we all lit the replica money of different dominations and waited for it to burn fully, which took a few minutes. It was a mixed atmosphere on the way back to the car and then the city. As we were getting closer to our hotel, Mr. Woo told Hong Wei the name of a restaurant where the two of us would meet them that night for dinner around 19:00.

We took it easy and relaxed in the company of Jin Yang, Wang Hao and of course, Hao Yang. They couldn't take up Mr. Woo's offer of dinner, because they had no babysitter. But they didn't mind that Hong Wei and I accepted the invitation from Mr. Woo.

When the time was right that evening, we made our way by taxi to the restaurant. I forget the name, but whatever. Mr. Woo, his wife, his son and his daughter and their other halves were all there as well as one or two friends. The prepared food was brought in on plates. I tasted some of it out of courtesy. Good Lord! This was spicy to the extreme! I just couldn't eat it, as much as I randomly tried what was on offer. But I did manage to eat some things, which kept my hunger at bay. I washed it down with a beer called Tuborg. The rest ate happily, but I knew where I stood. After dinner we were invited back to Mr. Woo's son, Woo Ting's house. We accepted the invitation. We had a few extra beers and chatted. It was then that I learned that his son Woo Ting was a radio presenter. I told him I was doing some radio work as well, which led to a most enjoyable conversation, with Hong Wei doing all the translating. Everyone got on great and it was a very friendly atmosphere. We left around 23:00, all the worse for a few extra beers.

Like Cinderella, my eyes closed on the pillow before the midnight hour. Before doing so, I wondered what the next day Friday would hold in this city and district of 32,000,000 people. Where would we be going, or what would we be doing?

We got up early on Friday and had breakfast. Surprisingly, after breakfast Jin Yang told us that we were moving hotel. We moved across the city to a hotel called The Bu-Jing. To this day I still don't know why I never even bothered to ask him why. We booked in and then departed on a scheduled trip that Jin Yang had arranged. It was to a former prison camp on the outskirts of the city, called *The Gele Mountain Revolutionary Martyrs Cemetery.* This was a very, very famous and historical place. We got a taxi and arrived there shortly after. This is a major attraction in this incredible city. This trip was to take us to the *Chongqing Hongyan Culture Centre* first.

As we made our way to the main entrance, I could see that there were a lot of other nationalities from all over the world there apart from Chinese and Japanese. It was initially a hideaway for monks, but then it was turned into a prison. We saw all of the outbuildings, just as they were and the furniture and fittings that were there and used at the time. Some of the outhouses you could go in around and others were closed to preserve what was there, although you could look in the windows and see a lot of photographs on view. The experience was chilling, and you could feel history there. It really was a special place to see and to know what history it contained. But you really need to check the history on this place yourself and it would fill you in on dates, facts and figures and what happened there. I was glad I went to see this unique place.

We had a small snack there before we left, as Hao Yang was getting tired and hungry. On our way back to the hotel, Hong Wei informed me that Mr. Woo's son (Woo Ting) and his friend Mr. Shee, whom we had met the previous night at the main meal, wanted to take Jin Yang and myself out for dinner and a few beers around 19:30. Hong Wei and Wang Hao didn't mind, as they were tired too. When we got to our hotel, the two lads were waiting to meet us. They said hello and were delighted to see us. Then they whisked myself and Jin Yang into a waiting taxi. I said to myself, this could be an interesting night, before it ends.

Within a few minutes we were on our way. But I was pleasantly surprised when they brought us to an uptown restaurant, where a private eating floor operated upstairs. This was grandeur to me, which I had not seen in any of my previous eight visits to China. I knew by the way this place was laid out and the number of people at each of the limited tables, this wasn't a cheap restaurant. But the two lads were personal friends with the owner. I guess that helped, because when the bill arrived some two hours later, it certainly did!

The menu meant nothing at all to me and the three lads had very little English. I just said that beef was my main choice and I was easy. They all ordered the same. They were prepared to show me what they had ordered, in case I wanted to sample it. The waitresses brought an individual little cooking stove for each of us over to the table. It was like a little Bunsen burner and it held a round funnel of flavoured water, and you added extra spices to make it stronger. I just kept mine plain and simple, as I was playing it safe. There were three separate types of sliced beef that arrived for me and I tried all three. I added them to the heated water and also added some carrots and some corn on the cob as well.

The three lads just threw all kinds of everything into their burners and left it simmer away. I wondered how they could have eaten it when I saw it. Their food was saturated with spices and practically black with the added flavours. Mr. Woo Ting produced a small bottle of wine from a red bag and asked me did I want to sample some. My reply was, "No thank you, I've tried it before and its dynamite." Even though I was replying in English, I think they got the message loud and clear. Mr. Woo Ting and Jin Yang had the wine and Mr. Shee and I had a few bottles of Tsingtao beer instead.

The conversation turned to football. Mr. Shee was a fan of the beautiful game. He communicated through his phone. Mr. Woo Ting and Jin Yang had not met for twenty years, with the exception of the previous night, and they had a lot to talk about. They all asked me my opinions on the beef. I graded it from one to two to three for them and they were happy. They were surprised when I called over the manager and informed him that I thought the beef was beautiful, which brought a broad smile to his face. The first bottle of wine didn't last very long. Soon Mr. Woo Ting produced a second one from his red bag again. I was happy to drink with Mr. Shee as we consumed our beer at a moderate rate.

But the two lads were burning the candle at both ends and adding a few glasses of canned lager to their tall glasses, as they were reminiscing about the past and growing up. I knew the devil was lurking in the background. When I saw the third bottle of wine appearing from the red bag, then I knew the end was near for both of them. Mr. Woo Ting's mum was Hong Wei's best friend and he lived with her in Anshan city, prior to coming back to Chongqing to live with his dad. We wound down the meal and I must say I enjoyed it. Mr. Shee and I polished off our remaining beers before the bang arrived, as I knew it would. Jin Yang came out the worst for wear I'm afraid, because when we came out the door of the restaurant, the night air hit him like a sledgehammer. But we picked up the pieces including Jin Yang and we eventually got dropped home safe and sound, by taxi. He made it to the bedroom door okay, how, I don't know to this day.

Yes, tomorrow was going to be another day, but with a difference. Our party were due to leave Chongqing on an early morning train the following day, to the neighbouring city of Chengdu. This was for a further few days, which Jin Yang had also arranged. This should be fun I thought, as my head was on the pillow for midnight. Another day would be dawning soon, and it would be another city to my collection.

The last word I will give you on Chongqing: It is still a magical city. When you think of it, 32,000,000 people there and spicy food is the first love to practically all of them! I'm afraid I wouldn't live there for any money. I'd be dead in a week, if that was my only choice of food, as I would be on hunger strike! I would still recommend it for a visit though. When you see this city running on all engines all at the one time, you could only marvel at it. I was glad to have had the experience to have visited Chongqing. But there was more in store for me, as there always is when I visit another city.

Saturday morning arrived and we were all up and ready as early as 07:30. I was surprised that Jin Yang was up (after the previous night) for the challenge that lay ahead. The devil was disappointed – he hadn't got his man this time! Jin Yang, Hong Wei, Wang Hao, Hao Yang and I were all ready to go, when the taxi arrived to take us to the train station. Jin Yang is a fantastic man to organise travel arrangements.

It was close to 08:00, when we found ourselves in the main flow of morning rush hour traffic. The four-lane traffic was moving on all streets like a giant octopus. Coming one way and going in the other. From my front seat observation point, I noticed a motorcyclist drawing up alongside of us. I had noticed over the years that motorcyclists in particular run out of patience fairly quickly. They see the gap and without staying in their proper lane, they head for it. This results in them weaving between the stop and go movement of cars, trucks, buses and other large vehicles. Being a professional bus driver for a number of years, I knew one day I would see the inevitable happen. This action is also through not having any patience and trying to save a minute or two.

The motorbike took off from where he was and continued with these actions that I have described. He clipped two cars as he was crossing lanes and was tossed onto the ground in front of us. Naturally the two cars stopped, put their hazard lights on and went about checking the damage to their cars. Meanwhile the motorcyclist was getting up off the road and looking at what was left of his bike. We were the next car amongst the hundreds of others in the flow and saw it all. The other traffic users just put on their indicators, left or right and went around the scene. As a professional bus driver myself, I asked myself the question: was it worth it? Where did it get the motorcyclist at the end of the day? He was in the wrong and was now going to be late for work. He would have had a lot of explaining to do when the police arrived.

The traffic was now like a moving heard of buffalo, it waited for no one. We got to the main railway station after that slight hold up. I saw thousands of people all over the main building and surrounding areas. They were all heading here, there and everywhere. What a sight to see and it was for real. This was to be our third trip on the bullet train and the adrenalin was still the same for me. Our trip to Chengdu was due to take just one and a half hours. I said I would put my time to good use and catch up on my notes, as I had fallen a bit behind. I still kept an eye on the amazing scenery that meets your eye wherever you travel to on this magic train. Hao Yang was wide alert and excited as the train pulled away from the station. Hong Wei was keeping a close eye on her much-loved grandson too. The technology of it just amazed me and still does! We got in on time – to the minute in fact.

Jin Yang hailed a taxi in a matter of minutes and after discussing a price with the taxi man, we were on our way to our hotel which was called Jinjiang Inn. Most of the taxies here were a lime green colour and they were a Volkswagen Jetta. The hotel was on a narrow little trading street and the taxi driver found it hard to find it, but eventually he did. We booked in and within thirty minutes we were in a taxi and on our way to the world-famous *Chengdu Research Base of Giant Panda*. For me to see this conservation centre was a major plus.

We arrived at the gates of this impressive entrance and I could see that there were tourists from a lot of countries there, other than Chinese or locals. Some days they can be as much as 100,000 visitors pass through the gates. This place covers a lot of ground and you are free to walk anywhere that is not out of bounds. There were signs everywhere indicating where you were. It had all different sections where the pandas were at all different age groups. They had breeding areas, feeding areas and exercising areas. All of these indoor and outdoor areas were there for a purpose. The pandas have never lost their magical appeal.

Crowds flocked from all over to get to the viewing areas, where you got their names and individual history on fixed display boards. Hao Yang was very excited to see pandas all over the place and being so close to them. We saw pandas ranging in ages from six months to six years and a lot older too. There were eating and toilet facilities all over this huge complex as well. Scenic pathways brought you from one place to another. Some of the earlier buildings we were in gave you a history of this world-famous place and a detailed account of the work being carried on there. All of this work of course is in an attempt to keep this lovable species in existence. Funnily enough Michelle Obama and her two daughters had been there recently, as a few giant posters around the visitors' centre indicated. The atmosphere amongst the western visitors that I spoke to all had the one train of thought: what a wonderful place this was and praise for the brilliant work being done there by scientist and a whole host of qualified people. We spent about four hours in there, with a small snack break and a rest in between. It was a very interesting place and a must if you ever find yourself in the vibrant city of Chengdu.

Hao Yang had the last word when his dad Jin Yang bought him a giant panda on the way out. The gates were closing and the stall sellers were gathering up the last of their unsold bits and pieces. I'm sure their money was made earlier in their long, but profitable day. Jin Yang bargained with them and got the panda at a knock down price. This panda was big, really big and cuddly and Hao Yang held him tightly and wouldn't let him out of his sight. We got dropped off back at one of the eating malls. There were fast food stalls and restaurants scattered all over the place. I tried a few meaty things on sticks and from bowls. The food was not as spicy as it was in Chongqing, but I still couldn't handle it. The other four ate all around them, including Hao Yang.

When we got back to the hotel, I had six bottles of Tsingtao beer in my possession. They had a short shelf-life that night and I had a good sleep, even if it was on an empty stomach.

We had an early start on Sunday, with plans to visit a city called Liashon. We had to get a shuttle bus from a certain pick up area in Chengdu. We snatched a quick breakfast from a restaurant across the road from the pick area point and made our 08:30 departure on time. This bus ride was nearly three hours long. It was going to be tiring and a long day at that. This particular place we were going to had several places of interest to see. But most notably it was home to the biggest outdoor stone Buddha in the world.

We had a female tour guide on board the bus, who told everyone about the history of this place that we were bound for. When we got there, she conducted the tour from the bus to the main entrance of this mountainous region. She brought us to the main Buddhist temple first, where luckily for us, the monks were just finishing their prayer session. They all spilled out from a side hall and some took up positions selling souvenirs, relics and other items that they had made themselves. I saw others freely talking to people, but they all stayed within a confined area. There were other statues to past Buddha's and scholars around the place. I suppose the monks continually explain all of this to the countless visitors that pass through this historical place every day. We had a look around at other unusual buildings and small temples, which made up this historical mountain sight.

One of the main points of interest that I thought was fascinating was the viewing area on this mountain, where you can actually see the three rivers meeting. Most people would say and understandably so, how could you see this. When you look at a certain spot in the river, you can see this happening. There are three different mud colours combined. One of the rivers looked very brown, another looked very grey and the other looked a little green. You have to look carefully, closely and you can actually see the point where the three of them meet. I thought it was tremendous to see this phenomenal sight with my own eyes. There were hundreds of tourists scattered all over this mountainous region.

Not far from this point, there is another viewing area, where you can see the top of the giant Buddha's head and his upper body. But you are restricted by your viewing position and the drop of his giant body, such is the height and it is also in between two huge cliff faces, with hundreds of visitors all cramming for a glimpse from that limited spot. The *Leshan Grand Buddha* is in a sitting position and looked to me to be a least one hundred feet in height. There was a walkway that brought you down the side of this mountain, which would enable you to see the complete size of this gigantic Buddha, but it was crammed with people going down and coming up. It would have taken us a week to get up and down and Hao Yang had to be considered too. We saw what we could and left it at that. The time was running a little against us, as our scheduled shuttle bus was due to leave from our pickup point at 16:00.

On our way back from this historic mountain, Jin Yang sprung a surprise on us with unexpected tickets for the sightseeing cruise. They travel up and down this river, where they go to the face of the mountain and from there you can get a perfect view of the giant stone Buddha. Back down the road from the entrance to this mountain, there is a pier on the banks of the river where these cruiser boats are moored up.

So Jin Yang led the charge, as we hurriedly made our way to the next available boat and boarded it with a few other tourists. We put on our life jackets and went up on the deck and waited for the cruiser to take off. The time was 15:00 when the skipper turned on the engines. This was definitely a bonus, as far as I was concerned. This was now going to give us a full clear view of the enormity of the biggest stone Buddha in the world. Just think about that for a moment, as I did.

After a few minutes going upriver, we saw ourselves getting closer to the giant stone figure of the Buddha. The skipper's boat brought us right up to the cliff face. He cut the engines. We were static in the water and able to take a few unique photographs. We could see the hundreds of people on the top of the mountain, where we had been an hour earlier. We could also see the railed path down the side of the rock face, but it was full of people trying to get up and others going down. We could see the full view of the Buddha from top to bottom. It was just an incredible sight. I wondered had anyone from my home city of Waterford seen this magnificent spectacle. I doubted it. How it was made and put there was a complete mystery to me. Unless someone tells me how this was done, I will have to carry it to the grave with me. The detail of the features in the stone were amazing and the Buddha was painted in a mostly light pinkish colour.

The skipper turned the cruiser around after a few minutes and within fifteen minutes we had returned to the pier docking area. We were back on dry land and made the shuttle bus with about ten minutes to spare. The courier lady looked a little worried at our late arrival, but the bus still didn't go until 16:00. We were the real winners here, have no doubt about that. Another three hours took us back to Chengdu, where we arrived at about 19:00. We were all tired and Hao Yang was knocked out. We got some food in another shopping mall, when Hao Yang came around. I ate a small bit, but I did wash it down with four bottles of Tsingtao beer. It had been a tiresome day for travelling, but I think in the overall context of what we had seen and in particular the giant Buddha, it was well worth it.

Monday October the 10th was my mother's birthday. How could I forget that, when I think of the mother I had? She would have been ninety-five years old, if she had still been alive. She was in my thoughts for most of that day. Yes, she was a mother in a million!

We had to vacate our hotel early, giving us a bit of time on our hands. We would be catching the train back to Chongqing at 17:00. Jin Yang being the wonderful organiser, suggested we see another museum in Chengdu city. It was called *The Wuhou Shrine Museum*. This was another wonderful museum which dealt mainly with a warlord called Liu Bei who joined forces with two other warlords. It's the story of the three kingdoms history and there are artefacts there that date back to 223 AD. We spent about three hours in there covering the whole area and it was well worth it for me to see what I saw. We got something to eat and then made our way to the main railway station. Even in this city of far less people than Chongqing, the main railway station was still packed with people. I suppose you could say everybody was going somewhere and the rest were arriving from everywhere. This train station had high security personnel too, but they are there for the safety and security of everyone.

On the bullet train it was only going to be a few stops really, so boredom didn't set in. We left on time and got in on time, as I expected. During transit, I caught up on my notes again and brought them all up to date. When we got to Chongqing, we had to get a taxi, find our hotel and get something to eat. We had a pleasant surprise when our taxi dropped us off at our hotel about an hour later. There was Mr. Woo's son, Woo Ting, waiting for us, with a message. His dad and family members insisted on us joining him in a nearby restaurant, which was a blessing in disguise.

When we got there Mr. Woo and his wife, and the rest of his family were delighted to see us. We didn't waste any time tucking into the self-service buffet food that was on offer. Surprisingly, the food was not as spicy as before and I wondered why. Mr. Woo informed Hong Wei that he had specifically picked this restaurant in my interest, as he was aware that I was on hunger strike (literally) and not eating as much food as I should, due to it being too spicy. What more could you say of the man and his wife, for being so thoughtful? We finished our dinner around 21:00 and thanked our hosts most sincerely. We were in bed and asleep for our usual time of 22:00.

Tuesday was our last day in Chongqing and it was to prove very interesting indeed. Mr. Woo and his good wife picked us up at our hotel after breakfast. It was a trip he had planned for us the night before, which I didn't know anything about. How could I with no Chinese! We had a long stretch in the day to fill, as our flight was not until 20:00 back to the city of Shenyang. He took us to one of the major attractions in Chongqing. It was to the *Great Hall of the People Building* first. What an impressive sight this building is from the outside. It looks down on a huge wide flat stoned open space. The building is used by the Chinese National Government for regular meetings. Unfortunately, the day we were there, it was closed to the public. Across from it is another impressive sight, Chongqing's *People's Assembly Hall.* The Chinese national flag was flying proudly in the wind from both buildings.

At the other end of this wide-open space and looking just as impressive is *Chongqing China Three Georges Museum.* As you know by now, I have seen other museums in my travels, but boy, was this one also impressive. When we went up the steps to this eye-catching entrance, it was saturated with security. Inside the main doors, all articles were x-rayed in the machine. The huge arena-like ground floor is in a cream colour marble, which is the same on the other three floors above ground level. Entry to these is gained from a massive wide-open staircase with marble steps in the same colour.

The structure and the layout of this building was just fabulous. Where do I start with the history within this building? It is all there to see and goes back as far as you want. There were sections there on paintings, culture, arts and crafts. There was information there on famous wars that were fought. There was also a section on authors and poets, plus past currencies and a section on the Chinese ethnic groups. Then there were the changing times of the famous Blaganzi River and the Three Gorges.

The real surprise for me was the making of the famous dam. It raises cargo shipping boats on a lift-like basis. The water comes in and the boats rise to the appropriate level. This took years to consider from successive Chinese leaders. It was a pioneering project where there was no room for error. Building the dam was an incredible piece of engineering. They have a model of the dam in the river and a continuous video of how it was made. The dam also serves for conserving water in the normal fashion. It blew me away that this could be made and so successfully. Even on the floors, there was a section with a glass surface with a model of the Ghangie River from its start, through to its finish. It's a length of about thirty feet that you could see straight through, when you looked down. It was like a glass map under your feet. It was an incredible piece of work to manufacture. We were there for about three hours and took in the three upper floors as well. Ah, this place just blew me away with its splendour surroundings and all that was displayed. It was easy to see why there was so much security in and around this fascinating museum. It is worth going to Chongqing alone to see this place. Mr. Woo and his wife knew that we were impressed. You couldn't but be impressed with what we had seen.

The time was moving on. We made a quick return to Mr. Woo's house, where he insisted on cooking some food for us before our departure for the airport. I had some Australian beef he had got for me. This was well cooked and beautiful, as the rest ate other food. What more could this man have done for us. But the clock moved on and so did we. At 17:30 Mr. Woo and his wife took us to the airport. We said our goodbyes to them and made our way to the check-in desk. There was a big crowd there and a lot of security people were evident when I was looking around. But a new experience was about to unfold before my eyes. It was the first time I was to witness a random security check in the queues of people waiting to check in. Anyone in any queue could be picked out at random. There was a guy with a torch like stick (like a baton) and a dog, observing everyone and he would just walk over to anyone and just tap your bag or case. I just had a gut feeling that he was going to tap my bag. Within a few minutes, I was next on his radar and it happened. I was clean, and he just walked elsewhere. I wondered whether it was because I was a westerner.

I think explaining yourself here if you broke the rules, would have been some experience. After the check-in, it was more security and then it was straight to our departure gate. The good news was, I was presuming the return flight would take five or six hours. So, I was pleasantly surprised when Hong Wei informed me that it would only take around three hours. The return flight from Chongqing to Shenyang goes direct. Our outward flight had gone the long way around, as it had a drop-off and a pickup. Boy, was I happy when I heard that news. I would consider Chengdu a great city to see and equally Chongqing a marvellous city to visit, but if you don't like spicy food, then I would suggest you search around for less spicy eating places. There are still other fabulous cities to see in China. But Chongqing has to be the capital of the world, when it comes to spicy foods, and what an experience it was for me to have visited this wonderful city.

It was Tuesday night and our plane was en route to Shenyang and closing in fast. Within a few minutes of landing on time, we had changed transport and were on our way to Anshan city. Hao Yang was in another world and fast asleep. But I was well aware that his big day, his 3rd birthday, was on Saturday and we were leaving on the Sunday. Still there were lots to do and see before then. The party wasn't over yet, but I knew my next party would be my retirement one in Anshan city in about three years' time.

Waking up on the Wednesday morning around 08:00 and having only arrived in from Shenyang at 01:00 that same morning, I was tired but happy to be back. My body ached from all the travelling, but it was still good that I had gone. After breakfast, Hong Wei and I had to go and see a cousin of hers who she was very close to. I knew her very well from previous visits. She was dying of cancer and we spent about two hours in her company, with Hong Wei doing all the talking. She was very happy to see Hong Wei and I was pleased. I just sat back and relaxed, watching a little television, even though it was in Chinese. We both knew that it would be the last time we would see her alive. It was a sad occasion, particularly when we were leaving and had to say goodbye. We gave her a hug and a kiss, but it was heart-breaking, knowing you weren't going to see her alive again.

We took it easy for the rest of the day and left our bodies thaw out. We had a dinner date at 18:00 that evening with three friends of Hong Wei. Just to eat food that wasn't spicy was a welcome relief. We ate at a restaurant called, believe it or not The Old Dock Road. Now don't tell me where that name came from, but it is there. I enjoyed the food and the beer went down well also. They all enjoyed their conversation in Chinese, as I enjoyed listening to them. The night wound down with a few photographs and a long goodbye.

We had an early night and were home by 21:15 but didn't hit the bed until 22:15. Three days to go and I knew it would be a hectic run into the finish. I was dreading Sunday, as we would be in the air at 13:00, having to say goodbye to family and friends, who always made our stay so enjoyable. Thursday was my last chance to get some presents for those back in the Emerald Isle (Ireland).

With breakfast over it was straight down to the main shopping area. There are hundreds of shops to choose from. I just wanted a few souvenir shops. There was no rush, as in my head I was winding down too. The green, green grass of home was starting to find its way to the brain cells in my head. Over the last few visits to China, I have learnt to let the women do the shopping. I just stay inside on a seat or outside, watching the world go by. On this occasion, when Hong Wei went into one of these giant shopping centres, I waited outside for the two hours while she was in there. I even watched workmen putting down concrete slabs to replace broken ones outside on the street. It was interesting to see what method they were using compared to the western technique. They were a little different in the tools they used. They used different shovels, trowels, floats and they mixed the sand and cement differently. They observed me looking at them and seemed friendly by nature. But the job was done while I was there. Then again, who would I be to tell the Chinese, of all people, how to lay stones. Most of their history is stone related, through The Great Wall, museums, buildings, monasteries and temples.

When Hong Wei emerged, I entered a small souvenir shop close by and was only five minutes inside purchasing a few things. We then went to one of her sister houses', where her other sisters were present. They all played Ma Jiang. Then we had dinner in the early afternoon, after which they resumed their game. I kept up on my notes and relaxed with some television channels. I knew there was still a lot to write about before 13:00 on the Sunday, when there would be no turning back. We stayed there until around 20:00 that night, with another snack in between.

When we got back to Jin Yan and Wang Hao's apartment, there was a World Cup qualifying game on the telly between Poland and Armenia.

I watched that and the rest of the highlights from other games before I retired at 23:00. Hong Wei had long since departed to her pillow, as she had to get her beauty sleep. All was well, that ended well.

Friday came as it always comes, but I think and have always thought that Friday is different than any other day in the week. I think people are more relaxed, particularly if they are off over the weekend. It started with breakfast outside Jin Yang's apartment on the side of the road, at around 08:00. Pan Pan was picking us up at 08:30.

It was from a little well-known cooking stall where the passing trade was for all those rushing to work and only had a few minutes to spare. They made little crispy fritters with eggs and flour. They were like long pastries without the cream. It was something similar to making pancakes, where they keep pouring on the hot mix like a rotating system onto a big hot giant saucepan. I had four of them and they were nice and filling. A bottle of Pepsi-Cola washed them down. Hong Wei chose carefully with her own selection and a drink of hot water. The two cooking stall attendants made two or three other pastry items as well, which they cooked in hot cooking oil. This was a little bonus for me to see and eat from it to.

Pan Pan picked us up on schedule at 08:30. I did not know where we were going until Hong Wei informed me. Hong Wei and her sisters had to go back to say a final goodbye to her late parents and brother. We met Mr. Liu and her sisters at a certain place en route. It was the same routine as before, only this time they brought fruit, wine and cigarettes. When we got there and stood in front of the headstone, they peeled the fruit, lit the cigarettes, which they left there and then they poured a little of the wine over the perimeter of the base. I presumed it was an offering of what their parents liked. I was able to handle my emotions a lot better than the first time. We spent a few minutes there and then went down to the end of the road and carried out the burning of the money ritual again. Then it was back to visit their brother again at the Buddha Temple. I stayed in the car and chatted as best I could with Mr. Liu until they returned.

We got back to Anshan city and we all had lunch in the restaurant called Com.ie. The beef was nice and done on a rotating chain-like machine where it keeps rotating on the skewers. For a change I stayed on Pepsi-Cola, just to give the body a break. Mr. Liu and Hong Wei's sisters went their separate ways after lunch. You might say what happened next was a little out of routine, but I was open to anything that was suggested. When we were finished at the restaurant, Pan Pan gave us a lift to a hairdresser that Hong Wei had an appointment with.

You might say is this worth talking about? Well it was if you saw this hairdresser guy in action. He was so busy, that you only got to see him through a strict appointment. He was tops at his profession and he gave Hong Wei his undivided attention. I could see that this guy had been hairdressing for a long time, as his attention to detail was that of a perfectionist. He was chatty to Hong Wei, as she filled him in on our relationship and marriage. He had a good sense of humour, which I could see from his body language. If this guy was in Ireland and working in one of the big cities, he would do well. As he was coming to the end, I just sat there in the salon watching in amazement at the transformation he had made in Hong Wei's appearance. This guy was tops at his profession, it stood out a mile! When that was finished and Hong Wei looking like a million dollars, this happy and conscientious hairdresser was still paid in Yuan.

We had another appointment, as Pan Pan picked us up and the two girls wanted to see a cousin of theirs who had a stroke a few years ago and was now getting home help. I had met this man before briefly but didn't know whether he was still alive or dead. They stopped on the way at a supermarket and got three boxes of special milk for him. I thought it was a very charitable act of kindness from them. When we got to the old apartment complex and knocked on the door, his carer opened it. The old man was thrilled to see them both, as they gave him a loving hug.

It made me think about life and what can happen in the blink of an eye. A million things can happen at any stage in one's life. So, make the most of it folks, while your health is okay and live every day as if it was your last.

I saw how incapacitated the old man was. He was delighted to see his two nieces and have them spend nearly two hours with him in the presence of his carer. We eventually had to go. The carer thanked Hong Wei and Pan Pan for coming. I was only an onlooker in the visiting episode. Both of them gave him a kiss and a hug before we left and then retreated down the darkened steps. I asked Hong Wei what they had spoken about and she just said they reminisced about the past. Thoughtfulness and a little bit of kindness can go a long way. It was nice for me to have witnessed it.

We made something to eat when Pan Pan dropped us back at Jin Yang's apartment and relaxed until it was time for bed. The next day was Saturday, but with a difference. It was D-day, as it was Hao Yang's third birthday. This was the other main reason we had stayed on for the extra week. I thought at the time it was going to be a day that I was not going to forget in a hurry. How right I was, in making that judgement. Hong Wei's grandson's big day arrived as Saturday kicked in.

When Hao Yang woke, he went straight in to see his mum and dad and then Hong Wei to see his presents. To see the excitement on his face is what it's all about. He was more than delighted with what he got. After a light breakfast, plans had been put in place for a party in a very nice restaurant. We took it easy until we departed from the apartment at 11:00. We collected this birthday cake, in a rather impressive large box from a specialised baker on the way to the restaurant. Hao Yang was naturally excited, as it was his special day and he knew it.

We arrived at 11:25 and the families were all waiting to congratulate him and give him his presents. We were ushered into this rather large private spacious room. It had two massive rotating glass-top tables. But the orders were one for men and the other for women and children. This was the first time in all of my travels to China that I was not sitting at the same table as Hong Wei, while having food. But Mr. Liu was next to me and it was, as always, great to see him.

We all went with the flow and the wide selection of food was the exact same on both tables. There was a great buzz as the Tsingtao beer flowed on our table by the bottle. Mr. Liu and I kept our elbows busy, as our small glasses were continually topped up with beer. One thing I did notice on this occasion and it surprised me, was that lamb was the main meat on the menu list. Normally beef is the more common on the menu. What was even more surprising was that nobody was eating much of the lamb. They were all sticking to their other original foods and what they were accustomed too. I was more than happy to tuck into the lamb, as given the choice, I would prefer it to beef any day. There were other choices that I sampled, but the lamb took a hammering.

The occasion was all about Hao Yang on his third birthday. I said a few words and stressed that we were delighted to be there, even though it was on our last day. Hong Wei passed the words on to the attendance. With all the main food consumed, I suppose it was inevitable that our attention turned to the cake. When they opened the cake, it was a sight to behold. Hao Yang got the first slice which he tucked into. The rest of us took our turn and it was worth waiting for. It was a sponge cake and it just oozed with cream and jam. If I had to think about the calories, I would never have eaten it. After a good three hours of drinking and eating, we finished with a rendition of Happy Birthday to Hao Yang. He had loads of photographs taken with everyone and I think he was aware of all the commotion his birthday had caused. That brought an end to the proceedings on that occasion, for another year.

The five of us returned back to the apartment. I watched some Chinese football on the telly, as Hong Wei and Jin Yang had the task of packing our four suitcases in the afternoon. I would get annoyed and run out of patience doing that. As the few hours passed and teatime approached, I wanted to go for one last meal to my favourite restaurant called 'Da Han' that has the best beef in Anshan city, in my opinion. I passed these comments on to Hong Wei and she passed them onto Jin Yang, who in turn said, "No problem Billy, we will do that." He said he would book a table at the restaurant for 19:30.

When the clock struck 19:30, we were all seated in the restaurant and ready to be served beef from the charcoal fire, with the steel grill taking the flames. The three steaks made an appearance and after a few minutes under the intense heat, they were done to perfection. Another three followed the first three, with the same result. There was another table there, where the rest of the other foods were cooked. The owner made an appearance when he heard from the manager that I had selected his restaurant for our last supper. But the real reason, and he knew it, being I was there was for the quality of his beef. He gave us a free choice of anything else on the menu which the others availed of.

I was happy, as Hong Wei and Jin Yang had some noodle dish and Wang Hao and Hao Jang had something else. I was full of beef and was more than happy. We finished up and I gave my complements to the manager on the way out. We were home at our favourite time of 22:00 and asleep by 22:30. That was the last supper over, tomorrow Sunday was yet to come. It would be our last day on Chinese soil for a while. On this occasion, I really was dreading Sunday. But it would arrive after a few hours' sleep and we had to be ready for the long goodbye.

We were up early at 08:00 and had a decent breakfast. Our suitcases were packed from the previous day. What they contained, I didn't know and to make it better, I didn't care either. Hong Wei's family arrived in four cars and my good friend Mr. Liu was present in one of them. Around 09:00 our convoy of four cars headed out of Anshan city on the one-hundred-mile route to Shenyang airport, which takes about two hours comfortably. We got there for 11:00 and checked in straight away. Boy, was I glad to see those four suitcases gone, out of sight. We had a waiting time of two hours to kill. Hong Wei's family members always stay to the end, which makes saying goodbye all the harder. Over the years they have been so good to me, but we had to let go eventually. And boy, was it hard. I hugged and kissed the females and shook hands with the males and lastly, with my great friend Mr. Liu. That brought a tear to my eye as the space between us grew with every step.

Security was tight and thorough, which was nothing new at airports and railways to us. But all our papers were in order and we proceeded to the next security screening. Hong Wei's family were now out of sight and just a memory. Here again, everything was strict and thorough. Then we made our way to the last security checkpoint where a surprise awaited me. Hong Wei went through without a hitch. The Chinese policewoman checked my ticket and then my passport, where she unexpectedly said to me, "Will you wait there please, sir?" With a wave, she summoned a second senior female official from a desk behind her. I said to myself, this is all I need now.

The second official took my passport back to her desk and started to check things. This was the first time that this had happened to me in eight previous visits. But I remained cool, as the first official looked straight through me as I waited. After a few minutes the second official left her desk and made her way back to the checkpoint and instructed the girl to wave me through. I never asked her what the problem was, nor had there been one. No, I just politely said, "Thank you." and moved on. Of course, I breathed a sigh of relief as I passed through the checkpoint and the waiting Hong Wei breathed an even bigger one when I drew level with her. She asked me was there a problem. To which I replied, "There was no problem. Let's go."

Within minutes, we were up and away, as the city of Shenyang was now just a memory. Our first flight was to Beijing and then a ten-hour flight to Amsterdam in Holland. The final part was the usual, from Amsterdam to Dublin in Ireland. I was looking forward to it like a hole in the head. It's the one thing that turns me off before every trip. It's the length of the flights and the layovers. We had to kill some time in Amsterdam, before we got our flight back to Ireland. We passed through emigration and customs no problem, and then it was a three-hour bus ride back to Waterford city. As I said earlier, its twenty-four hours travelling time from door to door. We arrived on our own doorstep at 03:00. This was immediately followed by the usual marathon sleep.

When we both woke up, there was no late breakfast from the now departed Fengqin. That was strange in itself as both of us dearly missed her. But she has settled back in London, England now and we keep in touch with her. To think that she went to China and found Hong Wei for me in my hour of need. Like in Gilbert O'Sullivan's great hit song *Alone*

Again Naturally, one of the lines says: I*n my hour of need, I truly am indeed, alone again naturally.* But in my case, I really was not alone again. Such things could only be written, where else only in the Gods.

Coincidently, in the month of February in 2018, my time with Bus Eireann (the national bus company) came to an end. This was following my retirement after twenty-two years' service, and forty-nine years' working in total. What will I do with myself? Plenty! I never doubted this situation for a second.

I had been doing a bit of radio work previously, co-hosting a sports show once a week. I enjoyed this work and the challenges it threw at me. Unfortunately, that radio station ran out of funding and closed down. I just took it in my stride, like the other things I accepted in my life and just got on with it. A few months passed and things started to happen again in the media world for me. What is the saying you hear sometimes? When one door closes, another opens.

At the time of writing this, I'm doing sports media work and am involved with Waterford's number No. 1 radio station, WLR FM. I have been a regular contributor on the WLR FM podcast show 'Keane on Sport' since September 2018. This show has proved extremely popular with listeners all over the world, especially Waterford exiles. I also broadcast as an analyst with WLR FM on live football match coverage during the season. This work takes up some of my week doing revision, checking on results, reports and noting facts and figures on football. There is a challenge there every week and I like doing it.

The rest of my time is spent watching most sports. I do a bit of reading, my favourites being autobiographies, as I find them interesting and relaxing. I also do a small bit of cycling once or twice a week, plus a bit of gardening when the sun shines. On the weekends, I relax and have a few beers with a few friends of mine.

Now, an all too familiar route

Hong Wei and I went back to China in March of 2019 to see her much-loved family and friends. Her son Jin Yang and daughter-in-law, Wang Hao, had an addition to their family in 2017, a daughter called Yue Yue to join their son, Hao Yang. This was to be my tenth visit to China, and it was as exciting as the other nine. It was another experience for me, which I was to enjoy, as usual.

On Saturday the 23rd of March, Hong Wei and I flew out of Dublin on the now familiar route to Amsterdam, on to Beijing and then finally to Shenyang. At our final destination, after passing through security and customs, the arrivals area presented itself to us yet again. As expected, all of Hong Wei's family were there waiting. In that initial moment when you see them, the excitement was still the same for everyone.

As was the usual practice, there were hugs given out freely. As expected, her two grandchildren got the biggest hugs. Hao Yang was now six and his sister Yue Yue had just gone over the one-and-a-half-year mark. It was also great to see my good friend Mr. Liu, Hong Wei's brother-in-law. Her four sisters, her niece Hong Hong with her son Yang Ren, and her nephew Niu Niu were all present.

We arrived back in Anshan city and went to a certain hotel, where a welcome home party had been arranged. I gave a speech specifying how delighted we were to be back amongst Hong Wei's family and friends after a two-and-a-half-year absence. We enjoyed the occasion. I recognised all the familiar dishes and their contents that were on display. Tiredness played its part shortly after, as I knew it would.

As usual, we were staying with her son, Jin Yang, his wife Wang Hao and the two children. We had planned to go to Shanghai and two other cities during our stay. Hong Wei was staying an extra month, as I was returning to Ireland at the end of April to take in Newcastle United's last home game against Liverpool. This was a ritual that I had done for the previous thirty-two years and the fixture was somewhat more important this year, with Liverpool going for the title.

I could see over the following days, just what it meant for Hong Wei to be here amongst her family and friends. I just went with the flow and sampled the familiar tastes of food, but always on the lookout for something new.

Two events were pencilled in for definite. Hong Wei's birthday party on April 25th and I had promised myself a retirement party on my next visit. The weather was beautiful, which surprised me. The days passed as sure as night followed day. The familiar sights around Anshan city that greeted me were still the same. I noticed that 90% of the taxies had changed from red and grey to lime green and grey. When we went shopping with Jin Yang, Wang Hao and the two children in the supermarket, I noticed something that I had not seen before. On the steep incline escalator with a full shopping trolley to a lower level, I noticed that the trolley was stopped in one spot. There are magnetic wheels on the trolleys, so your trolley does not run away on you. You'll agree a very good idea, which I had not experienced before.

On one of the days, Hong Wei had to meet a friend that she had not seen for years. We had a pleasant afternoon eating dinner in a restaurant called Jin-Da-Lai. I just listened to them talking in Chinese and still wondered how they speak the language. I gave up trying to learn it a long time ago. Hong Wei was enjoying every minute of her stay and that was important from my point of view. The days passed and to see the enjoyment Hong Wei got with her two grandchildren was worth the trip alone.

Over the following few days, we visited aunts and uncles in rotation. They were all glad to see her. All of these people I had met before, on previous visits.

On the first Saturday (March 30th) Mr. Liu brought us to see the local football team, Liaoning, playing Shenyang in Shenyang on a supporters' minibus. The fans on the bus were friendly and welcomed us warmly. Surprisingly with the previous few days having been beautiful, the weather was changing slightly as we left Anshan city at around 11:00. This was a 100-mile trip north and as we approached Shenyang city it was colder, and it actually snowed. I found that amazing, but the light snow did not dampen the supporters' spirit, nor mine. Security at the grounds was tight, as it always is, but the banter between the fans is always great to hear. Liaoning deservedly lost the match 3–0, as they were caught on the break three times. To make matters worse, they also had a man sent off for a straight handed right uppercut to an opponent.

By the time the match was over, the snow had stopped, but it was freezing cold and my feet were nowhere to be found. On returning to the warmth of the bus, things got better. My feet came back to life. After some two hours on the road, everyone was still in good spirits as we approached Anshan city.

Shanghai was still on our itinerary, it was just a case of when Hong Wei's son, Jin Yang, would book it. As before, our daily routine remained the same until we finally got a departure date of April 9th.

Another thing I had learnt and had not heard before was that Chinese people consider walking over manhole covers to be bad luck.

Something else that had escaped me before for some reason was the collection of cash from banks. Within a few days as we passed certain banks, we saw routine cash collections with a difference. A security company called 'Security of China' pulled up outside of a bank in a black transit van with darkened windows and a side door. Within seconds, this door opened and four men in black uniforms emerged in military fashion. Two of them had machine guns and one of them entered the bank with the two carriers. The other armed guard stood at the entrance door. After a few minutes the three of them emerged from the bank, two of whom carried cases which they dispatched in a rear hatch at the back of the van under the watchful eye of the armed guard. The other armed guard at the bank door covered everything else that moved. The three then got into the side door of the van, as their armed colleague at the bank door simultaneously left his post and entered through the side door also. His machine gun was at the ready at all times and from my observation point, I would say, had the need arose, he would not have hesitated to have used it.

Moral of the story, 'Don't mess around with these guys!'. The whole operation only took a few minutes in full view of the passing general public. I'm sure it was a daily sight for Chinese people, but for me, it was an experience to see it in the course of a few days.

On Sunday the 7th of April we had a different engagement, as Pan Pan and her husband Dong Bin hosted all the family to dinner in a country restaurant. This was definitely going to be a new experience for me. Everyone had arrived at the predetermined time of 12:30. The sun was shining brightly as we turned in from the main road a few miles outside of Anshan city. This venue had a driveway to it and was surrounded by trees in a garden. It really was picturesque with a few separate eating cabins for different numbers of guests. There were twenty-one of us, but we got a cabin to accommodate everyone in our party. The selection of food as always was a broad range and excellent. My favourite beer has always been (Tsingtao) and that was available. It was drunk at a steady rate by Mr. Liu. Mr. He, Dong Bin and myself. I believe over the course of our meal, we drunk a lot of this bottled beer. When the meal was over and everyone was satisfied and full, there was karaoke on offer. The good thing was we didn't even have to move anywhere, as this was catered for within the building.

The Chinese just love singing and are not shy when it comes to exercising their vocal cords. This karaoke session brought the best out in all the participating singers, even the bad ones like me. I even attempted a few Elvis Presley numbers and I didn't scare anyone out the door, because the songs were obviously in English. Hong Wei treated those was present with a few songs using her excellent voice. She didn't need karaoke. After three hours with the singers and non-singers, the karaoke session came to an end. But this was not the end of the proceedings, as two tables were cleared for the popular board game of Ma Jiang. I don't know how to play it, but I love looking at them playing it. The time passed away, during which I had taken a long walk. But darkness did eventually descend on this unique restaurant. When we came outside to get into the cars for our journey back to Anshan city, the place was transformed with a dazzling display of lit Chinese lanterns. It was beautiful to see and added to these unique surroundings.

On Tuesday the 9th, the six of us departed for Shanghai from Shenyang airport with an early evening two-hour flight. I thought to myself before boarding the plane, this could be interesting. What was I going to experience on this trip?

We arrived into Shanghai's busy airport on time, which was great. Jin Yang had a car hired at the airport in Shanghai for when we arrived. Even though it was dark, the infrastructure and bright lights guided us into this famous city. They were neon lights flashing atop every high rise commercial or industrial building. Apartment blocks were scattered across the city's skyline, as we neared our hotel accommodation. It was with the excellent hotel group called Jinjiang Inn Hotel. This successful company have hotels all over China. We booked in and got our heads down, as the two grandchildren were now in the land of nod. Hong Wei and I closed our eyes in the darkness within a few minutes of hitting the bed.

What was in store for us tomorrow, I wondered.

I had heard so much about Shanghai, it was going to be a case of judging it for myself. One of the most famous cities visited by tourists in the world with a population of around twenty-six million people. I was not to be disappointed, for what followed.

Hiring the car, proved to be the best move we could have made, as we were free to come and go as we pleased over the following few days.

On awakening and having breakfast, it was to be a long day that was on the itinerary. Shanghai Disneyland was the first choice that Jin Yang had picked out. It's situated not too far outside the city, but boy, was it impressive as we approached it from the motorway. It had the main feature (The Castle) towering into the sky and instantly recognisable. The car park alone was divided into sections for cars and buses. Was it big? It was huge, about the size of twenty-five football pitches, if not bigger!

Everybody parked in strict rotation under the directions of the stewards that were in attendance. We walked the two miles to the main entrance and waited with the other people, to go through security. We then went through another security area. The crowds were in their hundreds, but if you counted who passed through in the course of a day, it would have to be thousands.

It was a day to remember, from opening time in the morning at 11:00 until 21:00 that night on our feet. Ten hours of walking around to all of the magical sights that greeted us. All I can say is, if you're ever in Shanghai, do go and see it. When we finally got back to the car, I felt like I had been through an Olympic marathon walk. Having seen the lot and the excitement on the two grandchildren's faces throughout the day, it was worth it. I also knew I would not be back this way again.

The next day was more of the same. An early start after breakfast was the order from Jin Yang. He drove us to an underground car park and when we surfaced, a place called The Bound Walkway greeted us. From here you get a view that is most commonly seen on every one of the Shanghai skylines from across the river. Again, huge crowds thronged this familiar walkway with every nationality you could think of, to be seen. I think everyone on it had a camera phone, a camera or a video recorder and they were all in constant use.

In the afternoon, we took in the unreal world-famous Yuyuan Garden Malls. There were thousands of tourists walking on foot through this vast array of shops, market stalls and eating places. We spent hours there and I was beginning to get shorter by the hour from two days of continuous walking. I even saw groups who had stopped off from their world cruise. At the end of that experience, the night-time brought relief to my feet, with the help of food and a few Tsingtao beers.

Those two days were followed with a visit to the Wildlife Park Zoo, where the magic never seems to disappear. Another six hours were spent in there on foot, like most of the other visitors. The grandchildren, Hao Yang and Yue Yue had great fun seeing all of the animals on view. There were loads of side shows there also with wonderful effects. We got a lot of those in and I thought the thinking and planning behind the ideas was mind-boggling.

As evening approached and darkness fell, we made our way over to the Shanghai Tower. All I can say is if you ever want to see the whole of Shanghai in one place, this is where to go. It was 19:00 in the evening when we arrived and there was no shortage of sightseers. What must it have been like all day, with the continuous flow of tourists? Again, security checks were extremely tight with several checks on our way to the ground floor lifts. This was one hundred and eighteen floors to the observation area. Yes, straight up in fifty-five seconds. That's why this tower has the fastest elevators in the world.

When we got there, the area was wonderfully done in a circular fashion with reinforced glass, which gives you a view like nothing I had ever seen before in my life. I remember looking out over all the other high-rise buildings which dwarfed this spectacle. I walked around the circumference with Hong Wei and marvelled at the views by night. Ah, this had to be seen to be believed. We also looked down on the surrounding river and the lit up cruise boats travelling at a romantic speed.

The traffic below was one big gigantic movement of lights on the streets. It was incredible to see the motorways stretching out as far as the eye could see and all the different lights on the ground and on the buildings below. Jin Yang, Wang Hao, Hao Yang and Yue Yue had seen all of these sights too. We spent a good hour up there, before making our way down to the eating floor, with our numerous photos taken from on high. Here you had a pick of restaurants to choose from. We all duly picked from the wide range of food and tucked into it without hesitation.

Our last day in Shanghai was just spent relaxing, as we had a lot of mileage to do in the hired car over the following few days.

The next day after breakfast it was all six of us into the car, as the city of Suzhou beckoned, with a surprise stop on the way. After only a few short miles from the disappearing Shanghai skyline, we turned off the main road. It was approaching high noon and the sun was out in force.

The run through the countryside was a very enjoyable experience and the scenery was at times breath-taking. But there was the added bonus of stopping off at a rather famous ancient town called Zhou Zhuang in Jiangsu province. It was in actual fact a town built on water, stretching back in history to some nine hundred years.

After a little soul-searching we found this magical place. This was a completely hidden-away town, with its own entrance through a street with a maze of shops on it. This turned out to be rather unique, as on getting there, I thought it was just a few market shops with a boat or two on a single canal. Going over one small bridge brought us into another area where there were canals with lots of gondola-like boats on them. These were operating for tourists to enjoy the views from the water. The place was thronged with people and a multitude of shops greeted our eyes. I asked myself how this place could be built on water. It was just amazing to see the canals running through it and around it. There were hundreds of people at the shops that were selling everything from an anchor to a needle. I really couldn't believe what I was seeing.

The six of us made our way through the maddening crowds and began looking at several famous houses from a historical point of view. Jin Yang and Wang Hao were fantastic in looking after Hao Yang and Yue Yue in a pram. These were all narrow little pathways, crammed with tourists. I guess this was China's answer to Italy's' Venice. We did get some food at one of the countless food stalls that were operating there. After spending several hours there, it was time to go. We must have covered every inch of this fascinating place.

Back up on the main street of this town where the traffic passes through, the twentieth century comes back into view. This was easily one of the most amazing places I had ever seen!

On returning to our car with our bellies full, we continued under the cover of darkness towards the city of Suzhou. Eventually the city did come into view and as we toured the darkened streets, Jin Yang found our accommodation. It was another Jinjiang Inn Hotel and after checking us in, the land of nod arrived rather quickly for all of us.

The water town was still on my mind. How I could ever forget seeing that! Tomorrow would be another day, what would it hold?

At early light, my first impressions from our fourth-floor view (what a contrast to the Shanghai tower) told me that this was a big city. For most of the day we just looked around the city centre, with its hundreds of shops and restaurants. The taxies that I saw here were mostly light blue in colour. The footpaths were continually thronged with people doing their own thing. Again, there seemed to be more motorbikes than bicycles. We got dinner that evening and had a few beers. Jin Yang said, tomorrow would be a long day. I wondered what he meant.

When morning came and breakfast was finished, we made our way to the central area of this city. We were going to visit two world cultural heritage sights where gardens featured prominently. After queuing amongst the large number of tourists that were present, Jin Yang bought the tickets for us to gain entry. Security is always tight at these places as you are talking about history and heritage from way back through the ages.

It was called *The Lion Forest Garden* which consisted of hundreds of rock formations mixed with pathways woven into gardens that also had underneath caves. There were water canals which passed through and around these halls and pavilions. Surprisingly, there were also small waterfalls scattered around this unique place. Two or three little bridges got you from one place to another. A lot of different fish had made it their home as they swam around with complete security. There were houses and garden retreats there from past emperors. I noticed in most walking areas, there were thousands of small stones individually made up the many paths that were beneath our feet. All of this was quite interesting to see, because it was unique. We only saw two westerners there amongst the hundreds of tourists, obviously from other parts of China.

The other place in close proximity was called *The Humble Administrators Garden,* which dates back to 1513. After Jin Yang got our tickets, we made our way through the mass crowds. The sun was glorious, and the settings were ideal to be amongst gardens, ponds and canals. It was a place with natural beauty. You could feel the tranquillity there. We spent about two hours there and the two children enjoyed the freedom amongst the picturesque settings.

Yes, two quite interesting places to see, with a lot of history attached. The rest of the day was spent in a relaxed mood.

The next day, we just took it easy and did a little shopping. The following day, the city of Thoushan was next on our travels. It was a case of leaving early in the car, as there was a lot of road between these two cities. But I was looking forward to it, like the first time you go anywhere there is excitement within.

The five-hour car ride was interesting in itself, as there was a lot to see. We passed loads of heavy good vehicles, all laden down with their goods going to different cities by road. The infrastructure was impressive and not a sweet paper was to be seen on this eight-lane highway. When we eventually got to our destination, we had crossed a number of suspension bridges over several rivers. These bridges were feats of engineering, the likes of which I had never seen anywhere else in the world. Some of them were two and three miles long. Thoushan was another big city from my first observation. But tomorrow was another day and tiredness ruled after an early dinner.

The following morning it was raining and spoiled our plans for the day. But two days rain out of twenty-four wasn't bad. We just toured around and looked out at the passing streets through our rain dropped windows. As dinner time approached, a new experience was about to greet my eyes. Jin Yang turned off a main street and there was a long line of fish restaurants on this street. It was easy to recognize them, as they each had lots of see-through glass fish tanks on public view. These tanks held every kind of live fish and shellfish that you could think of. On view over the glass tanks there were lots of fish menus.

We stopped the car and I said to Hong Wei, "I don't believe what I am seeing."

She said to me, "Are you hungry, Billy?"

"Not now," I replied, as I suddenly lost my appetite. As you know by now, fish and I don't mix. That's just me and my personal taste. Prawns would be as far as I would go. But hunger took over the mind-set of the rest and in we went to one of our choosing. Jin Yang ordered for everyone, while I looked after myself. Luckily the restaurant had potatoes on the menu. I ordered some and had a few Tsingtao beers to wash them down. They all tucked into their chosen food from their bowls and we enjoyed our choices. We finished our meal and then left on our continued tour of Thoushan city. I did notice that most of the taxies I saw were orange. After a few hours of sight-seeing, night-time did come and it was lights out. Tomorrow was to be a memorable and unforgettable day.

A bright sunny day greeted Hong Wei and I as we pulled back the curtains in our bedroom. As Hong Wei and I were sitting down alone to a late breakfast in the restaurant, a funny thing happened. You know the way you might be listening to a bit of music in the background when you are having your breakfast. Well to my complete surprise, what song came over the airwaves only one of the great Irish ballads *The Foggy Dew*. I couldn't believe my ears. I wondered was it for the only Irishman in the restaurant. Incidentally, it is one of the songs that will be played at my funeral.

After breakfast, Jin Yang started the car and informed his mother, who then told me where our destination was. We were on our way to a famous female Buddhist shrine (Guan-Yin, the Goddess of Mercy) on Putuo Shan island. Most people go to this place by boat and it is one of the four most sacred mountains of Chinese Buddhism. It was another glorious day with the sun shining down on us for free.

We drove to this car park area, and then made our way to this huge departure ferry terminal. This place was huge with hundreds of people there. All had the one purpose of visiting this very, very sacred place. I noticed a huge percentage of them had travelling cases. Hong Wei informed me that people stay overnight there for one or two nights, or whatever they decide. Jin Yang again purchased the tickets for this trip as we took our place in the long lines of people waiting until their turn came to board. There were lots of tourists, but mostly Chinese, from what I could see on this particular day. Like us, all of them were eager to see this special place.

Eventually our turn came to board these very high-powered ferry cruisers which operate continuously over and back to the island, from dawn until dusk. With the amount of people wanting to visit this place, this is a big daily operation. The ferries were thronged with people, but I could see there were strict guidelines as to the correct number of passengers (being counted) for each ferry and this was adhered to rigidly through the boarding system procedure the stewards had in place. We managed to get seats on this twenty-minute journey. Looking at the two grandchildren, Hao Yang and Yue Yue, I knew they were excited to be travelling by boat and Hong Wei was very happy to be in their company. On the journey over to the island, you can actually see this Buddhist way up on the summit of Mount Putuo.

Upon our arrival at the docking area, there were hundreds of people waiting to make the return journey, having paid their homage to this Buddhist in the one day or they could have stayed over. The amount of people coming and going to this sacred place really surprised me. We had a choice to make, which was to either walk to the shrine or wait for one of the many shuttle buses that operate all day. It was all uphill. The obvious choice was to wait with the other intending travelling passengers for a bus. Like the ferry, our turn came eventually. We boarded for the short ten-minute journey. The drop-off point leaves you with a little walking to do, but that wasn't a problem.

We arrived at the shrine amidst hundreds of worshippers. Most of them lit incense sticks from a huge big iron collecting trough and then paid homage to the Buddhist from this area. They then walked up the stone steps and across the open space, up to the statue. I'm sure over the course of the day, that revolving figure of tourists added up to thousands. This was a sight that I had never seen before, with so many people worshipping this Buddhist. The sun was really inflicting its rays on the worshippers below, this being the hottest part of this particular day. I wandered up to the Buddhist in my own time, just to see her at close quarters. She was huge in appearance. Then I went in under this structure where there were a number of smaller Buddha's all lined up in individual openings in the surrounding walls. All of the worshippers did their own thing there and I respected them for that. I knew this was quite a unique place to see and I felt privileged to have seen it.

Between going and returning to this special place, it took us about eight hours in total. On returning to Jin Yang's car in the early evening, we had a long drive ahead of us to the city Hangzhou in Zhejiang province. We got to our hotel in Hangzhou very late and bedded down without delay.

The following morning, our bodies succumbed to the hotel beds – we missed breakfast, as we never made it down in time. My body was close to meltdown, between tiredness and fatigue. But we did surface around midday and got something to eat. We took it easy in the city centre and browsed around the shops. Everyone took it easy that evening, which gave Jin Yang time to plan our itinerary for the following two days.

One of the main tourist attractions in the city of Hangzhou is the bridge that spans the famous Qiantang River. You might ask what is particular about that? Well, if you saw a bridge with a highway on top of it and with railway tracks below, you might say it would be interesting. It was the first highway and railway combined bridge ever built in China. It is known as the double-decker bridge.

On the following morning we took in a few historical museums, one of which contained the history and background of the man who designed the double-decker bridge. His name was Mao Yisheng and what brilliant and confident foresight he had to design this magnificent spectacle. Other interesting features there were relating to soldiers who had lost their lives in the war and people who had contributed handsomely to the city of Hangzhou. Other features were about a major fire that happened. Everything was in Chinese, so I had to figure it out from the displayed photographs that were on view.

Outside there was a giant white statue of a soldier in a battle pose, but I could not pick up from anyone who he was or what he represented. Then we made our way to the giant Liuhe pagoda that dominates the skyline. What an impressive sight this was to see. Hong Wei, Hao Yang and I decided to have a look at this impressive pagoda. It has thirteen floors, but we were only allowed to climb to the seventh, as there was no access to go any further. By the time we got to the seventh floor, I don't think we had any energy left anyway. They were stone steps practically straight up, from floor to floor. My sixty-five years told on me in the going up part. We had to watch Hao Yang like a hawk as his enthusiasm was to get to the next floor before Hong Wei and me. He needn't have worried, as we weren't a threat.

When we got there the view from the seventh floor was breath-taking. We could see the city from all four sides, especially the double decker bridge and the Qiantang River in full flow. Ah yes, it was beautiful sights that greeted our eyes. Funnily enough the coming down was quite precarious, in the sense that it was better and safer to come down backwards holding a railing – the steps were that steep. There was a bit of fun attached to it though, if anyone had seen Hong Wei and me on our descent! Hao Yang managed it no bother, in fact at times, he found it funny too.

I noticed over the few days, that the blue grey and the green grey taxis in this city looked like they were equally divided. Jin Yang hiring the car was a master stroke, as we could come and go as we pleased. Later we all went for dinner in a restaurant, where Jin Yang and I sunk a few Tsingtao beers. This was followed by an early night, as tomorrow would hold another experience for me.

Friday was to be our last day in Hangzhou city, on this twelve-day break, as we were due to return to Anshan city on the Saturday. After a late breakfast, Jin Yang, Wang Hao and Yue Yue all stayed behind, as Hong Wei, Hao Yang and I ventured to one of the biggest lakes that this city prides itself on.

When we got there on foot, a massive lake greeted us. This was a huge tourist attraction and I could see why. The sun was beating down on us all, but it was beautiful. There were thousands of tourists and locals there. On the section where we were standing, there were dozens of gondola-like boats, paddle boats, motorboats (a little different than the ones we had seen in the Watertown) and other large ancient boats that were specifically built for the visitors. All of these vessels were operating in their own areas and being occupied for a certain amount of time until the clock ran out on their passengers. We could see on our walk that the people there were enjoying the day that was in it.

There was a route around this huge lake where you had golf buggies and they would bring you around the full circumference. These buggies could hold about a dozen people at a time and were in continuous use, as they dropped off and picked up people according to their times. They were a little pricey, but worth it knowing the chances of me being back this way again were remote, also my legs were feeling the pinch now. My body was not for walking and Hao Yang would not have lasted long either. We flagged down an empty buggy and got a front seat much to Hao Yang's delight.

Hundreds of people were walking on this path and got on and off these buggies at their ease. It was great to experience the full circumference of this lake while sitting down and taking in some of the attractions that we saw en route. There were a lot of people there and the time literally flew. It was late afternoon when we made our return to our hotel, had dinner and took it easy. It had been a long and tiring day in the sun and fatigue won out again.

Our flight to Shenyang from Hangzhou airport was booked for 21:00 on the Saturday night. With this in mind, we took it easy for the day and just relaxed. With the flight over us and the hundred-mile road journey over us too, Anshan city awaited our arrival at 01:30 in the morning. It was Sunday, a week to go, as we entered Jin Yang and Wang Hao's apartment.

It was going to be a busy week, with the gang of eleven waiting to meet us on Monday evening. My retirement party, as I had promised myself two and a half years earlier, and then there was Hong Wei's birthday party on Thursday 25th.

On Monday at 18:00 we arrived at the hotel to see the gang of twelve. Mr. E was missing through a family matter that was unavoidable. But he sent word that he would see us on the Wednesday night. Those that were there were all delighted to see us, and pleasantries were exchanged in the following hours. Their kindness and humour were the same as always in their company. A great night was had by all and a lot of Tsingtao beer was drunk.

Recovery was slow on Tuesday, as you would expect, from the previous night. I took it easy all day and changed my routine by us going for a pizza. I'm not a big pizza lover, but I felt my body needed a change of fuel. Hong Wei didn't mind and went with the flow. Being in the last week, we were now on the countdown to our departure date, something I never looked forward to.

Wednesday morning was set aside for a little shopping. Wang Hao came along with Hong Wei and me. I left them off and just waited outside in the glorious sunshine and watched the world go by. I had time to think about being away for the twelve days and the four cities we visited.

My opinion was, they were all nice places to see and I was glad I did, but the pace of them was quicker. Anshan city, to me, was a much more relaxing place to be. That evening it was great to see Mr. E and the few of the gang of twelve that were available. He was delighted to see us, as always. We had a great night, with Hong Wei busy interpreting for me, for most of it. What would I have done without her? Can you imagine!

Thursday April 25th was Hong Wei's birthday and I wanted to make it a night for her to remember. She actually shares her birthday with my third brother, Paul. What none of them were aware of, (until I told them) was that they also share it with the famous late footballer, Holland's greatest-ever player Johan Cruyff! A cake was ordered, and a hotel room was booked in advance. It was just for her immediate family and that totalled around twenty-five.

On Thursday night everybody in attendance wished her well and the arrival of the birthday cake topped off the night. All I can say is the Chinese sure know how to bake a cake and are excellent in the confectionary trade. I can still see the cream on top of the sponge!

She took all of the good wishes that were showered on her in her stride. It was a most enjoyable night and I was glad for her. Mr. Liu, Dong Bin, Mr. He and I all drank a lot of Tsingtao beer. The body was feeling the pinch now, but it had to be done. Chinese wine was on offer, but I declined, as I had learned my lesson once before. My retirement party was the next day, (Friday) but I didn't need any cake. Guests wise, it was a repeat of the previous night. I just gave a small speech about how much I was enjoying my retirement and then everybody enjoyed the rest of the proceedings. My body was being pushed a little further down the line, with food and Tsingtao beer. The night ended a little earlier than the previous night, but fatigue played its part in that.

Saturday morning arrived and Saturday night also arrived several hours later. Being the last day, it was a family gathering. I gave my thoughts to those present on the previous five weeks and the experiences we encountered and saw along the way. The night finished early with lots of photographs being taken. I suppose you could say Hong Wei and I were the main participants. When I closed my eyes shortly afterwards, the end of my tenth trip to China was into its final hours.

Sunday was departure day and when it arrived, there was a slight change in the proceedings. I was returning solo and Hong Wei was staying for another month, much to her family's delight. The weather had been fantastic for my five-week stay, with the exception of two day's rain. Most of Hong Wei's family travelled with us, in convoy. Mr. Liu was a definite attendee.

We left Anshan city at 12:30, as we had to be at the airport in Shenyang for 14:00. My first flight was at 17:00 to Shanghai. Then it would be continued with my second flight to Amsterdam. After that my last flight would take me to Dublin in Ireland. The one-hundred-and-ten-mile bus ride home to Waterford city was the last thing on my mind. On arrival at the airport, I checked in my two suitcases and then we all just relaxed and waited for Father Time to move on.

The clock ticked away, and it finally pushed on to goodbye time. It was strange on this occasion, as the previous goodbyes were of the two of us departing.

I said my goodbyes to the others, and left Hong Wei until last. I felt bad and sad when the moment came. But letting go had to be done, amidst a lot of tears. The security guard had his instructions as I passed him, then I suddenly found myself on my own. Hong Wei and those present continued waving, as I continued on my path to the first security desk. After my clearance there and a final wave to everyone, they disappeared from view. While waiting at my departure gate, I reminisced about a lot of things that had gone on in my life. Yes, fate has played its part, of that I'm certain. Particularly after that chance meeting with Fengqin at the bus stop on that September day, way back in the year of 2003.

Shortly after and on time, my plane took off. The city of Shenyang below disappeared from sight. I wondered when I would see it again.

I got back to Waterford city by the now familiar route, and as usual I was shattered when I got there. I counted the days, all thirty-one of them, until I was on my way to picking up Hong Wei at Dublin Airport on her return home.

So that my friends, is just about where my story is at. I hope you have enjoyed reading it, as much as I have enjoyed bringing it to you. Perhaps someday some of you will get the chance to go and see this magical country with the most resilient of people. The history, the culture, the scenery and its people have to be experienced. Do go and be open-minded. You won't be disappointed, that I can promise you.

Life can be funny and at times, strange. I believe fate has played its part to a fair degree in my life. Everything that happens is for a reason. Life is about the choices we make. This was the predicament that faced me all those years ago. I believe if you give up, you go under and you only become a statistic. I'm only too aware of the alternatives. So in life, do make the most of it and if you get a second chance, take it with both hands. Embrace it. Value it. Appreciate it. Never look back and be grateful to have gotten it. I know I did!

This was written by:

Billy Costine

E-Mail address: bcostine@hotmail.com

Owner of all copyrights